Saving Soldiers or Civilians?

Concerns for the lives of soldiers and innocent civilians have come to underpin Western, and particularly American, warfare. Yet this new mode of conflict faces a dilemma: these two norms have opened new areas of vulnerability that have been systematically exploited by non-state adversaries. This strategic behaviour creates a trade-off, forcing decision-makers to have to choose between saving soldiers and civilians in target states. Sebastian Kaempf examines the origin and nature of this dilemma and, in a detailed analysis of the US conflicts in Somalia, Afghanistan and Iraq, investigates the ways the US has responded, assessing the legal, moral and strategic consequences. Scholars and students of military and strategic studies, international relations and peace and conflict studies will be interested to read Kaempf's analysis of whether the US or its adversaries have succeeded in responding to this central dilemma of contemporary warfare.

Dr Sebastian Kaempf is Senior Lecturer in Peace and Conflict Studies at the School of Political Science and International Studies at the University of Queensland, Australia. His research interests are in international security, peace and conflict studies, the ethics and the laws of war, and the impact of digital new media technology on contemporary security. He has won an Australian national award for teaching excellence (AAUT) and is the convener of the massive open online course (MOOC) 'MediaWarX' (see: https://www.edx.org/course/global-medi a-war-technology-uqx-mediawarx-0).

Saving Soldiers or Civilians?

Casualty-Aversion versus Civilian Protection in Asymmetric Conflicts

Sebastian Kaempf

University of Queensland

CAMBRIDGE
UNIVERSITY PRESS

CAMBRIDGE
UNIVERSITY PRESS

University Printing House, Cambridge CB2 8BS, United Kingdom

One Liberty Plaza, 20th Floor, New York, NY 10006, USA

477 Williamstown Road, Port Melbourne, VIC 3207, Australia

314–321, 3rd Floor, Plot 3, Splendor Forum, Jasola District Centre, New Delhi – 110025, India

79 Anson Road, #06–04/06, Singapore 079906

Cambridge University Press is part of the University of Cambridge.

It furthers the University's mission by disseminating knowledge in the pursuit of education, learning, and research at the highest international levels of excellence.

www.cambridge.org
Information on this title: www.cambridge.org/9781108427647
DOI: 10.1017/9781108551816

© Sebastian Kaempf 2018

First published 2018

Printed in the United Kingdom by Clays, St Ives plc

A catalogue record for this publication is available from the British Library.

ISBN 978-1-108-42764-7 Hardback

To my parents, Ulrike and Michael

Contents

Acknowledgements

Writing the acknowledgements to this book in a little café in Berlin (some things never change) on a cold, rainy autumn afternoon makes me aware of two things. On the one hand, it has been a remarkable, fun, and intellectually thrilling but also long and exhausting journey that began in Aberystwyth in the UK and that ended half way around the globe at the University of Queensland (UQ) in Australia – with two longer research stints at Brown University in Providence, RI and Humboldt University in Berlin. On the other hand, I realised how fortunate I have been to come across so many amazing people in the course of that intellectual journey. To various degrees they have all fostered my enthusiasm for this topic, helping me develop critical thoughts and the ability to question, which have resulted in this end product.

At the same time, many of those who have contributed to this intellectual journey have also become close friends whose support and company have been exceptional and who are very dear to me. Maybe every book project is an emotional roller coaster ride; mine certainly felt like it. It has been comforting to know that there has been this tremendous support through highs and lows, through enchanting moments and moments of frustration, personal loss, and illness.

Even though I am right now feeling exhausted from a redrafting process which seemed never ending, the tremendous feeling of gratitude prevails for all those who I have been fortunate enough to get to know and who have made this the remarkable experience it has been for me.

First and foremost, I want to thank my two PhD supervisors, Nick Wheeler and Alastair Finlan. It is difficult to put into a few lines the amount of gratitude and admiration I feel for your exceptional support, the outstanding supervisions, the spot-on yet always very constructive criticism, and your commitment to what was the beginning of this research project. At this point I also want to thank Jan Selby for his great job as secondary supervisor in my first two years before his move to Sussex.

What made the Interpol Department in Aberystwyth such an extraordinary place for me was the number of staff and fellow PhD students whose advice and support I could always seek and on whose expertise I was able to draw (and of who many became good friends). Here, I am particularly grateful to Mike Williams, Andrew Linklater, Rita Abrahamsen, Jenny Edkins, Martin Alexander, Gerry Hughes, Andrew Priest, Richard Wyn Jones, Will Bain, Toni Erskine, Cian O'Driscoll, Roland Vogt, Sabrina Schulz, Columba Lennon Peoples, Chrissi Yeung, Stig Hansen, Touko Piiparinen, Gemma Collantes Celador, Wolfango Piccoli, Melanie Wagner, Darren Brunck, and Ilan Zvi Baron.

Furthermore, particular thanks go to Christopher Coker, Dominique Jacquin-Berdal, and Margot Light for being partially responsible for sparking the early enthusiasm for my subject and who have been extremely generous in their support during and after my time at the LSE.

At Brown University, I would like to thank James Der Derian, Tom Biersteker, Neta Crawford, and Annick Wibben for their wonderful generosity, their great and inspiring discussions, their very valuable advice, and for giving me a chance to experience the Watson Institute.

At UQ, my intellectual home for over a decade now, I very much want to express my enormous gratitude to Alex Bellamy, Roland Bleiker, Ian Clark, Andrew Phillips, Matt McDonald, Emma Hutchison, Richard Shapcott, Cindy O'Hagan, Marianne Hanson, Sarah Teitt, Phil Orchard, Richard Devetak, Tim Dunne, Chris Reus-Smit, Stephen Bell, Kath Gelber, Al Stark, and Gillian Whitehouse. Many of you have proofread some of the earlier drafts, have given me a lot of personal support and advice and have pushed me at times when I needed pushing (which was a lot!). It speaks to the intellectual powerhouse that UQ has become that I could draw on such diverse and rich expertise among colleagues in the offices just around me! But I need to single out five colleagues in particular: Matt McDonald, Andrew Phillips, Chris Reus-Smit, Roland Bleiker, and Jason Sharman. In different ways, each of you has gone above and beyond what anyone could expect in supporting me intellectually, personally, and strategically.

I was also blessed to be granted a research sabbatical by my Faculty (thanks Tim and Richard) which allowed me to finish this monograph while being based at Humboldt University in Berlin. Here, I am extremely thankful to Herfried Münkler both for being my host and for long lunchtime discussions about my project. I am also deeply indebted to Jason Sharman, Felix Wassermann, Paul Williams, Luke Glanville, Roger Stahl, Parag Khanna, and Dan Menchik for proofreading some of my draft chapters and for a lot of strategic advice.

Beyond the confines of the academic world, I would like to express my deep thanks to a group of close friends whose company I have held dear for many many years and who have continuously supported me through this journey: Leana Islam, Volker Schimmel, Steffi and Stefan Kaufmann, Emma and Flocki Scheding, Isi and Jojo Meyer, Mikey Slivka, Parag Khanna, Ines Rocha, Marco Mohwinckel, Evi Kreutz, Jan Stegemann, Eva and Guillaume D'Homme, Fernanda Torresi, Mariano Griva, and Helen and Matt McDonald. You might not have realised how much your support has meant to me, but looking back now I feel a level of gratitude that I struggle to put into words.

I would also like to thank John Haslam and Toby Ginsberg at Cambridge University Press for their guidance, diligence, and patience. It has been a real pleasure working with you. And I would like to thank the two anonymous reviewers for their insightful, critical, and very constructive and helpful feedback.

Finally, and most importantly, I want to express my deepest gratitude to my aunt Christine, my uncle Rolf, and especially my sister Steffi, my brother-in-law Oli, and my parents Ulrike and Michael. You have always encouraged me to follow my interests and supported me in this endeavour without any trace of doubt. Where others might have objected, you have generously financed my long years of study without questioning and you have made sacrifices that are truly exceptional. Most importantly, you have always been driven by the unique belief that you should try everything to foster my curiosity and to allow me to pursue my interests. I could not have wished for anything more. I am endlessly thankful. Mum, Dad, I dedicate this to you.

★★★

Some sections of this book have been published previously and I would like to thank the publishers for granting me copyright permission to use some of this material in this monograph.

In particular, some parts of Chapter 1 have been published in Kaempf, S. (2009). 'Double standards in US warfare: Exploring the historical legacy of civilian protection and the complex nature of the moral-legal nexus'. *Review of International Studies*, 35 (3): 651–674. See also: www .cambridge.org/core/journals/review-of-international-studies/article/dou ble-standards-in-us-warfare-exploring-the-historical-legacy-of-civilian-p rotection-and-the-complex-nature-of-the-morallegal-nexus/AF7A11C B95C6547413C6F6B118D3564A.

Some sections of Chapter 2 have previously been published in Kaempf, S. (2014). 'Postheroic U.S. warfare and the moral justification for killing in war'. In Amy E. Eckert and Caron E. Gentry (eds.), *The Future of Just*

War: New Critical Essays, pp. 79–97. Athens, GA: University of Georgia Press.

Some parts of Chapter 3 have previously been published in Kaempf, S. (2011), Lost through non-translation: Bringing Clausewitz's writings on 'new wars' back in. *Small Wars and Insurgencies,* 22 (4): 548–573.

And finally, some parts of Chapter 4 have previously been published in Kaempf, S. (2012) US warfare in Somalia and the trade-off between casualty-aversion and civilian protection. *Small Wars and Insurgencies,* 23(3): 388–413.

Abbreviations

ARVN	Army of the Republic of Vietnam
AWSS	allocated weapons storage sites
CENTCOM	United States Central Command
CIA	Central Intelligence Agency
Delta	Forces Army's First Special Forces Operational Detachment-Delta
DEVGRU	Naval Special Warfare Development Group
DMZ	Demilitarised Zone
DOD	Department of Defense
FRY	Federal Republic of Yugoslavia
ICRC	International Committee of the Red Cross
IDP	internally displaced people
IHL	international humanitarian law
INGO	international nongovernmental organisation
JCS	Joint Chiefs of Staff
JDAM	Joint Direct Attack Munitions
JSOC	Joint Special Operations Command
JWT	just war tradition
LIC	low intensity conflict
MACV	Military Assistance Command, Vietnam
NATO	North Atlantic Treaty Organisation
NGO	nongovernmental organisation
NLF	National Liberation Front
NSC	National Security Council
OAF	Operation Allied Force
OEF	Operation Enduring Freedom
PAVN	People's Army of Vietnam
PLO	Palestine Liberation Organisation
POW	prisoner of war
Psy-Ops	Psychological Operations
QRF	Quick Reaction Forces
RMA	revolution in military affairs

RoE	rules of engagement
RPG	rocket-propelled grenade
SNA	Somali National Alliance
SNM	Somali National Movement
SOF	Special Operations Forces
SSA	Somali Solution Alliance
TFR	Task Force Ranger
UNITAF	United Task Force
UNOSOM	United Nations Mission in Somalia
UNSC	United Nations Security Council
UNSCR	United Nations Security Council Resolution
UNSG	United Nations Secretary General
USAF	United States Air Force
USC	United Somali Congress
USN	United States Navy

Interviewees

Bacevich, Andrew	26 January 2005
Bearden, Milton	21 June 2005
Bergen, Peter	4 December 2005
Borchini, Charlie	17 June 2005
Bowden, Mark	14 November 2004
Conetta, Carl	4 December 2004
Dobbins, Jim	18 December 2004
Durch, Bill	30 November 2004
Finel, Bernard	30 November 2004
Garstka, John	18 December 2004
Gray, David	28 February 2005
Grissom, Adam	2 December 2004
Hammes, TX	21 December 2004
Hartley, Aidan	12 February 2005
Hirsch, John	15 January 2005
Howe, Jonathan	6 January and 21 June 2005
Ikins, Chuck	30 November 2004
Ishimoto, Wade	18 December 2004
Johnston, Robert	11 January 2005
Jones, Seth	2 December 2004
Kennedy, Kevin	1 March 2005
Miller, Reid	12 March 2005
Montgomery, Thomas	16 March and 24 June 2005
Oakley, Robert	30 November 2004 and 15 June 2005
Pirnie, Bruce	21 December 2004
Pudas, Terry	17 June 2005
Rababy, David	21 December 2004 and 13 January 2005
Radcliffe, David	30 November 2004
Richburg, Keith	12 March 2005
Starr, Jeoffrey	15 June 2005
Wright, Ann	12, 19 March and 31 May 2005

Introduction

While the United States has not lost its appetite for war, the way in which its conflicts are being waged has changed dramatically. Over the past few decades, US warfare has lost much of its cruelty on two particular fronts. First, thanks to advances in military technologies and the gradual loss of the popular belief in war as a force that requires sacrifice, US warfare has become 'post-heroic'.[1] 'Post-heroic' means that the American people no longer affirm their humanism through violent acts but have instead become unwilling to accept the risk of dying in combat.[2] Humanism had previously turned war into an experience that gave meaning and authenticity to American citizen-soldiers.[3] Yet today, very few Americans still conceive war as a source of asserting one's existence and as a source of individual transformation.[4] This growing 'post-heroic' attitude manifests itself in the so-called 'body bag syndrome' and in a general casualty-aversion among US political and military decision makers.[5]

Second, due to technological innovations and the growing acceptance of universal legal restraints on the use of force, US warfare has largely come to comply with the legal principle of non-combatant immunity.[6] The protection of innocent civilians in target states has become a central concern in US military operations. As a result, the prevailing concern for the lives of US soldiers and enemy civilians has come to normatively underpin contemporary American warfare.[7]

---

[1] Luttwak 1995, 109–122; Luttwak 1996, 33–45.
[2] Luttwak 1995, 109–122; Luttwak 1996, 33–45; Ignatieff 2000c; van Creveld 1996; Coker 2002b; Gelven 1994; Ehrenreich 1998.
[3] Van Creveld 1996; Hedges 2002, 3–17; Gelven, 1994; Nietzsche 1981, 74.
[4] Chapter 2 will provide a detailed definition and analysis of the aspect of humanism in general and in the context of contemporary American warfare in particular.
[5] Record, 2000; Mann 1988, 184–185; McInnes 2002, 69; Shaw, 1991.
[6] Coker 2001, 1–45; Ignatieff 2000c, 197–201; Shaw 2005, 4–28; Farrell 2005, 177–179; Bacevich 1996, 37–48; Wheeler 2000.
[7] Renz and Scheipers 2012, 17–43.

Yet, this new mode of warfare faces a fundamental problem because of the inherent tension that exists between the two norms of casualty-aversion and civilian protection. This could be seen, for instance, during the 1999 Kosovo War, where casualty-averse attitudes categorically ruled out the deployment of ground forces and lead to a bombing campaign from such high altitudes which (while it made US pilots safe from Serbian anti-aircraft fire) significantly reduced the precision of the 'smart bombs' and thereby exposed Serbian civilians to larger risks.[8] Conversely, allowing US fighter pilots to fly at lower altitudes would have increased the risks to American military personnel but would also have resulted in lower numbers of 'collateral damage'.[9]

Most importantly, once the particular interactive dynamics of asymmetric conflicts are taken into account, this inherent tension turns into a devilish dilemma: The two norms have opened new areas of vulnerability that have been systematically exploited by non-state adversaries, who have identified the two norms (casualty-aversion and civilian protection) as the centre of gravity of US warfare.[10] Here, the US norm of casualty-aversion has translated into a renewed conviction among non-state adversaries that killing even a handful of US soldiers can trigger political repercussions and can ultimately lead to US withdrawal. And the perceived need for US warfare to comply with International Humanitarian Law (IHL) has lead non-state adversaries to systematically manipulate these norms by deliberately placing non-combatants in harm's way. It is this strategic behaviour by non-state adversaries that exacerbates the tension inherent in these two norms, forcing US decision-makers to have to choose between exposing enemy civilians to larger risks and increasing the combat risks to its own soldiers.

Against this backdrop, this book examines the origin and nature of this dilemma. It investigates – through interviews with key stakeholders in these conflicts – the ways in which the US has responded to this dilemma, and assesses the legal, moral, and strategic consequences. Has the US military been able to wage its post–Cold War asymmetric conflicts in ways that achieved highest levels of casualty-aversion while also safeguarding enemy civilians? Or did the asymmetric strategies employed by its non-state adversaries force US decision-makers to decide on one norm at the expense of the other? And if so, what were the legal, moral, and strategic consequences of such decisions?

---

[8] Cornish 2003, 121; Walzer 2004, 17.

[9] See for example, Münkler 2004; Habermas 1999; Wheeler 2003, 197–198.

[10] Bohrer and Osiel 2013, 747–822; Cordesman 1998; Gentry 2011, 243; Cornish 2003, 121.

It is with a view to addressing these issues that this study first develops a novel conceptual framework, drawing on the existing literature on the rise of 'post-heroic' American warfare, the solidification of norms of IHL, and the growth of unconventional asymmetric security challenges. This framework is then applied to three detailed empirical cases examining the asymmetric conflicts between the US military and non-state actors in Somalia (1992–1994), Afghanistan (2001–2002), and Iraq (2003–2011).

Examining these issues is significant because they have been at the forefront of contemporary asymmetric conflicts (of which conflicts between the US military and its non-state adversaries constitute the most extreme constellation). Such a focus provides answers as to why many of the post–Cold War conflicts unfolded and ended in the way they did – something the existing literature in International Relations has not yet been able to do.

Existing Literature

The last two decades have seen the release of several important studies that address – to varying degrees – the three core concepts on which this book focuses: the rise of a post-heroic, casualty-averse American mode of warfare;[11] the strengthening of and increasing compliance with the principle of non-combatant immunity within US warfare;[12] and the nature and particular interactive dynamics generated by asymmetric conflicts between state and non-state actors.[13] While drawing inspiration from and building on the insights of these essential works, this book is distinguishable from them in two important ways.

First, while most sources have provided good insights into the socio-historical causes behind this recent transformation of American warfare and the specific interactive nature of asymmetric conflicts, they have tended to place their emphasis on only one of the three key concepts. Put differently, instead of examining and critically contextualising all three phenomena, they focused on either the rise of US casualty-aversion, the strengthening of the principle of non-combatant immunity, or the interactive nature of asymmetric conflicts.

For instance, the body of literature presented by Andrew J Bacevich, James Der Derian, Edward Luttwak, Jeffrey Record, Charles Moskos,

---

[11] Mann 1988; McInnes 2002; Shaw 2005; Coker 2002b; Ignatieff 2000c; Der Derian 2001; Bacevich 2005; Singer 2009; Enemark 2014; Buley 2008; Münkler 2004.

[12] Thomas 2001; Ignatieff 2000c; Shaw 2005; Farrell 2005; Coker 2001; Walzer 2004; Crawford 2013; Bellamy 2006; O'Driscoll 2008; Renz and Scheipers 2012, 17–43.

[13] Arreguin-Toft 2005; Strachan 2007; Münkler 2014; Chaliand 1994; Van Creveld 1991b; Griffith 1992.

Martin Shaw, Michael Mann, Karl W Eikenberry, Christopher Coker, Michael Ignatieff, and Colin McInnes has made a groundbreaking contribution to the socio-historical understanding of the rise of US casualty-aversion over the last decades – insights on which the book will draw.[14] Yet, while generating valuable understanding and developing a consensus that the American military – following the Vietnam War – has tended to wage riskless wars, this subsection of the International Relations literature has generally failed to relate its research findings to, and discuss them in the context of, the simultaneous strengthening of the principle of non-combatant immunity and how it is impacted upon by enemy behaviour.

At the same time, the body of literature that has focused on the humanising trend underway in contemporary US warfare has tended to do so without contextualising its findings in light of the rise of casualty-aversion.[15] For instance, Ward Thomas's *The Ethics of Destruction*, Theo Farrell's *The Norms of War*, Michael Ignatieff's *Virtual War*, Neta Crawford's *Accountability for Killing*, and Maja Zehfuss' *Killing Civilians* all have generated very valuable understanding of the socio-historical reasons as to why American military operations in recent decades have come to comply with IHL – and the book will draw on these extensively.[16] With its particular research focus, however, this existing material has stopped short of discussing its findings in relation to the simultaneous rise of casualty-aversion and in the context of the interactive dynamics of asymmetric conflicts.

While such a focus on the dynamic interaction at the heart of the nature of war tends to be marginalised by the body of literature reviewed above, it can nevertheless be found in the strategic studies literature. From the work of Carl von Clausewitz, Thomas Edward Lawrence, Mao Zedong, and Vo Nguyen Giap to more contemporary thinkers such as Martin van Creveld, Herfried Münkler, Christopher Daase, or Ivan Arreguin-Toft, strategic studies has explored the nature of interactions between adversaries.[17] Yet, these insights have rarely departed from the realm of hard strategy to the issues of law and morality as pertaining to American warfare.

Thus, while generating valuable understanding of each of these three phenomena in and of itself, the majority of the existing literature has failed to relate its research findings to, and discuss them in the context of

[14] Record 2000; Moskos 2002; Eikenberry 1996; Mann 1988; McInnes 2002; Shaw 2005; Coker 2002b.
[15] Thomas 2001; Wheeler 2002; Shaw 2005; Farrell 2005; Bacevich 1996; Ignatieff 2000c.
[16] Thomas 2001; Ignatieff 2000c; Farrell 2005; Zehfuss 2012, 423–440. See also Thomas W Smith 2002, 355–374; Boot 2003; Coker 2001, 1–45.
[17] Clausewitz 1984; T.E. Lawrence 1994, 880–891; T. E. Lawrence 1962; Griffith 1992; Giap 1977, 23–55; Arreguin-Toft 2005; Münkler 2004; Daase 2003, 17–35.

the other two concepts. This is problematic, this book argues, because today's asymmetric conflicts are essentially contestations – by both sides – over the two norms of casualty-aversion and civilian protection. On the one hand, the legitimacy and ultimate success of US warfare hinges on its ability to wage 'humane' or 'costless' wars (with lowest levels of risks to both enemy civilians and American military personnel). On the other hand, the strategies of non-state adversaries – compelled to adjust due to their military inferiority – have aimed at preventing the United States from waging war in this way; here, the two norms of casualty-aversion and civilian protection have become the core target. In other words, contemporary asymmetric conflicts are essentially conducted over and decided by the ability or inability to wage these wars in ways that are costless to both American soldiers and enemy civilians. Therefore, if we seek to fully understand the legal, moral, and strategic nature of contemporary conflicts, we need to combine and critically address all three elements together: the norms of casualty-aversion and civilian protection and how they are impacted upon by the interactive dynamics that are inherent in asymmetric conflicts.

The book rectifies this by examining the relationship between all three concepts. It thereby demonstrates that any systematic theoretical as well as empirical investigation into the trade-off between US casualty-aversion and civilian protection cannot afford to ignore the particular dynamics generated by the interactive nature of war. By not taking the role of the adversary – and the notion of the interactive nature of war – into account, most of the literature has implicitly assumed that the trade-off inherent in US warfare is immune from the actions taken by the adversary. Yet, by ignoring this important aspect, it has failed to explore how the balance between these key American values has been exacerbated by the behaviour of US adversaries. During the Bosnian War and NATO's campaign against Serbia over Kosovo, for example, Slobodan Milosevic deliberately placed command posts and military anti-aircraft guns into the densely populated residential areas of Belgrade or chained unarmed UN monitors onto military equipment during the siege of Sarajevo in order to deter US bombings.[18] Such an intentional exploitation of the American compliance with the principle of non-combatant immunity by ruthless and indiscriminate adversaries has generated severe challenges for US strategy. More will be said about these types of challenges in detail; these examples merely serve to illustrate that war is never waged upon a lifeless mass, but always on an animate agent who responds.[19] In the

[18] Skerker 2004, 29–30; Ignatieff 2000c, 28, 195, 200; Dunlop 1999, 29.
[19] Clausewitz 1984, 77.

unpredictable, non-linear, and interactive nature of war, 'the enemy has a vote, too.'[20]

Not to take this aspect into account significantly distorts any analysis of the conflicting values within contemporary US warfare in the same way that an analysis of a football match would be limited if it tried to explain the performance of one side without reference to the performance of the opposing team. Such an analysis would be insufficient as one side's performance can always only be as good as the other side permits. In other words, the interaction between the US military and its adversaries has to be addressed because the character of a conflict is not shaped autonomously or independently of the adversary, but in response and in reaction to the latter. In war, both adversaries act according to their strengths, they respond to their opponents' actions and adopt their own strategies accordingly. They are seeking to shape the character of the conflict and the responses of their adversaries, but are also, in turn, being shaped by the changed character of the conflict.

Furthermore, the book argues that the lack of focus on these interactive dynamics is particularly problematic in conflicts waged under conditions of asymmetry. These conditions have highlighted another central feature of American warfare as there are no adversaries resembling the level of US military might in the post–Cold War world.[21] This means that all warfare involving the American military superpower (especially when waged against semi-/non-state actors in Somalia, Afghanistan, and Iraq) cannot be described in any other way than as highly asymmetric in character.

Conditions of asymmetry are inherently unstable because they compel the disadvantaged side to adjust its strategy and tactics accordingly. They therefore generate a qualitatively different interactive dynamic between adversaries than would be the case in symmetric wars.[22] Not to take these particular dynamics into account distorts the analysis of whether it has been possible for the United States to wage war in ways that produced low American casualty rates while at the same time ensuring high levels of civilian protection.

Second, while a handful of publications in the field of International Relations have begun to explore some forms of relationship between these three concepts (casualty-aversion, civilian protection, and the interactive dynamic of asymmetric conflicts)

---

[20] Clausewitz 1984, 86; Beyerchen 1992, 59–90; van Creveld 2000, 116; Skerker 2004, 27–39; Arreguin-Toft 2005.
[21] Bacevich 2005, 16; Kennedy 2002; Kahn 1999, 1–6.
[22] Kahn 2002, 2–9; Bacevich 1996, 45; Van Creveld 1991b, 58.

and thereby have generated extremely valuable insights,[23] such analyses nevertheless have been deficient in the following ways: they have either not provided a systematic and comprehensive engagement with this trade-off; have focused specifically on a single empirical case; or have remained purely theoretical by not relating innovative conceptual ideas to empirical cases. As a result, they have often remained so narrowly focused on one particular military campaign that they have failed to generate theoretical knowledge beyond one particular case – something this monograph rectifies by cross-examining three empirical case studies. Furthermore, a number of theorists, most notably Michael Walzer, Martin Shaw, and Paul W Kahn, mainly tend to be exclusively interested in theoretical reflections upon these questions that their theoretical strength is at the detriment of a detailed empirical focus. Thus, they tend to lack empirical evidence as a means to test, and thereby substantiate, their theoretical findings.[24]

And finally, some of existing sources have focused very broadly on the 'West' and the 'Western way of war' rather than pursuing a specific focus on contemporary American warfare.[25] This book, on the other hand, is not concerned with the notion of 'Western' warfare, but merely with the specific theoretical and empirical aspects of contemporary asymmetric conflicts involving the United States and non-state actors in Somalia, Afghanistan, and Iraq. Given the importance of the specific interactive dynamic generated by asymmetric conflicts, focusing on US warfare allows the monograph to examine these dynamics under the most extreme constellations available in world politics today: where the world's most powerful military state actor (the US) is fighting with non-state military actors (warlords in Somalia, terrorists and insurgents in Afghanistan and Iraq), these specific interactive dynamics become visible most clearly.

Building on the existing literature, this book rectifies the shortcomings identified in the sources above by bringing together the strategic and legal/moral strands of the available literature to develop a systematic theoretical framework to assess and analyse the trade-off at the heart of US warfare before applying this framework to the three comparative case studies of the US interventions in Somalia, Afghanistan, and Iraq.

---

[23] Walzer 2004; Crawford 2013; Bellamy 2006; Duffield 2001; Thomas W Smith 2008, 144–164; Bohrer and Osiel 2013, 747–822; Walzer 2009, 40–52; van Creveld 1991b; Kaldor 1999; Coker 2002b; Ignatieff 2003c; Walzer 1992; Coker 2001; Shaw 2005.
[24] Walzer 1992; Kahn 2002, 2–9; Shaw 2005.
[25] Münkler 2004; McInnes 2002; Van Creveld 1991b; Shaw 2005; Coker 2001.

Detailed Chapter Synopsis

Chapter 1 examines how – by breaking with the historical double standards regarding civilian protection in conflicts – by the end of the 20th century, US warfare has come to comply with IHL. Yet, civilians are still being killed. This has sparked controversies over what constitutes legitimate targeting practices and as to whether higher levels of civilian protection could be achieved. Through an engagement with these debates, including an exploration of the evolution of the norm of non-combatant immunity with specific reference to US warfare, the chapter shows how IHL does not provide fully satisfactory answers to these issues as it is too permissive in relation to the killing of civilians. The chapter proposes that more stringent moral guidelines, such as those underpinning the idea of 'due care', have the potential to go much further in providing protection for the innocent in war. By drawing on the moral idea of 'due care', the chapter asks whether the US military has made a positive commitment (including an increase in combat risks to its soldiers) to spare enemy non-combatants or if other factors, primarily American casualty-aversion, have compromised the level of protection afforded to civilians in target states.

Chapter 2 explores the socio-historical reasons as to why the American willingness to sacrifice large numbers of its citizens in modern wars has been replaced by the rise of casualty-aversion following the Vietnam War. And yet, the chapter also shows, in contrast to the general intolerance among military and political leaders towards exposing American military personnel to the risks of combat, Special Forces continue to view war in heroic terms, that is, as a source of individual transformation. Considering the central roles played by these Special Forces in contemporary US warfare in general, and during the interventions in Somalia, Afghanistan, and Iraq in particular, the chapter identifies the tensions between the heroism of US Special Forces and the general casualty-aversion among US leaders: Does the prevailing political quest for minimum casualties override the warriorhood of US Special Operations forces? Or, are they permitted to expose themselves to larger risks than the rest of the American military personnel?

Having identified the rise of the casualty-aversion and civilian protection as key norms of contemporary US warfare, Chapter 3 focuses on the inherent tension between these two norms. Crucially, however, it argues that this inherent tension is exacerbated further by US adversaries, who have identified US concerns for body bags[26] and collateral damage as the centre of gravity of US warfare and have adjusted their strategic behaviour

---

[26] 'Body bags' originally were a way through which militaries measured progress towards victory: a way to count the numbers of enemy soldiers or men killed. Because of the way in

accordingly. In other words, US war is never waged upon a lifeless mass, but always on a living agent who responds. Enemy behaviour is a factor external to and yet crucially affecting the US ability to wage its wars with both features of civilian protection and casualty-aversion intact. Therefore, to answer the book's overall question of whether the US military has been able to wage its wars in risk-averse and humane ways, the particular dynamic interaction between the US and its non-state adversaries needs to be taken into account. How have non-state adversaries, in the face of overwhelming US military might, adjusted their strategies accordingly? And how have these strategic adjustments exacerbated the tension between US casualty-aversion and civilian protection, thereby forcing US decision makers to choose between saving US soldiers and enemy civilians? And what were the legal, moral, and strategic consequences of such decisions?

The empirical, in-depth case studies (Chapters 4 to 6) of the volume answer the above questions by comparing and contrasting the US military interventions in Somalia, Afghanistan, and Iraq. By selecting these three cases over other interventions, the book deliberately explores cases in which the United States waged war against semi-state and/or non-state actors rather than states. This allows the book to investigate the interactive dynamics generated in asymmetric wars under the widest possible gap between two military actors. In these cases, the particular interactive dynamics generated by asymmetric wars have been most profound, thereby providing a rich field through which to explore the book's main research questions.

Chapter 4: Somalia (1992–1994)

Besides being the first major asymmetric conflict the US was involved in since Vietnam (and Lebanon), the importance of focusing on a case like Somalia is that in contrast to other US interventions throughout the 1990s, US ground forces were directly placed in harm's way. American soldiers (especially Special Forces) were inserted into a strategic environment where the technological might of the US military could not as easily secure the goal of casualty-aversion as was the case with, for example, Bosnia, Kosovo, or Libya.

---

which this measuring became discredited in Vietnam, the US military at least officially stopped counting enemy bodies. Instead, 'body bags' have since referred to the number of US soldiers killed in conflict. While this change will be addressed in passing in Chapters 2 and 3, this manuscript uses the term 'body bags' with reference to killed US soldiers and therefore to the norm of casualty-aversion.

The case study covers the period from the beginning of the US intervention in December 1992 until the loss of eighteen US Rangers in October 1993. It thus focuses on the American-led United Task Force (UNITAF), also known as 'Operation Restore Hope', and the pre-eminent US role in the UN-led United Nations Mission in Somalia (UNOSOM II).

Drawing on new primary interview material with key stakeholders, it examines how the asymmetric strategies employed by Somali warlord Muhamed Farah Aideed compelled US commanders to choose between saving US soldiers and Somali civilians before investigating the legal, moral, and strategic consequences of this choice.

Chapter 5: Afghanistan (2001–2002)

By drawing on extensive and new primary interview material, the case study covers the US decision-making process in the wake of the 9/11 attacks and 'Operation Enduring Freedom' from October 2001 until 'Operation Anaconda' in April 2002 (when major American military operations ceased for over half a year).

The case study explores how the asymmetric strategies by the Taliban and Al-Qaeda brought about the dilemma for US commanders – the inability to wage Operation Enduring Freedom with low risks to both US military personnel and Afghan civilians. Focusing on the US response to this dilemma, the case study examines the legal, moral, and strategic consequences of US operations.

Chapter 6: Iraq (2003–2011)

This third and final case study empirically evaluates the violent clash between American military forces and its adversaries in Iraq. The chapter distinguishes between three combat phases over the course of 'Operation Iraqi Freedom' (OIF): the overthrow of Saddam Hussein's regime (19 March–1 May 2003), the insurgency (May 2003–December 2006), and the so-called 'surge' (December 2006–December 2011). The case study advances our understanding of how the strategies of US adversaries exacerbated the US ability to operate in ways that ensured low risks to American military personnel and high levels of civilian protection. The chapter critically evaluates US military operations through the prism of IHL and examines whether American forces started prioritising casualty-aversion over the safeguarding of Iraqi civilians. Finally, the chapter examines whether lower numbers of Iraqi civilian deaths could have been achieved if marginal increases to the risks faced by US soldiers had been accepted and if different military strategies had been chosen.

Why Somalia, Afghanistan, and Iraq?

The empirical part of the book answers the central research question by comparing and contrasting three US military interventions: one in the immediate post–Cold War era and two since 9/11. The three case studies have been chosen to provide a comparative investigation of the legal, moral, and strategic challenges facing the US military when it intervenes in conflicts where the local actors are not sensitive to international norms of civilian protection in war.

The types of intrastate conflicts encountered in Somalia, Afghanistan, and Iraq posed a major challenge to American warfare. This challenge has arisen from the specific operational environments that tend to give advantage to unconventional forms of warfare such as guerrilla tactics and hit and run strategies.[27] The United States is likely to find itself increasingly operating in urban settings (as experienced in Mogadishu and Iraq) and in mountainous environments (such as the campaign in the Hindukush). In other words, urban and mountainous guerrilla warfare has become the predominant theatre of operations in the twenty-first century.[28] In that sense, Somalia, Afghanistan, and Iraq are likely to resemble the type of strategic environments in which the US military will conduct operations in the years and decades to come.

Furthermore, because of the focus on the dynamic interactions under conditions of asymmetry, these cases were selected over other US interventions in the post–Cold War world such as Bosnia, Kosovo, or Libya. Admittedly, the American armed forces have maintained military capabilities so far in excess of those of any would-be (state- or non-state) adversary to the extent that it easily dwarfs the capabilities of a number of competitors combined.[29] This historically unprecedented level of asymmetry is unbridgeable in conventional terms and seems to render any American adversary, whether state or non-state actor, to a status of military helplessness.[30] By selecting the cases of Somalia, Afghanistan, and Iraq over other interventions, the book deliberately explores cases in which the United States waged war against semi and/or non-state actors rather than state actors. This allows the monograph to investigate the interactive dynamics generated in war under the widest possible gap between two military actors: it is in these cases that the particular interactive dynamics generated by conditions of asymmetry should become most profound.

[27] Griffith 1992; Giap 1977, 23–55; Laqueur 1977, 187–243.
[28] Lieven 2001, 1–8; Kaplan 2000, 8–58.   [29] Bacevich 2005, 16.
[30] Kahn 2002, 2–9; Münkler 2006, 60.

Part of the empirical research focuses on the immediate post–Cold War era because it is generally regarded as a period of 'disinterested' wars, that is to say wars that were not justified and legitimised in terms of vital US security interests.[31] Instead, humanitarian rationales were a prominent feature of US interventionism in this period (Northern Iraq from 1991 to 1993, Somalia from 1992 to 1993, Bosnia from 1992 to 1995, and Kosovo in 1999).[32]

The importance of focusing on a case like Somalia is that it sets up a framework for comparison with US military interventions after 9/11. The latter have taken place in a period of 'interested' wars.[33] These are wars which are not fought for humanitarian purposes (even though humanitarian rationales were in play) but – at least according to the Bush and Obama Administrations – for purposes of self-defence against the forces of terrorism with a global reach.[34] The question guiding these cases is whether 9/11 has changed the context for US casualty-aversion and civilian protection from the era of humanitarian interventions: Did the US military in Afghanistan and Iraq adopt a different approach to force protection than in Somalia given that the US was fighting both wars with perceived vital national interests at stake? How far were military operations conducted in a *less* casualty-averse manner? And what were the implications of this for civilian protection? Was everything done to reduce the level of harm for enemy civilians? Or, could more civilian lives have been saved by accepting higher levels of risk to American military personnel? What was the strategic reasoning of American adversaries? And to what extent did the asymmetric strategy employed by al-Qaeda, the Taliban, and Iraqi insurgents exacerbate the US ability to wage these wars in a riskless and humane way?

By considering – through the cases of Somalia, Afghanistan, and Iraq – the reality and nature of the conflict environments into which the US has intervened, the research critically examines how enemy behaviour impacted on the trade-off between US casualty-aversion and civilian protection.

Methodological Orientation

Instead of following one overarching qualitative social science research method, the monograph is rather eclectic in its choice of methodological approaches.

---

[31] Mueller 1996, 31; Krauthammer 2002; Bacevich 2002, 143.

[32] Walzer 2004, 100–101; Wheeler 2000.   [33] Krauthammer 2002.

[34] Elshtain 2003, 1–45; *The 9/11 Commission Report: Final Report of the National Commission on Terrorist Attacks upon the United States* (New York: W. W. Norton & Company, 2004), p. xvi.

Chapters 1 and 2, for instance, illustrate the socio-historical evolution of American casualty-aversion and civilian protection by employing a genealogical approach as pioneered by Friedrich Nietzsche and Michel Foucault. This permits the book to critically investigate and explain the conditions under which certain values or practices emerge, grow, and change.[35] A genealogical approach absolves the research from the need to recount the entire history of a phenomenon and restricts itself to historical episodes that are of decisive importance in understanding a phenomenon in terms of its key issues. For that reason, a genealogical methodology is concerned with questions of 'how' rather than 'what'. It asks how the norms of casualty-aversion and civilian protection have originated, changed, and finally evolved into their respective forms. By principally focusing on the causes of change, a genealogical method provides the most appropriate approach in order to achieve the objectives set out in Chapters 1 and 2.

Due to the focus on the dynamics that occur during US conflicts with semi-/non-state actors and on how the interaction impacts on the trade-off in US warfare, Chapters 3 to 6 employ a methodology which broadly fits within the school of social constructivism. Yet, these chapters neither follow any specific strand of social constructivism, nor aim at making any original contribution to the debates in which social constructivists are currently engaged. Instead, these chapters expose a conception of the interactive nature of war that is generally in line with constructivists' claims that agents and structures are mutually constituted.[36] Stressing the socially constructed nature of agents and structures, constructivists emphasise how agents can shape, reproduce, and change their material and ideational environment, yet are constrained and shaped by it.[37] In other words, the constructivist premise of agents and structures, inter-ests and identities, ideas and beliefs being 'mutually constituted' under-lines the basic understanding of war's interactive dynamic as being mutually constituted by both adversaries.

The material for the empirical research is drawn mainly from two sources. On the one hand, the analysis makes extensive use of the diverse secondary literature on the nature of the local conflicts in Somalia, Afghanistan, Iraq and contemporary US warfare. Besides drawing on existing secondary and web-based sources of these American interven-tions, the research draws on new primary source material which has been gathered through thirty-eight semi-structured interviews with former and current American military planners, service personnel, and foreign policy

---

[35] Nietzsche 1995; Foucault 1977, 139–164.   [36] Wendt 1992, 391–425; Giddens 1984.
[37] Price and Reus-Smit 1998; Zehfuss 2001, 54–75; Wendt 1992, 391–425.

makers. In addition to that, sources have been collected from journalists (print media and television) who reported on Somalia, Afghanistan, and Iraq during the respective operations and who therefore have directly experienced the reality and nature of US interventions on the ground (*Christian Science Monitor*, *The New Yorker*, *The Atlantic Monthly*, *The New York Times*, *The Washington Post*, Reuters, CNN, NBC, BBC). Finally, sources have also been collected from the vast pool of experts and scholars in US East Coast universities (Brown University, Georgetown University, George Washington University), think-tanks, research centres, and public policy-focused institutions (RAND Corporation, The Brookings Institution, United States Institute of Peace, The Carnegie Endowment for International Peace, The International Peace Academy, The Carnegie Council on Ethics and International Affairs, and The Project on Defence Alternatives).[38]

---

[38] For details of the interviewees, see list.

1 US Warfare and Civilian Protection

> Nagasaki was an embarrassment to the art of war ... I think what will
> happen in the not-too-distant future is that we will have humane wars.
>
> Don DeLillo, *End Zone.*

Introduction

This book examines the trade-off between US casualty-aversion and
civilian protection in contemporary asymmetric conflicts. In order to
assess the central research question, the book develops a novel theoretical
framework of the trade-off between protecting enemy civilians and saving
US soldiers (Chapters 1 and 2) in the context of the interactive dynamics
generated by asymmetric conflicts (Chapter 3).

This chapter investigates the different forms civilian protection has
taken in nineteenth- and twentieth-century American warfare. It traces
the eradication of the double standards regarding civilian protection that
have characterised US warfare throughout most of its history. To do so,
the chapter employs a genealogical approach as pioneered by Friedrich
Nietzsche and Michel Foucault. This permits the chapter to critically
investigate and explain the conditions under which certain values or
practices emerge, grow, and change.[1] A genealogical approach tracks
the evolution of a value system by restricting itself to historical episodes
that are of decisive importance in understanding a phenomenon in terms
of its key issues. For that reason, a genealogical methodology is concerned
with questions of 'how' rather than 'what'. It asks – ex post facto – how the
aspect of civilian protection has originated, changed, and finally evolved
in its current form.

Employing a genealogical approach to trace the evolution of civilian
protection is very different from a commitment to a progressivist, linear,
let alone Whiggish interpretation of history. This does not mean that the
role of civilian protection in US warfare has not been strengthened

---

[1] Nietzsche 1995; Foucault 1977, 139–164.

compared to practices in the past, nor does it mean that its current role remains uncontested or could not be subject to regression. Rather, as this chapter will show, tracing the contours of civilian protection in the history of US warfare reveals a non-linear development subject to both chance and contingencies. The current role civilian protection is playing in US warfare therefore is not an endpoint or a 'pinnacle'. Instead, employing a genealogical approach essentially means to ask how we arrived at the form that civilian protection currently takes in US warfare. It traces the evolution of civilian protection through pivotal moments that impacted on it, whether it was for better or worse.

The chapter also draws on the historical-sociological approaches to International Relations, in particular Norbert Elias' and Andrew Linklater's works on the 'civilizing process' and the 'problem of harm'.[2] Their respective analyses of how attitudes towards cruelty, violence, and human suffering have changed across different historical eras and how emotional identification between different societies have increased, provide for the wider context through which to trace what Linklater calls the 'fundamental changes in thinking about what is permitted and what is forbidden in war'.[3]

By principally focusing on the causes of change, this genealogical method shows how the double standards in US warfare between the concepts of Bellum Romanum and Bellum Civile have slowly been eradicated in the aftermath of World War II (WWII) in a process through which the principles of Bellum Civile have become universalised. As a result, by the end of the twentieth century, US warfare, no matter where and against whom it is being conducted, has largely come to comply with the principle of non-combatant immunity.[4]

Yet, enemy civilians are still being killed, oftentimes at large numbers. This has sparked controversies over what constitutes legitimate targeting practices and as to whether higher levels of civilian protection could be achieved if US forces were exposed to greater risks. Through an

---

[2] Two points of clarification need to be made here. While the approach by both Elias and Linklater are useful methodologically in analysing changing attitudes towards harm and violence, their focus is on Europe and world politics. This book focuses more narrowly on the United States. Second, while both Linklater and Elias believe that 'advances' have been made in world politics, they do not commit to a linear, progressive, or Whig interpretation of history. Instead, their work stresses that civilising processes are always attended by decivilising dangers and regressions into barbarism. See for instance Elias 1996, 24–25; Linklater and Mennell 2010, 404–405.

[3] Linklater 2002, 336. See also Elias 1998.

[4] In this book, terms like 'non-combatants' and 'civilians' are defined along the lines of the 4th Geneva Convention, according to which civilians constitute 'people who do not bear arms' and who therefore are regarded as a subset of non-combatants, i.e. 'persons taking no active part in the hostilities', see Green 2000, 124.

engagement with these debates, the second part of the chapter argues that International Humanitarian Law (IHL) does not provide fully satisfactory answers to these issues as it is too permissive in relation to the killing of civilians. Instead, the chapter proposes that more stringent moral guidelines, such as those underpinning the idea of 'due care', have the potential to go much further in providing protection for the innocent in war. By drawing on the moral idea of 'due care', the chapter asks whether the US military has taken positive steps (including increased combat risks to soldiers) to spare enemy non-combatants or if other factors, primarily American casualty-aversion (examined in Chapter 2), have compromised the level of protection afforded to civilians in target states.

Bellum Romanum and Bellum Civile and the Double Standard towards Civilian Protection

A key feature of American warfare until the end of the twentieth century was the existence of a double standard regarding the levels of restraint towards enemy civilians. Originating in ancient Greece and Rome, drastically different levels of respect for civilian protection (located in the concepts of Bellum Romanum and Bellum Civile) had profound effects on European and – by extension – American warfare. This double standard was finally eradicated in the late 1980s and 1990s, resulting in a significant strengthening of the principle of non-combatant immunity.[5]

To investigate this current humanising trend, the chapter examines the different forms civilian protection has taken throughout the history of US warfare. First, however, it traces the conceptual origins of the double standards in ancient Greece before examining how they came to shape the American use of force. This short detour is important, for US warfare was modelled on key aspects of ancient Greek (and Roman) warfare, including the conceptual double standards which informed how force was employed by the ancient Greeks against those who were conceived as humans and subhumans. Systematised by Roman law, these conceptual double standards were subsequently inherited by the Renaissance and the Enlightenment – and thereby became the legal foundation of Europe and, by extension, the United States.[6] In this process, the conceptual

---

[5] The chapter focuses exclusively on the American (rather than a general 'Western') conduct of war for the reason that the US has become the most dominant contemporary military actor, not only possessing unprecedented military capabilities but also being able to project them globally. More importantly, the United States, conceiving of itself as a unique historical actor, has tended to project its military capabilities in the language of norms and law – including the exception-less respect for the principle of non-combatant immunity.

[6] Rabkin 2011, 700–716.

differentiation between Bellum Romanum and Bellum Civile that had originated in ancient Greece and Rome and that had characterised European warfare, came to persist in US warfare.[7] The chapter employs the concepts of Bellum Romanum and Bellum Civile as a means to conceptually reconstruct the different normative and legal restraints with which military force was employed.

In the context of ancient Greece, when Greek warriors fought other Greek warriors, they generally observed the unwritten conventions of city-state warfare. The so-called 'Common customs of the Hellenes' ensured that a highly ritualised and restraining code was honoured in intra-Greek warfare.[8] The restraint enshrined in these Hellenic customs, however, was only shown in intra-Greek wars; they did not exist in wars between Greeks and non-Hellenes.[9] In conflicts against the latter, as during the Persian Wars (490–478 BC), Greek warriors waged unrestricted warfare.[10] The difference between these drastically different types of war was based on the concepts of Bellum Civile and Bellum Romanum.[11] The former codified the normative restraints on the use of force in order to maintain a high level of discrimination in war. In contrast, Bellum Romanum was a type of

[w]arfare in which no holds were barred and all those designated as enemies, whether bearing arms or not, would be indiscriminately slaughtered.[12]

This type of warfare was inherently indiscriminate.

In applying only to certain peoples and not to others, these early conventions in war were particularistic in nature as the protection afforded by them only applied to Greeks. Towards non-Hellenes, a Greek warrior could and did behave without restraint.[13] In other words, a double standard existed with respect to the normative restraints on the use of force.[14]

The reason why Bellum Romanum rather than Bellum Civile was practiced against non-Hellenes was located in a limited notion of humanity.[15] Those living inside the respective historical conception of

---

[7] Coker 2002b, 62; Linklater 2004b, 8–9.
[8] Howard, Andreopoulos and Shulman 1994, 13.
[9] Aristotle 1958, 16; Bryant 2016, 31–37.
[10] Herodotus 2003; Hanson 2000, 37; Parker 2005, 22–27.
[11] Colin S. Gray 1999, 275–276; Lindqvist 2002a. Although the terms Bellum Romanum and Bellum Civile were coined after the wars waged by the Roman Empire (in particular following Julius Caesar's campaigns in Gallicia), the existing literature tends to use them equally in reference to the wars fought by the ancient Greek city states. According to this view, the Romans merely formalised what the Greeks had already practiced.
[12] Howard, Andreopoulos and Shulman 1994, 3.
[13] Herodotus 2003; Phillipson 1911, 40; Bryant 2016, 31–37.
[14] Ignatieff 1999, 117; Elias 1996, 176.   [15] Aristotle 1958, 16; Phillipson 2011, 40.

humanity were regarded as human beings and therefore subjected to the principles of Bellum Civile. Those living outside the conception of humanity were seen as subhumans and were consequently subjected to the principle of Bellum Romanum. The limits and boundaries of humanity, or, in other words, the moral restraint on the use of force, were the fault lines between Bellum Civile and Bellum Romanum.

Bellum Romanum and Bellum Civile in Seventeenth to Nineteenth Century US Warfare

This normative double standard of restrained and unrestricted warfare was adopted throughout most of the European and – by extension – American history of warfare.[16] Humanity in the American context was defined as Christian, white, and civilised. All those outside these categories were dehumanised by labelling them infidels and savages. This distinction between intra- and extra-American standards of humanity inherited from the ancient Greeks, chivalric knights, and early European colonial powers resulted in the continued application of the double standard of morality in the use of force.[17] Within the American conception of humanity, normative restraints were increasingly complemented by legal restraints trying to salvage the decencies of chivalric warfare in the industrial age.[18] Yet, these decencies were neither morally respected nor legally binding in wars waged against those considered to be 'savages' and 'barbarians'.[19]

The limited conception of humanity was sufficient justification for the conduct of a type of war against those outside humanity that – had it been practiced in this form between Americans and Europeans – would have been considered as inhumane and unacceptable.[20] And precisely because the dehumanisation of these outsiders had become the norm, Bellum Romanum was the standard military practice by Americans during their imperial expansion.

Underpinning America's continental expansion were the religious 1630 vision of America being 'a city upon a hill' and the political rationale of 'Manifest Destiny'. A deeply religious nation, Americans perceived themselves as a Chosen People, forging a special covenant with God. Bestowed to them by Him, their destiny was to carve a New Jerusalem out of the wilderness.[21] 'Manifest Destiny' was an early nineteenth-century vision proclaiming that the American people must redeem the land to the

---

[16] Elias 1996, 461, 176; Braudy 2003; Rabkin 2011, 700–704; Downes 2006, 160–161.
[17] Dower 1993; Linklater 2010, 166.   [18] Roberts and Guelff 1999; Best 1983.
[19] Philip K Lawrence 1999, 6–34.   [20] Elias 1996, 154.
[21] Bacevich 2005, 122; Tony Smith 1995.

west, and extend their sovereignty to its natural frontiers.[22] Coined by John L O'Sullivan, 'Manifest Destiny' thus referred to the conviction that superior institutions and culture gave Americans the God-given right, even an obligation, to spread their civilisation across the entire continent.[23] In their quest to dominate the continent from ocean to ocean, Americans regarded the indigenous Indian population that they encountered as subhuman obstacles to their push westwards.[24] Early colonialists and settlers defined the Indian tribes of New England as savages, subjecting them to unrestricted warfare. For example, George Washington, the first US president, described Indians as 'beasts of prey, similar to the wolf, though they differ in shape.'[25] Lieutenant General William T. Sherman, the commanding general in the wars against several Indian tribes, argued that

The more [Indians] we can kill this year, the less will have to be killed in the next war, for the more I see of these Indians the more convinced I am that they all have to be killed or maintained as a species of paupers. Their attempts at civilization are simply ridiculous.[26]

During its westward expansion, the US government either dealt with Indian tribes by forcing their resettlement or by waging wars of total extermination against them.[27]

The 1832 'Grand American Desert' Plan and the 1834 'Indian Intercourse Act' signed by President Andrew Jackson compelled the indigenous population to move from their natural habitat to allocated territories (so-called 'permanent Indian country').[28] Whenever these measures of forced resettlement met with resistance by tribes like the Cherokees or the Seminoles in Florida (1836–1842), American forces by default waged unrestricted warfare against them.[29]

Following the 1843 Oregon Settlement and the Mexican-American War (1846–1848), the strategy of permanent resettlement became obsolete. With Indian country no longer marking the official boundary of the United States and unable to remove the indigenous population further West, the American government forced the remaining Indian tribes into reservations. Those tribes that were not in their allocated reservations by 31 January 1876 were assumed to be at war with the United States. US military reaction against the latter turned into a long range strategy of annihilation.[30]

[22] Porch 2001, 55.   [23] Jeffrey and Nash 1994, 427–428.
[24] Grenier 2005; Dower 1993, 148–149.   [25] Dower 1993, 150.
[26] Cited in Weigley 1973, 158.   [27] Williams 2005; Grenier 2005.
[28] Weigley 1973, 153–154.   [29] Chris H Gray 1997, 117.
[30] Zinn 2003a, 152–169; Chris H Gray 1997, 115; Weigley 1973, xxi–xxii.

In the zeitgeist of the colonial age there was – at least from the perspective of the coloniser – nothing wrong with launching indiscriminate warfare against 'savages'.[31] Bellum Romanum could be practiced against 'uncivilised' tribes as they were placed outside the conception of humanity. Theodore Roosevelt, who later became the twenty-sixth President of the United States, publicly supported the virtual extermination of the American Indians on the grounds that they were an uncivilised race:

> I suppose I should be ashamed to say that I take the Western view of the Indian. I don't go so far as to think that the only good Indians are dead Indians, but I believe nine out of ten are, and I shouldn't inquire too closely into the case of the tenth.[32]

In the Red River War (1874–1875) and in the wars against the tribes of the northern plains, the economic base of Indian communities (the buffalo herds) were destroyed and tens of thousands of Indians massacred. The result of waging Bellum Romanum was not only the annihilation of the military power of the Indian nations, but also the extinction of their independent way of life and culture.

At the same time, however, when American forces fought European powers as during the French and Indian War 1755–1763, the war of 1812, or the 1898 Spanish-American War, the unmitigated cruelty visited on the Indian nations by default gave way to a restricted way of fighting. White Europeans were generally regarded as living inside the conception of humanity and therefore had to be subjected to the principles of Bellum Civile.[33] The moral conventions as well as early rules of international law, designed to ensure a high level of humanity in wars between 'civilized' nations explicitly excluded colonial subjects from its provisions. International law only protected those deemed to be civilised, whereas 'barbarians' and 'savages' at best possessed rights to guardianship and punishment.[34]

American imperial expansion beyond the continent reproduced the same double standards. The United States had always thought of itself as different from European colonial powers. At least in its own mind, it saw imperialism as an accidental by-product of the victory over Spain in 1898. Yet, finding itself in the possession of Puerto Rico and the Philippines after the 1898 War with Spain, America was prepared to pick up what the poet Rudyard Kipling termed 'the White Man's Burden'.[35] This famous poem enshrined in the US perception an image of the Filipinos as 'fluttered folk and wild ... sullen peoples, half devil and

---

[31] Elias 1996, 154, 461.   [32] Cited in Dower 1993, 151.
[33] Lindqvist 2002a, 30–31; Rabkin 2011, 700–716.
[34] Roberts and Guelff 1999, 53–57.   [35] Zinn 2003a, 312–313; Boot 2002, 106–107.

half child.'[36] For Americans, there was a clear link between fighting Indians on the Western frontier and Filipinos in Asia. During the Philippine War (1898–1902), US forces under Major General Arthur MacArthur, a former Indian fighter on the Western plains, burned entire towns, tortured civilians, and slaughtered the local population.[37] His 'General Order 100' eliminated the neutrality of the civilian population and orders were given to kill everyone above the age of ten, slaughtering as many as 200,000 civilians in the process.[38]

The moral issues raised by this practice of unrestricted violence and – in the case of the Indian nations – genocidal warfare were insufficient to either rattle the confidence of the American people in their assumed right to extend the frontiers against the wishes of indigenous inhabitants or to penetrate their self-understanding of the modern world as progressive and peaceful.[39] The reason for this was that those on the receiving end of colonial violence were non-Whites, non-Christians, and subhumans who at best had to be treated as infants that needed to be educated and punished. As the zeitgeist of modern societies aimed at the remaking of mankind, the social engineering of humans and the annihilation of entire 'hordes of barbarians' were part of the progression of the modern human project. As a result, ethnic cleansing and genocide became constitutive of progress.[40] The perceived limits of humanity remained the fault lines between Bellum Romanum and Bellum Civile.

The Blurring of Bellum Romanum and Bellum Civile in the Age of Modern Industrial Warfare

Compared to the age of empire, the boundaries of humanity changed significantly in the age of modern industrial warfare, thereby shifting the fault lines between Bellum Civile and Bellum Romanum. The principal effect of Modernity was to further constrict this already limited definition of humanity. By further reducing the definition of humanity to exclusive groups such as the race, the ethnic group, the class, and the nation, the group of those living outside humanity was effectively enlarged and included White and non-Whites, Americans as well as non-Americans[41]. The boundaries of inside/outside therefore shifted with the result that the fault lines between Bellum Romanum and Bellum Civile went straight through the American and European continents. In other words, more human beings were excluded from the notion of humanity compared to

---

[36] Dower 1993, 151.   [37] Jeffrey and Nash 1994, 685–687.
[38] Lewis and Steele 2001, 38–39.   [39] Porch 2001, 176–177.
[40] Rubinstein 2004, 54–124.   [41] Dower 1993; Lindqvist 2002a; Thomas 2001.

the imperial age. Accordingly, Bellum Romanum, previously only practiced by whites against non-Whites, slowly started seeping into the wars
fought among Americans and Europeans.

Why did this happen? Modernity brought a displacement of metaphy-
sics from God onto History as the grand narrative.[42] It replaced a religious
division of humanity with a secular one. History was no longer preor-
dained or subject to divine intervention, but subject to humankind. In the
modern age, women and men were no longer objects but subjects of
History.[43] During the course of the Enlightenment, a dialectical struggle
over different concepts of Historical progress emerged in which
Liberalism and Rationalism gave rise to the powerful intellectual and
political currents of the counter-enlightenment that were outspokenly
anti-liberal and anti-positivist, such as Romanticism, Socialism, and
Fascism.[44] As a consequence, the modern age turned into a struggle for
History among those who saw themselves as agents pushing History into
the future by forging new world orders.[45] The race, the nation, the ethnic
group, and the class served as secular religions by offering an entire
worldview that justified sacrifice.[46]

In this dialectical struggle between different concepts of History,
war was more than a mere instrument of policy. War was a medium
for progress, social engineering, and political change because it was
through the means of war that the modern individual became an
agent of History.[47] According to Mark Mazower, the three major
concepts of History inherently shared the will to forge a New World
Order:

> The liberal Woodrow Wilson offered a world safe for democracy; Lenin offered
> a communal society emancipated from want and free of exploitative hierarchies of
> the past; Hitler envisaged a warrior race, purged of all alien influences, and
> fulfilling its historical destiny through the purity of its blood.[48]

In their quest to make History, no compromise was permitted. All three
ideologies believed in the final showdown where the forces of the future
would prevail over the forces of the past. All three saw themselves des-
tined to remake society and to remake the world in a New World Order
for mankind.

The total and uncompromising nature of modern ideologies allowed
for the dehumanisation of others outside their nationalistic, racial, and/or
ideological boundaries. They divided the universe into forces of light and
forces of darkness, thereby labelling outsiders as subhumans, beasts, or

---

[42] Joas 2003.   [43] Rorty 1989; Blumenberg 1985.
[44] Howard 2000; Horkheimer and Adorno 1973.   [45] Howard 1981.
[46] Coker 2004, 1–45.   [47] Howard 2000; Coker 1994.   [48] Mazower 1999, x.

barbarians.[49] The concepts of History laid the legitimate grounds upon which unrestricted warfare and unprecedented cruelty against entire societies could be waged in the course of the twentieth century.[50] Once other nations had been dehumanised, the lawlessness with which war was practiced outside the United States and Europe could no longer be kept from seeping into wars between them. As a result, the distinction between Bellum Romanum and Bellum Civile started breaking down.

Once the technology and scientific innovations of industrialisation could give full reign to killing, modern wars became total – encompassing every aspect of private and public life.[51] This rising curve of barbarism became most obvious in relation to civilians who became the proper, in some cases even the main target of the modern war machine.

Yet, it was the American Civil War (1861–1865) that provided the first modern glimpse of total war.[52] The Civil War witnessed the departure from customary practices that had previously prevailed in wars between 'civilized' armed forces. Confronted with unrestricted warfare, first attempts were made to salvage the decencies of Bellum Civile by codifying standards of civilised behaviour in legal terms. The 'Instructions for the Government of Armies of the United States in the Field' (which came to be known as the Lieber Code) were issued to the Union Army on 24 April 1863 and not only prepared the way for the calling of the 1874 Brussels Conference but also had profound effects on the shaping of the overall evolution of IHL as codified by the Hague and Geneva Conventions.[53] But even though the Lieber Code aimed at reigning in the worst annihilationist tendencies of the Civil War, it failed to prevent the degeneration of the conflict.[54]

This degeneration was slow but gradual, evolving from the early restraint in Union and Confederate practices to increasingly directing military force at the enemy's economic resources and civilian population. The strategy of annihilation of General Ulysses S Grant emerged out of the realisation that wars of attrition made the attainment of decisive victory in battle more difficult and that conciliatory politics had failed to bring the Secessionists back into the Union.[55] Although the Civil War was still far off the later contests of rival productive capacities like those during World War II, the logistical requirements of both mass armies had already become big enough to make war against the enemy's resources and support base begin to appear a tempting prospect.[56]

---

[49] Ehrenreich 1998, 200–203.   [50] Shaw 2003, 54–144.   [51] Pick 1993.
[52] Hagerman 1988; Farrell 2005, 76–77.
[53] Roberts and Guelff 1999, 12–13; Gade 2010, 221–226.   [54] Weigley 1973, 128–152.
[55] Weigley, 139–141.   [56] Chris H Gray 1997, 116.

The resulting strategy of Union forces, executed by Generals Grant, Sherman, and John Pope, was not only designed against the enemy industry and land, but also developed into a deliberate strategy of terror directed at the civilian population. As Sherman argued, '[w]e are not only fighting hostile armies, but a hostile people and must make old and young, rich and poor, feel the hard hand of war.'[57] This understanding of modern war as a conflict between peoples beyond the contest of armed forces led to campaigns, most famously Sherman's March to the Sea as well as the forced evacuation and the burning of Atlanta, which aimed at carrying the destruction of war straight to the enemy people.[58] By arguing that 'war is hell', Sherman saw himself entitled to do whatever he considered militarily necessary to defeat the Confederate Army.[59] The Union's objective became the complete destruction and total submission of the South, causing the practice of Bellum Romanum to seep into conflicts between white Americans.

The United States and – shortly thereafter – modern Europe experienced a type of war that aimed 'not just [at] the overthrow of the enemy's political power but [at] the physical destruction of his entire society.'[60] In World War II, political and military decision makers on the sides of the Axis and Allies alike regularly used arguments of military necessity to override concerns for civilian protection, as during the strategic bombing campaigns and the dropping of the atomic bombs.[61] As modern war was waged as a struggle for the survival of the state and the political community, the ideological threats posed by those outside humanity were regarded as so horrific and imminent as to make concern for civilian protection redundant.

But even within total warfare, important differences existed in the level of respect for civilians shown by the participating armed forces. For example, Hitler's Blitzkrieg campaigns in Western Europe and Africa remained relatively restrained compared with the ideologically driven 'Vernichtungskrieg' in the East that aimed at the total annihilation of the 'Jewish-Bolshevik Revolution'.[62]

In the American case, a similar difference existed between the levels of restraint shown by US soldiers in the European and Pacific theatres of the war. Although America waged total war on both societies, several studies show how racial and ideological factors help explain why US behaviour against imperial Japan was considerably more unrestricted and barbaric than against Nazi Germany.[63] Despite Hitler's orgy of violence on the

[57] Cited in Weigley 1973, 149.   [58] Walzer 1992, 32–33.   [59] Walzer 1992, 32–33.
[60] Howard, Andreopoulos and Shulman 1994, 8.
[61] Shaw 2003, 126–144, Philip K Lawrence 1999, 87.   [62] Bartov 1985.
[63] Mitchell 1997, 312; Farrell 2005, 89.

Eastern Front and the execution of the Holocaust, it was the Japanese rather than the Germans who were dehumanised as vermin, 'beastly little monkeys' or 'apes in khakis'.[64] Analysing the role that race played in shaping American attitudes during the Pacific War, Theo Farrell argues that

Racist images of the other – of the enemy as subhuman – made it possible for the Marine Corps to prosecute a brutal ground war against Japanese forces, and the US Army Air Force to conduct a horrific air campaign against Japanese cities.[65]

No Japanese equivalent to the 'Good German' existed in the American consciousness; instead, they were seen as a race or even a species apart.[66] The Japanese were saddled with racial stereotypes that Americans had applied to non-Whites for centuries during their conquest of the New World, the slave trade, the Indian wars, and the US conquest of the Philippines.[67] Such dehumanisation not only made possible the decision to make the Japanese population the direct target of US conventional and nuclear attacks, but also explained why the American war in Asia was more unrestricted and merciless than in the European theatre.[68]

To give an example, under the Executive Order 9066, signed by President Roosevelt on 19 February 1942, the US government incarcerated 110,000 Japanese-Americans en masse but failed to take any comparable action against residents of German or Italian origin. In Europe, but not in the Pacific, one distinct feature was the lack of racial hatred for the enemy; the average American GI was found to hate Germans less than 'Japs'.[69] These racist undertones were also reflected in American bombing policies as well as the treatment of (and refusal to take) Japanese Prisoners of War (POW).[70] Moreover, the United States Air Force (USAF) often held to comparatively restricted bombing practices over Germany (such as flying daytime raids in order to ensure higher levels of precision and using lower numbers of incendiary or napalm bombs).[71] No such considerations of restraint existed in the American campaigns over Japan.[72] Even within total war, therefore, important differences existed in the levels of respect the United States showed to civilian populations.

The modern age reduced the boundaries of those considered to be humans and thereby enlarged the group of those who were considered to be outside humanity. The fault line of those outside humanity now included Whites and non-Whites (anyone belonging to a different race or

[64] Dower 1993, 84.   [65] Farrell 2005, 87.   [66] Mitchell 1997, 312.
[67] Lewis and Steele 2001, 144.   [68] Dower 1993, 11; Farrell 2005, 89.
[69] Mitchell 1997, 313.   [70] Farrell 2005, 84–89.
[71] Tami D Biddle 2004, 253; Thomas 2001, 131–133.   [72] Thomas 2001, 134–135.

following a different ideological Weltanschauung). The process of the decline of moderation in wars between Western industrialised powers marked the breakdown of the distinction between Bellum Romanum and Bellum Civile, for it steadily regressed modern societies into an age of barbarism. Comparing America's modern industrial wars with its earlier colonial wars reveals a clear dehumanising trend.

The Humanising Trend

This dehumanising trend in modern US warfare was reversed in the post-1945 world.[73] The resulting humanising process, however, was slow to evolve and only grew gradually.[74] The first indications of this long process towards the strengthening of the principle of non-combatant immunity came through the Geneva Conventions of 1949 and could be witnessed on the Korean Peninsula and in Indochina. It was during the Korean and (crucially) Vietnam Wars that the racial undertones and ideological absolutes that had previously been employed to justify the American practice of Bellum Romanum gradually started ringing hollow.

For a considerable period of time, however, racial hatred still coloured American views of both conflicts in ways that often found expression in language, imagery, and practices not dissimilar from the racism of the Philippine and Pacific Wars.[75] Moreover, it was in abstract ideational terms that Americans saw both conflicts as a test of their nation's will and readiness to confront and ultimately contain Communism. Based on the 'domino theory', Korea and Vietnam were conceived as part of the Cold War Manichean struggle between the forces of good and evil in which the US had to prevail in order to save humanity from Communism.[76]

On this ideological level, the Korea War and (in its early phase) the Vietnam War deeply appealed to America's sense of historical mission and duty to test its character and destiny against an enemy that was the antithesis of everything it stood for – Communism.[77] Americans were prepared to support the 'Long Twilight Struggle', which required sacrifice and justified unrestricted warfare against the indigenous population of both countries.[78]

Despite the invocation of racial and ideological absolutes analogous to the ones that had justified the dehumanisation of US adversaries in earlier conflicts, a new American sensitivity towards civilian casualties could

---

[73] Zehfuss 2010, 543–566; Kahl 2007b, 7–46.
[74] Renz and Scheipers 2012, 17–43; Rabkin 2011, 700–716; Gade 2010, 223–230.
[75] Dower 1993, 311; Lindqvist 2002a, 267–275.
[76] McCrisken 2003, 21–22; McNamara, Blight, and Brigham 1999, 22.
[77] Neu 2000, 11.   [78] Herring 1986, 144.

nevertheless be detected in the Korean War. In his study of the 'bombing norm', Ward Thomas shows that

By the time of the Korean War, an international sensibility was emerging that bombing attacks resulting in many civilian deaths, even if they were not aimed at the civilian population per se, were not a legitimate means of warfare.[79]

The sources of this emerging international sensibility in part came from the horrors and devastating suffering caused by World War II. In particular the Nazi atrocities, the indiscriminate nature of Allied strategic bombing as well as the dropping of the atomic bombs on Japan had started to render such military practices unjustifiable in the eyes of the international community.[80] Both the proclamation of the Universal Declaration of Human Rights of 1948 and the Geneva Conventions of 1949 were designed to recognise the equality of all human beings and to endow civilians with legal protection from wanton violence. The four Geneva Conventions in particular, building upon and expanding the rules of modern war as set out in the Lieber Code and the Hague Conventions of 1899 and 1907, codified the norms prohibiting the targeting of civilians in wars.[81] The codification of these humanitarian norms, Farrell argues,

Followed the logic of appropriateness: states agreed to be bound by the norms because by the mid-twentieth century, the alternatives – mistreating civilians, wounded, and prisoners – were no longer considered acceptable behaviour by the international community.[82]

This is not to deny that the American military subjected Korean cities to strategic bombing and incendiary raids that aimed at weakening civilian morale and that resulted in hundreds of thousands of deaths. In fact, Thomas acknowledges that the emerging norm of civilian protection was not only far from being internalised by the US military but also not powerful enough to prevent the use of strategic bombing despite growing international criticism. Post–WWII, in other words, a new norm was emerging which was bumping up against the old norm of Bellum Romanum. At the same time, however, the new norm

[w]as beginning to force [American decision-makers] to limit the means by which they could [use airpower to wither enemy morale] and make them consider the political costs they might incur by offending international opinion on the issue.[83]

This newly emerging norm could also be witnessed in the nuclear taboo that came to shape US policy following the bombing of Hiroshima and

---

[79] Thomas 2001, 151.   [80] Shaw 2005, 18–19; Mueller 1990, 117–131.
[81] Roberts and Guelff 1999.   [82] Farrell 2005, 155.   [83] Thomas 2001, 151.

Nagasaki. As Farrell shows in his study on the origins and institutionali-
sation of the nuclear taboo, American policy-makers recognised
a normative prohibition on the use of nuclear weapons (except as a last
resort in retaliation for a nuclear attack) soon after World War II.
US Presidents from Harry S Truman to George H W Bush conceived
the use of atomic weapons against non-nuclear powers either as morally
wrong *per se* or as unacceptable by (world) public opinion.[84] In relation to
strategic bombing and the use of nuclear weapons, the era of the Korean
War therefore saw the beginning of a change in American attitudes
towards the safeguarding of enemy non-combatants.

Concerns for civilian protection became even more evident in the
Vietnam War. Far more than in Japan or Korea, the growing sensitivity
about civilian casualties served as an important constraining factor on
America's bombing strategies.[85] In Vietnam, the same fear of a potential
Soviet or Chinese Communist intervention that had already influenced
US decision makers during the Korean War placed significant limitations
on US bombing practices in North Vietnam.[86] The US only started to
escalate its military operations in Vietnam (such as the mining of
Haiphong Harbour and the Christmas Bombing) after the opening to
China and détente with the Soviet Union was already underway by 1972.
This demonstrates the constraining effects that the fear of escalation with
Moscow or Beijing had on US warmaking. In contrast to the Korean War,
however, the targeting of densely populated areas such as Hanoi and
Haiphong or the country's dam and dike systems was generally avoided
throughout the war, indicating a far greater emphasis on the avoidance of
civilian casualties than in Korea.[87] By imposing significant restrictions on
target selection, the civilian authorities in the White House and Pentagon
not only tended to overrule the US military, but also rejected the requests
by the Joint Chiefs of Staff (JCS) and General William Westmoreland,
Commander of American Forces in Vietnam (1964–1968), for further
escalation and, as in 1967, for an all-out war.[88] Both President Johnson
and his successor Richard M Nixon were acutely aware of the political
costs that resulted from collateral damage and accordingly placed considerable emphasis on avoiding civilian casualties. As a result, many
targets that could have been lawfully struck were placed off-limits such
as the 'restricted' and 'prohibited areas' around Hanoi and Haiphong.[89]

The evidence of the bombing practice in Vietnam suggests that the
sensitivity about civilian casualties had grown since World War II and the

---

[84] Farrell 2005, 106–110; Tannenwald 2007, 1999, 433–468.   [85] Boot 2002, 291.
[86] Summers 1982, 87–88.   [87] Thomas 2001, 147–156.   [88] Logevall 1999, 375–414.
[89] Summers 1982, 83–86; Herring 1986, 170–177.

Korean War. The relative constraint in the use of air power against Vietnam indicated the beginning of a shifting of boundaries between those inside and outside the American definition of humanity. The norm of non-combatant immunity began to impose restraints on the killing of enemy civilians who had previously been located outside humanity. Subjecting the Vietnamese people to the unrestricted warfare of Bellum Romanum in the form of strategic bombing could no longer be legitimated.

In contrast to this change in bombing practices, the overall American conduct of the ground war in Vietnam remained indiscriminate and inhumane. Relying heavily on artillery and airpower to dislodge the enemy, the United States waged a furious war against Vietcong and North Vietnamese base areas. In the course of the Indochina War, the United States dropped seven million tons of bombs, more than twice the total bomb load dropped by all the nations in WWII combined.[90] In addition, American counterinsurgency campaigns saw the establishment of free-fire zones in South Vietnam (in which all persons who remained within them were targeted without restraint). Villages suspected of harbouring Vietcong were subjected to 'search and destroy' operations or forced to resettle in the strategic hamlet relocation project.[91] Combat pressure for a high body count, the belief by many US soldiers in the 'mere-gook-rule' (i.e. that Vietnamese life was expendable and not protected by IHL), and the semi-official rule that 'as long as it's dead and Vietnamese, it's Vietcong', resulted in an inhumane and indiscriminate ground campaign.[92] The symbolic failure of the ground campaign came on 16 March 1968 at My Lai, when 571 unarmed Vietnamese civilians were massacred by a platoon of US soldiers.

The Vietnam War therefore did not clearly fit into the category of either Bellum Romanum or Bellum Civile. The relative restraint practiced during the US bombing in Vietnam in comparison to previous practices in World War II and Korea indicated a level of humanity that went beyond the practice of Bellum Romanum. However, the relatively unrestricted conduct by US forces on the ground fell well short of the practice of Bellum Civile. Thus, the Vietnamese people were subjected to a US strategy that fell somewhat uneasily between Bellum Romanum and Bellum Civile. However, this nevertheless indicated – in comparison to earlier US wars – a shift in the location of the fault lines between those previously considered inside and outside of humanity.

Despite these significant changes, the public outcry at the cruelty American soldiers visited upon the Vietnamese people also demonstrated

[90] Boot 2002, 301.   [91] Moran 2002, 200.   [92] Gibson 2000, 93–154.

the extent to which the conduct of the war was out of line with the public's moral expectations at the time. According to Michael Walzer, the feelings expressed by most of the war's opponents 'had to do with the systematic exposure of Vietnamese civilians to the violence of American warmaking'.[93] In other words, opponents of the conduct of the war argued that US military operations did not sufficiently protect Vietnamese civilians.

Such sentiments can be explained through the socio-political changes occurring globally and within the United States. On a global level, the 1948 Universal Declaration of Human Rights had started to shift notions of obligations towards outsiders, in particular towards civilians.[94] And within the United States, legal racial discrimination started coming to an end in the mid-1950s. On May 17, 1954, in the case of 'Brown v. the Board of Education', the US Supreme Court ended federally sanctioned racial segregation in public schools by ruling unanimously that 'separate educational facilities are inherently unequal.'[95] A groundbreaking case, the ruling overturned the decree of 'Plessy v. Ferguson' (1896), which had declared 'separate but equal facilities' constitutional and which had been used for generations to sanction rigid segregation.[96] However, the landmark ruling in 1954 merely referred to public education facilities, leaving other areas of public life unaffected. Furthermore, implementation of the Supreme Court decision was slow, especially in the South where resistance to desegregation was the strongest. The most visible confrontation erupted in Little Rock, Arkansas in 1957, when President Dwight D Eisenhower had to send the National Guard to protect the newly gained rights of African Americans.[97] Over the course of the next two decades, however, the National Association for the Advancement of Coloured People (NAACP) used the precedent of 'Brown v. the Board of Education' to challenge segregation in other areas of American society. It thereby gradually expanded black civil rights and provided the legal foundations of the grassroots Civil Rights Movement that started taking shape in the mid-1950s and 1960s.[98] Thus, by the time of the Vietnam War, the Civil Rights Movement had made important strides and brought about significant change. The dehumanisation of African Americans had been declared unconstitutional at home, thereby undermining racial arguments that previously sanctioned indiscriminate force against indigenous people abroad and at home.

[93] Walzer 2004, 7.   [94] Linklater 1998; Rorty 1989, xvi.
[95] www.nationalcenter.org/brown.html, accessed on 5 July 2006.
[96] Zinn 2003a, 450–451.   [97] Jeffrey and Nash 1994, 957.
[98] Zinn 2003a, 450–451; Jeffrey and Nash 1994, 956–957.

Against this wider context, and in addition, the ideological arguments which had justified the dehumanisation of others and the cruelty against them started disappearing.[99] Americans' unfettered ideological belief in the containment of Communism, the Domino Theory, and the spreading of liberty, which had mobilised the nation in Korea and during the early years of Vietnam, started breaking down with the Tet Offensive of 1968. With the old racially and ideologically motivated arguments no longer ringing true, the ability of the American public to dehumanise others became significantly reduced.[100]

The Tet Offensive was the 'military and political continental divide' of the Vietnam War.[101] It shattered US optimism and formed the turning point in the public and media support for the war, both of which turned from neutral and supportive to critical towards and fully against the continued involvement in Vietnam.[102] In the eyes of the US public, the media, and the majority of the political class, Tet symbolised what Vietnam had become in spring 1968, a quagmire where military operations did not necessarily have anything to do with the perception of the value or course of the war.

The media coverage reinforced this transformation of the American conscience for it implicated the American people in the conduct of the war for the first time.[103] Throughout the conflict, camera teams and war photographers captured the cruelty visited upon the Vietnamese people in the name of containment. This footage severely disenchanted the American people for it created a dissonance between their image of themselves as noble, innocent liberators and the savage reality generated by their soldiers on the ground.[104] The war in Indochina was not only delegitimized because of the mounting numbers of US body bags, but also because it was fought inhumanely.

What had changed in the late 1960s in US society was that the enemy was increasingly recognised as a fellow human being rather than being dehumanised on the grounds of political affiliation, race, religion, or colour. This development slowly started to alter the conscience of the American people regarding the cruelty directed against the Vietnamese. The changes in racial and ideological understanding slowly caused Americans to re-evaluate their relationship with the Vietnamese people. The latter became part of an expanding notion of humanity as Americans started gaining what Richard Rorty calls the imaginative ability 'to see strange people as fellow sufferers'.[105] This process of 'self-reflexivity' lies

---

[99] Linklater 2010, 155–178.   [100] Coker 2001, 30–31.   [101] Record 1996, 55.
[102] Herring 1986, 203.   [103] Coker 2001, 30–33.   [104] Neu 2000, 19.
[105] Rorty 1989, xvi.

at the heart of the refusal to recognise humanity as the incarnation of something larger than the individual such as God, religion, race, or ideology. In other words, the old ideational absolutes have been eroded as a justification for the legitimacy of Bellum Romanum.[106] Instead, Christopher Coker argues,

[w]e have put humanity back at the centre of our philosophical and ethical systems of thought – hence the interest in humanitarian warfare, and the importance attached to humanity in the wars we now fight.[107]

This is important for it removes any philosophical or moral defence of cruelty.

Yet the war in Vietnam created a dissonance precisely because the conduct of the war – as seen on TV every day – was out of line with the public feeling that the limits imposed on the use of force were morally insufficient.[108] This gap between military practice and public moral expectations was particularly interesting because US military practice in Vietnam was comparably more discriminate than during the wars against Japan and Korea. This means that despite the early indications of a historical trend towards higher levels of respect for the principle of non-combatant immunity, US warfare in Vietnam was not discriminate enough to be legitimate in the eyes of the American people. Thus, US warfare was forced to close the gap between its own practice and public expectations in order to become legitimate again. Whatever the moral argument, there was now a strategic reason for the US military to fight justly if it wanted to maintain public support at home.[109] The direct result of the political fallout from Vietnam was the beginning of the systematic internalisation of the principle of non-combatant immunity into US military doctrine, training, and even the development and procurement of weapons systems.[110]

This humanising trend in US warfare continued to gather strength after the end of the Cold War.[111] During the 1991 Persian Gulf War a historically unprecedented emphasis was placed on minimising direct casualties to civilians.[112] Limiting the risks to enemy civilians was a major objective shared among American military and political leaders.

---

[106] Coker 2001, 5.   [107] Coker 2001, 5.   [108] Walzer 2004, 9.   [109] Walzer 2004, 9.
[110] Here, the Peers Report (which had investigated the underlying causes of the My Lai massacre and located the disrespect for civilian immunity in the systematic failures of military training) led to the 1974 Department of Defence Directive ('DoD Law of War Program') which had a profound impact on the internalising non-combatant immunity in the military. For more details, see Bacevich 2005, 148–174. See also Roland Arkin 2010, 337.
[111] Rabkin 2011, 700–716.
[112] Thomas 2001, 158–159; Renz and Scheipers 2012, 17–43.

By carefully differentiating between the Iraqi regime and the Iraqi people, the rhetoric of key decision makers displayed a principal understanding that the war was to be conducted between armed forces and that civilians should be shielded from the violence.[113] The president and his generals believed that the American people would not tolerate the slaughter of civilians. For Walzer, the readiness of the American leadership to employ moral arguments and rationalisations that

in the past had come from outside the armed forces – clerics, lawyers, professors, just war theorists – [is] a clear indication of the triumph of Just War Theory.[114]

As Walzer goes on to show, President Bush and Generals Norman Schwarzkopf and Colin Powell incorporated a way of rationalising and justifying their way of making war that had remained external to American decision-makers during Vietnam.[115]

The difference of the situation in the early 1990s from that of the Vietnam era was not merely rhetoric but was also reflected in the way in which US strategy was designed to minimise collateral damage. The American air campaign for instance excluded numerous potential targets because they were considered culturally or religiously sensitive. Furthermore, all other targets underwent extensive legal review for their proximity to civilians, school, hospitals, or mosques.[116]

Overall, these concerns for civilian protection translated into a highly restrained and precise targeting strategy which produced around three thousand civilian casualties – a low figure compared to both the number of civilian casualties in previous American wars and the amount of ordnance dropped.[117] It is for that reason that Operation Desert Storm has been interpreted as one of the most intense and simultaneously most discriminate air campaigns in history.[118]

The 1991 Persian Gulf War showed the extent to which the dehumanising trend in American warfare had been reversed in the course of five decades. The changes in US targeting practices indicate a clear progression of the importance of civilian protection since WWII.[119] This humanising trend was slow to evolve and only accelerated after the Vietnam War.[120] Yet by the end of the Cold War, American warfare progressed substantially towards closing the gap that opened in Vietnam between indiscriminate military practices and the public's expectations of how war should be conducted. In other words, US warfare transcended the racism as well as the ideological Weltanschauung that had previously

---

[113] Ignatieff 2000c, 199; Chris H Gray 1997, 31–37.   [114] Walzer 2004, 9.
[115] Walzer 2004, 9.   [116] Ignatieff 2000c, 199.   [117] Werrell 1992, 46.
[118] Bacevich 1996, 45.   [119] Walzer 2004, 10–11.
[120] Renz and Scheipers 2012, 17–43.

dehumanised others and had justified the fundamentally indiscriminate practice of Bellum Romanum. This tectonic shift – in combination with improvements in weapons technology – has elevated the avoidance of collateral damage to one of the central features of contemporary American warfare.[121] The 'happy marriage', as Farrell termed it, of Western-derived norms of international law with American precision military technology, has permitted the United States to limit civilian deaths during contemporary conflicts for it possesses 'unprecedented capability to create discriminate destruction.'[122] Due to the acquisition of new military technology and the restructuring of its forces following the Vietnam War through the Revolution in Military Affairs (RMA) and net-centric warfare, the US military has been able to emphasise precision in the pursuit of minimal civilian casualties.[123]

Today, American firepower is concentrated on the enemy's military and efforts to minimise the level of harm to non-combatants in target states have informed US targeting policies.[124] The increased involvement of military lawyers in the target and weapons selection process during and since the Gulf War has contributed significantly to US operations falling in line with IHL.[125] This development is historically important for it has reversed the long twentieth-century dehumanising trend in American campaigns.

Contemporary US Warfare and the Legal-Moral Nexus

Civilian Protection and IHL

Despite the strengthening of the principle of non-combatant immunity and the improved adherence to IHL, however, the United States has not been able to wage war without enemy civilians getting killed. Inflicting harm on enemy civilians is not necessarily a breach of IHL.[126] Under the 1977 Additional Protocol I to the 1949 Geneva Conventions, enemy civilians can justifiably be killed provided that their death was neither the outcome of a deliberate attack, nor the result of a disproportionate use of force.[127] This legal compromise between the principle of discrimination and the proportionality rule on the one hand and the recognition on

---

[121] Der Derian 2001, xv–xvii; Zehfuss 2010, 543–566; Rabkin 2011, 700–716.
[122] Farrell 2005, 179.   [123] Thomas W Smith 2002, 355–374.
[124] Zehfuss 2010, 543–566; Coker 2001, 1–45; Farrell 2005, 177–179;
[125] Kahl 2007b, 7–46; Bacevich 1996, 37–48; Ignatieff 2000c, 197.
[126] Gross 2006, 555; Johnson 2006, 167–195.
[127] 'Additional Protocol Additional to the Geneva Conventions of 12 August 1949, and relating to the Protection of Victims of International Armed Conflicts (Protocol 1)', available at www.unhchr.ch/html/menu3/b/93.htm, accessed on 3 March 2006.

the other hand that even the most restricted military operations can hardly be executed without inflicting some level of harm on non-combatants is generally referred to as the doctrine of double effect.[128] Double effect is a moral doctrine that is enshrined in the legal framework of The Hague and Geneva Conventions. Defined by Walzer as a 'way of reconciling the absolute prohibition against attacking non-combatants with the legitimate conduct of military activity',[129] the doctrine permits non-combatant deaths as long as the military objective of the action is just, i.e. if civilian deaths are unintended and if the military effects out-weigh the unintended effects on non-combatants.[130] These conditions are legally enshrined in the Additional Protocol of 1977.

The practical constraint on the doctrine of double effect is the propor-tionality rule. Enshrined in Article 57 (2)(iii) of the 1977 Protocol I of the Geneva Conventions, it prohibits attacks

[w]hich may be expected to cause incidental loss of civilian life, injury to civilians, damage to civilian objects, or a combination thereof, which would be excessive in relation to the concrete and direct military advantage anticipated.[131]

This creates a legal obligation for military commanders to consider and weigh the potential effects on civilians with the anticipated military advantage. This is emphasised further in Article 57 which requires belli-gerents to take constant care 'to spare the civilian population, civilians, and civilian objects', including doing 'everything feasible to verify that the objectives to be attacked are neither civilians nor civilian objects'.[132] According to this conventional interpretation of the doctrine of double effect, non-combatants can be killed but not deliberately or directly attacked.[133]

US interventions in the post–Cold War period have sparked irresolva-ble controversies among international lawyers over what constituted a legitimate target and whether the proportionality rule had been satisfied. The problem with the way in which the doctrine of double effect has been

---

Although the United States has neither signed nor ratified the Additional Protocol, US forces have nevertheless officially aimed to adhere to its provisions regarding dis-crimination and proportionality. Thus, the Additional Protocol I is not regarded as customary international law in its entirety, though the US military has regarded these two specific provisions as such. See Thomas W Smith 2002, 360.

[128] Gross 2006, 557–558.   [129] Walzer 1992, 153.   [130] Johnson 1999, 119–120.

[131] 'Additional Protocol Additional to the Geneva Conventions of 12 August 1949, and relating to the Protection of Victims of International Armed Conflicts (Protocol 1)', available at www.unhchr.ch/html/menu3/b/93.htm, accessed on 3 March 2006.

[132] 'Additional Protocol Additional to the Geneva Conventions of 12 August 1949, and relating to the Protection of Victims of International Armed Conflicts (Protocol 1)', available at www.unhchr.ch/html/menu3/b/93.htm, accessed on 3 March 2006.

[133] Shaw 2005, 134; Wheeler 2002, 208; Zehfuss 2010, 543–566; Gross 2006, 557–558.

enshrined in IHL is that it leaves what critics have called 'an important space of indeterminacy' within which conflicting yet plausible legal claims can compete for validation.[134] NATO's targeting of dual-use facilities in the Federal Republic of Yugoslavia (FRY) during 'Operation Allied Force' provides a good example of the scope for conflicting and indeterminable judgements over the permissible limits set by the doctrine of double effect.[135] NATO's air campaign attached a similar, if not even stronger, significance to the avoidance of collateral damage as Operation Desert Storm.[136] The important role military lawyers played during the latter had only foreshadowed their centrality during the Kosovo campaign. In 1999, they were integrated into every phase of the campaign, and their legal scrutiny – in combination with a much larger share of precision-guided weapons systems than in Iraq – resulted in a very surgical intervention.[137] Postwar surveys suggested that the number of civilian casualties inflicted by the bombing campaign was around five hundred.[138]

Yet, NATO's escalation of the air campaign to include dual-use facilities inside the FRY sparked a debate as to whether the Alliance had violated IHL.[139] Disagreements over the interpretation of IHL (in particular over what counted as legitimate targets and whether the proportionality rule had been violated) between human rights NGOs and NATO member states proved unbridgeable.[140] This was even more surprising considering that all those involved in the controversy accepted the existing framework of IHL and yet ended up drawing opposing conclusions.[141]

According to Wheeler, the fact that the Alliance and the NGOs 'drew radically different conclusions from applying the same body of law illustrates the problem of legal indeterminacy'.[142] This outcome demonstrates more generally the limits of the existing legal framework to provide a sufficient framework for protecting non-combatants from harm.[143] The insufficiency here stems from IHL's inability to provide

---

[134] Wheeler 2003, 210; Svendsen 2010, 367–371.   [135] Thomas 2006, 9.

[136] Thomas 2001, 162–168.   [137] Ignatieff 2000c, 197–198; Farrell 2005, 159–160.

[138] This figure is disputed by the Yugoslav Government, NGOs, and some researchers who have claimed the number of non-combatant deaths ranged from 1,200 to 5,000. Most sources, however, have come to agree to the figure of five hundred civilian dead during NATO's Kosovo campaign. For further details, see Shaw 2002, 343–360; Human Rights Watch 2000; Conetta 2001.

[139] Johnson 2006, 189; Farrell 2005, 159–162.

[140] 'Final Report to the Prosecutor by the Committee Established to Review the NATO Bombing Campaign Against the Federal Republic of Yugoslavia', available at www.un .org/icty/pressreal/nato061300.htm, accessed on 1 June 2006.

[141] Wheeler 2003, 189–216. See also Svendsen 2010, 367–370.

[142] Wheeler 2003, 214; Kaufmann 2003, 186–191.   [143] Rowe 2000; Plaw 2010, 3–6.

a clear answer to the question of whether everything has been done to spare civilian lives. As a result, the legal permissiveness of the doctrine of double effect allows states to perform acts that are likely to have evil consequences, such as the killing of civilians.[144]

The key condition of the doctrine that the good act is sufficiently good to compensate for its effects on civilians is a weak constraint, for it can justify large numbers of unintended yet foreseeable civilian deaths.[145] Michael Walzer notes this most strongly when he writes:

We have to worry, I think, about all those unintended but foreseeable deaths, for their number can be large; and subject only to the proportionality rule – a weak restraint – double effect provides a blanket justification.[146]

The proportionality rule, Wheeler argues, leaves the door sufficiently open so that 'any state can justify the killing of innocent civilians as an unintended consequence of attacks against legitimate military targets.'[147] The problem of the legal rendering of the proportionality rule is its vagueness, as it offers no clear guidance or method for deciding when the threat of collateral damage is indeed 'excessive'.[148] It is this vagueness that results in the legal permissiveness for injuring non-combatants provided it can be shown that a legitimate military target was hit during an attack.[149]

Civilian Protection and the Moral Idea of 'Due Care'

The controversies over the targeting of dual-use facilities and collateral damage show, however, that this legal permissiveness has not eliminated the moral judgements associated with military violence. Compliance with IHL has been an attempt to reduce complex issues of morality into technical issues of legality. In the case of US warfare, Michael Ignatieff writes,

The Geneva Conventions have become a casuist's bible, and close readings of their fine print are supposed to eliminate the moral and political risks associated with military violence. Yet, moral questions stubbornly resist being reduced to legal ones, and moral exposure is not eliminated when legal exposure is.[150]

---

[144] Crawford 2003; Kaufmann 2003, 186–191; Gross 2006, 558.

[145] Crawford 2007b, 187–212; Zehfuss 2010, 543–566; Walzer 1992, 153; Gross 2009, 322.

[146] Walzer 1992, 153.

[147] Wheeler 2002, 209; see also Walzer 1992, 153; Svendsen 2010, 371.

[148] Bellamy 2006, 183.

[149] Bellamy 2005, 288; Kaufmann 2003, 186–191; Schwenkenbrecher 2014, 97.

[150] Ignatieff 2000c, 199.

In other words, while general compliance with the legal constraints on waging war has been an important achievement, it has failed to fully address the complex questions of morality arising from American military interventions. If the conduct of war is considered clean and humane from a legal point of view, it does not necessarily follow that it fulfils all moral requirements. Inflicting collateral damage or targeting dual-use facilities remains a sensitive moral issue.[151]

To give an example, during the 1991 Gulf War, US forces dropped two laser-guided bombs on the Al-Amiriya shelter in Baghdad, which at the time was thought to be an Iraqi command and control centre.[152] However, unknown to the Americans, the military facility also served as an air raid shelter for four to five hundred Iraqi civilians who died in the attack (130 of them children) on 13 February 1991. The bombing – the largest single incident of collateral damage of the war – satisfied the principle of discrimination and the proportionality rule as defined by IHL.[153] As long as the intention behind the attack was the destruction of the military facility and not the intentional harming of civilians (the American military did not know of the presence of civilians at the time), it was legally permitted.

In the case of the Al-Amiriya bombing, the legal issue at stake therefore was not over whether the proportionality rule had been violated. Rather, serious legal questions in this case arose over the provisions set in Article 57 (2)(i) with regards to the adequacy of the US efforts to get accurate intelligence about who was occupying the bunker at the time of the attack. In the ensuing debate over whether the US military had done 'everything feasible' to verify that the bunker was no civilian – or, in this case, dual-use – object before engaging the target, competing legal claims arose. The US government, while admitting that it 'knew that the [Al-]Amiriyah facility had been used as a civil-defence shelter during the Iran-Iraq War',[154] argued that by 10 February 1991, it had received clear evidence that it had become an alternative command point which had shown no sign of being used as a civilian bomb shelter. It argued that through signals intelligence and spying satellites, the movement of military peoples and vehicles in and out of the site had been verified.[155] By contrast, Human Rights Watch argued that US intelligence was insufficient and that interviews with neighbourhood residents would have revealed that the Al-Amiriyah bunker was 'plainly marked as a public shelter and was used throughout the air war

---

[151] Crawford 2007b, 187–190; Barber 2010, 467–500.   [152] Boot 2003.
[153] Thomas 2001, 88.   [154] Human Rights Watch 1991.
[155] White House, 'Crafting Tragedy', available at https://georgewbush-whitehouse.archives .gov/ogc/apparatus/crafting.html#3, accessed on 6 January 2017.

by large numbers of civilians'.[156] Furthermore, its report stated, even if changes in the protected status of the bunker had occurred, it would have required alerting the occupants to the attack and that the 'United States' failures to give such warning before proceeding with the disastrous attack ... was a serious violation of the laws of war.'[157]

These competing legal interpretations of whether 'everything feasible' had been done to verify the exact status of the target and whether the attack violated IHL remained unresolved. And yet, the controversy revealed two important aspects: not only does the indeterminacy and vagueness of IHL leave the door sufficiently open for varying legal interpretations to arise over the adequate levels of verification, it also demonstrates, from the US reaction to the bombing, that the infliction of collateral damage was seen not as a legal but as a moral concern.

The Al-Amiriya bombing became a big American public relations disaster as scenes of burnt bodies being pulled out of the devastated shelter and of distraught relatives were broadcast around the world. And the subsequent outcry revealed to the US Administration the extent to which military action it considered to be legally permissive had fallen significantly short of the moral expectations of Arab and Western publics and governments. Recognising this sensitivity, General Colin Powell, Chairman of the Joint Chiefs of Staff, voiced his concern that 'another massacre like this would destroy the allies' moral standing'.[158] Henceforth, Powell and General Norman Schwarzkopf exercised their personal approval of all sorties in Baghdad and placed all bunkers that could potentially serve as civilian air raid shelters off limits for the rest of the war.[159] The drastic reaction from Western publics and the self-imposed restrictions by the military indicates that the real issues at stake were not necessarily legal but moral.

From a moral standpoint, IHL is too lenient and vague, for it fails to adequately restrain the use of force in terms of its effect on civilians. The legal permissiveness of accidental (i.e. unintended) killings of civilians like the Al-Amirya bombing therefore raises important moral questions, especially since the infliction of collateral damage has become a key characteristic of American military campaigns in the post–Cold War world.[160]

More restrictive moral interpretations of the doctrine of double effect, like those offered by Just War theorists such as Walzer, Wheeler, Alex Bellamy, Steven Lee, and Anne Schwenkenbrecher argue that it is not

---

[156] Human Rights Watch 1991.   [157] Human Rights Watch 1991.
[158] Cited in Atkinson 1993, 288.   [159] Bacevich 1996, 45.
[160] Crawford 2007b, 187–190; Zehfuss 2010, 543–566; Patricia Owens 2003, 595–616.

enough to simply *not intend* the deaths of non-combatants.[161] Instead, non-combatants have the moral right to something more – the right for 'due care' to be taken with their lives.[162] What they look for in military campaigns is, as Walzer points out, 'some sign of a positive commitment to save civilian lives'.[163] This more stringent interpretation of the principle of discrimination tries to resolve the moral inadequacy of the doctrine of double effect (as enshrined in existing IHL) by supplementing it with a positive commitment to spare civilian lives.[164] Soldiers therefore must make some positive efforts to avoid harming civilians, and this requires considerably more than simply not intending to directly and intentionally harm them.

International lawyers and critics might charge that Walzer's (and some of the discipline's) reading of IHL is selective and that it thereby omits other concrete measures that IHL already requires soldiers to take which – if taken on aggregate – actually generate something very close to Walzer's idea of 'due care'.

One such existing measure, for instance, can be found in Article 57(1) of the 1977 Additional Protocol to the Geneva Conventions, which requires that

[i]n the conduct of military operations, constant care shall be taken to spare the civilian population, civilians, and civilian objects.[165]

A second, more concrete measure, can be found in Article 57(2)(i) which requires that

[t]hose who plan or decide upon an attack shall . . . do everything feasible to verify that the objectives to be attacked are neither civilians nor civilian objects and are not subject to special protection.[166]

The argument made here is that – besides the proportionality rule – IHL already has in place additional provisions that on aggregate generate provisions that come very close to the moral idea of 'due care'.

And yet, even when these additional legal requirements are taken into account, there remain a number of problems that are not dissimilar to the

---

[161] Walzer 2009, 40–52; Bellamy 2005, 287–289; Walzer 1992, 151–159; Wheeler 2002, 208–210; Lee 2004, 235–236; Schwenkenbrecher 2014, 94–105.

[162] Mayer 2007, 221–223; Bellamy 2005, 288.

[163] Walzer 1992, 156; Barber 2010, 467–500.

[164] Schwenkenbrecher 2014, 97; Johnson 1999, 132–133; Plaw 2010, 3–6.

[165] 'Additional Protocol Additional to the Geneva Conventions of 12 August 1949, and relating to the Protection of Victims of International Armed Conflicts (Protocol 1)', available at www.unhchr.ch/html/menu3/b/93.htm, accessed on 3 March 2006.

[166] 'Additional Protocol Additional to the Geneva Conventions of 12 August 1949, and relating to the Protection of Victims of International Armed Conflicts (Protocol 1)', available at www.unhchr.ch/html/menu3/b/93.htm, accessed on 3 March 2006.

issues surrounding the proportionality rule. First, Articles 57(1) and 57(2)(i) are relatively vague and provide a weak restraint on double effect. For instance, the legal requirement of Article 57(2)(i) to 'do everything feasible to verify ...' is very imprecise: What exactly does 'everything' include? What exactly does 'feasible' mean in the context of military operations? The vagueness of the formulation leaves the door sufficiently open for legal interpretation. This is not to discount the pathbreaking nature of the 1977 Additional Protocol in setting stricter guidelines and rules around military attacks and civilian protection.[167] As Adams and Guelff note, Additional Protocol 1 contains 'controversial innovations ... spelling out unprecedented rules relating to discrimination in the conduct of military attacks'.[168]

Despite these advancements compared to earlier conventions, however, they remain imprecise and vague. This issue had already been subject to significant discussions during the negotiations of the Additional Protocol. As outlined in the ICRC's Legal Commentary to the Additional Protocol (published in 1987), military commanders expressed deep concern over the fact that these provisions were 'relatively imprecise and [were] open to a fairly broad margin of judgement.'[169] Interesting here is that criticism over the vagueness came from two very different interest groups. One the one hand, several states feared that the imprecision left the door open for legal interpretations that 'failure to comply with Article 57 may constitute a breach and may be prosecuted as such.'[170] Here, the vagueness was seen as opening the door for prosecution more easily and that a greater degree of precision was actually required so that anyone would know whether he/she was committing a grave breach. These delegations saw the Article 57 as 'dangerously imprecise'.[171] On the other hand, some delegations argued about Article 57 in general, and about Article 57(2)(i) in particular, that the wording 'everything feasible' was 'too broad' regarding the protection to civilians.[172] Specifically, they expressed 'reason to fear' that by being able to invoke the success of the military operation in general, 'one might end up ... neglecting the humanitarian obligations prescribed'.[173]

The same issue over the imprecise wording of 'everything feasible' and the 'precautions commanders have to take in making decisions' was also reflected in the official reservations signatory states expressed towards Additional Protocol I, in particular regarding articles 51, 57, and 58.[174] For instance, with regard to Article 57, Australia and New Zealand felt

---

[167] Roberts and Guelff 1999, 420.   [168] Roberts and Guelff 1999, 420.
[169] ICRC 1987.   [170] ICRC 1987.   [171] ICRC 1987.   [172] ICRC 1987.
[173] ICRC 1987.   [174] Gaudreau 2003, 156–159.

compelled to emphasise that 'military advantage ... also included a variety of considerations, including the security of attacking forces.'[175] Here, some states stressed the issue of force protection which had not been mentioned as a factor at all.

In other words, the vagueness of provisions and expectations set out in the Additional Protocol, particularly in Article 57 and subclause (2)(i), generated concern among negotiating delegations and ratifying state that its imprecise formulation neither provided for clear enough guidelines to soldiers, nor that it sufficiently constrained the doctrine of double effect.[176]

But there is a second, arguably more important issue. Adding to the problem of Article 57 is that it fails to make any mention of the need to increase the risks to the lives of soldiers in order to ensure higher levels of discrimination and civilian protection. It thereby leaves out any reference to whether 'taking constant care to spare civilians lives' and whether 'doing everything feasible to verify that targets are not civilian objects' actually includes accepting higher levels of risk to soldiers at all. Nothing in the law says that the lives of soldiers need to be risked, let alone to be risked more. What this means is that, from a legal point of view, soldiers can claim that they did everything feasible to protect civilians even when their actions fell short of even considering risking their own lives. The law is silent on the risk levels soldiers are expected to take, or as Walzer puts it, 'the laws of war say nothing about such matters'.[177]

In other words, Article 57, while requiring soldiers to take constant care to spare civilian life provides a weak restraint on the doctrine of double effect, it allows – due to its vagueness and imprecision – for large numbers of unintended but foreseeable death among civilians. And, most importantly, it remains silent on the obligations of soldiers to accept higher levels of risks provided that such extra risks increase the safeguarding of civilians. Legally speaking, 'everything feasible' does not include any requirement to increase the risks to soldiers in order to spare civilians.

By contrast, the need to explicitly factor in a potential increase in the risks soldiers face is precisely what the moral idea of 'due care' does.[178] For the latter, 'doing everything feasible' explicitly includes the possible need to accept higher risks to soldiers.[179] Factoring in this possibility, rather than leaving it out, signals a different understanding of costs and expectations attached to care. It is this different level of care for civilians

[175] Gaudreau 2003, 156; ICRC 1987.
[176] Gaudreau 2003, 156–159; Roberts and Guelff 1999, 420.   [177] Walzer 1992, 152.
[178] Lee 2004, 235–237.
[179] Bellamy 2006; Thomas W Smith 2008; Walzer 1992; Wheeler 2002; Lee 2004; Schwenkenbrecher 2014.

and the expectations surrounding risk taking for soldiers that differentiates 'due care' from IHL.[180] Due care therefore is an attempt to further constrain the doctrine of double effect, one that is designed to further strengthen the safeguarding of civilians than the existing laws of war currently do.

These differences between IHL and 'due care' might at first sight appear to be small, but they are important. And they stem from what ultimately drives their respective objectives: in the case of the law, it is designed to permit military activities while attempting to limit the harm caused to civilians; in the case of 'due care', the starting point is the concern for civilian protection that – while not unlimited – is seen as paramount over military action. As Lee puts it,

> The moral concerns of the two principles are different: the concern of the principle of proportionality is the sum of harms and benefits of an action, while the concern of the principle of discrimination is the rights of persons not to be harmed, unless they have done something to surrender those rights.[181]

In other words, in spite of the seeming similarity between the legal and moral elements of 'due care', the latter remains more restrictive than the former.

In practical terms, the moral idea of 'due care' obliges commanders to take active steps to reduce the risks to civilians even if this means increasing the risks to their own soldiers.[182] This moral requirement arises, it is argued, from the basic understanding that soldiers cannot kill unless they are prepared to accept the risk of dying in return.[183] In other words, the idea of 'due care' requires military commanders to accept a higher risk to their soldiers if such a commitment would protect civilians from harm.[184] As Walzer puts it, 'if saving civilian lives means risking soldier's lives, the risk must be accepted.'[185]

When Walzer introduced the idea of 'due care', he suggested that the risks to civilians should be reduced 'as far as possible'.[186] This raises the question regarding the threshold, or the exact levels of extra risk that soldiers can reasonably be expected to take in order to spare civilian lives.[187] Walzer recognised that reducing the risks to civilians as far as possible would not always be morally feasible as it would imply a potentially open-ended increase in the risk to combatants.[188] Complicating matters, military commanders also have moral obligations

---

[180] Walzer 1992, 152.   [181] Lee 2004, 236.
[182] Thomas W Smith 2008, 144–164; Shaw 2005, 134.
[183] Kahn 2002, 2–9; Walzer 2009, 40–52.   [184] Mayer 2007, 221–223.
[185] Walzer 1992, 156.   [186] Walzer 1992, 155.   [187] Johnson 2006, 189.
[188] Walzer 1992, 156.

towards the soldiers under their command: they can neither expose them to disproportionate risks nor jeopardise military missions by prioritising civilian protection over the safety of their own forces.[189] Put differently, there is no moral obligation to give such attention to civilian protection that it significantly reduces the chances of military success – that it, as Walzer writes, 'doom[s] the military venture'.[190] Rather, the idea of 'due care' requires soldiers not to be sent beyond the point at which the risk they expose themselves to becomes so catastrophic that it endangers the entire mission.[191]

At the same time, however, combatants are required to accept higher risks to themselves if risking their lives means saving civilians.[192] According to Walzer,

[t]he principle is this: when it is our action that puts innocent people at risk, even if the action is justified, we are bound to do what we can to reduce those risks, even if this involves risks to our own soldiers.[193]

What the idea of 'due care' therefore expects is for soldiers to not only refrain from intending to harm civilians, but also to take positive and active steps to reduce the threat to non-combatants as far as possible, even if that means accepting a 'marginal' increase of risk to their own lives.[194] Yet the burden of the precautions that have to be taken should not involve too great a sacrifice of either soldiers' lives or the military objectives.[195]

Regarding the upper limits of increases in risks that combatants have to morally accept, the literature on the idea of 'due care' has remained relatively vague. Critics like Lee and Shaw therefore charged that limiting the risks soldiers would be expected to take in such undefined terms in fact provided an 'escape clause' for Western strategists.[196] While such criticism is not unjustified, the vagueness of the idea of 'due care' requires further judgement on the application of such general rules to particular cases. In its current definition, the idea of 'due care' does not enable consideration of precisely what levels of sacrifice a military actor has to take in order to reduce the risk of harm to civilians.[197] 'Due care' proponents are in agreement that no specific figure or percentage point can be attached to what the upper limits of risk increases should be.[198] In that regard, 'due care' is diametrically opposed to black letter law. Instead,

---

[189] Cornish 2003, 123; Thomas W Smith 2008, 144–164; Walzer 2004, 73.
[190] Lee 2004, 241.   [191] Barber 2010, 467–500.   [192] Walzer 1992, 156.
[193] Walzer 2004, 17.
[194] Unfortunately, Walzer leaves the term 'marginal' undefined (Walzer 1992, 152–159).
[195] Walzer 1992, 152–159; Hart 1963, 130.   [196] Shaw 2005, 134; Lee 2004, 239–241.
[197] Hart 1963, 129–130.
[198] Bellamy 2006; Thomas W Smith 2008; Walzer 1992; Wheeler 2002; Lee 2004; Schwenkenbrecher 2014.

'due care' is deliberately context-specific and thereby only provides general guidelines for moral (not legal) judgement that require careful application to empirical cases. The primary principle thereby is the idea that the possibility to increase soldiers' risks should be part of the military calculation. By how much such risks should be increased is seen as a secondary question that requires judgement of specific military operations.

It is in the situational context of specific operations like the Al-Amirya bombing or Operation Allied Force that we can investigate if the American military succeeded or failed to take 'due care' to avoid inflicting injuries on Iraqi civilians. By placing the vague and indeterminate definition of the upper limits of 'due care' into the context of specific cases, it can generally be investigated whether the US military took positive steps to reduce the risk to non-combatants, even if this meant accepting a marginal increase in the levels of risk faced by American combatants. The questions arising out of this are: Could the United States could have achieved an even higher level of civilian protection by placing US soldiers at higher risks? Were such increased combat risks (while not required legally but morally) even considered, let alone implemented? Or would such a positive commitment have created disproportionate levels of risk to US soldiers that it would have endangered American military objectives?

These context-specific moral questions will be examined in the empirical cases of the US interventions in Somalia, Afghanistan, and Iraq. Before that, however, the book needs to investigate the role casualty-aversion has come to play in US operations, which is the subject of the next chapter.

Conclusion

The chapter identified and contrasted the different forms civilian protection has taken in the history of US warfare. It was shown how respect for the lives of enemy non-combatants has undergone substantial transformations. By locating the boundaries of humanity as the fault lines between Bellum Romanum and Bellum Civile, the chapter traced the shifting of these boundaries historically. The changes clearly indicate two broad historical trends in the period under investigation.

From the early Indian Wars to the age of modern industrial warfare, the boundaries of humanity shifted considerably, resulting in a dehumanising trend in US warfare. In the modern age, racism and ideology increased the group of those who had previously been considered to be outside humanity and against whom unrestricted warfare could be waged. This reduction of humanity translated into an increasing disrespect for civilian protection. Civilians became the deliberate target in total wars.

This dehumanising trend in American warfare was steadily reversed in the period between the 1950s and the 1990s. The resulting humanising process evolved once the racial and ideological abilities to dehumanise others started ringing hollow due to domestic changes. This domestic transformation coincided with and was reinforced by the Vietnam War which exposed the US public to the cruelties their soldiers visited upon the local population in the name of containment. With the possibility of dehumanising outsiders breaking down, unrestricted warfare could no longer be justified. In other words, the Vietnam War exposed a legitimacy gap between public expectations and the reality of US military operations on the ground. After the US military lost the war, it began closing the gap between its military practices and public expectations by strengthening its compliance with IHL. This process slowly eradicated the double standards between Bellum Romanum and Bellum Civile that historically had underpinned US warfare and – at the same time – elevated the avoidance of civilian casualties to one of the central features of contemporary American warfare. The 1991 Persian Gulf War showed the extent to which the practice of Bellum Civile has become universalised.

Despite the growing recognition among American leaders as to the close adherence to IHL, it is also increasingly the case that Western publics, Just War theorists, and Human Rights groups oftentimes want more protection than these laws provide. The chapter illustrated how IHL and the doctrine of double effect, with which US warfare has largely come to comply, remain too permissive regarding the risks to civilians. It showed how even if the American conduct of war satisfied the conditions set by IHL (the vagueness and legal indeterminacy of this particular issue were illustrated), it does not necessarily follow that all the moral requirements have been fulfilled. In fact, the legal permissiveness regarding collateral damage raises the important moral question of whether an even higher level of civilian protection could have been achieved. By examining the issues of this legal-moral nexus pertaining to the protection afforded to civilians, the chapter drew on Michael Walzer's idea of 'due care'. The latter – in spite of its debated limits – provides a moral framework through which the book examines if the US military has taken 'due care' to spare enemy non-combatants or whether other factors, such as American casualty-aversion (introduced in the next chapter), compromised the level of protection afforded to civilians in target states.

We had 500 casualties a week when [the Nixon Administration] came to office. America now is not willing to take casualties. Vietnam produced a whole new attitude.

Henry Kissinger, 1999

During the Gulf War, it was more dangerous to be a young man back in the United States, with all its car accidents and urban murders than to serve in combat. Thus, almost 300 soldiers had their lives saved by serving in Desert Shield and Desert Storm. The United States effectively saved American lives by going to war.

Chris H. Gray

Introduction

The previous chapter traced the importance of the norm of non-combatant immunity in contemporary American war making. This chapter critically investigates how far the value of US casualty-aversion has undermined what can be achieved in terms of civilian protection.

It shows how the US changed from a modern society that accepted huge numbers of casualties among its own military personnel to a postmodern society that has become increasingly unwilling to sustain such losses. This process is illustrated through the transformation of the aspect of humanism that took place during and after the Vietnam War. First found in ancient Greek mythology and warfare, humanism constituted a dimension that turned war into an act of self-realisation for warriors. It ensured that warriors accepted sacrifice, including the risk of dying, for it allowed them to invest their lives with meaning. The chapter illustrates the vital role played by humanism in giving meaning to and permitting large scale sacrifice in the modern wars waged by the US (such as the Civil War, World Wars I and II, and the Korean War).

The chapter then examines how the widespread loss of humanism translated into an unwillingness to sacrifice lives. The causes for this and the subsequent rise of casualty-aversion are analysed through the socio-historical changes of American society during the Vietnam War. Particular focus is placed on the disenchanting and alienating nature of the Vietnam War, which no longer allowed US soldiers to experience humanism, and on the rise of postmodern risk societies.

Moreover, it is shown how the 'body bag syndrome' has impacted on American military operations in the post-Vietnam era. The chapter thereby investigates the extent to which the growing political necessity to wage 'post-heroic warfare'[1] has impacted on the different branches of the American military with a particular emphasis being placed on the role of US elite forces. It identifies the tension between so-called 'niche warriors' and the predominantly casualty-averse political class and asks whether political (and military) concerns for zero tolerance have prevented 'niche warriors' from waging war in a less casualty-averse way.

In the final part, the findings of the chapter are discussed and problematised in the context of civilian protection. The transformed attitudes towards casualties among their own soldiers and among enemy civilians as well as the tension between the two have become key characteristics of contemporary US warfare.

Humanism and the Warrior

The instrumental dimension of warfare stands for the attainment of rational ends by rational means. It is mostly associated with Thucydides and Carl von Clausewitz who conceived war as a deliberate act of policy and as a rationally planned means for the attainment of certain political or economic goals.[2] It signifies the political purpose of war, the political reason why a certain state decides upon armed conflict with another – or in the famous words of Clausewitz:

War is not merely an act of policy but a true political instrument, a continuation of political intercourse, carried on with other means.[3]

Thus, the instrumental dimension in war means that war is conducted by the state as a tool to achieve political ends.

The problem with Clausewitz's notion of the instrumental is that he overlooked how war has never been purely instrumental, but also humanistic.[4] Though Clausewitz seemed to have sensed the humanistic

---

[1] Luttwak 1995.   [2] Von Clausewitz 1984.   [3] Von Clausewitz 1984, 87.

[4] Van Creveld 1996, 497–499; Coker 2002b, 15–44; Gelven 1994; Keegan 1993. What I prefer to call 'humanism' or 'humanistic' (for reasons that will become obvious later on) has been termed differently by other writers. Van Creveld termed it 'expressive', Coker 'existential' and 'humanistic', Gelven 'existential'. As I am referring to the warrior type stemming from the literary canon of ancient Greece, I prefer to use their term which was

dimension in the nature of war, he only touched upon it briefly by acknowledging the importance of 'moral factors' such as courage, determination, endurance, 'friction', chance, and a willingness and callousness that enabled a soldier to bear his and others' sufferings. But he neither tried to provide a systematic analysis of the humanistic dimension itself, nor to discuss it in the context of the instrumental.[5] As a result, Clausewitz ended up overemphasising the instrumental dimension of war, for he largely understood war as a purely rational undertaking purged of humanism.[6]

This has not been a problem merely confined to Clausewitz's writings. The instrumental dimension in war has generally tended to be more pronounced in Western thinking because of the crucial role war has played in bringing about, in preserving, and in breaking the social institution of the state. From the Greek city-state to the nation-state of the late nineteenth century – to paraphrase Charles Tilly – war made the state, and the city/nation-state made war.[7] Thus, the analytical emphasis within the Western literary canon has tended to be on the political aspects of wars waged by states rather than the humanistic aspects of wars waged by warriors.

In pointing out this particular oversight in Clausewitz's universe, Martin van Creveld, one of the most radical reinterpreters of armed conflict since the Prussian General, suggests that the humanistic aspect should be added to our philosophical understanding of war.[8] And although no systematic account of 'humanism and the warrior' has been produced yet, he argues that the notion of humanism

> may be found in writers such as Homer through Shakespeare all the way to Friedrich Nietzsche ... From Henry V in front of Harfleur to the Übermensch playing with danger, the starting point is the romantic idea that war does not primarily consist of killing; instead, it hinges on the willingness to die if necessary. For a person to lay down his life for his interest – let alone that of somebody or something else – is logically absurd. On this obstacle, von Clausewitz's entire strategic theory collapses like a house of cards.[9]

This willingness to die, or at least the acceptance of the risk of dying, cannot be fathomed through an instrumental understanding of war. From

---

'humanism'. The difference between terms such as existential and expressive is one of aesthetics, not of content or meaning.

[5] Humanism was never Clausewitz's central focal point as he was primarily interested in war (and not warriors) as a theoretical concept and its practical use as an instrument of statecraft.

[6] Ehrenreich 1998, 7; Van Creveld 1991b.

[7] Tilly 1975, 42; Giddens 1985 and Giddens 1990.

[8] Van Creveld 1991b and Van Crfeveld 1996, 497–499.   [9] Van Creveld 1996, 498.

the perspective of the warrior, the motivation to accept the risk of dying must be found somewhere else.

The humanistic conception of war allows for an understanding of how coping with danger is a source of joy and how – for the warrior – war is the greatest joy of all.[10] War, in other words, is an experience that gives meaning and authenticity to warriors. For warriors, war is not so much fought to achieve justice or to right a wrong (war as instrumental), but to achieve meaning for oneself (war as humanistic).[11] Thus, war is not exclusively a question of gaining rational ends by rational means because ultimately the willingness to die in war derives its force from the human soul.[12] This aspect of humanism as opposed to the instrumentality and rationality of war can also be detected in Machiavelli's writing on 'Fortuna', Janowitz's account of the 'heroic' and Lawrence's thoughts on the 'spirit'.[13] War needs to be understood as the intrinsic part of a humanistic discourse, which aims at the existential idea of becoming and overcoming. War makes warriors aware of unexpected dimensions of themselves. War is a source of asserting one's own existence and a source of individual transformation.

The Origins of Humanism

Understanding how humanism evolved historically in the context of US warfare is best illustrated by employing the same genealogical approach as used in the previous chapter. Such an approach asks how humanism has originated, changed, and finally evolved in its contemporary American form.[14]

In a Nietzschean fashion, such a genealogy needs to start with the ancient Greeks. It is through the warriors of ancient Greece such as Achilles, Hector, Pericles, and Agamemnon that the notion of war as humanistic entered the Western and therefore American literary canon.[15] At the heart of this literary canon stand Homer's two epics of the Iliad and the Odyssey, which have influenced American ideals of the humanistic warrior ever since.[16] Besides Homer's epics, the warrior penetrated the Western consciousness through Greek lyric poetry of the Archaic Age (seventh and sixth century BC). The poems of Kallinos, Archilochos,

---

[10] Hedges 2002, 3–17; Gelven 1994.   [11] See Nietzsche 1981, 74; Jünger 2000.
[12] Coker 2002b, 45–60.   [13] Cited in Chris H Gray 1997, 94.
[14] Employing a genealogical approach to tracing the evolution of casualty-aversion is very different from a commitment to a linear or Whiggish interpretation of history. Rather, tracing the contours of casualty-aversion in the history US warfare reveals a non-linear development subject to both chance and contingencies.
[15] Gelven 1994, 15; Coker 2002b, 61–82.   [16] Braudy 2003, xix; Ehrenreich 1998, 151.

Mimnermos, and Tyrtaios gave voice to the newly emerging hoplite democratic warriors, who – equipped with their trademark shields – fought decisive battles in the massed ranks of the phalanx.[17] Here the heroic Greek warrior was born, imagined, and idealised. Generations of warriors over subsequent centuries and millennia (including today's American Special Operations Forces) have understood themselves in a lineage that binds them to these warriors of ancient Greece.[18] For while the Greeks regarded war as part of the human condition, they nevertheless conceived it as something humanistic, as an act that produced meaning and authenticity.[19] Their lust for battle and contest was not only part of political life, but was also expressive of their humanism. For them, it was their humanism that made intrastate wars different from the ones fought between barbaric non-Greek tribes. Their grounding in humanism made them self-consciously aware of their difference from the barbarians living outside the Greek civilisation of city-states.[20] And the reason why the ancient Greeks conceived war as a humanistic experience was rooted in the following three features: agency, subjectivity, and inter-subjectivity.[21]

Agency

The Greek classics describe warriors as moral agents. Mortal heroes such as Pericles, Achilles, or Agamemnon, hazard all in battle, including their lives. Achilles' enemies were not the enemies of the city-state or of Greek civilisation, but his own. The battlefield was the place where warriors were discovered and where they discovered themselves. For Nietzsche, the Iliad is expressive of war as an act of will, the will to power, that makes one an agent of one's own destiny.[22] Central to the feature of agency is Agamemnon who stated that

If by avoiding death we could make ourselves immortal, then I should not fight. But we must die someday, so let us go to win glory ourselves or to serve the glory of others.[23]

For the warrior, life measured solely by its length falls short, but a life shortened by honour reaches its fullest measure.[24] Peace exposes a void, a space emptied of a sense of existential purpose, whereas war offers

---

[17] Hanson 2000, 41–43.   [18] Toffler and Toffler 1994, 133; Rutherford 1978, 54.
[19] Coker 2002b, 17.   [20] Hanson 2000.
[21] Gelven 1994; Van Creveld 1996; Nietzsche 1995 and 1981; Ignatieff 1999; Coker 2002b; Howard 1976.
[22] Nietzsche 1995.   [23] Cited in Griffin 1983, 177.   [24] Gelven 1994, xii.

excitement and instils meaning.[25] Through agency, warriors experience life to the fullest – and only in battle does the shallowness and vapidness of much of their lives outside war become apparent.[26] Agency permits the warrior to gain a coherent understanding of who he is, like Shakespeare's Hamlet who – by grasping the nature of war – is able to grasp himself.[27] Risking his life in war allows the warrior to test the limits of human agency, the limits in which excellence could be won. Agency in war allows for an awareness of the unexpected dimensions of the warrior himself.

Subjectivity

This feature of humanism stands for the need for one to discover warfare subjectively. In ancient Greece, the free citizen was expected to fight for the city. As part of this duty, the necessity of war was never questioned, though the Greeks often questioned a certain war's morality as can famously be studied in the Melian dialogue during the Peloponnesian War.[28] War was not separate from political life – it was political life and fighting was regarded as the supreme act of citizenship. Victor Davis Hanson shows how the ferocious and destructive head-on clashes between hoplite Greek phalanxes were designed for the same outcome as consensual government – an unequivocal and instant resolution of political disputes. This style of fighting had resulted from the rise of constitutional governments in the city states between 650 and 338 B.C. Greek citizens voted for and against going to war and by voting for war, they committed themselves to fighting in it.[29] And precisely because a warrior ultimately fights for himself, he gains respect and honour from his community. The Greeks, for instance, celebrated the hoplite's bravery and glorified his sacrifice through literature, philosophy, paintings, and sculptures. One of the core aspects of subjectivity is to be commemorated by those whom the warrior leaves behind. In the moment of heroic death, subjectivity allows the warrior to live on eternally.

Inter-subjectivity

Inter-subjectivity refers to the relationship of the warrior with his enemy under the condition of the reciprocal imposition of risk. In order to be humanistic, a warrior must honour his enemy. Homer's Hector serves as the prime example of a warrior who – despite his objective to defeat his

---

[25] Arendt 1998b, xii.   [26] Hedges 2002, 3.
[27] Gelven 1994, 8; Kaplan 2002; Hedges 2002.
[28] Thucydides 1974, 400–408; Walzer 1992, 4–12.   [29] Hanson 2000, vii.

enemy – does not humiliate him. Instead, his enemy deserves respect for both share a community of fate in which they have accepted the reciprocal risk of dying. This community of fate requires the true warrior to respect and even hate his enemy, but never to despise him. According to Nietzsche,

> You may have enemies whom you hate, but no enemies whom you despise. You must be proud of your enemy: then the success of your enemy shall be your success too.[30]

If the warrior disrespects his enemy, he himself cannot be honoured by his enemies and those he leaves behind. If, however, the warrior takes pride in his enemy as Hector did, then to be defeated by one's enemy is no disgrace. The Greek warrior respected and recognised his Greek adversary as someone like himself.[31]

The acceptance of the reciprocal imposition of risk established the internal morality of the relationship between warriors. Warriors are allowed to kill one another precisely because they stand in a relationship of mutual risk. Only this reciprocal condition morally licences the warrior to kill another warrior.[32] Each warrior possesses the licence to kill because each acts in self-defence vis-à-vis the other.[33] This requirement of reciprocity lies at the heart of inter-subjectivity. This inter-subjective community of fate binds warriors together in a brotherhood of death.

The features of agency, subjectivity, and inter-subjectivity are essential to turn war into a humanistic experience. Humanism and warriorhood cannot be separated but have to be thought of as two sides of the same coin.[34] Due to the humanistic dimension, the warrior located himself in a humanistic discourse that aimed at the existential idea of 'becoming' and 'transforming'. As a result, war has served as a drive for authenticity, for meaning, and for the discovery of the warrior's worth as human being. The ancient Greek hoplite was a

> free man who, [having mortgaged his life to his liberty], must be ready to risk his life on the battlefield if the mortgage is to be redeemed.[35]

It is this readiness of the ancient Greek warriors to accept the risk of dying on the battlefield that invested their lives with a heroic quality. It is through this humanistic discourse that warfare provided meaning. Humanism allowed the warrior to discover his truer self, his identity, and his authenticity.[36]

---

[30] Nietzsche 1981, 75.   [31] Ehrenreich 1998, 141.
[32] Kahn 2002, 2–9; Walzer 1992, 34–44; Lazar 2010, 180–213.
[33] Kahn 2002, 2–9; Johnson 1999, 124.   [34] Hanson 2000.   [35] Hanson 2000, xiii.
[36] Gelven 1994; Van Creveld 1996; Ignatieff 1999; Keegan 1993.

The ideal warrior was a man who went to war not for the utilitarian purpose of serving the state, but to serve himself. Nietzsche's Zarathustra preached that nothing meaningful and worthwhile ever came about without strife. War allows every human being – equipped with the 'will to power' – to assert itself. Struggle, strife, and war are inevitable expressions of being alive.[37] But life, for warriors, is not the highest good. War, in other words, is not only an acceptable means, but also an important end in itself: it is an act of self-realisation. Placing himself in a humanistic discourse, the warrior's existence always entailed an acceptance of the risk of dying. Humanism ensured that the warrior accepted this risk precisely because it allowed him to become, to transform, and to invest his life with meaning.

The European knights of the Middle Ages saw themselves in a lineage that bound them to the ancient warrior cultures of Athens and Rome.[38] They represented special warrior classes which understood war as a humanistic experience. For the chivalric knight, ancient heroes like Hector, Alexander, Scipio, and Caesar were quintessential examples of ideal warriors.[39] The book 'On Military Matters' by the Roman military writer Vegetius, for instance, was translated as 'The Book of Chivalry' in the thirteenth century and became the single most important authority on strategy, tactics, and behaviour to European knights.[40]

Warriors of the Middle Ages were an exclusive group whose status was protected by the emerging 'jus militares', the laws of the knights.[41] Their protected status as warriors obliged them to live by a strict set of codes of conduct known as the code of chivalry or the Warrior's Honour. The concept of Christian chivalry originated in the poetry of the troubadours in the twelfth century. These early accounts celebrated the virtues not only of courage but also of honour, gentleness, and courtesy:

The chevalier not only had to be sans peur but sans reproche. Knighthood was a way of life, sanctioned and civilised by the ceremonies of the Church until it was almost indistinguishable from the ecclesiastical order of the monasteries. Indeed in the twelfth century military orders – the Templars, the Knights of St. John, and the Teutonic Knights – were established in conscious imitation of the monastic foundations. The sword-belt and spurs set the knight apart ... and in the mythical figures of Parsifal and Galahad priest and knight became indistinguishable, equally dedicated, equally holy, the ideal to which medieval Christendom aspired.[42]

Because of the militarisation of the church and the sacralisation of war in the course of the Middle Ages, the chevaliers regarded war and religion as

---

[37] Nietzsche 1981, 73–75.   [38] Van Creveld 2000a, 46–70.
[39] Stacey 1994, 27; Ehrenreich 1998, 144.   [40] Stacey 1994, 27.   [41] Stacey 1994, 31.
[42] Howard 1976, 4–5.

inseparable elements.[43] The Warrior's Honour thus allowed the humanistic features of agency, subjectivity, and inter-subjectivity to live on within an elite warrior class.

The chivalric knights fought to achieve personal glory, just as Achilles or Hector did, and to uphold the honour of their noble lineage.[44] Because of the elitist status of the chevalier, none of these humanistic possibilities would be accessible to the common person until the modern age invented a new type of warfare based on nationalism, ideology, the 'levee en masse', and the draft.

Humanism in Modern American Warfare

The advent of modern warfare was possible due to the dual effects of the technological and political revolutions that swept through America and Europe between the sixteenth and nineteenth century.[45] In his analysis of mass industrial warfare from Napoleon to the Cold War, Theo Farrell identifies 'mass mobilization and industrialisation [as] central features' of modern war.[46] The technological innovations caused by the Industrial Revolution reduced the common man to the level of a tiny component within the larger war machine fought by bureaucratised armies.[47] Here, the American Civil War (1861–1865) provided the first glimpse of the disenchanting nature of modern war.[48] But at the same time, the American and French Revolutions invested the common man with the kind of opportunity for humanism and glory that was once exclusively reserved for the warrior elite.[49] Through the Revolutionary Army under George Washington, the 1793 levee en masse, and the 1798 Jourdan Law (which established the first system of universal conscription), the warrior ethos was extended to the entire nation. Nationalism made it generally possible for the average citizen to be a soldier.[50] And the American and French armies came to represent the highest ideals of their Revolutions for they stood for 'sacrifice for the common good, careers open to talent, fraternity among equals'.[51]

The effects of the technological and political revolutions sweeping through early modern America as well as Europe are well summed up by Ehrenreich:

In the early modern period mass armies had proletarianized the foot soldier, reducing him from status of the peasant to cog in the machine. Revolutionary

---

[43] Ehrenreich 1998, 166–174.   [44] Ignatieff 1999, 117.
[45] Hobsbawm 1999; Chris H Gray 1997; Philip K Lawrence 1999.   [46] Farrell 2005, 71.
[47] Pick 1993; Coker 2002b, 56–57.   [48] Weigley 1973, 130–146; Hagerman 1988.
[49] Parker 2005, 213.   [50] Coker 2002b, 55.   [51] Parker 2005, 196.

armies of the 18th and 19th century noble-ized him, allowing for shots at glory and receiving medals.[52]

In other words, Modernity was both liberating and alienating. The modern age saw a diffusion of humanism downwards from the elite warrior to the average citizen soldier. Notions of glory and sacrifice were no longer confined to an exclusive hereditary class of warriors. Yet, despite this diffusion, the difference between the vanishing old warrior class and the emerging modern citizen soldier was significant. Highly individualised and elitist warriors were no longer viable because industrial warfare ceased to depend on their individual strength and talent as a precondition for success. Instead of undisciplined individuals who charged across the battlefields pursuing their own agenda, modern warfare required disciplined, organised soldiers who swore allegiance not to themselves but to the state.

The type of glory achieved in modern wars was also different from the one sought by the ancient Greeks and the chevalier of the Middle Ages because modern industrial wars were spiritually disenchanting and alienating.[53] The mechanisation and the serial slaughter of modern war experienced by US soldiers significantly challenged and transformed humanism.

Agency

Heroism implies a death freely chosen. The warrior by definition chooses between going and not going to war. He prefers risking a heroic death on the battlefield to ordinary life because those on whose behalf he dies will honour his heroism eternally. This in turn makes the warrior a free agent in his own war. By contrast, the citizen soldiers of the modern age lacked this particular feature of agency as they were ordered to fight for the state rather than fighting for their own cause. Nevertheless, those Americans entering the Civil War and World War I (WWI) at first went with the expectation that

their war would [still] engage them in personal decisions and adventures, and that they would find occasions for personal combat, personal courage, personal killing, and, if necessary, personal dying, personally chosen and accepted.[54]

But once they found themselves fighting in the trenches in Virginia and the battlefields of Europe, they felt a disillusioning sense of strangeness, an unimaginable otherness of war from the past.[55] Modern industrial warfare neither seemed to allow for individual agency in the way that

---

[52] Ehrenreich 1998, 191.   [53] Coker 2004, 27.   [54] Hynes 1998, 48.

[55] This is not to deny that premodern wars were not horrific. Yet, the particular alienating and disenchanting experience of modern industrial warfare was significantly different – a difference that was clearly reflected in the fiction and poetry written by those who experienced it firsthand. For detailed accounts, see Hynes 1998.

wars between Greek hoplites, the knights of the Chivalric Age had been fought, nor for aristocratic cavalry charges with lances and sabres.[56] Modern soldiers felt alienated by the technology of industrial warfare, which increasingly distanced themselves from their opponents. They felt truly estranged by a war machine that drove millions to death. Modern technology and a mechanised way of thinking, Christopher Coker writes, not only exploited nature but also man himself as a resource, reducing him to an insignificant mosaic in a large canvas.[57] The nature of war had become a passive suffering that denied men in the trenches the type of individual agency that had previously been the key marker of warriorhood.[58] This is not to claim that individual soldiers did not at times act bravely and even decisively (and more will be said about this). Generally, however, modern man became the victim of the industrial war machine.

Modern industrial war could only offer a strangely depersonalised version of humanism as agency was transferred from the individual to the nation, from the warrior to the citizen soldier. The modern nation, not the individual soldier, gave war its transcendent purposefulness. The nation became a political religion. As Hans Kohn writes:

Messianic dreams of the nation at their centre put the nation into immediate and independent relation with the Absolute, and one of the main ways in which religion and nationalism are structurally similar is their ability to sanction sacrifice for the Absolute.[59]

Agency was transferred to the American people and to an ideological sense of mission that was assumed to be bestowed upon America by history.[60] These ideational absolutes provided for the transcendental purposefulness of modern wars and for the idea of a collective warrior organism in which every American citizen could now claim membership.[61] But by depersonalising warfare, by robbing war of its agency, modern war became a 'Materialschlacht' (battle of material) that turned soldiers into 'Kanonenfutter' (cannon fodder).

Industrial war (with a few exceptions) ceased to serve as a drive for meaning and authenticity. The modern battlefield no longer seemed to be a place where the citizen soldier could discover himself in the way warriors had been able to. It increasingly stripped away personal glory, heroism, and the feeling that the soldier could control his own fate. Instead of fighting for themselves, men in modern war were fighting in service to

---

[56] Prins and Tromp 2000, 214.   [57] Coker 2004, 18–21.   [58] Hynes 1998, 57.
[59] Quoted in Elbe 2003, 47.   [60] Bauman 2000b; Coker 1994; Bacevich 2005, 122.
[61] Ehrenreich 1998, 201.

technology and their abstract notions of the American people or in order to 'make the world safe for democracy'.

Subjectivity

The warrior accepts the risk of dying because he has a heightened sense of risk to the average citizen. Premature death, in that sense, is his destiny, the natural completion of his life.

It is [his] guarantee of immortality (or death transcended), the act by which [the warrior] is remembered by his community. It is the supreme act, which sets him apart from ordinary men.[62]

Modern warfare no longer allowed for the 'transcendence of death' as modern soldiers suffered an anonymous death on the battlefield. This anonymity, however, was not confined to the butchery of mass warfare; instead, it was part of modern life with its assembly line, Fordist time-tables, and mechanisation.[63] Modern life largely denied subjectivity for individuals who became cogs in the wheel, reduced to a condition and a system. Just as the engine had destroyed the dignity of human labour, Coker observes,

[t]he machine had destroyed the dignity of soldiering as well: war was no longer 'a pure trial of wills', a test of character, a duel between warriors, but a matter of impersonal calculation.[64]

Life in modern society was alienating – and so were the wars fought by these societies. Accountable to scientific axioms and mechanising rules, war was robbed of its soul and passion that previously had allowed the warrior to experience war subjectively.

With modern warfare driving millions to death, it became largely impossible for the individual soldier to set himself apart. The number of US service personnel alone killed in the Civil War was 498,000 (Union and Confederate forces combined). In the twentieth century, 53,402 died in World War I, 404,997 in World War II, 33,651 in the Korean War, and 58,168 in the Vietnam War.[65] Death on the battlefield was no longer individualised, but anonymous. The soldier who was remembered after the Civil War, two world wars, and the Korean War was anonymous.

---

[62] Coker 2001, 34.
[63] Harley 1999; Pick 1993. On the 'fetishism of the machine', see Farrell 2005, 76–80, 88.
[64] Coker 2004, 3.
[65] Available at www.cwc.lsu.edu/other/stats/warcost.htm, accessed on 16 July 2006; available at www.va.gov/pressrel/amwars01.htm, accessed on 16 July 2006. See also Eikenberry 1996, 112.

The monuments to 'The Unknown Soldier' of the Great War, Hannah Arendt wrote,

bear testimony to the then still existing need for glorification, for finding a 'who', an identifiable somebody whom years of mass slaughter should have revealed. The frustration of this wish and the unwillingness to resign oneself to the brutal fact that the agent of the war was actually nobody, inspired the erection of the monuments to 'The Unknown Soldier', to all those whom the war had failed to make known and had robbed thereby, not of their achievement, but of their human dignity.[66]

The anonymity and the serialisation of death on the modern battlefield robbed war of any subjective meaning for the individual American soldier. Modern industrial warfare severely de-individualised warfare.

A warrior accepts that his life entails the risk of dying on the battlefield because those on behalf of whom he dies will honour his heroism eternally.[67] By de-individualising and dis-enchanting war, however, industrial warfare became mass carnage in which the life of the individual counted for nothing.

In his writings Nietzsche was concerned about the utilitarian ethic that he detected on modern battlefields. The replacement of warriors by citizen soldiers, he feared, had led to the death of humanism: 'I see many soldiers: if only I could see many warriors!'[68] Nietzsche was particularly concerned with war losing its humanistic dimension and with modern soldiers becoming pure instruments of the state. The reality of modern war seemed to confirm his fear that the modern citizen soldier would no longer be able to fight for himself – instead he became the instrument of the state's war machine.[69] The nature of industrialised warfare and the sheer scale of killing did not allow for individual commemoration by those he left behind.

Inter-subjectivity

Inter-subjectivity for the ancient Greeks referred to the relationship between the warrior and his (Greek) enemy. Because the enemy shared the same community of fate, the warrior had to honour him. In the warfare of the chivalric knights

The ties of [religion, marriage,] class and kinship that linked elite warriors on both sides made it difficult to think of the enemy any other than human. By the 20th century, all this had changed.[70]

---

[66] Arendt 1998a, 181.   [67] Hynes 1998, 207; Coker 2002b, 45–60.
[68] Nietzsche 1981, 74; Hobsbawm 1998, 337.   [69] Hobsbawm 1998, 337.
[70] Ehrenreich 1998, 203.

With the advent of mass society, democracy, and nationalism/modern ideologies, respect tended – with some exceptions[71] – to be replaced with disrespect and hatred of entire nations and races. With the introduction of nations as organisms, Americans and Europeans came to see the adversary as a monster or a beast. They learned to hate their enemy in the abstract.

Modern war was no longer predominantly fought as a hand-to-hand battle or a duel. Instead, modern war meant to kill and to be killed by an enemy the soldier hardly ever set an eye on. Death in modern war came from a distance and at random. It was, Hynes observed in his study of the experiences of American and British soldiers in modern wars,

no longer a fate you chose, for your cause or your country, or because it was your job; it was something done to you, an accident, as impersonal as the plague.[72]

The growing distance between modern soldiers and the overwhelming technology used severely challenged the inter-subjective relationship between warriors that was considered to be crucial for the warriors of ancient Greece and the chivalric knights.

Compared to the humanism of the Greeks and the knights of the age of chivalry, modern war largely ceased to be humanistic. The general conclusion drawn by those who experienced the reality of modern war was that it was alienating.[73] The technological dynamic and application within which the soldier was subsumed 'totally instrumentalised the traditional warrior ethos by robbing war of its [humanistic] appeal'.[74] Modern war was mostly reduced to butchery, robbed of its romance and its humanism. There was nothing Homeric about industrial killing at either the Somme or Iwo Jima. The industrial battlefield made a mockery of the warrior's dreams of Greek-like Homeric struggles that had inspired generations of warriors in the past.

Yet, even though modern industrial warfare turned battlefields into slaughterhouses that did not leave much space for individual humanism, war still provided meaning to Americans. By elevating the entire society into a warrior organism, modern ideology offered the American people – not necessarily the individual – a chance to become an authentic people.[75] The glory of the individual was anonymous because it was the glory of the nation, and through warfare modern man could become a more authentic member of the nation. The nation had become a warrior organism. Thus, the features of agency, subjectivity, and inter-subjectivity were depersonalised and transformed in such a way that they merely became

[71] Bourke 2000.   [72] Hynes 1998, 70.   [73] Mueller 1991, 1–28; Fussell 1975.
[74] Arendt 1998a, 180–182; Coker 2004, 46.   [75] Bacevich 2005, 122; Tony Smith 1995.

attributable to the ideational level of the collective as a Hegelian organism. If the individual soldier could no longer find individual space for humanism in modern war, then the nation and ideologies served him as a secular religion by offering an entire worldview that justified collective, if depersonalised, sacrifice.[76] In the modern age, the features of humanism could – in most cases – only be found on the level of the nation and ideologies.

The Transformation of Humanism in Vietnam and the Rise of US Casualty-Aversion

The American disenchantment with the modern ideational justification for sacrifice did not come in the trenches of the Civil War, two World Wars, or the Korean War, but in Vietnam. The experience of the war in the jungles of Indochina for the individual US serviceman was so disenchanting that he no longer experienced war as an act of either individual or national self-realisation, authenticity, and transcendental meaning. The Vietnam War came to mark the great divide between those Americans who had come of age in the heroic triumphant atmosphere of the Second World War and those growing up in the landscape of moral confusion and transformation of Vietnam.[77] The average US soldier could no longer find agency, subjectivity, and inter-subjectivity in the Indochina War. This loss of humanism has made US casualty-aversion one of the core tenets of US war making ever since.

Agency

The feature of agency in modern war has been transformed from the individual to the collective idea of the nation or ideology that gave modern war its transcendental purposefulness. It was in these abstract ideational terms that Americans initially saw Vietnam as a test of their nation's will and readiness to confront and ultimately contain Communism. Americans were prepared to support Presidents John F. Kennedy's and Lyndon B. Johnson's 'Long Twilight Struggle' which required sacrifice.[78] Based on the 'domino theory' the Vietnam War was conceived and legitimised as part of the Cold War Manichean struggle between good and evil.[79] On this ideational level, Vietnam deeply appealed to Americans' sense of mission and duty that was

[76] Toynbee 1957, 18; Bacevich 2005, 9–11.   [77] Bacevich 2005, 34.   [78] Neu 2000, 11.
[79] McCrisken 2003, 21–22; McNamara, Blight, and Brigham 1999, 22; Morris 2003.

bestowed upon them by history, promising them a test of their character and destiny.[80]

The generation of Americans who came to fight in the jungles of Vietnam were born between 1945 and 1953 and thus had grown up in a zeitgeist that conditioned them to think of Vietnam as their generation's natural turn to install national glory, to defend liberty, and to renew America's virtue.[81] Philip Caputo, who was among the first Marines to be sent to Vietnam in 1965, captures this zeitgeist well when he writes that

We believed in all the myths created by that most articulate and elegant myth-maker, John Kennedy. If he was the King of Camelot, then we were his knights, and Vietnam our crusade.[82]

The ideal knight of Caputo's generation was John Wayne, whose agency and sacrifice in the 1949 movie *The Sands of Iwo Jima* were present in the minds and narratives of those serving in the early stages of the Vietnam War. The death of this modern day Achilles in the Pacific War was conceived as meaningful and heroic as it served a transcendental purposefulness for the American people. His sacrifice was conceived as justified on the ideational level for it was made in defence of life, liberty, and the pursuit of happiness.

As the Vietnam War progressed, however, especially after the 1968 Tet Offensive, the initial ideal of sacrifice started giving away to a growing unwillingness to sacrifice. The ideational purpose which had not only mobilised the American nation in the past, but that had also legitimised its costs in lives and material, began losing its appeal.[83] As Andrew J. Bacevich argues,

For the Americans who came of age in the 1960s and 1970s . . . Vietnam was the defining event, the Great Contradiction that demolished existing myths about America's claim to be a uniquely benign great power and fuelled suspicions that other myths might also be false.[84]

For the average 19 year-old conscript, the war was emptied of meaning, values, coherence, reasons, and romance. Those serving on their one-year

---

[80] Tony Smith 1995; Coker 1989.
[81] Isaacs 1997, 7; Neu 2000, 11–13; Hynes 1998, 183.   [82] Caputo 1996, 69–70.
[83] One area this disenchantment was reflected in was polls. In October 1967, the tide began to turn with more Americans (47%) for the first time saying that it was a mistake to send troops to Vietnam than not (44%). Following Tet in 1968, the majority of Americans for the first time (53%) opposed the Vietnam War; by 1969 and 1970, opposition to the war averaged 55%, and by 1971 and 1973 it was as high as 60%. President Johnson's approval ratings dropped from 58% (October 1967) to 24% (April 1968) – which analysts believe was due to the effects of the Tet Offensive. Available at www.gallup.com/poll/18097/Ir aq-Versus-Vietnam-Comparison-Public-Opinion.aspx, accessed on 5 December 2016.
[84] Bacevich 2005, 34.

tour in Vietnam increasingly felt that they could no longer discover themselves through the same agency that they had seen in John Wayne. Instead, there is much evidence in the literature and in the oral history on Vietnam that 'John Wayne was the Hollywood-in-their-heads, exposed and mocked by the real, bitter thing.'[85] Here, the iconic figure of John Wayne is omnipresent, yet always as a sign of how completely the old values of heroism had become an anathema, everybody's example of how not to fight a war because it would lead to death.[86]

Wayne's name was used to describe heroic acts in movies, but which would bring death on the battlefield. The icon of American courage and heroism became a joke, an anti-hero, and everybody's example of how not to fight a war.[87]

The notion of the Vietnam hero was no longer of a man who through his agency could gain authenticity, or of a man who chose death in order to realise his truer self, but of a man whose ingenuity, endurance, efficiency, and competitiveness helped him survive. Death was no longer freely chosen but avoided. Joseph Heller's 1961 novel *Catch-22* in this respect became the central and most popular novel of the Vietnam War generation, for it captured the prevailing feeling that there was no space for heroes in modern war. The real hero was the anti-hero, the one who successfully overcame the risks of warfare and survived, for it was in surviving and not in dying that the US serviceman in Vietnam triumphed.[88]

The warriors of the ancient Greeks accepted the risk of dying on the battlefield by their own will because it promised the natural – if premature – completion of their lives. The Vietnam soldier, in contrast, became an icon of alienation and scepticism seeking individual survival as the supreme value. Due to the perceived lack of agency, he preferred to live, raise a family, and see the future (embrace the 'boredoms of ordinary life') rather than accepting the risk of dying for an ideology that had started ringing hollow.[89]

Subjectivity

This feature of humanism stands for the need for oneself to experience war subjectively and the need to be commemorated by those who are left behind. Subjectivity for warriors, Coker writes, only ends at the moment that they are no longer honoured by their fellow citizens:

[85] Hynes 1998, 183.   [86] Kovic 1977; Caputo 1996; O'Brien 1999; Herr 1991.
[87] Neu 2000, 18.   [88] Isaacs 1997, 19, 24; Coker 2001, 35–36; Hynes 1998, 214–215.
[89] Bacevich 2005, 28–35, 124.

Warriors live in the recognition of their fellow citizens; in the story told of their lives after they are gone; in the esteem in which they are held by their bravest enemies.[90]

By experiencing war for himself, the warrior gains respect and honour from the community on whose behalf he risks his life. By being commemorated, the warrior at the moment of death lives on eternally.

Among the American youth at the time of the Vietnam War, there was no desire to discover war subjectively. In Vietnam, contrary to WWII and Korea, it was not regarded by a large section of society as dishonourable to avoid the draft.[91] Rather, the dishonourable thing to do was to serve in a war in which the faith in the good cause had leaked away. As a consequence, draft evasion and desertion were commonplace. To give a few examples: over the course of the war, 209,000 military-aged men defied the draft by moving to Canada; another half a million refused military induction Vietnam; and by 1972, more young men were exempted from the draft than were inducted into military service.[92] Vietnam was the first American war from which the affluent middle classes were substantially exempt. It demolished the notion of military obligation traditionally associated with US citizenship.[93]

In Vietnam itself the military morally disintegrated because US soldiers in Vietnam felt abandoned and betrayed by their nation on whose behalf they were supposed to risk their lives.[94] Instead of being honoured and respected, they were increasingly cast by American public culture, art, music, media, and intellectuals back home as symbols of national failure and shame.[95] The war had become the longest and most unpopular war in American history and as it continued and the faith in the good cause had disappeared, they had become an anti-war myth of national dishonour, a fall from grace. In Vietnam, mutinies and 'fragging' were commonplace.[96]

The use and abuse of drugs was a means that allowed conscripts to escape from the disenchanting reality of the war, a clear expression of the

---

[90] Coker 2004, 9.   [91] Scott 1966.
[92] A comparison of the ratio of conscientious objectors to actual draftees across the major wars the US fought prior to Vietnam is quite instructive: during World War I, per 100 inductions, there were 0.14 conscientious objectors; in World War II, the ratio was 0.15. In Vietnam, these ratios went up to 25 by 1970 and to 130 by 1972. See Baskir and Strauss 1978, 67–69.
[93] Bacevich 2005, 28, 99.   [94] Hynes 1998, 180.   [95] Coker 2005, 10.
[96] Zinn 223b, 245. 'Fragging' (a term referring to the shooting or hand-grenading of a superior American officer by an American soldier) incidents are uncertain. Between 1969 and 1973, the US Army reported at least six hundred officers being murdered. In 1971, there were an estimated 1.8 fragging incidents for every one thousand US soldiers deploying in Vietnam. See Walker 2009, 113.

end of the desire to experience war subjectively. A random sample of drug testing in 1971 showed that 67 per cent of American soldiers used marijuana and 45 per cent hard drugs (such as heroin). Of the 2,500 casualties delivered to hospital in September that same year, 55 per cent were hospitalised not because of battlefield wounds but because of drug abuse.[97]

The feeling of abandonment and betrayal was confirmed by the silence that awaited them back home after their one-year duty. In the past, US veterans had been welcomed back by the American people through celebrations, medals, and memorials. What separated Vietnam veterans like Ron Kovic from previous generations was their sense of alienation from a country on whose behalf they were forced to risk their lives but which itself refused to give its name to the war.[98] Instead of celebrations, there was silence. Instead of commemoration, there was a refusal to honour them and even build a memorial. In fact, the Vietnam War Memorial, erected at the Mall in Washington, DC in 1982, was financed and built by the Vietnam veterans themselves.[99] Thus, in order to live on eternally, those who served in Vietnam, rather than the society they served for, had to ensure that they were not forgotten by their own nation.

Inter-subjectivity

Traditionally, this feature refers to the relation a warrior has with the enemy. As both share an inter-subjective community of fate that binds them together in a brotherhood of death, the enemy deserves respect. For most US conscripts, however, the Vietnam War was not fought as a duel or hand-to-hand battle. The enemy was elusive, hidden, and generally tended to evaporate into the jungle before US soldiers could set an eye on him or her. Caputo captures this widespread experience when he asks, 'I thought we were fighting phantoms . . . where were these fabled guerrillas, the Vietcong?'[100] US troops felt that they were fighting an invisible enemy who regularly killed and wounded them through mines, booby traps, and sniper fire.

The unfamiliar nature of the enemy's defensive guerrilla strategy was extremely disorientating and created a dissonance in the minds of Americans. From movies, history classes, and books, they had absorbed that war was linear, something that progressed through successive battles and campaigns towards a conclusion. But the war in Vietnam offered neither such a story line nor frontline, just fragments of violence. The asymmetric nature of the war turned out to be entirely different from the expectation of

[97] Herring 2000, 60.   [98] Kovic 1977.   [99] Hynes 1998, 207.   [100] Caputo 1996, 56.

inter-subjectivity that most US soldiers had brought to South East Asia. The resulting dissonance was heavily reflected in American fictional and oral history that came out of Vietnam. It is filled with the prevailing sense that the war had no clear chronology, no beginning or ending, and no continuity.[101] To the Americans the war appeared to be random, chaotic, incoherent, and without a narrative logic. It was a war without direction, a story without a plot. They saw the war, as in Michael Herr's *Dispatches* (1991), as a series of vignettes, arranged like a surrealist movie that created one long disorientating image of events. The Vietcong was a nebulous and elusive enemy, appearing to be nowhere and everywhere, blending into the local population, but hardly ever – as Clausewitz put it – materializing as a concrete body.[102] The Vietcong denied their adversaries the establishment of any inter-subjective relationship.

With all three features of agency, subjectivity, and inter-subjectivity fundamentally transformed by the nature of the conflict, the average US soldier could no longer experience humanism in the Vietnam War. In that respect, the war marked the great divide regarding US humanism. The nation that had entered the war was different from the one that left it. The war had changed the mental and spiritual landscape of America. In the Civil War, WWI, WWII, and the Korean War, America had been prepared to expend vast numbers of lives, yet casualty-aversion had not been the central issue. In Vietnam, however, it became the central issue.[103]

When the conflict developed in unexpected ways, the true nature of the larger ideational purpose of America itself was increasingly doubted. Widely held national myths such as innocence were challenged and the belief in exceptionalism fundamentally shaken.[104] Vietnam became, according to Isaacs, 'the era's most powerful symbol of damaged ideals and the loss of trust, unity, shared myths and common values'.[105] On the deepest ideational level, it was waged not only on a distant battlefield, but also in the unchartered depth of the American psyche and soul. It disrupted America's story, its own explanation of the past and vision of the future.[106] 'Vietnam', as Richard Nixon observed, 'tarnished our ideals, weakened our spirit and crippled our will.'[107] Ideational foundations like containment, the Domino Theory, and the spreading of liberty, which had not only mobilised the nation in the past, but had also legitimised sacrifice, were demolished.[108]

Historical sociologists explain this disruption with the past more generally through the rise of reflexive or liquid postmodernity.[109] The modern

---

[101] Isaacs 1997, 31; Coker 2001, 31–33.   [102] Clausewitz 1984, 481.
[103] Bennett and Flickinger 2009, 587–590; Record 2000.   [104] Bacevich 2005, 34, 124.
[105] Isaacs 1997, 6.   [106] McCrisken 2003, xiii–xiv.   [107] Cited in Simons 1998, 13.
[108] Shaw 2005, 79–80.
[109] Beck 1992; Beck, Giddens and Lash 1994; Baumann 2000a.

age, according to thinkers such as Ulrich Beck, Anthony Giddens, and Zygmunt Baumann, had forced societies to undergo a dual process of dis-embedding and re-embedding.[110] Ushered in by the Enlightenment, the modern age had dis-embedded societies previously based on religious absolutes in order to re-embed them into secular absolutes such as nationalism and modern ideologies. By the 1970s, with the rise of postmodern risk society, however, this dual process was starting to be disrupted: processes of dis-embedding still occurred, but they were no longer followed by processes of re-embedding.[111] This, according to Baumann, meant that societies started moving from the modern era of pre-allocated reference groups into a postmodern epoch in which the destination of individuals has remained undetermined.[112] Postmodernity no longer furnished any beds for re-embedding these dis-embedded individuals. As a result, the modern ideational foundations that had mobilised the American people were giving way to postmodern individualisation.[113]

This means that the transformation of humanism in Vietnam coincided with the rise of America as a postmodern society structured around the avoidance and management of risks.[114] Distributional conflicts over 'goods' such as jobs, social security, and income (which dictated the traditional agenda of modern politics) have given way to distributional conflicts over 'bads'; that is the risks created by threats to individual life, health, and well-being.[115] By transforming from a modern into a postmodern society, the US has become increasingly risk averse. American politics and the way politicians have conducted war, has been about the control and prevention of such risks.[116] These societal changes in conjunction with the transformation of humanism translated into an unwillingness to sacrifice, thereby increasingly turning the US from an inherently heroic into what Edward Luttwak called a 'post-heroic society'.[117] Reflecting the emergence of risk society, casualty-aversion has become institutionalised in the way in which the US has waged wars ever since.[118]

Casualty-Aversion and US Warfare Post-Vietnam

In 1973, President Nixon abandoned conscription in response to the rampant unpopularity of the draft and replaced it with an all-volunteer force.[119] The Vietnam War thus became the last war in which American

---

[110] Beck, Giddens and Lash 1994, 23–45.   [111] Beck 1999.
[112] Baumann 2000a, 10–17.   [113] Rorty 1989; Harley 1999.   [114] Beck 1992.
[115] Beck 1992.   [116] Coker 2002a, 57–59.
[117] Luttwak 1995, 109–122; Luttwak 1996, 33–45.
[118] Shaw 2005, 79–80; Bacevich 2005, 57; Record 2002, 10–14.
[119] Eikenberry 1996, 112; Herring 2000, 64.

conscripts were sent into battle. From that moment onwards, Michael Mann argues, wars no longer mobilised the American nation as a player, only as a detached spectator: '[American] wars no longer involve real or potential sacrifice, except for professional troops.'[120] Physical sacrifice, in other words, ceased to be an obligation of American citizenship and instead became the voluntary business of citizens-turned-professionals.[121]

The all-volunteer force effectively put an end to the unity between modern society and universal conscription that had begun with the levée en masse in the late eighteenth century. This transcendence of traditional forms of militarisation and participation ushered the emergence of what Martin Shaw calls 'post-military society'. Transferring the risks of combat exclusively onto professionals, Shaw argues, undermined the Clausewitzean understanding of the relationship between state, army, and the people and challenged the modern understanding of military service.[122] In the American and French Revolutions, the fraternal unity of the nation-state was established by eradicating the boundaries between the elite warrior community and society. The establishment of an all-volunteer force and the army's move to 'Total Force'[123] structure symbolised the break with this fraternal unity and was designed at the time to detach the American public from the emotions and sacrifices of war.[124] Vietnam demolished the notion of military obligation and, as Bacevich writes, 'brought the tradition of the citizen-soldier to an end'.[125] As a consequence, modern war began to transform into a spectator sport in which a risk-averse society was no longer coerced or expected to participate physically. The American public could spectate war from a distance without the risk of suffering.[126] For American society post-Vietnam, the exposure to the risk of dying in war became voluntary.

Yet confining the risk of combat to volunteers was merely the immediate first step in attempts by American political and military decision makers to re-legitimise warfare with the US public. The Vietnam disaster affected US leaders so deeply that it has lurked behind most of what has been thought and done in American military affairs since. It has become a reference point of what to do in order to prevent the United States from getting embroiled in similar quagmires. It was principally in this context, but also in immediate response to the 1983 killing of 241 US Marines in

[120] Mann 1988, 184–185.
[121] McInnes 2002, 69. An exception to this rule can be found in the National Guard.
[122] Shaw 1991.   [123] For details on 'Total Force', see Duncan 1997.
[124] Bennett and Flickinger 2009, 587–589; Dauber 2002, 70.
[125] Bacevich 2005, 99; Mann 1988, 184–185.
[126] Ignatieff 2000a; Der Derian 2005; McInnes 2002, 2, 29.

Beirut, that US decision-makers came to perceive public support for any military operation as conditional upon minimum US casualties.[127]

In the fall of 1982, US President Ronald Reagan had sent US Marines into Lebanon's raging civil war as part of a multinational peacekeeping force to oversee the withdrawal of Syrian troops and PLO fighters from Beirut as well as the restoration of the authority of the Lebanese government.[128] After initial successes, violence soon returned, culminating in the suicide bombing of buildings housing American and French forces on 23 October 1983.[129] The bombs took the lives of 241 US Marines, marking the deadliest single day death toll for the US Marine Corps since the Battle of Iwo Jima in World War II. Following the suicide attack, the US President withdrew American peacekeeping forces. This disastrous mission not only heightened military caution and deepened the service's misgivings about deploying US forces for unclear goals in muddled, complicated foreign conflicts, but also demonstrated that the limits to the American will to sacrifice exposed by the Vietnam War remained.[130]

Following the peacekeeping mission, Reagan's Secretary of Defence, Caspar Weinberger, in 1984 presented six conditions that were to be satisfied before US military power could be employed in the future. The Weinberger Doctrine, as it came to be called, was essentially an articulation of the military's desire to ensure that it would 'never again' find itself fighting under circumstances similar to those in Vietnam and Lebanon.[131] The specific criteria to govern decisions regarding the use of force set out that US armed forces should only be committed to combat when the purpose was 'deemed vital to our national interest'; there was a 'clear intention of political will to win'; any use of American force must be 'sufficient to achieve victory'; have 'clearly defined political and military objectives'; the rational guiding the use of force 'must be continually reassessed and adjusted if necessary'; be approved by the American people and 'their elected representatives in Congress'; and going to war must be 'a last resort'.[132]

The doctrine attempted to codify the lessons on the use of force learned by US military officials from the wars in Vietnam and Lebanon. Its conditions reflected, according to Cori Dauber, the military's interpretation (represented by Harry G. Summers book 'On Strategy')[133] of what went wrong in both conflicts and inverted the analysis:

[127] Luttwak 1995, 116; Record 2002, 10–14.   [128] Zinn 2003b, 359–360.
[129] Michael Smith 2006, 94–95.
[130] Isaacs 1997, 73; Cornish 2003, 125; Luttwak 1996, 37–39; Neu 2000, 70.
[131] Neu 2000, 70; Bacevich 2005, 48; McCrisken 2003, 111.
[132] McCrisken 2003, 106–107. See also Luttwak 1995; Bacevich 2005, 51–52.
[133] Summers 1982.

While Summers' analysis is an assessment of what not to do, Weinberger instead produced a checklist of what *to* do in order to produce successful military operations.[134]

In other words, any decision to intervene was to require policy-makers to advance a plausible case for meeting all these tests.[135] The failure to do so was to constitute a de facto veto. Thus, the purpose of the Weinberger Doctrine was not to facilitate the effective use of American military power, but to insulate the armed services from another Vietnam-like disaster.[136]

Among the six conditions, public support was identified to be the most crucial and therefore irreducible one.[137] The other five conditions were not seen as intrinsic criteria in themselves, but as political conditions that needed to be met in order to ensure continued public support.[138] With a clear sense of the public's general casualty-aversion following Vietnam and Lebanon, the Weinberger Doctrine conceived public support as conditional upon a minimum of US casualties.[139] It therefore linked continued public support directly with a minimum level of casualties. In other words, casualty-aversion was officially institutionalised as the single most important condition that needed to be met in order to make American warfare acceptable to what US decision-makers viewed as an increasingly casualty-averse public.[140]

Besides codifying the paramount lessons of Vietnam in what was intended as a permanent and comprehensive statement of policy govern-ing the use of force, the military also ushered in a period of massive reforms that aimed at the moral reinvigoration of the troops and retrieving legitimacy among the public. This journey of renewal, which was to culminate temporarily in the 1991 Gulf War, aimed at sustained innova-tion that left few parts of the armed forces untouched. Beginning with General Creighton Abrams's 'Total Force' policy and the 1982 AirLand Battle doctrine, the military tried to salvage the American profession of arms (that was left thoroughly discredited and dishonoured in Vietnam by events such as the My Lai Massacre) as well as to refocus from peripheral proxy wars to the Cold War confrontation in the 'Central Region' of Europe.[141] These early reform policies of the late 1970s and early 1980s aimed at retrieving professional legitimacy by avoiding future campaigns even remotely resembling the Vietnam War.[142]

---

[134] Dauber 2002, 70 [Italics in original]; Gentry 1998, 180.   [135] Murray 2007, 44.
[136] Bacevich 2005, 42.   [137] Record 2002, 12; Luttwak 1996, 38–39.
[138] Record 2002, 12.   [139] McCrisken 2003, 38.
[140] Knickerbocker 2003; Luttwak 1995, 112; Simons 1998, 7; Record 2002, 12.
[141] For a good account of post-Vietnam reforms undertaken by the US Army, see Clancy and Franks 1997, 84–127.
[142] Sechser and Saunders 2010, 507; Zambernardi 2010, 21–27.

The AirLand Battle doctrine offered a formula according to which US forces would turn back a full-scale non-nuclear Soviet attack by relying on superior tactics and technology to compensate for the enemy's larger numbers.[143] The doctrine adopted a distinctly new American style of warfare, drawing on advanced technology (first used in the last stages of the Vietnam War) and the concentration of overwhelming force from unprecedented distances.[144] This ground-breaking reform created the nucleus of what in the 1990s became known as the 'Revolution in Military Affairs' (RMA) and net-centric warfare: the integration of computer technology and knowledge management systems to improve battlefield command and control, the development of precision-guided weapons technology as well as the deployment of new types of armour, stealth systems, and unmanned platforms.[145] Most importantly, to make the weapons of this new technology-driven warfare acceptable politically, Michael Ignatieff argues, it was essential

to increase the precision of their targeting; to minimize the collateral or unintended consequences of their use; to reduce, if not eliminate, the risk to those who fired them, by keeping them as far away from the battle-line as was consistent with accuracy. From the beginning, therefore, technology was in search of impunity.[146]

The objective of this process of military reinvigoration therefore lay in creating risk-free and high-precision warfare that could be waged from ever-increasing distances.[147]

The driving force behind these post-Vietnam reforms that led to the contemporary US approach to warfare was to bring the use of force in line with what was perceived as a casualty-averse public. Advanced technology was used to reduce American exposure to the risks of combat while heralding lesser risks to enemy non-combatants. It aimed at producing a new grammar of killing in which the spilling of American blood became de-emphasised.[148] This journey of renewal developed over the period of a decade and its cumulative effects were fully unveiled for the first time during Operation Desert Storm.[149]

---

[143] Clancy and Franks 1997, 84–127; Bacevich 2005, 36–47.
[144] Gentry 1998, 187; Ignatieff 2000c, 164–177; Sechser and Saunders 2010, 507.
[145] For a detailed account of the RMA and net-centric warfare, see Eliot Cohen 1996, 37–54; Arquilla and Ronfeldt 1997; O'Hanlon 2000, 7–31; Krepinevich 2001, 76–89; Der Derian 2001, 28–33, 126–161.
[146] Ignatieff 2000c, 164.   [147] Bacevich 2005, 159; Ignatieff 2000b.
[148] Coker 2005, 10–16; Bohrer and Osiel 2013, 803–809.
[149] Chris H. Gray 1997, 36–50; Ignatieff 2000c, 168.

The Persian Gulf War and American Casualty-Aversion

Operation Desert Storm was the first American war in which, from the beginning, securing the goals of high levels of casualty-aversion and civilian protection were key operational objectives.[150] The formulation of war aims and the conduct of military operations were governed by the fear among American leaders that the loss of too many American military and Iraqi civilian lives would erode public and congressional support for the war.[151] To the extent that American military and political decision makers were haunted by the memories of Vietnam and were preoccupied with avoiding a repetition of the same mistakes, the 1991 war was not only fought to overthrow Saddam Hussein's aggression against Kuwait but also to conquer and overcome America's troubling memories of Vietnam.[152] The Gulf War, according to Herring,

> was more about Vietnam than Kuwait for a political and military leadership that sought vindication, to prove that they had learnt from their failures in Vietnam.[153]

Close adherence to and internalisation of the Weinberger Doctrine ensured that the ghost of Vietnam would not cast its shadow over the Gulf War. Starting from the build-up to the war, President George H. W. Bush and his administration set out to mobilise public support with a conscious and explicit campaign to free the country from the legacy of Vietnam. The president had repeatedly stated that Iraq would not be 'another Vietnam' and that the paralysis this war had caused would be overcome.

The successful performance by the US military in winning quickly and with a minimum of casualties certainly vindicated the reforms undertaken in response to Vietnam in the 1970s and 1980s. President Bush emphasised this point in his victory speech on 1 March 1991 when he triumphantly declared the Vietnam Syndrome to be kicked once and for all: 'The spectre of Vietnam has been buried forever in the sands of the Arabian Peninsula.'[154] Senior military officers also situated Desert Storm in this larger story of redemption. 'This war didn't take one hundred hours to win', Major General Barry McCaffrey stated, 'it took fifteen years.'[155] These and other statements from American officials implied that the historical judgement which had lingered ever since the defeat in the jungles of Vietnam had been overturned.[156]

---

[150] Record 2002, 4.   [151] Eikenberry 1996, 113.
[152] Simons 1998, 20–21; Ignatieff 2000b; Record 2002, 10–14.   [153] Herring 2000, 77.
[154] Cited in McCrisken 2003, 150.
[155] Cited in Bacevich 2005, 34. See also Ignatieff 2000b.
[156] For a listing of various public statements, see Chris H Gray 1997, 46; Bacevich 2005, 33–35.

Yet, by complying to the letter with the Weinberger Doctrine, the United States was far from kicking the Vietnam Syndrome. On the contrary, the American military had succeeded in reinventing warfare in a way that has made it acceptable to the US public, politicians, and the military. It thereby helped restore the respect and prestige of the armed forces within American society and provided a longed for opportunity for redemption. The US conduct of war post-Vietnam therefore embodied rather than defeated the Vietnam Syndrome.[157]

In the Gulf War, the potential death of US military personnel has been instrumentalised as a risk to be avoided, which is profoundly at odds with the humanist message at the heart of the warrior tradition. Warriors by definition accept the risk of dying. They hazard all, including their lives, in war. America's postmodern society, which is structured around the avoidance of risk in every aspect of social life, fought this war in ways that aimed at minimising precisely these risks.[158] In this new postmodern warfare, most servicemen and servicewomen are no longer moral agents in the way the ancient Greeks understood the term. Instead, they have become machine- and technology-assisted agents, trained for and fighting a particular mission by virtual reality and computer simulation. Such virtual wars, Bacevich writes, are 'not conducted by specially empowered and culturally distinctive "warriors" but by computer-wielding technicians'.[159] Trained in and assisted by such technology, they are no longer required to feel courage, to experience fear, or to show the type of endurance that was regarded as the defining marker of agency.[160]

The war fought in the Persian Gulf was mediated by machines and information technology.[161] The postmodern battlefield was largely electronic with the actual war being waged not over real territories but virtual maps and geographies generated by computer simulations and data supplied by satellites.[162] Thus, the reality of the postmodern battlefield is mediated largely through technology. For James Der Derian, the Gulf War constituted the beginning of 'virtual cleansing', a process of the sanitisation of violence that aims at overpowering the mortification of the human body.[163] By enlisting US soldiers and the US public in virtual and virtuous ways, this newly evolving postmodern warfare has not only altered subjectivity through the means of technology but has also sought to evade the fact that postmodern warfare is still about killing others.[164] American warfare has achieved lethal perfection with a degree of

---

[157] Simons 1998, 6; Record 2002, 10–14.   [158] Beck 1992; Coker 2001, 51–61.
[159] Bacevich 1996, 47.
[160] Bowden 2002; Luttwak 1995, 116; Der Derian 2005; Ignatieff 2000a.
[161] Virilio 2002.   [162] Chris H Gray 1997.   [163] Der Derian 2001, 120.
[164] Der Derian 2001, xvi–xvii; Virilio 2002.

impunity that is unprecedented. Waged increasingly by computer technicians and high-altitude specialists, it is becoming increasingly abstract, distanced, and virtual. This phenomenon of 'virtual cleansing' was also noted by Michael Ignatieff:

> War thus becomes virtual, not simply because it appears to take place on a screen but because it enlists societies only in virtual ways. Due to nuclear weapons, it is no longer a struggle for national survival; with the end of conscription, it no longer requires the actual participation of citizens; ... and as a result of the exponential growth, it no longer draws on the entire economic system. These conditions transform war into something like a spectator sport. As with sport, nothing ultimate is at stake: neither national survival, nor the fate of the economy. War affords the pleasure of a spectacle, with the added thrill that it is real for someone, but not, happily, for the spectator.[165]

In other words, new networked computer systems, simulations, and precision-guided weapons systems have created an experience of war that no longer requires humanism and therefore can be experienced virtually without the need to accept the risks of dying.

Victor D. Hanson interpreted this lack of humanism in the new US warfare as the ending of the warrior tradition of ancient Greece. Greek warriors despised the archers and javelin throwers of the Persian armies for their lack of humanism as they could kill effectively from a distance but with little risk to themselves. Avoiding close infantry battle, something that was disdained by the ancient Greeks, had become one of the central tenets of the 1991 US campaign. Relying on weeks of massive aerial bombardment and precision-guided missile technology before a mere four days of ground campaign brought an end to the war, the United States avoided fighting at close quarters and instead waged war from afar with little risk to its own soldiers.[166] Like the Persians, Hanson concluded, the Americans 'suffered from that most dangerous tendency in war: a wish to kill but not to die in the process'.[167] Due to its technological might, the US military has come close to realising this wish; for it now has the capacity to apply force without suffering the risk of reciprocal injury.[168] At the heart of the postmodern US warfare that evolved in the Gulf War, Der Derian writes, 'is the technical capability and ethical imperative to threaten and, if necessary, actualise violence from a distance – *with no or minimum casualties*'.[169] Whereas risk taking in the past was an illustration of bravery, the hallmark of a warrior's true nature, by the end of

---

[165] Ignatieff 2000c, 191.   [166] Hanson 2000, 6–11.
[167] Hanson 2000, 10; see also Kahn 2002, 2–9.   [168] Kahn 2002, 7; Ignatieff 2000a.
[169] Der Derian 2001, xiv–xv [Emphasis in original]; see also Gentry 1998, 179.

the Cold War it had become a measure of irresponsibility for American decision-makers and the average citizen.

Interestingly, US political and military elites have generally proven to be even more casualty-averse than the US public. Polling data taken at the time of the Gulf War revealed the extent to which America's political and military elites have convinced themselves that public intolerance towards US casualties was much higher than actually was the case.[170] Yet, despite a number of surveys of this phenomenon, the general assumption among US decision-makers about the casualty-averse nature of the US public has remained the same.[171] The high levels of casualty-aversion, which resulted in only 382 US personnel being killed in the Gulf War (235 of which were caused by accidents and friendly fire incidents),[172] seemed to reinforce the lesson that only minimum numbers of US casualties could prevent the erosion of public support.

Despite casualty-aversion becoming one of the key characteristics of contemporary US warfare, American warriors are not entirely dead. Although their numbers even within the US armed forces are extremely small, they have survived in what Alvin and Heidi Toffler call 'a niche market'.[173] In 1998, these 'niche warriors' consisted of about twenty-one thousand Special Operations Forces (12,500 Army, 5,800 Air Force, and 2,700 Navy).[174] They comprised a number of highly specialised units such as the Green Berets and the Army Rangers, the Navy Seals, and the Air Force Special Relations Command. In addition, the Joint Special Operations Command (JSOC) consists of three units whose existence the Pentagon has refrained from officially acknowledging: the Naval Special Warfare Development Group (DEVGRU, also known as 'SEAL Team 6'), the Air Force's 24th Special Tactics Squadron, and the Army's First Special Forces Operational Detachment-Delta (Delta Forces).[175]

Thomas K. Adams defined Special Operations Forces (SOF) as

specially organized, trained and equipped military and paramilitary forces that conduct special operations to achieve military, political, economic or informational objectives by generally unconventional means in hostile, denied or politically sensitive areas.[176]

They are made up of volunteers and able to cover an array of situations ranging from reconnaissance, information as well as psychological

[170] Farrell 2005, 90; Record 2002, 10–14; Kull and Destler 1999; Gartner 2008, 95–101.
[171] Hyde 2000, 17–27; Eliot Cohen 2001, 55–56; Shaw 2005, 34–35.
[172] Ignatieff 2000b.   [173] Toffler and Toffler 1994, 105–107.   [174] Adams 1998, 9.
[175] Kibbe 2004, 109–110.
[176] Adams 1998, 7. For an overview of the various attempts to define SOF, see Horn 2004, 3–34.

operations, to sabotage, rescuing hostages, psychological warfare, (coun-ter-) insurgencies/terrorism, and support for humanitarian and civic actions operations.[177]

These 'niche warriors' were first deployed during WWII, the wars in Korea and Vietnam, and were also active during the Gulf War where they comprised merely seven thousand out of the 540,396 American troops deployed.[178]

In contrast to the rest of the US military, which has declared 'force protection' its watchword,[179] which employs technology to increase the distance between itself and the enemy, and whose members display a growing unwillingness to accept the risks of dying,[180] 'Niche warriors' are trained specialists in close hand-to-hand combat, operating in small teams and at high risks.[181] They are specifically designed and deployed for human contact with the enemy in situations where their degree of specialisation exceeds that available through technology or where the use of conventional force is not considered a military option.[182]

What sets them apart goes beyond the skills that can be taught to conventional military forces. Rather, they are highly adaptable and cap-able individuals who display independent thought, initiative, as well as mental agility and demonstrate a level of leadership and toughness exceeding that found in regular forces. In short, their status pertains to their intellectual and philosophical capabilities and their distinct belief that no mission is too dangerous and no task too daunting.[183] As McRaven observes, 'their aspiration of glory, however unpalatable that may seem, [is] essential to their success on the battlefield.'[184] This means that those who join SOFs do so with the expressed purpose of accepting and taking extraordinary risks to their lives in combat. The humanism of 'niche warriors' represents the last link to the warrior cultures of ancient Greece and Rome. According to Coker,

[t]hey still represent human agency, battling against the odds and exercising their own discretion. They are still subjective beings who experience danger by operat-ing behind the lines and by enduring more, both physically and emotionally, than other soldiers ... and they are still inter-subjective beings who are more likely to honour or understand the fighting qualities of their enemies in the hand-to-hand battle, the one-on-one encounters in which they often engage.[185]

---

[177] Horn 2004, 9.
[178] Horn 2004, 21–22; Toffler and Toffler 1994, 108. For a history of American SOF, see Adams 1998.
[179] Record 2000, 4–11; Hyde, 2000, 17–27.   [180] Finlan 2008; Keegan 1978, 71.
[181] Michael Smith 2006.   [182] McRaven 2004, 66.
[183] Adams 1998, 25; Coker 2002b, 80–83; McRaven 2004, 61–78.
[184] McRaven 2004, 67.   [185] Coker 2002b, 82.

In contrast to the average US soldier, 'niche warriors' still conceive war as the intrinsic part of a humanistic discourse that aims at the existential idea of becoming. For them, war has remained a source of individual transformation.

Yet, their humanism places them at odds not only with the rest of the American military that has come to view soldiering as a profession rather than a vocation, but also with a society that finds the loss of life increasingly difficult to justify and in which humanistic ideas of sacrifice have waned.[186] The exceptional humanism of 'niche warriors' generates tensions with a predominantly casualty-averse military and with the wider 'post-heroic' American public. Yet, considering the centrality of SOFs in post–Cold War conflicts, these tensions raise important questions regarding the acceptable risks 'niche warriors' are permitted to take in contemporary American warfare: Does the prevailing political quest for minimum casualties override the warriorhood of US SOFs? In other words, do political and military concerns for zero tolerance prevent them from fighting in a less casualty-averse manner – are they policed by 'post-heroic' standards external to their humanism? Or, are 'niche warriors' permitted to expose themselves to larger risks than the rest of American military personnel?

Conclusion

The chapter analysed the evolution of casualty-aversion as one of the key characteristics in contemporary US warfare. This process was illustrated by examining the transformation of humanism as the force that traditionally allowed warriors to experience war as an act of self-realisation and to accept sacrifice. Here, the chapter showed how in the course of the twentieth century, the US developed from a society that accepted large numbers of casualties in modern wars to a postmodern risk society that has become increasingly reluctant to sustain any military casualties in war. The big turning point that brought about a fundamental reduction in humanism and at the same time witnessed the advent of the body bag syndrome was the Vietnam War.

The lessons drawn from the political defeat in the jungles of Indochina ushered in a period of groundbreaking reforms that had the aggregate effect of institutionalising casualty-aversion as a means to re-legitimate warfare with the American people. For the US public was conceived by political and military decision makers as intolerant to future body bags and yet crucial to support in any future conflict.

[186] Shaw 2005, 79; Luttwak 1996, 33–45.

Despite the centrality of casualty-aversion to contemporary US warfare, the chapter also showed that pockets of humanism have survived in American SOFs. In contrast to the general intolerance towards exposing the US military to the risks of combat, these 'niche warriors' continue to view war (and the acceptance of the risk of dying) as a source of individual transformation. Considering the centrality of elite forces in the US interventions in conflicts such as Somalia, Afghanistan, and Iraq, the chapter raised questions regarding the tensions between their humanism and the general casualty-aversion among US forces that will guide investigations in the empirical chapters.

In the wider context of the book, the rise of the body bag syndrome to become a key characteristic of American warfare has created fundamental tensions with the other defining feature of US military practice, respect for the norm of non-combatant immunity. By employing Michael Walzer's idea of 'due care' as a moral framework, the subsequent chapters investigate how far it has been possible for the United States to wage wars since the 1990s that satisfied its values of casualty-aversion and civilian protection. Or, has the decline in humanism and the simultaneous rise of casualty-aversion led to a type of warfare that is only riskless to US soldiers at the expense of the safeguarding of civilians? In other words, does the US, in making war more riskless for itself, make it less humane for non-combatants?

Yet, before investigating the legal-moral nexus pertaining to this tension between US casualty-aversion and civilian protection in the specific cases of Somalia, Afghanistan, and Iraq, an additional dimension needs to be introduced in the next chapter: the crucial fact that war is never waged on a lifeless object, but on an adversary who acts and responds. This means that war by its very nature is interactive and that it generates a particular dynamic precisely because 'the enemy has a vote, too'.

In Vietnam and Lebanon, the Americans experienced the interactive nature of war and subsequently embarked on a series of fundamental military reforms that were principally designed to overcome the interactive dynamic of warfare on their own terms. The introduction of electronic systems and information technology through the RMA as well as net-centric warfare aimed at distancing US forces from the enemy (thereby ensuring the highest levels of protection for US military personnel) while using precision-guided information technology to kill with overwhelming yet highly discriminate firepower (thereby guaranteeing the safeguarding of civilians in target states).

Coming to the fore for the first time during the 1991 Gulf War, this postmodern American warfare was celebrated not only as effectively overcoming the Vietnam syndrome but also as transcending the factors of 'friction', chance, unpredictability, and the fog of war. It was viewed (by some) within the US military as proving Baron Antoine Henri de Jomini right and Clausewitz wrong.[187] In contrast to the latter, Jomini believed that the scientific component of war could be elevated to the point of rendering the artistic components of war irrelevant.[188] The Gulf War seemed to constitute a major step towards the realisation of that vision.[189]

Yet, such triumphant perspectives were obscured by the important fact that the war against Iraq proved to be atypical for the type of interventions to come.[190] Critics have argued that Saddam Hussein proved to be a strategically incompetent commander-in-chief and that Iraqi forces, lacking any air cover and unable to hide in the desert, were sitting ducks for US aircraft.[191] Moreover, in the course of the next decades the US military found itself using military force against semi-/non-state actors in wars under conditions of asymmetry rather than fighting symmetric interstate conflicts. The RMA and net-centric warfare, however, were strategically designed for open plain defence against an attack by the Warsaw Pact, and therefore seen as a means to engage a conventional enemy rather than an unconventional one. Saddam's Iraq, in that sense, turned out to be an exceptional match.[192]

Wars under conditions of asymmetry, however, generate fundamentally different interactive dynamics between conflicting parties. Any examination of the tension-ridden relationship between US casualty-aversion and civilian protection therefore cannot ignore the particular dynamics generated by such wars. Not to take these particular dynamics into account distorts the analysis of whether it has been possible for the United States to wage war in ways that produced low American casualty rates while at the same time ensuring high levels of civilian protection. For this reason, the next chapter investigates the nature of asymmetric warfare with a particular focus on the often neglected role of the adversary.

---

[187] Ignatieff 2000b.   [188] Watts 1996.   [189] Bill Owens 2000.   [190] Adams 1998, 1.
[191] Mueller 1995.   [192] Mueller 1995, 77.

3   The Interactive Dynamics of Asymmetric Conflicts

> A picture of war as a whole can be formed by imagining a pair of wrestlers.
>
> Carl von Clausewitz

> I never thought it would go on like this. I didn't think these people had the capacity to fight this way ... to take this punishment.
>
> Robert S. McNamara

> The struggle must build, however, slowly. The way to win is by small defeats, one after another until the coup de grace.
>
> Vo Nguyen Giap

Introduction

This book investigates how asymmetric enemy behaviour (the interactive dynamics of war) affects the inherent tension between the American values of casualty-aversion and civilian protection to such an extent that it leads to a trade-off between saving US soldiers and enemy civilians. In order to fathom this phenomenon, the chapter seeks to generate understanding and demonstrate the importance of the specific interactive dynamics underpinning asymmetric conflicts. The argument put forward is that any systematic investigation of the tension-ridden relationship between US casualty-aversion and civilian protection cannot ignore the particular dynamics generated by conditions of asymmetry.

The chapter is structured in the following way. Drawing on Clausewitz's metaphors of 'War as a Wrestling Match' and 'War as a True Chameleon', it analyses his understanding of the interactive, non-linear, and transformative nature of war.

It then examines how Thomas Edward Lawrence's and Mao Zedong's creativity as theorists of guerrilla warfare lay in their successful application of Clausewitz's writings to conditions of asymmetry. Their deep understanding of Clausewitz's insights on War as a Wrestling Match and the relationship between offence and defence allowed them to raise guerrilla warfare from a concomitant strategy employed in large-scale war to the level of a political-military strategy in its own right. Their conceptual contribution demonstrates the validity of the Ringkampf (wrestling match) as a metaphor for understanding the interactive dynamics of warfare under conditions of asymmetry.

The final part of the chapter applies these insights to the Vietnam War. It thereby concentrates on the interactive nature of the Ringkampf under the condition of asymmetry between the Clausewitz-driven, conventional US military giant and its Mao-inspired, guerrilla-fighting/unconventional Vietnamese adversary. By analysing the dynamic interaction between the American and Vietnamese strategy that aimed at imposing their respective wills on their adversary, it is shown how a militarily disadvantaged Vietnamese side employed asymmetric strategies that won the war politically.

'War as a Ringkampf'

Clausewitz understood war as inherently non-linear in nature. Non-linearity implies that war tends to change its characteristics in ways that cannot be analytically predicted. Such notions can be found in Clausewitz's writing on chance, uncertainty, 'friction', and the fog of war. Writing in an age grounded in scientific positivism, his understanding of war as inherently non-linear in nature was revolutionary.[1] In contrast to Baron Antoine Henri de Jomini and Dietrich von Bülow, who both believed that elements of uncertainty and chance in war could be eliminated and that war could be made predictable,[2] Clausewitz asserted right at the beginning of *On War* that war was continuously and universally bound up with the element of chance.

Absolute, so-called mathematical factors never form a basis in military calculations. From the very start there is an interplay of possibilities, probabilities, good luck and bad.[3]

Non-linear elements, probability, and chance are never absent and therefore turn war into a gamble.[4]

No other human activity is so continuously and universally bound up with chance. And through the element of chance, guesswork and luck come to play a great part in war ... Therefore only the element of chance is needed to make war a gamble and that element is never absent.[5]

---

[1] Handel 2001, 43.   [2] Colin S Gray 1999, 95; Paret 1986, 190–191.
[3] Clausewitz 1984, 85, 86.   [4] Clausewitz 1984, 85.   [5] Clausewitz 1984, 85.

Clausewitz's non-linear conception of war, which stood in contrast to the positivist and linear zeitgeist of his time,[6] was an essential tool allowing him to write the most comprehensive philosophy of war to date.

Linearity is the result of proportionality (the idea that changes to the system output are proportional to the changes in system input) and additivity (the whole is equal to the sum of its parts). Non-linearity, on the other hand, disobeys proportionality and additivity. It exhibits erratic behaviour through disproportionately large or small outputs; or it involves synergetic interactions which on the whole are not equal to the sum of its parts.[7] As a consequence, the system's variables cannot be effectively isolated from one another and from their contexts. This means that linearisation is not possible because of the dynamic interaction at the centre of the system.

Clausewitz's definition of war is marked by non-linearity: 'War is nothing but a duel [Zweikampf] on a larger scale ... an act of force to compel our enemy to do our will.'[8] As each opponent is equally trying to impose his will on his enemy, war is marked by dynamic interaction. This aspect of interaction is crucial to Clausewitz because war

is not the action of a living force upon a lifeless mass (total non-resistance would be no war at all) but always the collision of two living forces.[9]

War thus is not an exercise of will directed against an inanimate matter but of will directed at an animate object which responds by actions of its own.[10] Fundamentally, war therefore becomes a duel between two independent minds:

War is not an exercise of the will directed at inanimate matter, as is the case with the mechanical arts, or at matter which is animate but passive and yielding, as is the case with the human mind and emotions in the fine arts. In war, the will is directed at an animate object that reacts.[11]

The interplay between action and reaction of animate objects allows Clausewitz to locate 'interaction' at the heart of the nature of war. This interaction provides war with a distinctive, inalienable dynamic and grammar.[12]

Introducing Hegelian dialectical thinking to the nature of war was one of Clausewitz's great contributions.[13] This methodological step allowed

---

[6] Beyerchen 1992, 59–90. For the impact of Hegel on Clausewitz, see Paret 1976, 147–208.
[7] Beyerchen 1992, 62; Beyerchen 1997.   [8] Clausewitz 1984, 75.
[9] Clausewitz 1984, 77.   [10] Van Creveld 2000, 116.   [11] Clausewitz 1984, 149.
[12] Colin S Gray 1999, 92–93.
[13] Paret 1986, 194. See also Schering 1939, 89–93; Heuser 2002, 6–8; Paret 1976, 147–208.

him to see the enemy not as an inanimate object, but as someone who will try to complicate and upset one's plans by doing the unexpected, by exploiting one's weaknesses, and by luring the enemy into a trap.[14]

> The ultimate aim of war [to impose one's will on the enemy by rendering him incapable of resistance, i.e. destroying his will to resist] ... must be taken as applying to both sides. Once again, there is interaction. So long as I have not overthrown my opponent I am bound to fear he may overthrow me. Thus I am not in control: he dictates to me as much as I dictate to him.[15]

Throughout Book One of *On War*, Clausewitz's reflections clearly indicate that he conceived of war as a form of social intercourse where two animate forces not only react but also take independent actions of their own.

Most importantly, however, he understood that the interactive nature of war produces a chaotic system which – at least theoretically – can lead to limitless extremes of mutual exertion and limitless efforts to defeat the opponent.[16] The course of the war therefore does not become the sequence of intentions and actions of each opponent separately. Instead, the shape and course of a particular war is generated by mutually hostile intentions and simultaneously consequential actions. The contest is neither the sum of adversaries' actions added together – something that the linear factor of additivity would imply; nor is the dynamic outcome of the interaction proportional to the input – something that the factor of proportionality would imply. Rather, it is the dynamic set of patterns made in the space between and around the adversaries.

The implications of this observation might not be immediately evident if we continue utilising the metaphor of the traditional duel with swords or pistols. But it becomes more obvious if we think of a wrestling match, which is how Clausewitz himself suggested we should imagine the struggle between two opponents in war:

> War is nothing but a duel on a larger scale. Countless duels go to make up war, but a picture of it as a whole can be formed by imagining a pair of wrestlers [Ringer].[17]

War is a wrestling match (Ringkampf), a match between two wrestlers, each of whom tries to compel his adversary to do his will.

The importance of this metaphor is not merely due to its capacity to generate a better understanding of the dynamic nature of war (as this chapter will show), but also due to its centrality in the philosophical understanding of American elite forces.[18] Regarding *On War* as 'the

---

[14] Van Creveld 2000, 123–124.   [15] Clausewitz 1984, 77.   [16] Brodie 1984, 652.
[17] Clausewitz 1984, 75.
[18] US Marine Corps 1997, 3–19; see also Michael Smith 2006; Haney 2003.

definitive treatment of the nature and theory of war',[19] the US Marine Corps' warfighting doctrine, for example, defines war as a struggle between 'a pair of wrestlers locked in a hold, each exerting force and counterforce to try to throw the other'.[20] In other words, Clausewitz's appreciation of the dynamic interplay between opposing human wills is essential to the philosophical understanding of the nature of war by contemporary American Special Operations Forces (SOF).

Despite the recognition of the role of the opponent's will in the interactive dynamic of the Ringkampf, however, *On War* says more about how 'to impose our will on the enemy' than about the enemy's attempt to impose his will in return. As a result, Colin S. Gray argues that *On War* does not offer the careful analysis of the Ringkampf among calculating enemies that accorded with its importance in Clausewitz's thinking.[21] Building on this criticism, this chapter tries to demonstrate the usefulness of Clausewitz's metaphor by giving a balanced account of both 'wrestlers'. Clausewitz's metaphor generates a deeper understanding of how the dynamic interaction between both wrestlers leads to bodily positions and contortions that are often impossible to achieve without the counterweight and the counterforce of the opposing wrestler. Their interaction generates unique formations, positions, and shapes that neither wrestler could possibly create alone. The US Marine Corps' warfighting doctrine echoes Clausewitz's emphasis on the dynamic interaction by arguing that

[w]ar is thus a process of continuous mutual adaptation, of give and take, move and countermove. It is critical to keep in mind that the enemy is not an inanimate object to be acted upon but an independent and animate force with its own objectives and plans. While we try to impose our will on the enemy, he resists us and seeks to impose his own will on us. Appreciating this dynamic interplay between opposing human wills is essential to understanding the fundamental nature of war.[22]

Thus, the character of a particular wrestling match does not result from the sum of both wrestlers' strengths and weaknesses, but from the dynamic interaction as such. As a result, we can assess the individual characteristics of each wrestler, but we cannot use these assessments to predict what the actual wrestling match will look like. The reason for this lies in the interaction itself. The dynamic interaction affects the character of the wrestling match, and the altered character of the wrestling match feeds back into the way each wrestler engages his opponent. The implication of this insight for the book is that the important role played by US adversaries cannot be ignored. Not to take these particular

---

[19] US Marine Corps 1997, 97.   [20] US Marine Corps 1997, 3.
[21] Colin S. Gray 1999, 103–104.   [22] US Marine Corps 1997, 3–4.

dynamics into account distorts the analysis of whether it has been possible for the United States to wage war in ways that produced low American casualty rates while at the same time ensuring high levels of civilian protection.

This dynamic interaction renders wars inherently non-linear in nature.[23] The significance of the metaphor of the Ringkampf is that it precludes any predictions about a war's outcome. Clausewitz was aware of the discomfort his findings would cause, but he could not hide his fascination with non-linearity and unpredictability: 'Although our intellect always longs for clarity and certainty, our nature often finds uncertainty fascinating.'[24] The importance he attributed to the unpredictability of the wrestling match manifests itself in his writings on chance and 'friction'. Though a general emphasis on chance has not been unusual among strategic theorists, it was nevertheless given exceptional attention in Clausewitz's work. This allowed him, more than any of his predecessors, to conceive of war as 'the realm of uncertainty'.[25] Wrapped in a fog of uncertainty, the nature of the dynamic interaction at the heart of war can best be understood through his metaphor of War as a Wrestling Match.

War under the Condition of Symmetry

Clausewitz drew the metaphor of the Ringkampf as 'a duel on a larger scale'.[26] As he hardly studied wars in the historical periods that preceded the Treaty of Westphalia in 1648, he intuitively took it for granted that organised violence could only be called war if it were waged between states.[27] In accordance with the conventional understanding of his time, he therefore defined war as

merely the continuation of policy by other means ... War is not merely an act of policy but a true political instrument, a continuation of political intercourse, carried on with other means.[28]

War was an act of resolving political issues that could not be settled by means falling short of the use of force. By claiming war to be the instrument of policy, he deliberately subordinated it under the sphere of states and the relations between states. As a result, the 'political culture

---

[23] Handel 2001, 25–32.   [24] Clausewitz 1984, 86.   [25] Clausewitz 1984, 101.
[26] Clausewitz 1984, 75.
[27] Kinross 2004, 36; Van Creveld 1991b, 35–36. This is not to deny that wars were waged between states prior to 1648, but this period was not of a particular concern for Clausewitz's nineteenth century state-centric mindset.
[28] Clausewitz 1984, 87.

assumed in *On War* is state-centric.'[29] According to Christopher Daase, it is paradoxical that this state-centric concept of war was given its most valid formula at a time when the democratic *levée en masse* (mass uprising) and the people's war seemed to have begun replacing classical interstate warfare.[30] By analysing the political upheavals of the Napoleonic Wars, however, Clausewitz succeeded in developing a definition of war that left his holy trinity unaffected.[31]

By defining war as the continuation of policy by other means, he not only confined the metaphor of the Ringkampf to interstate warfare, but also to conditions of symmetry (war between two relatively equal adversaries).[32] His conception of the wrestling match was driven by the assumption that states met numerous conditions in order to bring about and ensure symmetry between them. In interstate warfare, both wrestlers acknowledged that they were 'on par with one another'.[33] According to Herfried Muenkler,

[t]his acknowledgement may come about by the adversaries' mutual inclusion in a system of values thus considered binding on them both (chivalry) or by their common subjection to legal rules (international law, laws of war), depends on the assumption of equality which needs to be largely satisfied: broadly similar weaponry, no strategic disparities in information, and a socially analogous form of recruitment and training of combatants.[34]

The ritualised and enshrined symmetry of conventional war allowed for the type of wrestling match where both wrestlers could accept the rules because they were equals. This underlying assumption of equality between states as the principal actors in war (as developed in *On War*) limits Clausewitz's metaphor of War as a Wrestling Match to war under the condition of symmetry.[35]

Limiting his definition of war to the symmetric realm of interstate conflicts had become the major source of criticism by the end of the Cold War.[36] Over 150 years after *On War* was published, the image of war, with

---

[29] Colin S Gray 1999, 102 (italics in original). See also Fairbairn 1974, 42.

[30] Daase 2001, 23.

[31] Van Creveld 1991b, 40. Clausewitz developed the concept of 'holy trinity' (wundersame Dreifaltigkeit) as his political framework for the study of war. It consists of the people, the commander and his army, and the government to which he attributed the elements of primordial violence, the mobilisation and commitment of the people respectively. He believed that any theory of war and any victory in war can be secured only if the proper equilibrium is achieved among these three dimensions. For further detail, see Handel 2001, 63–71.

[32] Fairbairn 1974, 42.   [33] Münkler 2003, 19.   [34] Münkler 2003, 19.

[35] Conditions of asymmetry can of course also exist between powerful and weak states. This distinction, however, did not feature in *On War*. Conflict between states was assumed to take place under conditions of symmetry.

[36] Keegan 1993; Van Creveld 1991b; Kaldor 1999.

which Clausewitz has been closely and rightly associated, has transformed fundamentally. Armed conflict has not remained within the traditional Clausewitzean parameters of warfare between states. Instead, wars between states and semi-/non-state actors or even conflicts excluding state actors altogether have evolved into the dominant form of military conflict.[37] This shift does not mean that wars between states have become a phenomenon of the past, but rather that they have become less likely statistically.

Increasingly what is replacing symmetric interstate conflicts are asymmetric wars (wars between two distinctly unequal adversaries) that are predominantly fought by guerrilla strategies that undermine the established rules and conventions of interstate warfare.[38] The terminology used to describe these asymmetric wars – 'new wars', 'intrastate conflicts', 'premodern wars', 'postmodern wars', 'civil wars', 'guerrilla conflicts'[39] – and the character attributed to them – 'dirty', 'savage', 'irregular', 'uncivil', 'amorphous' – imply the evolution of a phenomenon outside the norms and beyond the established state order.[40]

With the contemporary decline of interstate warfare and the simultaneous rise in wars between states and semi-/non-state actors, critics have argued that *On War* has been overtaken by the changing character of war.[41] Among the most prominent critics is Martin van Creveld, who claims that with the rise of 'Low-Intensity Conflict' (LIC), the 'Clausewitzean universe is quickly coming out of date and cannot provide us with the proper framework for understanding war'.[42] Clausewitz, he charges, did not understand that Trinitarian War only represented one of the many forms and shapes war has assumed.[43] In other words, for van Creveld and others, who discern a decline in the authority of the state, Clausewitz, as the pre-eminent philosophical thinker on Trinitarian war, has lost his validity.[44] Based on this rationale, the age of post-Trinitarian warfare signals the advent of the post-Clausewitzean universe.

Such claims are problematic for two reasons. First, these critics tended to ignore Clausewitz's earlier writing that was nearly exclusively dedicated to asymmetric wars, or what he called 'Kleine Kriege' (small wars), or guerrilla wars. The expertise found in his untranslated work in 'Meine Vorlesungen ueber den Kleinen Krieg' (1810/11) and

---

[37] Van Creveld 1991b; Kaldor 1999; Münkler 2004; Daase 2003, 17–35.
[38] Johnson 1999; Kaldor 1999.
[39] Kaldor 1999; Enzensberger 1993; Duffield 2001; John Keane 1996.
[40] Daase 2001, 25.
[41] Kaldor 1999; Keegan 1993; Mathews 1997, 50; Enzensberger 1993; Kinross 2004, 35–36; Kaplan 2000.
[42] Van Creveld 1991b, 57.   [43] Van Creveld 1991b, 57.
[44] Van Creveld 1991b; Enzensberger 1993; Kaldor 1999.

'Bekenntnisdenkschrift' (1812)[45] has mostly been ignored in the English and – to a lesser extent – German literature. It has hardly featured in the debates on the relevancy of the metaphor of War as a Wrestling Match under conditions of asymmetry, leading Christopher Daase to suspect that had they been known to post-Clausewitzeans, their judgements would have turned out more modest.[46] Ironically, had Clausewitz's widow not published *On War* posthumously (and against her husband's wishes) in 1832, he would have been known today – if at all – not as an expert on Trinitarian wars but as an expert on small wars.[47] His writings on small wars represent the first attempt at theorising the nature of conflicts between state and non-state actors.[48]

Second, even if these insights were ignored, such claims remain problematic: simply because war might no longer take place between states, it does not logically follow that Clausewitz's writing has become irrelevant in an age of wars between states and semi-/non-state actors. Instead, his metaphorical insights might still be relevant in a post-Trinitarian age. Neo-Clausewitzeans[49] such as Colin S. Gray for example have long argued that despite the state-centric focus of his work, Clausewitz's *On War* 'lends itself to application to any [premodern, modern, postmodern] period'.[50] Precisely such an application was eventually taken a century later by Thomas E Lawrence, Mao Zedong, and Vo Nguyen Giap.[51]

Connecting Clausewitz and Asymmetry

Through Lawrence's, Mao's, and Giap's respective military operations and theorising, the idea of guerrilla warfare as something more than just an auxiliary to state warfare started taking shape and acquired momentum.[52] In short, they succeeded in connecting Clausewitz's

---

[45] Clausewitz 1966b, 205–588; Clausewitz 1966a, 644–690.   [46] Daase 2001, 26.

[47] For more insights, see Daase 2001; Kaempf 2011, 548–573.

[48] It is important to note that Clausewitz regarded small wars as an adjunct to conventional war and not as an independent form of war in its own right. See Clausewitz 1966a, 704; Handel 2001, 124–125; Laqueur 1977, 101.

[49] Even though the term neo-Clausewitzean was originally coined by Anatol Rapoport in the introduction to his translation of *On War* (1968, 64–69), its usage in the thesis refers to thinkers such as Colin Gray, Stephen Biddle, Michael Handel, John Ferris or Martin Alexander, who – contrary to Martin Van Creveld, John Keegan, and Mary Kaldor – have not seen a problem in applying Clausewitzean analysis to sub-state, post-Trinitarian wars. Others, who do not see themselves as neo-Clausewitzeans, have argued that Clausewitz's relevance, especially his Trinity, can be conceived of even without the state. See Paret 1986, 202; Münkler 2004.

[50] Colin S Gray 1999, 102.   [51] Laqueur 1977, 100.   [52] Shy and Collier 1986, 838.

metaphors of War as a Wrestling Match and War as a True Chameleon with his insights on small wars, thereby widening the scale and scope to which the chameleonesque nature of war can be applied. Their collected writings on the Arab revolt of 1916–18 and on 'Protracted War' became the first comprehensive modern theory of guerrilla warfare as an independent type of warfare. Most importantly, in the case of the Vietnam War, General Giap demonstrated how close adherence to Mao's thought provided a successful strategy to defeat the United States.[53]

Lawrence's study of guerrilla or irregular warfare was based on the concrete experience of the Arab revolt against the Ottoman Empire.[54] His theoretical starting point was an analysis of Napoleon's, Clausewitz's, and Foch's understanding of war. Lawrence later confessed that Clausewitz, whom he read while studying at Oxford, 'had subconsciously inspired him in his own thinking'[55] – sometimes to such an extent that Lawrence seemed to have directly applied Clausewitz's ideas from his chapter 'The People in Arms'.[56] Applying this background in military history to the specific conditions that the Arab forces faced in Saudi Arabia helped him understand how the zeitgeist of modern warfare required that military victory could only be achieved by the physical destruction of enemy forces. The Turkish military – like most European armies at the time – was obsessed with the dictum that the ethic of modern war was to seek the enemy's forces, its centre of gravity, and destroy it in battle.[57] According to this conventional strategic wisdom, irregulars were incapable of forcing a decision in warfare as they could neither destroy the enemy's forces nor defend a line or point when attacked.

Yet, Lawrence devised a strategy that allowed the Arabs to prevail. Recognising the military inferiority of the Arab forces of Sherif Hussein and carefully analysing the strengths and weaknesses of the enemy, he realised that any successful guerrilla strategy had to break with Napoleon's doctrine of maximum concentration. Due to the prevailing technological, organisational, and numerical conditions of asymmetry, any major battle with the enemy was seen as a strategic mistake because the virtue of the irregular lay neither in force nor concentration.[58] According to Lawrence, any major military clash was 'an imposition on the weaker side that had to be avoided at all costs'.[59] Consequently, he creatively devised a strategy that deliberately deprived the enemy of

---

[53] Giap 1977, 23–55; MacDonald 1993, 78–90; Arreguin-Toft 2005, 37; Shy and Collier, 1986, 847–848.

[54] T. E. Lawrence 1994, 880–891.   [55] Heuser 2002, 138.

[56] For parallels between Clausewitz and Lawrence works, see Clausewitz 1984, 479–487; Weintraub and Weintraub 1967, 100–119; T. E. Lawrence 1962.

[57] Moran 2002, 31–33.   [58] Fairbairn 1974, 43–44.   [59] T. E. Lawrence 1994, 887.

contact with the Arab forces. The guerrillas refused to follow the conventional principle of the concentration of forces in space and time. Instead, they dispersed their forces geographically and extended the duration of the conflict. In other words, Lawrence refrained from fighting a conventional war and waged a small war instead. The basic strategy was not to confront the adversary where he could bring his military advantage to bear, but instead confront him in areas where his weakness and vulnerability had been identified. According to Lawrence,

The Turkish army was an accident, not a target. Our true strategic aim was to seek its weakest link, and bear only on that till time made the mass of it fall.[60]

This shows how much Lawrence's thinking was shaped by an acute recognition of conditions of asymmetry. His strategy of 'detachment', operating from secure bases in the desert and using hit-and-run tactics not only denied the enemy the opportunity to physically destroy the Arab forces but also forced him to stretch out.[61] In the process of dispersing (becoming less concentrated), the Ottoman forces became increasingly more vulnerable. Granted mobility, time, and space, irregular action thus started turning the qualities of organisation and discipline of regular armies into liabilities.[62] This forced the Ottoman army onto the defensive and allowed the Arab forces to regain the initiative.

Using the metaphor of guerrillas as operating like 'a cloud of gas' as the key to victory, Lawrence drew on Clausewitz's belief that guerrilla war should take the shape of a nebulous essence that never condensed into a concrete body:[63]

Suppose [the Arabs] were an influence, a thing invulnerable, intangible, without front or back, drifting about like gas? Armies are like plants, immobile as a whole, firm-rooted, and nourished through long stems to the head.[64]

By remaining largely invisible, by hiding in remote and inaccessible places and by relying on dispersion and mobility to escape after hitting the enemy, Lawrence showed how guerrilla warfare could bring its strengths to bear against the adversary's weaknesses. Channelling Clausewitz, Lawrence wrote that:

[i]n general, guerrillas ought to avoid head-on clashes with the enemy's main body. Instead they were to operate against his flanks, his foraging parties, the garrisons ... all the while relying on speed and surprise to concentrate their own forces, do their worst and disappear again ... Logistically speaking they were to be sustained partly from the countryside and partly by taking arms and equipment

---

[60] T. E. Lawrence 1994, 886.   [61] Townshend 1997, 161.
[62] See also Van Creveld 2011, 48–54.   [63] Clausewitz 1984, 481.
[64] T. E. Lawrence 1994, 883.

away from the enemy, thus making it unnecessary to have permanent, and vulnerable, bases.[65]

But the key to his success was ascribed to forging a national conscious-ness, a true people's war, through propaganda ('the printing press is the greatest weapon in the armoury of the modern commander')[66] – an indication of the centrality of the war taking place in the hearts and minds of the people. The centrality of propaganda was important in a conflict that was not so much physical as moral.

It is important to emphasise that the Arab revolt against the Ottoman Empire was not decisive in the context of the overall war (even though it tied down large numbers of Ottoman regular forces), as these decisive battles took place in Europe and not in the Middle East. Lawrence's conceptual work nevertheless succeeded in connecting the elements of the wrestling match with conditions of asymmetry that had remained disconnected in Clausewitz's writings.

Lawrence was primarily concerned with the tactical and operational aspects of guerrilla warfare. Subsequent authors had little to add to these two fields. But what the other important writer on modern guerrilla war-fare, Mao Zedong, did was to establish a theory of the relationship between the guerrillas and the people, as well as the 'three-step theory' about the way in which the campaign ought to proceed.[67] Writing before the back-ground of the Japanese invasion and the Chinese civil war and drawing on his experiences in both, Mao built a new doctrine that elevated peasant-based guerrilla warfare to an independent form of warfare.[68]

According to Samuel B. Griffith and Beatrice Heuser, Mao was not only familiar with Lawrence's work but also an ardent student of Clausewitz and highly influenced by the latter's conceptual connection between war and politics.[69] In resemblance to Clausewitz's famous pas-sage in *On War*, Mao wrote in 'On Protracted War' that war was action with a political character: 'politics is war without bloodshed, war is politics with bloodshed.'[70] Thus, his work bore resemblance to Clausewitz in conceiving of politics and war as inseparable.

Yet Mao developed Clausewitz's idea significantly further by stressing the primacy of political over military concerns. This hallmark of his

---

[65] Cited in Van Creveld 2000, 201.   [66] Lawrence cited in Laqueur 1977, 170.
[67] Griffith 1992; Townshend 1997, 164–166; Van Creveld 2000, 204.
[68] Münkler 2006, 58–63; Shy and Collier 1986, 839.
[69] Griffith 1992, 136–137; Heuser 2002, 31, 138–139. Interestingly, Michael I. Handel points out that 'although Mao was strongly influenced by Sun Tzu, the main elements of [the former's] theory on guerrilla warfare can be found in the first pages of Clausewitz's chapter "The People in Arms"' (Handel 2001, 124–125).
[70] Cited in Griffith 1992, 55.

writing was born out of recognition that the prevailing military asymmetries of his time compelled him to 'adjust guerrilla strategy to the enemy situation'.[71] Guerrillas, weaker than both the Japanese army and the forces of the Guomindang, could not be effective or even survive without strong and well-organised popular support. Successful mobilisation of such support turned the civilian population into the sea in which the guerrilla could swim:

With the common people of the whole country mobilized, we shall create a vast sea of humanity in which the enemy will be swallowed up . . . The popular masses are like water, and the army is like a fish. How then can it be said that when there is water, a fish will have difficulty in preserving its existence?[72]

The civilian population would provide shelter, food, and intelligence while the very same political mobilisation process would ensure that the authority and limited legitimacy of the adversary would steadily be undermined.[73]

Mobilising that level of popular support, however, was a political rather than a military task. Mao therefore subordinated the military to the political struggle. This emphasis on popular support became an asymmetric means to overcome military inferiority politically.[74] Without the means to win a quick military victory, a 'protracted struggle' at least promised to exhaust the enemy politically.[75] In that respect, he diverged markedly from conventional military thought with its distinctions between war and peace, and between political and military factors.

Mao – not dissimilar to Lawrence – also diverged in other important respects, especially regarding the values attributed to the factors of space and time.[76] Mao recognised that any conventional battle against superior forces would be suicidal: 'Defeat is the invariable outcome where native forces fight with inferior weapons against modernised forces on the latter's terms.'[77] After all, this had long been the fate of indigenous forces in combat against colonial troops. Referring to Clausewitz in his reflections on 'luring the enemy into the interior of the country', Mao acknowledged that

---

[71] Mao Zedong 1992, 73, 121; Van Creveld 2011, 48–54.

[72] Cited in Schram 1969, 289.

[73] This is a good example of how – not only in the case of Mao, but more broadly among any partisans and resistance fighters – the civilian population has served a strategic purpose for militarily disadvantaged non-state actors. Good examples of this kind of exploitation of the civilian population (and relatedly, the norm of civilian protection) include the Spanish resistance against Napoleon, Yugoslav and Soviet partisans against the Wehrmacht, and anti-colonial resistance fighters in Algeria and Vietnam.

[74] Münkler 2006, 58–63; Shy and Collier 1986, 839.   [75] Griffith 1992, 55.

[76] For further details on the similarity of Lawrence's and Mao's understanding of the factor of space, see Fairbairn 1974, 43–44.

[77] Cited in Arreguin-Toft 2005, 34.

A foreign military expert once said that in the strategic defensive one should in general initially avoid decisive battles if they would occur under unfavourable circumstances, and seek them only when favourable circumstance have been established. This is entirely correct and we have nothing to add to it.[78]

For success to be achieved by the disadvantaged side, it was necessary not only to subordinate the military to the political struggle, but also to exploit the advantages of space and time.[79]

Mao realised that such a strategy would never be a rapid process, which is why he believed that a deceleration of war provided an opportunity for successful armed resistance against a superior enemy. He sought to exploit his own geographical and demographical advantages. He turned the strength of the invading colonial powers, such as velocity, time, and space into a disadvantage by slowing down and turning the struggle into a protracted conflict. According to Herfried Münkler,

Mao's creativity lay in his refusal to join in the race for greater acceleration of hostilities [the basic logic of Trinitarian war], as his peasant army would not have been able to win a war of that kind. Instead, he rejected the principle of acceleration and, turning weakness into strength, made slowness his watchword, defining guerrilla warfare as the 'long war of endurance'.[80]

Such a protracted struggle exhausted the enemy politically, thereby providing the disadvantaged side an asymmetric means to overcome its adversary's military superiority. Similarly, trying to hold territory would be suicidal for guerrilla forces. But by operating in vast and inaccessible terrain, they could entice, mislead, and wear their conventional enemies down and thereby create chances for small, yet on aggregate, very effective surprise attacks.

By slowing down and de-territorializing a conflict, guerrilla warfare – similar to symmetric warfare – tries to break the will of the opponent. Yet, the latter's will is broken by avoiding his military strength and bringing one's own strengths (popular mobilisation, time, and space) to bear on the adversary's centre of gravity. 'In guerrilla warfare', Mao wrote,

[s]elect the tactic of seeming to come from the East and attacking from the West; avoid the solid, attack the hollow; attack; withdraw; deliver a lighting blow, seek a lighting decision. When guerrillas engage a stronger enemy, they withdraw when he advances; harass him when he stops; strike him when he is weary; pursue him when he withdraws. In guerrilla strategy, the enemy's rear, flanks, and other vulnerable spots are his vital points, and there he must be harassed, attacked, dispersed, exhausted, and annihilated.[81]

---

[78] Quoted in Heuser 2002, 139.   [79] Van Creveld 2011, 48–54.   [80] Münkler 2003, 9.
[81] Griffith 1992, 46.

Because of the logic of asymmetric warfare, the guerrillas do not have to win militarily; instead they only need to obtain and sustain themselves as an inextinguishable threat in order to be successful. 'If guerrillas do not lose the conflict militarily', Raymond Aron wrote,

they win it politically; whereas if their opponents fail to achieve a decisive military victory, they lose the war politically and therefore militarily.[82]

By making this logic the hallmark of his operations as well as writing, Mao discovered an innovative strategy through which guerrilla warfare could balance the asymmetry in military vulnerabilities. His creativity combined with a deep understanding of War as a Wrestling Match provided a strategy for the weak to overcome the disparity posed by conditions of asymmetry. Moreover, his understanding of the different forms War as a Chameleon could actually take allowed him to elevate guerrilla warfare from a concomitant strategy of conventional warfare to the level of a political-military strategy of its own right.

Both Lawrence and Mao thereby revealed the conceptual applicability of Clausewitz's metaphors beyond the confined realms of interstate warfare. This theoretical widening of the scale and scope to which the chameleonesque nature of the wrestling match can be applied is of tremendous significance for research focusing on US warfare. Employing the Ringkampf as a methodological tool helps to uncover how US adversaries adjust their behaviour to US military superiority by exploiting the latter's vulnerabilities. Mao's operational success and theoretical writing became a model that was consciously imitated first by the North Vietnamese and then by disadvantaged sides throughout the world more generally.[83]

The Ringkampf in Vietnam

The condition of asymmetry in the Vietnam War which pitted the United States, alongside its South Vietnamese ally, against the People's Army of Vietnam (PAVN) and the Vietminh (Vietcong) resulted in a Ringkampf between 'the most powerful nation on the face of the earth and a tenth rate backward nation like North Vietnam'.[84] Rather than being a wrestling match between two wrestlers, it was therefore a conflict between a giant and a small actor, each of whom tried to compel his adversary to do his will.[85]

---

[82] Cited in Laqueur 1977, 40.
[83] Arreguin-Toft 2005, 37; Fairbairn 1974, 174–209; Shy and Collier 1986, 847–848.
[84] Summers 1982, 18.   [85] Zinn 2003b, 213.

Given the transformative effect the Vietnam War has had on US warfare (as analysed in Chapters 1 and 2), the War provides an important case of how the condition of asymmetry led each side to pursue diametrically opposed strategies and tactics in order to break the will of their adversary. By analysing the American and Vietnamese strategies through the prism of the Ringkampf, it can be shown how the US military generally failed to adjust to the particular nature of the war, whereas the militarily disadvantaged North Vietnamese employed asymmetric strategies that won the war politically.

When the US Marines were sent to the beaches of Da Nang in March 1965, US decision-makers and the public were driven by a sense of invincibility and optimism following World War II (WWII) and – to some extent – the Korean War. Based on those successes of the immediate past, the American political and military leadership assumed that the mere application of its vast military would be sufficient to destroy the enemy's military means decisively and quickly.[86] The belief among US commanders and military analysts was that the Vietnamese would give up all hopes for victory when they recognised the vast superiority of American technology.

The expectation that this technology would eventually produce victory precluded those managing the US war in Indochina from learning about Vietnamese culture, its history, and social structure.[87] As a result, they principally failed to adjust their conventional military means to the unconventional nature of their Vietnamese adversary.[88] In other words, instead of trying to adopt an appropriate strategy for the type of war it was fighting in Vietnam, the United States tried to fight the type of war it wanted to fight.[89] This American tendency to find conventional solutions to an inherently unconventional guerrilla war had already prevailed prior to the massive military built up between 1965 and 1968.[90] Well before US President Lyndon B. Johnson ordered the amphibious landing of the Marines in 1965, US military advisors and the Central Intelligence Agency (CIA) had tried to organise the South Vietnamese armed forces as a miniature version of the American military.

General William C. Westmoreland, who commanded US military operations, the so-called Military Assistance Command, Vietnam (MACV) from 1964 to 1968, was highly experienced in conventional wars but not in the type of war fought in Vietnam. A veteran of WWII and Korea, he was not, as one observer put it, 'a "small arms manual" but

---

[86] Herring 1986, 144; Isaacs 1997, 5.   [87] Gibson 2000, 97; Record 1996, 55.
[88] Hanson 2001, 390; Griffith 1992, 5.   [89] Krepinevich 1988, 131.
[90] Boot 2002, 288.

rather an army's "field manual operations" guy',[91] a shortcoming that resulted in considerable misjudgements of the nature of the adversary and of the US strategy and tactics needed to defeat the latter. In 1964, Westmoreland and the Pentagon thought that the National Liberation Front (NLF) and the Vietcong were fighting a conventional war according to phase three of Mao Zedong's three-stage theory, whereas Hanoi at the time was fighting a guerrilla war as prescribed in phase two and only moved to stage three in 1968, 1972, and 1975.[92] The strategy the Pentagon devised accordingly reflected traditional army doctrines of warfare, which would have been the right ones against a conventional enemy, but were maladjusted to guerrillas following Mao's strategic thinking.

Moreover, the US military was reluctant to deploy its Special Operations Forces systematically and effectively. Despite the very successful operations of a test unit, they were never seen by the Joint Chiefs of Staff as more than just a tactical adjunct to big unit warfare.[93] The enthusiasm of the Kennedy Administration for the role of Special Forces in counterinsurgency operations was not shared at all by the Johnson Administration.[94] In fact, the army fiercely and successfully resisted embracing counterinsurgency operations,[95] convinced that, as Army Chief of Staff George Decker remarked, 'any good soldier can handle guerrillas.'[96] This prevailing attitude was cemented during the Honolulu conference in 1966, which ratified a division of labour between the conventional war fought by US forces and the pacification and counterinsurgency operations conducted by the allied Army of the Republic of Vietnam (ARVN).[97]

'Search and destroy', as the US strategy between 1965 and early 1968 came to be called, aimed at locating and eliminating the Vietcong and the North Vietnamese regular units. In practical terms it meant that villages suspected of harbouring Vietcong were burnt, men of military age killed, and women, children, and old people relocated to refugee camps or strategic hamlets.[98] Relying heavily on artillery and airpower to dislodge the enemy, the United States waged a furious war against Vietcong and North Vietnamese base areas.[99] In the course of the Indochina War, the US dropped seven million tons of bombs, more than twice the total bomb load dropped by all the nations in WWII combined.[100] This strategy

---

[91] Boot 2002, 294. [92] Boot 2002, 294. [93] Adams 1998, 59–60.
[94] Freedman 2002b, 287–398; Griffith 1992, 4. [95] Summers 1982, 83–92.
[96] Cited in Krepinevich 1988, 37. See also Adams 1998, 60. [97] Gibson 2000, 101.
[98] Zinn 2003b, 224; Moran 2002, 200.
[99] Van Creveld 2011, 48–54; Herring 1986, 151.
[100] Zinn 2003b, 224; Boot 2002, 301.

relied on escalation, the steady increase of US forces (the build-up reached over 550,000 in 1969), and the exploitation of its technological superiority to cope with the peculiar problems of guerrilla warfare.[101] For instance, one hundred million tons of herbicides were used to deprive the Vietcong of their natural cover, and IBM computers were programmed to predict times and places of enemy attacks. Based on computers, statistical techniques of system analysis, and new scientific management methods, the United States waged science-based technological warfare that aimed at imposing its will on Hanoi.[102] Dominated by an ideology of system analysis and founded on the blind faith in the technology of destruction, the Pentagon measured success or failure quantitatively.[103]

In essence, the United States waged modern industrial warfare in Vietnam. Its science-based and technology-prone strategy, however, left no room for Clausewitzean notions of friction and unpredictability. In that sense, the US warfare in Vietnam was reminiscent of de Jomini, who had believed that the elements of chance and uncertainty in war could be eliminated by scientific positivism.[104]

The Vietnamese Communist revolutionary doctrine as implemented under the political and military leadership of Ho Chi Minh, General Vo Nguyen Giap, and Truong Chinh was generally based on ideas from the Chinese military tradition and in particular on Mao Zedong's writings in 'Protracted War' and 'Guerrilla Warfare'.[105] Chinh, the key Vietnamese strategic thinker, and General Giap, commander-in-chief of the Vietcong and the PAVN, thus envisaged a gradual progression from insurgency via guerrilla to conventional military victory as prescribed by Mao's three-stage theory.[106] Their defeat of the Japanese in WWII, of the French in 1954, and the separation of Vietnam into two states seemed to have validated the adoption of Mao's prescriptions.[107]

Between 1954 and 1965, the North Vietnamese strategy slowly progressed from stage two (guerrilla warfare) to stage three (conventional warfare), building up the PAVN while undermining the South Vietnamese government through Vietcong infiltration and insurgency. In December 1963, Ho and Giap decided to change the nature of the war by sending regular forces south.[108] Thus, what had begun by the 1940s as a low-grade and militarily self-sustaining insurgency would by the early 1960s have evolved into clear-cut conventional warfare waged by Hanoi.

---

[101] Herring 1986, 151; Gibson 2000, 95.   [102] Morris 2003.
[103] Gibson 2000, 93–154; Heuser 2002, 169.
[104] Watts 1996; Colin S Gray 1999, 95; Paret 1986, 190–191.
[105] Giap 1977, 23–55; Aron 1980, 2–9; Summers 1982, 83–92; Arreguin-Toft 2005, 37.
[106] Stetler 1970, 277–284; McNamara, Blight, and Brigham 1999.
[107] Giap 1977, 23–32; Stetler 1970, 11–36.   [108] Summers 1982, 83–85.

The conventional operations conducted by the Communist forces in 1963–64 (and again later in 1975), however, proved nothing about the nature of the war against the US during most of the 1960s. Westmoreland, who arrived in Saigon after the North Vietnamese had started sending regular forces south of the Demilitarised Zone (DMZ), believed that Hanoi had already entered stage three as prescribed by Mao's theory. Following the entry of the US military giant into the Vietnamese Civil War in 1965, however, Ho and Giap realised that due to their own weaknesses and the vast military and technological superiority of the US they would be unable to confront their adversary conventionally. As a result, Giap switched back from conventional war to revolutionary guerrilla warfare.[109]

This flexible change in strategy by Hanoi is a good example of how conditions of asymmetry force the inferior side to innovatively adapt to the enemy's capabilities. As dedicated students of Mao, the North Vietnamese leadership was acutely aware that under the conditions of asymmetry as they existed in 1965 they could not win this Ringkampf militarily.[110] By contrast, the practice of guerrilla warfare allowed them to break out of the conventional duelling grounds, to redefine the front lines, and generally to find asymmetric ways to adjust their strengths to exploit the weaknesses of the conventional American warfare.[111]

In their need to balance the asymmetric levels of vulnerability posed by the US military, the leadership in Hanoi knew that it could not compel the United States to do its will by destroying the latter's military means. If anything, decisive confrontations with the US military needed to be avoided by any means. Instead, they put all their efforts into breaking the political will of the United States to continue fighting.[112] Early on they identified the will of the US public as the enemy's most vulnerable point.[113] They understood better than their counterparts in Washington that

The centre of gravity for the American war effort were not Westmoreland's legions traipsing around the Central Highlands but US domestic public opinion.[114]

Hanoi conceived of its strengths in politics in its resolve to out-will the United States in a long war of endurance. Giap and Ho had already spent twenty years fighting and defeating two colonial powers. They therefore

[109] Krepinevich 1988, 164–193; Heuser 2002, 172–173.
[110] Giap 1977, 23–32; McNamara, Blight, and Brigham 1999, 33.
[111] Arreguin-Toft 2005, 37; Fairbairn 1974, 174–209; Shy and Collier 1986, 847–848.
[112] McNamara, Blight, and Brigham 1999, 32–34; Boot 2002, 316.
[113] MacDonald 1993, 291.   [114] Record 1996, 60.

believed that because of the higher stakes in the Ringkampf's outcome for Hanoi than for Washington (the Indochina War was total for the former and limited for the latter), the willingness to sacrifice would ultimately be higher on the Vietnamese than on the American side.[115]

The difference in the willingness to sacrifice, combined with the factor of time, was seen by Hanoi as a strategic advantage which could be used. Hanoi's means of rebalancing the levels of vulnerability was to exploit the perceived lack of US humanism through their own superior resolve and will to sacrifice. Thus, they decelerated and lengthened the Ringkampf by swimming as fish in the sea, by avoiding decisive battles, and by refusing to fight tactical engagements unless they were born out of their own initiative. Their overall defensive strategy skilfully combined with offensive tactics was designed to 'nibble on the edges' of the South Vietnamese and American armed forces in the hope that Americans, over time, might become weary of the war and the sacrifices it required.[116]

Therefore, until the Tet Offensive in early 1968, the North Vietnamese army and the Vietcong consciously refrained from seeking territorial acquisitions and instead sought population control and the winning of hearts and minds of local South Vietnamese who served as the sea in which the guerrillas could swim.[117] They routinely refused combat except under the most favourable conditions. Despite the US strategy of 'search and destroy', the initiative remained with Hanoi. The Vietnamese determined the initiation of as much as 88 per cent of all the tactical engagements with US forces throughout the war.[118]

In a guerrilla war fought without frontlines and territorial objectives and against an elusive enemy, conventional American measurements of progress such as the gain or the loss of a particular territory were useless. The United States could never hold the territory it had cleared and as a consequence was condemned to scan the same countryside again and again. In order to measure its success, Vietnamese body counts and killing ratios became the index of progress for the US military.[119] As Philip Caputo argued,

---

[115] Stetler 1970, 319–327; MacDonald 1993, 291; McNamara, Blight, and Brigham 1999, 23–24.

[116] McNamara, Blight, and Brigham 1999, 174–176, 226–227, 258–259.

[117] Heuser 2002, 173; McNamara, Blight, and Brigham 1999, 23.

[118] Boot 2002, 299; Moran 2002, 207; Herring 1986, 158; Krepinevich 1988, 188; Gibson 2000, 108–109.

[119] McCrisken 2003, 29; Moran 2002, 207. The practice of body counts became discredited as a result of the Vietnam War and the US military has continuously stated since that it 'do[es] not count bodies' (in reference to enemy soldiers and enemy civilians). See Broder 2003.

The measures of a unit's performance in Vietnam were not the distances it had advanced or the number of victories it had won, but the number of enemy soldiers it had killed (the body count) and the proportion between that number and the number of its own dead (the kill ratio).[120]

With an average of two hundred thousand North Vietnamese coming of draft age every year, the official US objective was to push Hanoi over the infamous 'cross-over-point', the point at which the US military would be able to kill enemy troops at a rate exceeding the Communist side's capacity to replace them. This attrition strategy depended on the US ability to force the Vietcong into battle. The latter, however, held the initiative. It could 'either refuse or accept battle on [its] terms and, in doing so, could control [its] casualty level'.[121]

The problem with this approach and the US strategy in general was that it assumed that attrition rates could be safely deducted from known factors such as firepower and the quantity of the equipment.[122] It presupposed a thoroughly predictable and static adversary rather than an understanding that in a Ringkampf, as Clausewitz had observed, 'the will is directed at an animate object that reacts.'[123] The Vietcong reacted by refusing 'to play Wehrmacht to Westmoreland's Patton'.[124] This failure to appreciate the interactive nature of the Ringkampf was reflected in a bitter story that made the rounds in Washington during the closing years of the Vietnam War:

When the Nixon Administration took over in 1969 all the data on North Vietnam and on the United States was fed into a Pentagon computer – population, gross domestic product, manufacturing capability, number of tanks, ships, and aircraft, and size of armed forces, and the like. The computer was then asked, 'When will we win?' It took only moments to give the answer: 'You won in 1964!'[125]

By aiming at fixed values and scientific system analysis, and by directing the approach to war exclusively towards physical quantities, the United States only considered the unilateral action, whereas war consists of dynamic interaction.

Recognising this flaw in American thinking, General Giap commented in 1969 that

The US has a strategy of the arithmetic. They question computers, add and subtract, extract square roots, and then go into action. But arithmetical strategy doesn't work here. If it did, they would have already exterminated us.[126]

---

[120] Caputo 1996, 168.   [121] Krepinevich 1988, 188.   [122] Morris 2003.
[123] Clausewitz 1984, 149.   [124] Boot 2002, 298.   [125] Summers 1982, 18.
[126] Cited in Olson and Roberts 1991, 145.

Attempting to quantify success through the managerial logics of the assembly line and computer science, the United States failed to understand the North Vietnamese will to resist because it could not conceive of the Ringkampf as a continuous interaction of opposites. This fundamental misunderstanding was reflected by General Maxwell Taylor who during the war expressed his puzzlement about

[t]he ability of the Vietcong continuously to rebuild their units and make good for their losses is one of the continued mysteries of this guerrilla war. We still find no plausible explanation of the continued strength of the Vietcong.[127]

No matter how much the United States attempted to escalate its techno-war, it did not succeed in breaking the Vietcong's will to resist. Nor did US strategy achieve its military objectives such as pushing the North Vietnamese beyond the notorious breaking point or stopping the infiltration into South Vietnam by the Vietcong. Official US estimates even conceded that infiltration increased in the period from 1965 to 1967 despite the bombing growing heavier and more destructive. The US enemy demonstrated great ingenuity and dogged perseverance in coping with the bombing, leading one American to comment with a mixture of frustration and admiration that 'Caucasians cannot really imagine what ant labour can do.'[128]

The big turning point, the 'military and political continental divide'[129] of the Ringkampf in Vietnam was the Tet Offensive of 1968. In November and December 1967, Giap changed strategy from stage two guerrilla warfare to stage three conventional war.[130] Despite taking the United States by surprise, the Tet Offensive was generally repulsed with devastatingly heavy casualties suffered by the North Vietnamese. In military terms, the Tet Offensive proved a disastrous outcome for Hanoi. Overall, an estimated forty thousand North Vietnamese died, compared to one to two thousand US servicemen killed in action.[131] Moreover, the popular revolutionary uprising in the South that was anticipated by Hanoi did not materialise. Instead, most South Vietnamese felt alienated by the atrocities committed by the PAVN and the Vietcong. By the time the offensive came to an end in April 1968, the Vietcong had been wiped out completely.[132] Following this disastrous military outcome, Hanoi shifted back to its defensive, protracted war strategy, sharply curtailing its level of military activity in the South and

[127] Cited in Record 1996, 61.   [128] Cited in Herring 1986, 148.   [129] Record 1996, 55.
[130] McNamara, Blight, and Brigham 1999, 193; Hanson 2001, 398–399; Herring 1986, 187–189.
[131] Krepinevich 1988, 248–251; Hanson 2001, 400.
[132] Summers 1982, 108–126; Moran 2002, 217.

even withdrawing some of its regular forces back across the DMZ.[133]
Realising that its attempted transition from stage two guerrilla warfare to
stage three conventional warfare had come too early, Hanoi starting
biding its time. The uproar in the US following the Tet Offensive probably reinforced its conviction that domestic pressures would eventually
force a US withdrawal.[134]

The successful military result for the Americans, however, did not
translate into political victory. Instead, it turned into political defeat due
to how Tet changed the US public's perception of the war.[135] As was
shown in Chapter 1, the Tet Offensive sent shock waves across the United
States because it demonstrated to the American people that Hanoi was far
from losing and the US far from winning the war.[136] Reflecting the public
view of the time, Townsend Hoopes, the Undersecretary of the Air Force,
wrote that

[o]ne thing was clear to us all: the Tet Offensive … showed conclusively that the
US did not in fact control the situation, that it was not in fact winning, that the
enemy retained enormous strength and vitality – certainly enough to extinguish
the notion of a clear-cut allied victory in the minds of all objective men.[137]

The will of the American public, understood by Hanoi as the centre of
gravity of the American war effort and therefore exploited accordingly,
was effectively broken by the Tet Offensive.[138]

Rather than seeking military victory, the US strategy after 1968 was to
search for an honourable way out of Vietnam.[139] While President
Johnson decided against running for re-election because of the war, his
successor Richard M. Nixon was voted into the White House promising
a secret plan to disentangle US forces from Indochina. Based on the
Nixon Doctrine, 'Vietnamization' became the official US strategy.
Already set up by the outgoing administration, 'Vietnamization' turned
the risks of war from US ground forces onto the ARVN, thereby effectively allowing US forces to be withdrawn (from peak mobilisation of
543,000 in April 1968 to thirty thousand in December 1972).[140] In other
words, President Nixon and his National Security Advisor Henry

---

[133] Krepinevich 1988, 250–257.   [134] Herring 1986, 226, 239.
[135] Isaacson 1996, 459; Moran 2002, 214–217; Hanson 2001, 393.
[136] Following Tet in 1968, the majority of Americans for the first time (53%) opposed the
Vietnam War and President Johnson's approval ratings dropped from 58%
(October 1967) to 24% (April 1968) – which analysts believe was due to the effects of
the Tet Offensive. Available at www.gallup.com/poll/18097/Iraq-Versus-Vietnam
-Comparison-Public-Opinion.aspx, accessed on 5 December 2016.
[137] Cited in Hanson 2001, 406.
[138] Karnow 1990, 131–135; MacDonald 1993, 291; Krepinevich 1988, 250; Herring 1986,
191, 200.
[139] Summers 1982, 105.   [140] Zinn 2003b, 231; MacDonald 1993, 300.

Kissinger did not end the war, but merely the most unpopular aspect of it, namely the killing of enemy non-combatants and the sacrifice of US lives in the jungles of Vietnam.[141]

At the same time, the Nixon Administration escalated the air war over North Vietnam in vain attempts to force Hanoi into a peace treaty. The so-called 'One War' strategy and the Phoenix Programme introduced by Westmoreland's successor, General Creighton W. Abrams, replaced 'search and destroy' with a new 'population control' approach which resulted in the systematic defeat of Hanoi's insurgent component in the South.[142] However, the North Vietnamese, knowing that the US president could no longer win the war politically, were prepared to wait him out, no matter what additional suffering it might entail.[143] Their conventional attack at Easter 1972 was once more countered successfully by massive US aerial bombardment and South Vietnamese ground forces. A few months later, the US withdrew completely. In April 1975, with the pictures of North Vietnamese tanks rolling through the streets of Saigon and the hasty and chaotic evacuation of US citizens by helicopters from the roof of the US embassy building, the Vietnamese Civil War finally came to an end. In the Ringkampf under the condition of asymmetry, the North Vietnamese defeated the US giant.

Writing on the topic of defeat in *On War* 150 years earlier, Clausewitz had recognised that

[n]ot every war needs to be fought until one side collapses. When the motives and tensions of war are slight we can imagine that the very faintest prospect of defeat might be enough to cause one side to yield. If from the very start the other side feels that this is probable, it will obviously concentrate on bringing about this probability rather than take the long way round and totally defeat the enemy.[144]

While Clausewitz wrote this particular passage with reference to symmetric interstate warfare, its applicability can be extended to wars fought under conditions of asymmetry. Applied to the Vietnam War, it illustrates how the Tet Offensive constituted more than just the 'faintest prospect of defeat' for the United States. The symbolism of Hanoi's resolve and vitality, the representation in the US media, and the perception by the American public led the United States to yield. Tet became the watershed of the Ringkampf as it broke the political will of America to continue fighting. Giap and Ho's asymmetric strategies had concentrated on bringing about this probability by avoiding the adversary's centre of strength (the US military) and by directing its own force at the latter's centre of vulnerability instead (the unwillingness of the United States to accept

---

[141] Isaacson 1996, 234–272; Zinn 2003b, 231.
[142] Hanson 2001, 310; Record 1996, 55; Zinn 2003b, 23.   [143] MacDonald 1993, 291.
[144] Clausewitz, *On War*, p. 91.

casualties). Unable to defeat its adversary militarily, Hanoi innovatively and creatively exploited America's casualty-aversion as a means to balance the asymmetric levels of vulnerability in the Ringkampf.

What mattered most to the American people was not the Vietnamese but the American body count. Accordingly, Giap's strategy was largely unconcerned with the human costs and sacrifices demanded by his own people[145] as 'his [was] not an army that sends coffins north; it [was] by the traffic of homebound American coffins that Giap measured success.'[146] In that sense, body count actually mattered, but on the American rather than the Vietnamese side.[147] Reflecting on the different attitudes towards casualties between Washington and Hanoi, Peter MacDonald argued that

[t]he US military were pressured to avoid them by politicians at home because pictures of coffins lined up on the runway ... waiting to be loaded for the return flight generated a near-hysterical reaction in the American viewing audience. On the other hand, Giap ... accepted deaths as part of the price they had to pay.[148]

In comparison to the 58,168 Americans killed in action, the North Vietnamese and Vietcong suffered disproportionate number of casualties. In the end, however, it was the American and not the North Vietnamese will that was eroded.

The US tactical successes in 1968 and 1972 did not prevent its strategic failure, while at the same time the tactical failures of Hanoi did not prevent its strategic success. In the words of Bernard Brodie, 'the side that lost completely in the tactical sense came away with an overwhelming psychological and hence political victory.'[149] This paradoxical outcome of the Ringkampf had resulted from the dynamic interaction between the US superpower and the Vietnamese guerrillas and is summed up well in a conversation that took place in Hanoi in April 1975 when the American Colonel Harry G. Summers defiantly told his North Vietnamese counterpart: 'You know you never defeated us on the battlefield,' to which the latter replied, 'That may be so, but it is also irrelevant.'[150]

The case of the Vietnam War shows how the Vietnamese adversary 'had a vote, too'. General Giap's and Ho Chi Minh's asymmetric strategy was a successful chameleonesque reaction against and adjustment to the prevailing military conditions. By successfully exploiting American vulnerabilities, Hanoi provided a strategic model that could be emulated by disadvantaged US adversaries in the future.

The particular dynamic seen in Vietnam is likely to stay as the vast conditions of asymmetry have been a key characteristic (and will continue

[145] Krepinevich 1988, 250.   [146] Lewy 1980, 68.   [147] MacDonald 1993, 291.
[148] MacDonald 1993.   [149] Cited in McCrisken 2003, 30.   [150] Summers 1982, 1.

to do so for the foreseeable future) wherever the US military intervenes.[151] By the end of the Cold War, the American armed forces had military capabilities far in excess of those of any would-be adversary or even a combination of adversaries. It dwarfs, as Andrew J. Bacevich argues, even those of its closest military allies.[152] For example, America's annual post–Cold War military budget of $260bn was not only the largest in the world, but also accounted for more (in absolute and in relative terms) than the next nine largest national defence budgets combined. Post–9/11 increases to the Pentagon's budget have made it as big as the annual military budgets of the next eleven countries combined.[153] In 2005, the United States accounted for 48 per cent of all the annual military expenditure worldwide – followed by the United Kingdom, France, Japan, and China with a share of 4–5 per cent each.[154] And its 2011 budget of $683bn exceeded the average Cold War average by 56 per cent, indicating that the gap in military spending (with the exception of perhaps China) will expand further in the years to come.[155]

As a result, American vulnerabilities in the post–Cold War world have hardly been of a military nature. Its investment in military technology not only created a military empire with unprecedented global reach (epitomised by airpower, satellite-guided cruise missiles, and unmanned predator drones), but also widened the levels of asymmetry.[156] As a consequence, the reciprocity of military risks has been reduced to such a historically unprecedented level that it has rendered US adversaries to a status of military helplessness in conventional conflicts.[157]

Compelled to adapt, US enemies try to recast the terms of conflict in ways that play to their advantages and exploit American vulnerabilities.[158] They are forced to seek ways of rendering US military superiority superfluous by seeking refuge in those areas where American military power cannot fully be projected (where US military superiority has to exercise considerable restraint) and where they can exploit US vulnerabilities (where American sacrifices are too costly). By the time of the Gulf War, these areas seem to have been located in the American need to fight wars that ensure the safeguarding of civilians while at the same time guaranteeing high levels of US casualty-aversion. As Chapters 1 and 2 have shown, this need for highly discriminate and post-heroic warfare has become the centre of gravity of contemporary

---

[151] Renner 2004, 87–113; Arreguin-Toft 2005, 19–20.   [152] Bacevich 2005, 16.
[153] Kennedy 2002; Der Derian and Wibben 2003.
[154] 'USA treiben Ruestungsspirale nach oben', *Der Spiegel*, 12 June 2006.
[155] Reid 2003; Mann 2003, 18.   [156] Kahn 1999; Bacevich 2005, 16–18.
[157] Kahn 2002, 2–9; Münkler 2006, 60.
[158] Bohrer and Osiel 2013, 803–806; Skerker 2004, 27–39; McInnes 2002, 136–141.

US warfare. Given the prevailing conditions of asymmetry, it can therefore be assumed that US adversaries will actively try preventing the
US from minimising its own casualties and at the same time seek to
place the US in a situation where it cannot escape inflicting high levels
of collateral damage.[159]

Conclusion

This chapter developed a methodological tool which allows for an analysis of
the ways in which the dynamic nature of war under the condition of asymmetry impacts on the tension between US casualty aversion and civilian
protection. In doing so, it critically investigated the insights of Clausewitz's
metaphors of War as a Wrestling Match and War as a True Chameleon.

The chapter then illustrated how T. E. Lawrence and Mao Zedong
took both of Clausewitz's metaphors beyond the confined symmetric
realm of interstate warfare. Their creativity allowed them to overcome
the disparity posed by conditions of asymmetry and to develop guerrilla
tactics and strategy as an independent form of warfare. Even though they
were only familiar with Clausewitz's major work, they nevertheless
showed how the applicability of Clausewitz's metaphors can be extended
to conditions of asymmetry.

The chapter then applied these ideas to the Vietnam War. This not only
illustrated the dynamic and transformative character of the wrestling
match in an asymmetrical environment, but also allowed for a better
understanding of how the militarily disadvantaged Vietnamese side
employed asymmetric strategies that allowed it to prevail against one of
the two superpowers of the time. This perspective on asymmetry and the
particular interactive dynamics it creates is important as the book concentrates on US conflicts with semi-/non-state actors, or conflicts that
provide the most extreme contemporary examples of asymmetry.

Given the research focus, the Ringkampf is central to assessing the
question of how the dynamics of the wrestling match exacerbate the
tension between US casualty-aversion and civilian protection. The next
three chapters investigate this question through the empirical cases of the
US interventions in Somalia, Afghanistan, and Iraq.

---

[159] This has even been recognised in the 2002 American army *Doctrine of Joint Urban
Operations* manual: 'Recent operations have shown potential adversaries may try to
take advantage of the fact that the American military forces will comply with the
requirements of the law of armed conflict' (Joint Staff 2002, 8).

4   The US Intervention in Somalia

Introduction

The theoretical part of the book introduced and analysed the two most distinctive characteristics of US warfare in the post–Cold War world. Chapters 1 and 2 have shown the inherent tension between casualty aversion and civilian protection that lies at the heart of contemporary American warfare. Moreover, the technological superiority of the US military creates conditions of asymmetry that generate particular interactive dynamics between the two conflicting parties (Chapter 3).

This chapter on the US intervention in Somalia offers the first of three case studies on how this trade-off between American casualty-aversion and civilian protection has been affected by the dynamics of the wrestling match. It examines the interaction between American forces and Somali warlords and the extent to which this conflict posed specific legal, moral, and strategic challenges to the American ability to wage war in both a casualty-averse and humane manner.

The following sub-questions guide the investigation of this case study: Has the US military been able to wage the war in Somalia in ways that achieved highest levels of casualty-aversion while also safeguarding Somali civilians? Or did the asymmetric strategies employed by Somali warlords force US decision-makers to decide on one norm at the expense of the other? And if so, what were the legal, moral, and strategic consequences of such decisions?

The chapter is divided into three parts. The first part briefly examines the historical background to the Somali civil war, the collapse of state structures, and the ensuing humanitarian crisis. This is important in order to understand the various factors that triggered the responses from the international community in form of the United Nations Mission in Somalia (UNOSOM) I and the US-led United Task Force (UNITAF).

The second part focuses on the period of the UNITAF mission from December 1992 to April 1993. It analyses the extent to which concerns for casualty-aversion and civilian protection informed key

US political and military decision-makers in Washington as well as on the ground. It critically examines how US policies and military strategies were designed and implemented to avoid potential clashes with local warlords or the alienation of the Somali people. As a result, UNITAF ensured low risks to US military personnel while at the same time generating high levels of civilian protection. This equilibrium between US casualty-aversion and civilian protection, however, came at the detriment of the resolution of the underlying causes of the Somali civil war.

The third part focuses on the United Nations Mission in Somalia (UNOSOM) II. The core emphasis is placed on the collision between the United States armed forces within UNOSOM II and the Somali warlord General Muhamed Farah Aideed, which turned into an all-out war between June and October 1993.[1] The UNOSOM II period thus provides for the specific empirical case of a Ringkampf under conditions of asymmetry. The chapter advances understanding of how Aideed's asymmetric strategies (which manipulated legal and moral norms by deliberately placing non-combatants in harm's way) made it increasingly difficult for the United States to operate in ways that ensured an equilibrium of risk between US personnel and Somali civilians. Given the local security environment created by Aideed, this part investigates if American forces started prioritising casualty-aversion over Somali civilian protection. Moreover, it asks if marginal increases to the risks faced by US soldiers could have resulted in lower numbers of civilian deaths.

The chapter concludes by relating the empirical findings back to the theoretical framework of the book, showing how the intervention in Somalia has impacted on US warfare in the post–Cold War world and setting up a framework of comparison with the US interventions in Afghanistan and Iraq.

Background to the Somalia Crisis

From 1969 onwards, Major General Mohamad Siad Barre had ruled Somalia. His one party dictatorship espoused 'Scientific Socialism' as its guiding ideology. He had maintained power through state control and irredentist, pan-Somalia nationalist claims on territory within the boundaries of neighbouring Kenya, Ethiopia (Ogaden), and Djibouti.[2] Following the disastrous Ogaden War with Ethiopia in 1977/78 and the

---

[1] Although UNOSOM II was a multinational peace-enforcement operation under UN command, the chapter almost exclusively focuses on the American contingent. Non-American contingents are only mentioned where their roles impacted upon US forces and vice versa.

[2] Birnbaum 2002, 59; Lewis 2002.

failed coup against his regime in 1978, Barre dropped his 'Greater Somali Concept'[3] and resorted to politics of clan favouritism.[4] These new policies involved placing clansmen and other loyalists into positions of power, wealth, and control while fuelling the rivalries with others.[5]

By altering the traditional balance of clan power within Somali society, Barre's post-1978 policies precipitated armed opposition that soon escalated into a nationwide civil war between factions based on clan affiliations.[6] Throughout the 1980s, Barre responded to political or armed resistance with violent crackdowns and serious human rights abuses especially against the clans of the Madscherten, Isaq, and Hawije. In one early example, Barre's forces completely destroyed the northern cities of Hargeysa and Burao (held by the rivalling Somali National Movement [SNM]), deliberately killing up to fifty thousand defenceless internally displaced people (IDP) and civilians in the process.[7] The brutal way in which the Barre regime tried to defeat the SNM's uprising has generally been interpreted as being a precursor to the increasingly cruel and indiscriminate warfare that came to haunt Somalia over the following years.[8]

Barre's methods of 'clan cleansing' altered the traditional laws and limits of conflict that – up until then – had tended to constrain violence among Somali clans.[9] For centuries, this traditional Somali code of conduct had differentiated between those who could legitimately be killed and those who had to be 'spared from the spear'.[10] In a predominantly pastoral society like Somalia, these unwritten conventions were effectively the equivalent to the modern day Geneva Conventions with their distinctions between combatants and non-combatants.[11] Breaking with this traditional warrior code, Barre set in motion strategies of 'clan cleansing' and banditry that were unprecedented in Somali conflicts. By deliberately employing indiscriminate force against enemy clans, he introduced an unrestricted way of warfare that was soon replicated by rival clans and militias.[12]

When his increasingly brutal and unpopular regime signed a Peace Accord with Mengistu Haile Mariam of Ethiopia in 1988, the last pretext for the Somali people to mobilise behind Barre's policies of irredentist

---

[3] The 'Greater Somali Concept' emerged in the 1960s in the form of policies aimed at uniting ethnic Somalis and eradicating tribalism and clan structures in favour of Somali nationalism.
[4] Lewis 2002, 248–251; Lewis and Mayall 1996, 100.   [5] Halim 1996, 72.
[6] Lyons and Samatar 1995, 14–21; Lewis 2002, 251–254.
[7] Peterson 2001, 14; Hirsch and Oakley 1995, 11.
[8] Birnbaum 2002, 68–77; Cann 2000, 160.   [9] Kapteijns 2008, 13–17.
[10] ICRC 1997.   [11] ICRC 1997, 2–3.
[12] Africa Watch 1993, 4–5; Lewis and Mayall 1996, 101; Hartley 2004, 184.

nationalism was removed.[13] Clan unrest erupted across Somalia, triggering a civil war during which the traditional restraint in conflicts broke down completely.[14] The ensuing civil war saw systematic practices of clan cleansing by all factions, the destruction of livestock, and the deliberate use of 'scorched earth' tactics. Barre, who had once declared that 'I arrived by the gun and I will only leave by the gun',[15] kept his word when he barricaded himself in his Presidential Palace with his artillery during the fight for Mogadishu in the late 1980s. Day and night he fired randomly into the city, demolishing whole districts until he ran out of ammunition and, on 26 January 1991, fled to his traditional clan strongholds near the Kenyan and Ethiopian borders to regroup.[16]

The emerging power vacuum was quickly filled by the violent power struggle between General Mohammed Farah Aideed and the interim Somali President Ali Mahdi Mohamad.[17] The collapse of the Somali state made the (sub)-clan the basis of authority, order, and organisational basis for armed defence.[18] Aideed and Mahdi, two former allies whose fragile coalition in the United Somali Congress (USC) had effectively ousted the ancient regime, could not agree on a power-sharing plan. Different sub-clan and family politics emerged, causing the dissolution of the coalition as both started competing for power in November 1991.

In Mogadishu, the traditional stronghold of their Hawije clan, a fratricidal war broke out between Mahdi's Somali Salvation Alliance (SSA) and Aideed's Somali National Alliance (SNA) that effectively divided the capital city along sub-clan lines.[19] Both warlords engulfed the city in a protracted blood bath during which fourteen thousand were killed and thirty thousand were wounded in the period from November 1991 to March 1992 alone.[20] The viciousness of the fighting was facilitated by a growing taste for the highly addictive narcotic khat, especially among teenage gunmen, who – after chewing it all day – would develop an uncaring aggressiveness. The import of the drug was controlled by Aideed's financier, Osmand Atto, who earned an estimated $1 million a month from this trade in narcotics.[21]

The UN-brokered ceasefire between Aideed and Mahdi, signed on 3 March 1992, geared up hopes that the supply of food by international

---

[13] Weiss 2004, 59.   [14] Lewis 2002, 257–266; Peterson 2001, 3–17.
[15] Cited in Hartley 2004, 190.   [16] Cann 2000, 161.
[17] Adam 1995, 69; Delaney 2004, 29. For a good account of the falling out between Aideed and Mahdi, see Cann 2000, 161.
[18] Adam 1995, 72–77; Lewis 2002, 263; Africa Watch 1993, 2, 6.
[19] Farrell 1995, 195; Peterson 2001, 15.
[20] Africa Watch 1993, 5–6; Lewis 2002, 264; Weiss 2004, 60.
[21] Birnbaum 2002, 47–52.

organisations could eventually proceed.[22] The optimism of the international community, however, was unfounded as Mogadishu descended into a state of lawlessness. Despite the fragile truce between the two major warlords, over forty different militias (some outside the control of either Aideed or Mahdi) roamed the streets on light trucks or jeeps fitted with machine guns, terrorising, killing, robbing, and looting.[23]

Close to the Kenyan border, Barre had regrouped his clan and counterattacked, thereby ravaging farms and food stock in three unsuccessful attempts to return to Mogadishu.[24] Both he and Aideed used 'scorched earth' tactics and starvation of enemy clans in a region that became known as the 'Triangle of Death' (the region between the three cities of Baidoa, Oddur, and Bardera). It was a harbinger of the tragedy to come: food was used as a strategic weapon against enemy clans. The destruction of agriculture and livestock production in Somalia's heartland in combination with a severe drought resulted in famine. The latter peaked in the period between April and June 1992, during which between 300,000 and 350,000 Somalis died, millions were displaced, almost 4.5 million were threatened by severe malnutrition and disease, and an additional 1.5 million were at immediate risk of starvation.[25]

Resulting from the increasing insecurity, most governmental, nongovernmental (NGO), and UN humanitarian organisations had evacuated their staff and suspended programmes in 1991 and 1992.[26] It was at this point that the UN intervened. In response to the humanitarian suffering and lawlessness, the United Nations Security Council Resolution (UNSCR) 751, passed on 24 April 1992, created a humanitarian operation known as the United Nations Mission in Somalia (UNOSOM) I.[27] It was comprised of fifty unarmed Pakistani observers who were sent to monitor the UN-brokered ceasefire signed by both warlords in March 1992. To counter the levels of banditry, five hundred armed peacekeepers were supposed to protect relief convoys.[28]

Yet, Mogadishu continued to descend into a state of banditry and lawlessness, forcing the UNSC to pass another resolution on 27 July 1992.

---

[22] The UN had withdrawn its personnel for security reasons when the major fighting broke out. A few International non-governmental organizations (INGOs) such as the ICRC, MSF, and CARE, however, had stayed on.

[23] Shawcross 2001, 67.   [24] Drysdale 1994, 22–26.

[25] Miller and Moskos 1995, 2; Halim 1996, 79; Lewis and Mayall 1996, 101–103.

[26] Weiss 2004, 61.

[27] UNOSOM I was originally called UNOSOM. However, in order to avoid confusion with the UNOSOM II mission following the UNITAF period, I refer to this mission as UNOSOM I.

[28] It took three months for the observers to arrive and the five-hundred-man Pakistani infantry battalion was not fully operational until September 1992.

UNSCR 767 approved an airlift of emergency relief supplies to alleviate the humanitarian crisis. Code-named 'Operation Provide Relief', the US Air Force began delivering massive quantities of food and aid.

Even though relief organisations sought to be non-partisan towards the various factions, the impact of the international aid deliveries was far from neutral regarding whether the conflict abated or worsened. In an environment ridden by civil war and famine, the humanitarian aid and the conflict started to interact in ways that were rarely understood even by the aid agencies at the time.[29] Food was a source of income and power.[30] Humanitarian aid got trapped in the conflict as factional fighting broke out over the control of food and supply routes. As the control of the distribution routes became a central factor in the political economy of militias and warlords, the flow of aid was interrupted, the lives of humanitarian workers were threatened, and the effectiveness of aid deliveries was greatly reduced.[31] Local warlords imposed heavy taxes on cargoes (10–20 per cent of incoming aid) and extorted unarmed international aid agencies by running protection rackets.[32] The International Committee of the Red Cross (ICRC), for example, paid $50,000 a month for security at the port of Mogadishu and throughout the south was forced to recruit 2,600 mercenaries to protect operations.[33] Depending on the region, 15–80 per cent of all international aid delivered was looted by local militias, criminal gangs, and warlords.[34]

In the context of this violence, any humanitarian aid given became part of that context and thus of the conflict itself.[35] The protection required by humanitarian aid agencies and offered by Somali guards led to a symbiotic relationship, or what Peterson termed

a Faustian agreement made by life savers who had no other way of carrying out their work and by the warlords who were making their work necessary in the first place.[36]

In other words, the famine had resulted from the Somali civil war, and the introduction of international humanitarian aid in a sense exacerbated the humanitarian catastrophe as it provided a new and effective source of power for the warring factions.[37] The starvation and malnutrition was thus not caused by a lack of aid, but because of the lawlessness, looting, and insecurity in the absence of international armed protection.[38]

---

[29] Lewis 1993, 1–3.   [30] Cran 1998.
[31] Farrell 1995, 195–197; Sahnoun 1994, 17; Lewis and Mayall 1996, 108.
[32] Wheeler 2000, 174; Delaney 2004, 29.   [33] Lewis and Mayall 1996, 108.
[34] Cann 2000, 164; Weiss 2004, 62.   [35] Mary Anderson 1999, 1.
[36] Peterson 2001, 31. See also Kapteijns 2008, 31.   [37] Shawcross 2001, 69.
[38] Wheeler 2000, 176.

On a broader scale, UNOSOM I demonstrated the problems of traditional peacekeeping operations to adjust to the new complex security environment of Somalia.[39] The limited mandate given to UNOSOM I by Resolution 751 was passed under Chapter VI of the UN Charter. It was thus not mandated to use force other than in self-defence and depended entirely on the consent of the warring factions.[40] And with Aideed refusing to guarantee the protection of the peacekeepers, the Pakistani blue helmets were holed up at Mogadishu harbour and did not leave their compound until the arrival of United Task Force (UNITAF) in December 1992.[41] Plenty of international aid therefore sat in a warehouse at the port as warlords controlled the streets.[42]

The paralysis of the Pakistani peacekeepers brought into stark relief the inability of UNOSOM I to carry out its mandate. It became clear that despite the introduction of massive international aid, the reason for the continued starvation of the Somali people rested in the institutional inability of UNOSOM I to operate in an ongoing intrastate conflict. Traditional peacekeeping was based on the assumption that there was a peace or ceasefire to be kept; that the warring factions had consented to the presence of peacekeepers; and that they would operate under strict neutrality.[43] In Somalia, where there was neither an accountable government nor a peace to be kept, UNOSOM I was rendered largely ineffective.[44]

In combination with growing public pressure to protect food convoys from looters – the international media had started to 'discover' the famine by August 1992[45] – there was growing political pressure on the international community to establish a secure environment for the delivery of international aid.

UNITAF and 'Operation Restore Hope'

Throughout the summer of 1992, US political and military decision-makers were strictly opposed to any direct military involvement in Somalia.[46] This opposition was reinforced by various warnings to stay out of Somalia, most strongly articulated by the US ambassador to Kenya, Smith Hempstone, who warned that Somalis were

---

[39] Weiss 2004, 63.   [40] Farrell 1995, 195.   [41] Miller and Moskos 1995, 4.
[42] Shawcross 2001, 69; Delaney 2004, 29–30.
[43] Berdal 1993; Otunnu and Doyle 1998; Goulding 1993, 451–464.
[44] Farrell 1995, 195; Albright 2004, 142.
[45] Dauber 2001, 211–214; Delaney 2004, 30.
[46] Telephone interviews with Ann Wright, 9 and 15 March 2005; Wheeler 2000, 178–179. Back in March 1992, the US had still opposed any UN peacekeeping force in Somalia.

[n]atural born guerrillas. They will mine roads, they will launch hit-and-run attacks. They will not be able to stop the convoys from getting through. But they will inflict – and take – casualties.[47]

Referring to the 241 marines killed in Lebanon in 1983, he cabled Washington, 'If you liked Beirut, you'll love Mogadishu.'[48]

By November 1992, however, the humanitarian situation in Somalia had deteriorated to such an extent that it put immense pressures on the Bush administration to respond more forcefully than just through the delivery of humanitarian aid.[49] According to Wheeler, the growing media coverage of the warlords preventing aid deliveries

[s]truck a powerful chord with a US public that wanted the administration to ride shotgun into Mogadishu and rescue the victims of lawlessness and starvation.[50]

The situation on the ground afforded more forceful action as it became apparent that UNOSOM I lacked teeth.

But to provide teeth to a failing UNOSOM I mission posed a particular dilemma for US leaders. Ever since the experiences in Vietnam and Lebanon, they had shied away from military operations that could not fulfil the conditions set out by the Weinberger Doctrine.[51] As Chapter 2 has shown, the Weinberger Doctrine had achieved what Cori Dauber identified as the 'status of hegemonic discourse' by the end of the Cold War.[52] It had become the 'controlling lens through which potential [US] deployments were debated and justified.'[53] A humanitarian intervention in Somalia would be in defiance of the control mechanism of the Doctrine, for no vital US national security interests were at stake.[54] Therefore, an intervention in Somalia, a country of no strategic significance to the United States after the end of the Cold War, was regarded as a 'disinterested' mission that made any US deployment difficult to justify.[55]

With the political and public pressure rising, however, it was not believed that there were intrinsic reasons as to why the use of force in a 'disinterested' mission was unacceptable in principle. It was simply

---

[47] Quoted in Peterson 2001, 53.   [48] Quoted in Peterson 2001, 53.
[49] Dauber 2001, 211–214; Delaney 2004, 30.   [50] Wheeler 2000, 180.
[51] McCrisken 2003, 106–111; Simons 1998, 6.
[52] Dauber 2002, 66; McCrisken 2003, 189.   [53] Dauber 2002, 68;
[54] Murray 2007, 563.
[55] The term 'disinterested' is used in contrast to 'interested' interventions as defined by the Weinberger Doctrine. The difference is therefore only in relation to the question of vital national security interests of the United States. It does not imply that in the absence of these vital national security interests, no other interests were at stake. From the perspective of US political and military decision-makers, these differences matter. See, Krauthammer 2002.

assumed as too risky politically because any potential sacrifice among US service personnel was understood to be unsustainable among the American public.[56] Thus – since the level of casualty-aversion among the US public was considered to be intolerably high – a purely humanitarian intervention could only be embarked upon if it were conducted with little or no risk to US military personnel.[57]

At the same time that Somalia became the pressing foreign policy issue, Bush also found himself accused for his failure to intervene militarily in the ongoing civil war in Bosnia. Boutros Boutros-Ghali, the United Nations Secretary General (UNSG), publicly attacked Western powers for fighting 'a rich man's war in the Balkans' while neglecting the biblical suffering of humans in Africa.[58] The call by President-elect William Jefferson (Bill) Clinton for military intervention in the Balkans was rejected by the Bush Administration on the grounds that the potential for a 'quagmire' and US casualties would be too high. General Colin L. Powell, Chairman of the Joint Chiefs of Staff (JCS), emphasised this point publicly when he argued that the complex situation in Bosnia not only lacked any clear political solution but would also necessitate a massive military intervention that was likely to result in large numbers of US casualties. Yet, even though Somalia did not reflect any major US national security interests either, Powell assessed that the latter at least afforded the merit of an achievable solution at limited risks.[59] An intervention in Somalia was therefore considered to be less risky than getting involved in the vicious civil war in the Balkans.[60] And the goodwill gained would help offset the widespread criticism of a lack of a US response to aggression in Bosnia. Lawrence Eagleburger, who served as Secretary of State during this period, recollected that the feeling in relation to Somalia among key policy-makers was that 'we could do this . . . at not too great a cost and, certainly, without any great danger of body bags coming home.'[61] Thus, Bush's motivation for intervention in Somalia was partially due to his desire to deflect attention from his inaction in the Balkans and the prospect that any intervention in Somalia was viable without risking the lives of US service personnel.[62]

As the architect of the 'New World Order', President Bush also understood that Somalia provided the ground to demonstrate the humanitarianism and leadership of the world's remaining superpower.[63] Acting as a lame-duck president, Bush conceived a riskless intervention as providing a high note on which to end his presidency. Following the Gulf War,

---

[56] Delaney 2004, 29–32.   [57] Wheeler 2000, 181.   [58] Tyler 1992.   [59] Powell 1992.
[60] Shawcross 2001, 66–67.   [61] Quoted in Minear, Scott, and Weiss 1996, 55.
[62] Hirsch and Oakley 1995, 42–43; Wheeler 2000, 181.   [63] Bacevich 2002, 143.

there was certainly a desire in Washington to demonstrate to the Muslim world that the Americas would not only be prepared to use force to liberate Kuwait and to secure the supply of crude oil, but that it was genuinely concerned for the well-being of Muslims.[64]

Consequently, when Colin Powell proposed a US military intervention in Somalia, he made it conditional on zero tolerance, a clearly defined exit strategy, a limited mandate, and the authority to use overwhelming force.[65] The White House and Pentagon in return made their approval of any involvement in Somalia conditional on ensuring a very limited UN mandate. This was seen as the only way to ensure that the costs in American lives in a conflict like Somalia would be virtually zero.[66]

In November 1992, the National Security Council's (NSC) Deputies Committee met and discussed Somalia four times; on 25 November 1992, President Bush decided to assemble a multilateral force in which the United States would take the leading role similar to the one taken in Operation Desert Storm.[67] This decision indicated a dramatic turnaround in the US position from only a couple of months earlier.

Due to casualty-aversion, American decision-makers were generally reluctant to become involved in the actual fighting in Somalia and under-took every effort to significantly limit the scale and scope of the UN mandate. During the negotiations over Resolution 794, Bush and Powell therefore insisted that the mandate was merely to stop the famine-related dying, to open up the supply routes, and to encourage the volun-tary decommissioning of arms. According to Chuck Ikins, who then worked at the Pentagon's Somalia desk,

[i]t was important that this mission was limited as this – according to the under-standing of the decision makers at that time – ensured that the risks to US forces were significantly reduced.[68]

The legacies of Vietnam and Lebanon were lurking behind the decisions taken by the Bush administration in November and December 1992.[69]

In concrete terms, the Bush Administration rejected any UN mandate that called for a comprehensively enforced disarmament of the warring factions. Instead, the resolution endorsed the offer by the United States to lead an international force to protect humanitarian relief operations in Somalia. The US intervention would merely establish a secure environ-ment in which the distribution of food could be secured and voluntary disarmament and reconciliation between the warring factions could

---

[64] Weiss 2004, 64.   [65] Lewis and Mayall 1996, 111; Shawcross 2001, 66–67.
[66] Mueller 1996, 31.   [67] Hirsch and Oakley 1995, 42–43.
[68] Interview with Chuck Ikins in Washington, DC, 30 November 2004.
[69] Bacevich 2005, 48; McCrisken 2003, 111; Delaney 2004, 31; Hyde 2000, 17–27.

begin. The mission would have a clear exit strategy and would be taken over by UN forces by January 1993 before the new US president came into office.[70] The ambitious agenda of disarmament, conflict resolution, and nation-building would be left for the subsequent UN mission.[71]

By adamantly opposing a concerted effort to disarm and demobilise any of the warring factions in Somalia, the American position contrasted sharply with that of the UNSG.[72] Boutros-Ghali viewed a comprehensively enforced disarmament and demobilisation of the Somali factions as a central rather than peripheral part of UNITAF.[73] He insisted that

> [w]ithout national reconciliation, involving the establishment of viable political structures and the disarmament and demobilization of the factional militias and armed irregulars, all the progress towards ending hunger would inevitably remain precarious and economic recovery would remain largely impossible.[74]

Driven by his 1992 *An Agenda for Peace*,[75] the Secretary-General viewed Somalia as a test case for post–Cold War peace-building efforts.[76] His argument for a resolution of the conflict – in which he was supported by most international non-governmental organizations (INGOs) – was diametrically opposed to the Americans who insisted on a limited mandate.

This fundamental disagreement came to the fore during the negotiations over the wording of UNSC Resolution 794 and manifested itself most forcefully in the debate over the question of what the 'establishment of a secure environment' in Somalia meant in concrete terms.[77] This disagreement is crucial, for it illustrated the overriding importance US political and military decision-makers placed on zero tolerance.

UNSC Resolution 794, adopted on 3 December 1992, authorised the UNSG and member states to use 'all necessary means to establish as soon as possible a secure environment for humanitarian relief operations in Somalia.'[78] The UNSG demanded that this term implied a complete and comprehensive disarmament of all warring factions by UNITAF whereas the United States insisted that the resolution made no specific reference to disarmament and demobilisation.[79]

By not clearly defining the tasks UNITAF was to undertake in order to establish a secure environment, however, the debate between the White

---

[70] Lewis and Mayall 1996, 111.

[71] It was understood by the Bush administration and other members of the UNSC that this subsequent UN mission would be given a much broader and more ambitious mandate in the Security Council than they were negotiating for UNITAF ('US and UN at Odds over Somalia', *Independent*, 12 December 1992; Bacevich 2002, 143).

[72] Lewis 2002, 269.   [73] Weiss 2004, 65.   [74] United Nations 1996, 37.

[75] Boutros-Ghali 1992a.   [76] Wheeler 2000, 193.   [77] Crocker 1995, 2–8.

[78] UNSC Resolution 794, 3 December 1992.   [79] Clarke and Herbst 1996, 71.

House and the Secretariat of the UN continued throughout UNITAF's mission. To give an example, in a letter to President Bush on 8 December 1992, Boutros-Ghali called for US forces to conduct a comprehensive disarmament program, arguing that

[a]ny forceful action by the international community in Somalia must have the objective of ensuring that at least the heavy weapons of the organized factions are neutralized and brought under international control and that the irregular forces are disarmed. Without this action I do not believe that it will be possible to establish the secure environment called for by the Security Council resolution or to create conditions in which the United Nations' existing efforts to promote national reconciliation can be carried forward and the task of promoting humanitarian activities can safely be transferred to a conventional United Nations peace-keeping operation.[80]

Bush responded to this letter by re-emphasising how the United States interpreted Resolution 794 as not calling for disarmament and demobilisation:

I want to emphasize that the mission of the coalition is limited and specific: to create security conditions which will permit the feeding of the starving Somali people and allow the transfer of these security functions to the UN peacekeeping force.[81]

For the United States, any resolution to the underlying causes of the humanitarian crisis was only to be addressed by the subsequent UN mission. A precondition for American involvement was limiting the objectives to such an extent that they could be accomplished with zero tolerance. More ambitious objectives like those demanded by the UNSG that would have addressed the underlying causes of the Somalia crisis were ruled out.

The White House and Pentagon clearly understood that Somalia was a disinterested third-order intervention where no vital national interests were at stake. If any military intervention were to take place, it could only be justified through the 'control lens' of the Weinberger Doctrine if the United States remained impartial and avoided being dragged into another civil war like Vietnam and Lebanon.

If limiting the scale and scope of UNSCR 794 was one way to ensure low risks to US military personnel, then gaining authorisation for overwhelming use of US force within the UN mandate was another. In fact, both were seen by US decision-makers as two sides of the same casualty-averse coin. General John Hoar, CENTCOM commander, and Lt. General Robert B. Johnston, US military commander of UNITAF, demanded using unprecedented Chapter VII authority for peace enforcement 'by all means necessary'. This would, according to Johnston,

Allow the on-scene commander maximum flexibility to determine what constituted a threat and what response was appropriate, including the use of deadly force.[82]

The UNSG was unable to move the Bush administration on either the issue of nation-building or disarmament and UNSCR 794 reflected the dominance of the US position. Even though it was unanimously adopted by the Security Council on 3 December 1992 under Chapter VII of the UN Charter (defining the humanitarian emergency in Somalia as a threat to international security), the resolution was explicitly limited in scope to the delivery of humanitarian relief and did not oblige UNITAF to disarm the belligerents.[83]

The ghosts of Vietnam and Lebanon were clearly present not only in the minds of the White House and the Pentagon,[84] but also among those in charge of UNITAF operations on the ground. UNITAF commanders had served in South Vietnam and Lebanon, two apprenticeships that now largely determined their approaches to the intervention. Ambassador Robert B. Oakley, whom Bush appointed Special Envoy to Somalia, had been a diplomat in Saigon in the 1960s and a former US ambassador to Somalia. UNITAF Commander Lt. General Johnston had not only served as a young Marine in Vietnam, but had also been part of the first Marine battalion that went into Lebanon. In fact, most of the Marines who arrived in Somalia had served in Beirut in the 1980s. Now, in December 1992, they raised the very same American flag at the UNITAF compound in Mogadishu that they had been forced to take down in Beirut in 1983.[85]

As a result of their past experiences, both conflicts continuously cropped up in conversations between UNITAF leaders.[86] Oakley recollects:

[t]he US military commander [Lt. General Robert B. Johnston] and I spent the first week [in Somalia] preparing notes about Lebanon and Vietnam. We had been in both places and we talked about the dangers, the traps and how to avoid them.[87]

---

[82] Telephone interview with Robert Johnston, 11 January 2005.

[83] For good discussions on the groundbreaking nature of UNSCR 794 see Greenwood 1993; Wheeler 2000, 182–187; Roberts 1993. At its height, UNITAF embodied 37,000 troops from 23 different countries. The US deployed twenty-eight thousand troops (10,000 soldiers and 16,000 Marines).

[84] Dauber 2002; Bacevich 2005, 48; McCrisken 2003, 111; Hyde 2000.

[85] Hartley 2004, 233–234.   [86] Dowden 2003.

[87] Interview with Robert Oakley in Washington, DC, 30 November 2004.

They concluded that what had gone wrong in both interventions was that the US military had been dragged deeply into a civil war and thereby had become a party to the conflicts.[88] The key lesson for Johnston was that

[o]nce you become perceived as the enemy, you have a totally different mission . . . I had experienced this very problem in Beirut and wasn't gonna get caught in that again.[89]

Therefore, they took measures to 'avoid being dragged into the conflict between the different Somali clan factions'.[90] They decided to resist any military and political actions that would turn Mogadishu into another Beirut or Saigon and instead set out to create a benign security environment for the intervening forces. In other words, they concluded that UNITAF should under no circumstances take sides among the Somali clans, that any confrontation (as long as UNITAF's mission was not compromised) and long-term animosity should be avoided, as this would have interfered with their objectives and would have increased the risk to US soldiers.

This was perceived as the only acceptable path for a casualty-averse US military to operate in Somalia. Johnston recalled:

[t]here is some natural casualty-aversion, but in the specific case of Somalia, we clearly didn't want to have casualties because it was a humanitarian intervention.[91]

Casualty-aversion dictated that Oakley, John Hirsch (Political Advisor to Johnston and Deputy to Oakley), Johnston, and Major General Anthony Zinni (UNITAF Director of Operations) were actively seeking the support of Somali warlords for the intervention.[92] This was regarded as vital in gaining legitimacy in the eyes of local actors that would significantly increase the protection of US soldiers as well as allow for the unhindered delivery of food.[93]

As a first step in his effort to create a benign security environment for US forces, Oakley met separately with Somali warlords Aideed and Mahdi on the 7 December 1992, two days before the planned amphibious landing of the Marines.[94] Aideed had been adamantly opposed to UNITAF. He was very suspicious and vociferous in his criticism of the UN involvement partly because of his genuinely strong nationalist feelings (Somalis are often described as a very proud people who have

---

[88] Hirsch and Oakley 1995, 156.
[89] Telephone interview with Robert Johnston, 11 January 2005.
[90] Interview with Robert Oakley in Washington, DC, 30 November 2004.
[91] Telephone interview with Robert Johnston, 11 January 2005.
[92] Lippman and Gellman 1993; Mersiades 2005, 206–208.
[93] Hirsch and Oakley 1995, 104.   [94] Stephen Smith 1993, 113.

successfully resisted foreign incursions throughout history).[95] More importantly, he feared that any outside intervention would hinder his plans to obtain power by any means necessary. Having ousted Barre from Mogadishu in 1991 and having defeated the latter's forces in the three subsequent campaigns, he naturally considered himself as the legitimate successor to Barre.[96] With his own forces more numerous and his military skills and experiences far superior to those of his ally-turned-rival Mahdi, Aideed believed that without outside international intervention he would have prevailed in the power struggle.[97] Moreover, Aideed had a strong personal animosity towards Boutros-Ghali, whom he considered responsible for Egypt's support of Barre during his terms as Egyptian Minister of State for Foreign Affairs.[98] But while Aideed resented outside interference from the UN, he did not specifically direct his animosity towards the United States (yet).[99] Oakley, who had a very good understanding of Aideed's thinking, successfully exploited the latter's attitudes towards the UN and the United States.

During the first meetings, Oakley explained to both warlords that the United States was intervening on humanitarian grounds under a limited UN mandate. He made them understand that America was not trying to work against them or to challenge their political roles, but instead was seeking – provided that it did not hinder UNITAF objectives – their participation in a political dialogue between the warring factions leading to voluntary disarmament. Oakley reassured Aideed that

[t]he mission was to facilitate humanitarian intervention by civilian organisations; it was not to rebuild Somalia ... Aideed told me 'You know, Mr Ambassador, I understand. In times of war I am a good general, like General Eisenhower. And in times of peace I am a good president, like President Eisenhower.' So I told him 'You got it right, so let's work on the peace side.' We made it clear to Aideed that he can get where he wants by peaceful means.[100]

In other words, Oakley emphasised that UNITAF would not become a political party to their power struggle. At the same time, however, he made an unambiguous threat to both warlords of what would await them

---

[95] Lewis 2002.   [96] Birnbaum 2002, 88–91.

[97] Cann 2000, 163. Ali Mahdi's genuinely positive response to UNITAF involvement was an indication that Aideed probably assumed correctly.

[98] Adam 1995, 85. In 1989, Boutros-Ghali visited Mogadishu to negotiate arms transfers to Siad Barre. Considering that Aideed was fighting the remnants of Barre's forces and his allies in Kismayu and Baidera at the time of the UNITAF intervention, his opposition to the UN was not only a remnant of the past but still relevant in December 1992.

[99] Gibbs 2000, 41–55; Hirsch and Oakley 1995, 19, 116; Peterson 2001; Birnbaum 2002, 96.

[100] Interview with Robert Oakley in Washington, DC, 30 November 2004. See also interview with John Hirsch in New York, 14 January 2005; Lewis and Mayall 1996.

if they decided to attack US forces or hinder the execution of UNITAF's mandate:[101] 'If you try military means you won't prevail cause it's gonna hurt you.'[102] Confronted with overwhelming US firepower and the promise by Oakley not to interfere politically, the warlords agreed that they would not oppose the outside intervention.

In the case of Aideed, however, the acceptance of UNITAF did not come without issuing his own warning. As Oakley recollects:

[t]he second day I was there before the Marines came in, a Somali of Aideed's entourage said to me: 'Look, we're not gonna oppose the landing because we understand the power of the US. On the other hand, we studied Lebanon, we studied Vietnam. We know how to get rid of you if we want to, by turning up casualties and public opinion.'[103]

If any warning of the potential dangers of the American intervention in Somalia was needed, this was the reminder. Aideed signalled that he understood the limited interests the United States had in Somalia and that he would cooperate only as long as the UNITAF mandate did not jeopardise his political interests.

On 9 December 1992, images of the amphibious landing of US Marines on the Somali coast were broadcast live around the globe. Except for a few gunshots, there was no resistance to the landing from any of the Somali factions.[104] Following the meeting with Oakley, Aideed had personally intervened with the Murasade, one of his highly armed allies who controlled the harbour of Mogadishu and the surrounding area where the landing took place. He had instructed them not to resist the landing of US Marines. Regarding UNITAF objectives to create a benign security environment that would ensure Washington's demand for zero tolerance, Oakley's meeting with the warlords started paying off.

Building upon this strategy, the UNITAF leadership deliberately fostered good relations with all Somali factions in general and with Aideed and Mahdi in particular.[105] Knowledgeable of Somali culture and sensitive to the explosive political environment, Oakley, Johnson, Hirsch, and Zinni understood that establishing permanent channels of communications with all factions and the Somali people was vital for creating a benign security environment for UNITAF.

Between 7 December and the UNOSOM II takeover in May 1993, Oakley would meet with and reassure clan leaders throughout Somalia

---

[101] Interview with Chuck Ikins in Washington, DC, 30 November 2004.
[102] Interview with Robert Oakley in Washington, DC, 30 November 2004.
[103] Interviews with Robert Oakley in Washington, DC, 30 November 2004 and 15 June 2005.
[104] United Nations 1996, 34.   [105] Stephen Smith 1993, 113.

before any UNITAF operation within their respective territories. UNITAF leaders also held daily meetings with Aideed's and Mahdi's factions. These measures were conceived as a means to ensure restraint, to demonstrate the exclusively humanitarian nature of the mission, to provide for an effective platform to avoid escalation, and thereby to minimise hostilities. To put this differently, Oakley's policy of embracing the warlords was primarily driven by casualty-aversion.

Hosting the first common meeting between both rivals on 11 December, Oakley discussed ways and means to avoid clashes between the various clans and UNITAF. At the end of the meeting Aideed and Mahdi signed a joint communiqué in which they renewed their commitment to a ceasefire and agreed to remove all heavy weapons and so-called 'technicals'[106] off the streets into 'Allocated Weapons Storage Sites' (AWSS), designed compounds where they would be inspected by UNITAF forces. It was understood that any heavy weapons or 'technicals' found outside the AWSS would either be confiscated or destroyed by UNITAF. The joint communiqué proved an important step for the establishment of a close working relationship as it allowed UNITAF to hold both sides accountable for their in/actions. To give an example: In mid-December 1992, Aideed tested UNITAF's resolve when some of his 'technicals' fired at US helicopters, only to be eliminated by the US response. Both Oakley and Johnston viewed their fierce yet proportionate response to this first clash as crucial for the rest of the UNITAF mission because it sent a clear message that defiance or violation of the communiqué would not be tolerated.[107] At the same time, however, UNITAF leaders ensured that this potentially divisive issue was addressed in the dialogue with the top military and political leadership of the different Somali factions.[108]

But dialogue did not only take place between UNITAF and the warlords but also with clan elders, women's groups, religious leaders, and humanitarian agencies, who also met on a daily basis in so-called joint committees.[109] Oakley's strategy was to revitalise Somali civil society and

---

[106] 'Technicals' were made by bolting custom-made mounts on the chassis of land cruisers, fitted with American 106 mm anti-tank cannons, smaller Chinese recoilless rifles, or Soviet anti-aircraft batteries that were adjusted horizontally for street battle (Peterson 2001, 24–25).

[107] Interview with Robert Oakley in Washington, DC, 15 June 2005; telephone interview with Robert Johnston, 11 January 2005.

[108] In this particular incident, Oakley met Aideed the next day and asked him for an explanation. The same day, Aideed's and UNITAF's radio stations issued a common statement declaring this incident an accident which was not in the interest of either side (telephone interview with Robert Johnston, 11 January 2005; interview with Robert Oakley in Washington, DC, 30 November 2004).

[109] Hirsch and Oakley 1995, 156–157.

thereby to set in motion processes to shift power away from the warlords.[110] Oakley termed this strategy 'plucking the bird'.[111] It was based on the assumption that if one took away one feather at the time, the bird would not notice it. If one continued this strategy, the bird would one day wake up and realise that it could no longer fly.[112]

Based on the understanding reached by the joint communiqué, the UN held peace talks between the fourteen warring factions in Addis Ababa at which two agreements were reached on 8 and 15 January 1993. These provided for a continuation of the ceasefire, the cantonment of heavy weapons under regular UNITAF inspections, and the framework for a comprehensive disarmament process.[113] Boutros-Ghali, who chaired the talks, assumed that UNITAF would start the process of disarmament whereas UNITAF leaders in Mogadishu and Washington rejected any such involvement as 'mission creep'.[114]

But while the United States continued to reject the Secretary-General's agenda, UNITAF nevertheless started confiscating weapons in urban areas, tried to shut down Mogadishu's arms bazaars by force, and raided one of Aideed's compounds.[115] These tougher practices in January 1993 started stretching the Bush administration's policy on not pursuing disarmament and not policing the ceasefire.[116] This was particularly the case when fighting broke out in Mogadishu and Kismayu in early 1993. In response, UNITAF found itself clashing with Somali factions in attempts to uphold the ceasefire.[117] These military operations, Wheeler argued,

[s]aw the US teetering on the edge of a slippery slope down which the USA was to slide, radically departing from its limited humanitarian mission, which had been the rationale for Operation Restore Hope.[118]

These moves to 'get tough' with the gunmen increased the level of tensions, and on 14 January 1993 the first US soldier was killed in an ambush.[119]

Despite the mounting tension between January and March 1993, UNITAF is a fascinating case because the United States conducted an intervention that overall ensured both low levels of US casualties and high levels of respect for the principle of non-combatant immunity. UNITAF

---

[110] Hirsch and Oakley 1995, 156–157.
[111] Lewis 2002, 269–270; interview with Robert Oakley in Washington, DC, 15 June 2005.
[112] Lewis and Mayall 1996, 72.   [113] Hirsch and Oakley 1995, 93–95.
[114] Lewis and Mayall 1996, 113–114; interview with Robert Oakley in Washington, DC, 15 June 2005.
[115] Noble 1993; Durch 1996, 323–324.
[116] Farrell 1995, 199–200. Oakley and Tucker 1997.   [117] Lyons and Samatar 1995, 93.
[118] Wheeler 2000, 192.   [119] Maier 1993.

only suffered 18 fatalities (8 combat, 10 non-combat related), and 24 US soldiers were wounded. On the Somali side, estimates range between 50 to 100 Somalis killed during the UNITAF period.[120] This outcome shows how the military strategies designed to de-escalate potential clashes and the highly discriminate procedures under which UNITAF operated minimised the levels of risk faced by both American military personnel and Somali non-combatants alike.

With the exception of the incidents in Mogadishu and Kismayu, UNITAF successfully avoided confrontation and generally operated in a very restrained manner. The low casualty rates on both sides were achieved because of a recognition of the humanitarian and therefore limited nature of the intervention and the deliberate attempts to avoid turning Somalia into another Vietnam or Lebanon.

Every UNITAF patrol and inspection was deliberately announced in advance by psychological operations (psy-ops) specialists through the UNITAF radio, the newspaper, and loudspeakers on helicopters. Sent by the Pentagon, these psy-ops countered the information sent by Aideed and Mahdi (who both called their respective radio stations 'Radio Mogadishu') and explained the nature of UNITAF's presence to the Somali people.[121]

UNITAF commanders assumed that operating cautiously, with advance warning, and overwhelming military force, would deter and – if needed – overwhelm any Somali aggression. This was understood as a means to ensure that none of the warlords' gunmen or militias was caught by surprise and opened a firefight. At the same time, this policy also provided enough prior warnings for civilians to clear the area of operations. The rationale behind this was that the success of UNITAF also depended on the support and the goodwill of the Somali people, who were under no circumstances to be antagonised.

These rules of engagement (RoE) decided by UNITAF leaders are interesting for operating under high visibility and prior warning was clearly designed to guarantee high standards of civilian protection and to avoid unintended clashes with local gunmen.[122] On the downside, however, any operation announced in advance potentially increased the risks to US service personnel by informing Somali factions of the exact time and place of UNITAF patrols. UNITAF commanders accepted the

---

[120] Hirsch and Oakley 1995, 82.
[121] UNITAF leaders showed a clear understanding that radio stations were critical sources of power for both warlords. Instead of closing them down – which in a society with a predominantly oral tradition would have amounted to a 'casus belli' – Oakley had simply decided to open UNITAF's own radio station.
[122] Dworken 1993, 1–27.

potentially higher risks to their own military personnel – even during the clashes in Mogadishu and Kismayu. The basic assumption behind these operating procedures was that with the establishment of a benign security environment, UNITAF would remain outside the domestic conflict and none of the Somali factions would have any strategic or tactical interest in clashing with UNITAF forces in the first place.[123] At the same time, there was a recognition that high levels of respect for non-combatant immunity were, according to Oakley, an essential means of 'ensuring low risks to US forces by minimising hostilities to the US.'[124] UNITAF's restrained operating procedures reassured the Somalis which in turn decreased the levels of risk to US forces. Thus, operating with potentially higher risks to US soldiers reinforced high levels of civilian protection which in turn guaranteed zero tolerance.

In comparison to other national contingents, US troops, with a few exceptions, were exceptionally well behaved.[125] While detailed evidence exists of how Pakistani, French, Belgian, and Canadian forces abused and even murdered Somalis, the disciplined behaviour by US forces was emphasised in subsequent reports on the standards of UNITAF.[126] The first two cases of US soldiers killing Somali civilians occurred in February 1993 and immediately led to court martials, sending a clear signal to US forces as to what behaviour was permissible within the RoE.

The United States was the only UNITAF contingent to open an office for Somali complaints and to make – in line with Somali traditions of behaviour in war – compensation payments to the families of Somali victims.[127] In the case of the US corporal who killed a Somali boy who had robbed his sunglasses, Oakley not only ordered a court martial, but also apologised for the violation via the UNITAF radio, and the United States paid compensation to the boy's family.[128] Enforcing high levels of restraint among US forces, punishing transgressors, and compensating Somali families proved to be an effective means to reassure the Somali people.

Thus, even though UNITAF found itself in two clashes with Somali factions towards the end of its mission, it successfully balanced the relationship between US casualty-aversion and civilian protection. The RoE and operating procedures established and implemented by the

[123] Dworken 1993, 9–12.
[124] Interview with Robert Oakley in Washington, DC, 30 November 2004.
[125] Farrell 1995, 198.   [126] De Waal 1998, 134–136; Miller and Moskos 1995.
[127] De Waal 1998, 136.
[128] Interview with Robert Oakley in Washington, DC, 30 November 2004; telephone interview with Robert Johnston, 11 January 2005; interview with John Hirsch in New York, 14 January 2005; interview with Chuck Ikins in Washington, DC, 30 November 2004. All participants independently recalled that incident.

UNITAF leadership ensured an equality of risk between US military personnel and Somali civilians. This was of course helped by the limited goals UNITAF had set itself. From the perspective of military effectiveness, the strategic goals associated with US military action had deliberately ruled out any major clashes with Somali warlords and were never designed to achieve any more ambitious goals other than facilitating the provision of humanitarian assistance.

UNITAF proved to be successful in fulfilling its mandate: the channels for the delivery of international humanitarian aid were reopened and secured, the famine had come to an end, and thousands of Somali lives were saved.[129] Mechanisms for voluntary disarmament were established during the first Addis Ababa meeting in January 1993 and political dialogue was fostered between various Somali groups. The process, however, remained deliberately voluntary for any UNITAF involvement was ruled out in Washington as potential mission creep.[130]

UNITAF's success in balancing US casualty-aversion and Somali civilian protection, however, came at the detriment of resolving the deeper and underlying causes of the Somali conflict. By not confronting the warlords, they were elevated in their status and power as they became a legitimate part of the political process.[131] Furthermore, they were allowed to keep most of their arsenals intact as no comprehensive disarmament took place. This was in sharp contrast to the agenda pushed by the UNSG that envisaged disarmament as the central step in preventing Somalia's long-term return to civil war and famine.

Among Somali civilians and even the warlords there had been an expectation that with the arrival of UNITAF, a process of comprehensive disarmament would begin that would bring an end to warlordism.[132] The United States thereby missed a small yet crucial window of opportunity which closed in the weeks to come. But as zero tolerance dictated that the United States generally kept away from any potential confrontation, all disarmament efforts remained voluntary.[133] For instance, UNITAF came to realise that Aideed had secretly relocated his technicals from the official inspection sites into the countryside. Although this was a clear violation of the December communiqué, Oakley and Johnston refrained from confronting Aideed over this issue, claiming that such acts did not pose a threat to the UNITAF mandate.[134] However, Oakley interpreted the UNITAF mandate less strictly and introduced mechanisms that also aimed at conflict resolution and the strengthening of civil

[129] Farrell 1995, 194–212; Roberts 1993; Weiss 2004, 94.
[130] Crocker 1995, 2–4; Lewis and Mayall 1996, 113–114.   [131] Kapteijns 2008, 31.
[132] Perlez 1992; Ransdell 1992; Smolowe 1992; Ellis 1993.   [133] Shawcross 2001, 99.
[134] Gibbs 2000, 45; Hirsch and Oakley 1995, 57.

society at the expense of the warlords. Here, considerable progress was made that tends to be ignored in the existing literature.[135]

The successful balancing between US casualty-aversion and Somali civilian immunity was achieved through a deliberate strategy that dictated cooperation over confrontation. Fostering consent with local warlords was to the detriment of the resolution of the conflict.[136] According to Michael Maren, 'The US force cleaned up the blood and put bandages on the body, but left the patient haemorrhaging inside.'[137] UNITAF ended up treating the symptoms, but never fully the causes of the disease.

UNOSOM II

This section concentrates on the collision course that developed between the UN/US and Aideed. Between May and October 1993, this clash provides an example of how the interactive dynamics of the Ringkampf impacted on the relationship between US casualty-aversion and civilian protection.[138]

In comparison with UNSCR 794, the mandate given to UNOSOM II in Resolution 814 (26 March 1993), was far more ambitious and authorised the UN to conduct a peace-enforcement mission under Chapter VII of the UN Charter.[139] If the former had been limited to protecting humanitarian relief, then the latter's call for disarmament, conflict resolution, nation-building, and democratic elections widened the mandate and aimed at resolving precisely those underlying causes of the Somali conflict that had been left unaddressed by UNITAF.

UNSCR 794 had remained limited because the casualty-aversion of the Bush administration had prevailed over the ambitious agenda pushed by the UN Secretary-General.[140] With the incoming Clinton administration, the American and UNSG's visions for Somalia converged rapidly. Instead of embarking on unilateral ventures, Clinton's 'assertive multilateralism' resolved to exert American power through multilateral organisations such as the UN. 'Assertive multilateralism' dovetailed nicely with Boutros-Ghali's *Agenda for Peace* vision of a more active UN, one willing to intervene in civil disputes for humanitarian reasons and for

---

[135] Farrell 1995, 194; Crocker 1995, 4–6; Durch 1996, 323–324.
[136] Western and Goldstein 2011, 48–59.   [137] Maren 1993.
[138] Given the research focus, the emphasis here is placed specifically on the American role within UNOSOM II. As will be shown, UNOSOM II was, despite the comparatively small US contingent, dominated by American military and political leadership, even to the point where UNOSOM II's mostly American leadership took orders directly from Washington rather than from New York.
[139] Goulding 1993, 451–464.   [140] United Nations 1996, 217.

nation-building. Somalia therefore presented itself as a case to which Washington's and New York's ambitious agendas could be applied.[141]

Yet, the Clinton administration still proved as anxious as its predecessor to extract American troops from Somalia. With Boutros-Ghali trying to ensure the continued US military commitment to UNOSOM II, the UN-US discussion in the end resulted in more US troop provisions to UNOSOM II than had been intended.[142] Clinton's pledge for continued American military support defied the 'control lens' of the Weinberger Doctrine, as the mandate given by UNSCR 814 resembled anything but the limited and impartial nature of UNITAF.[143] But conceiving Somalia as the test case for his 'assertive multilateralism', the new President believed that it merited not only political and financial, but also (limited) military commitments.[144]

Compared to the twenty-eight forces that comprised the American contribution to UNITAF, only 4,500 US troops remained to serve in UNOSOM II. These consisted of 1,150 Quick Reaction Forces (QRF) and three thousand logistical support staff.[145] But while the twenty thousand UN forces from twenty different nations were deployed under the military command of the Turkish Lieutenant General Cevik Bir, the QRF only operated on orders of Bir's Deputy Commander, American Major General Thomas Montgomery.[146] Thus, the US QRF (and the Delta and Army Rangers that were sent to Somalia in August 1993)[147] operated outside the UN command structure and took orders not from the UN but from senior decision-makers in Washington.[148] Retired US four star admiral Jonathan Howe was placed in charge of UNOSOM II as the Secretary General's Special Representative. A former Deputy National Security Advisor under President Bush, Howe also took his orders from Washington rather than New York.[149] As a result, the complex political and military command structures of UNOSOM II created confusion about the relative roles of the UN and the United States.[150]

Over the course of UNOSOM II, major operations undertaken on behalf of UNOSOM II would take place outside the command and control of the UN, disguising the fact that UNOSOM II operations at the core were dominated by Washington rather than New York. When

---

[141] Clarke and Herbst 1997, 193; Kapteijns 2008, 31.
[142] Hirsch and Oakley 1995, 111.   [143] Dauber 2002.   [144] Clinton 2005, 554.
[145] Farrell 1995, 202.   [146] Clarke and Herbst 1996, 73.
[147] The Delta Forces and Army Rangers reported neither to the UNOSOM II command nor to Montgomery but directly through their own commander, Major General William Garrison, to decision-makers in the US (Bacevich 2002, 145).
[148] Allard 1995, 18–19.   [149] Bacevich 2002, 143–144.
[150] Lewis and Mayall 1996, 116.

UNITAF's mandate officially ended on 3 May 1993, the follow-on mission remained a US political and military undertaking.

Despite relatively similar aggregate numbers of troops between UNITAF and UNOSOM II, the massive replacement of US forces by contingents from mostly developing countries made UNOSOM II considerably weaker militarily than UNITAF at a time when the mandate was dramatically expanded. This disequilibrium between military capabilities and political ambitions meant that UNOSOM II had to accomplish more than UNITAF with less potent forces.[151] The only real military muscle was provided by the US QRF that was barred from carrying out routine operations and was exclusively deployed to provide rapid assistance to other UNOSOM II forces.[152]

The debate over whether the attacks occurring in early June were inevitable or whether they were triggered by fundamental policy changes in New York and Washington is beyond the scope of this chapter.[153] It is a fact, however, that on 5 June 1993, Pakistani peacekeepers were attacked simultaneously at different locations in Mogadishu following the inspection of a UN-sanctioned Somali National Alliance (SNA) weapons storage site which was located next to Aideed's radio station. Twenty-four peacekeepers were killed and fifty-seven wounded.

The immediate response at UNOSOM headquarters, in Washington, and in the Security Council was to blame Aideed's SNA for the killings.[154] Although an official inquiry did not take place until July and then took several months to publish its results,[155] the UNSC in an urgent session on 6 June unanimously adopted Resolution 837 which condemned the murder of UN peacekeepers by forces apparently belonging to the United Somali Congress and the SNA.[156] The UNSC authorised that all necessary measures be taken against those responsible, including their arrest and detention for prosecution, trial and punishment.

The 5 June attacks marked the turning point, the official opening shot of the subsequent war between the US/UN and General Aideed. By adopting UNSCR 837, UNOSOM II transformed from a humanitarian mission into a counterinsurgency operation. According to John Hirsch, the Deputy Special Envoy of UNITAF, 'once 837 was passed, the whole operation shifted and in fact the UN declared war on

---

[151] Farrell 1995, 204–205.   [152] Bacevich 2002, 144.
[153] Lewis and Mayall 1996; Sloyan 1995.   [154] Lewis and Mayall 1996, 117–118.
[155] It concluded that the attacks were orchestrated by Aideed, yet no conclusive evidence was found that the attacks were pre-planned and pre-meditated (Wheeler 2000, 194–195).
[156] Clarke and Herbst 1996, 80.

Aideed.'[157] And by declaring war on the SNA, UNOSOM II transformed itself into the 15th clan in the Somali power struggle.

What followed were four months of escalating urban warfare as the United States brought its military capabilities to bear on locating the warlord and destroying his militia. US combat forces, who had not been much involved in operations prior to UNSCR 837, now spearheaded UNOSOM II operations.[158]

With the burden falling on the QRF, Montgomery orchestrated several operations that aimed at capturing the fugitive general and destroying his weapons depots. The initial attacks by American QRF in June and early July included air strikes and air ground searches against SNA weapons storage sites and facilities.[159] By continuing UNITAF's careful practices, these military operations – at the beginning – were generally very restrained and discriminate.[160] Overall, relatively high levels of civilian protection were achieved by illuminating targets from the air, using loudspeakers from helicopters, and giving early warnings to the local population.[161] But even the most proportionate and careful targeting could not avoid one hundred Somalis (including women and children) losing their lives.[162] What was important though was that the US QRF not only refrained from harming Somali non-combatants directly and intentionally. Rather, by accepting higher risks to their own lives (through giving advance warnings and operating under high visibility), American forces took active precautionary steps that reduced the risks faced by Somali civilians.

Yet, these operations failed to capture the warlord and did little to deter the SNA. Aideed's forces rather succeeded in escalating their own attacks and inflicting casualties on Moroccan and Italian contingents.[163] By mid-July, the Americans became more frustrated as frequent raids showed little effect on their adversary. Their operating procedures gave Aideed sufficient time to slip away. As will be shown, the use of firepower by US forces in the densely populated quarters of the Somali capital began to produce high levels of civilian deaths.[164] This begs the question of whether escalating US tactics in this conflict were compatible with the laws of war and the ethics of the use of force. In order to examine this question, we first need to understand how Aideed's asymmetric strategy posed a major challenge to American goals of achieving high levels of protection for both its soldiers and for Somali civilians.

[157] Interview with John Hirsch in New York, 14 January 2005.
[158] Allard 1995, 30–31; Bacevich 2002, 144.   [159] United Nations 1996, 391–392.
[160] United Nations 1996, 385.   [161] Wheeler 2000, 196.   [162] Church 1993.
[163] Durch 1996, 311–315.   [164] Wheeler 2000, 196–198; Bacevich 2002, 144.

Aideed's Strategic Thinking

Aideed's guerrilla strategy and insurgency tactics against UNOSOM II, and in particular the United States, evolved between June and October 1993. But several fundamental aspects of his strategic thinking were consistent throughout this period.

In general terms, the asymmetries in military capabilities and political interests dictated the nature of his strategy. Aideed had to acknowledge his military inferiority despite the relative military weakness of UNOSOM II in comparison with UNITAF. But while the differences in military capabilities favoured UNOSOM II and constrained the options of the SNA, he clearly appreciated his advantages over the former in the asymmetry of interests.[165] Here, his stakes in the conflict (political and physical survival) were ultimately much bigger than those of UNOSOM II. This allowed him to accept higher levels of sacrifice and to employ a range of tactics that UNOSOM II could not afford to take if they were to avoid increasing civilian casualties.

In addition to this, he was acutely aware of US sensitivities to casualties as well as its legal commitment to respect the principle of non-combatant immunity. Exploiting these two sensitivities became the central part of his strategy.[166] By inflicting casualties on UNOSOM II and especially US forces, the levels of sacrifice would become unacceptable and at least force the UN to accommodate to him or at best trigger withdrawal.[167] If the US/UN were provoked to respond with indiscriminate force, he could exploit this politically by rallying public support for his agenda.[168]

Mark Bowden argues that Aideed was acutely aware that civilian casualties worked to his benefit:

One way of putting pressure on an intervening force is to advertise the death and injury of civilians as this increases pressure on the latter .... It has become a standard part of these small scale wars to place civilians in harm's way on purpose. Aideed deliberately thrust civilians into this in order to exploit it because democracies are susceptible to pressure and public support can be made to evaporate.[169]

By inflicting casualties and by dehumanising the conflict, Aideed's strategy aimed directly at what he conceived as his adversary's centre of gravity: with America trying to fight humanely by minimising the harm caused to civilians, Aideed sought to maximise collateral damage (by deliberately placing Somali civilians in harm's way); with the need to

---

[165] Mack 1975, 175–200.   [166] Bowden 2000; Bohrer and Osiel 2013, 803–806.
[167] Peterson 2001, 96.   [168] Hirsch and Oakley 1995, 123.
[169] Telephone interview with Mark Bowden, 24 November 2004.

wage casualty-averse wars, he aimed at preventing the Americans from fighting that way.[170]

This strategic reasoning illustrates not only that the 'enemy has a vote, too', but also shows the importance of the dynamic interaction that lies at the heart of this conflict. If UNITAF created a benign security environment that allowed for zero tolerance and high levels of civilian protection, then Aideed now tried to create an environment in which it became increasingly difficult for US forces to operate in ways that ensured both casualty-aversion and civilian protection.

In the escalating conflict, Aideed's men were always several steps ahead of UNOSOM actions. Part of the reasons was that UNOSOM II raids in June and early July were announced in advance, which undermined the element of surprise. But the failure to capture him was also due to the warlord's vastly superior intelligence sources.[171] He had gone underground, started changing locations every night, merely moving by foot, and avoiding electronic means of communication which he knew would be picked up by American signals intelligence. The result was impressive: from 28 July until after the 3 October firefight, the warlord was neither sighted nor did the Americans receive any signal intelligence of him.[172]

The frustration resulting from the failing manhunt was exacerbated by the deteriorating security situation on the streets. Whenever UNOSOM forces ventured outside their compound, they encountered harassment, demonstrations, mob actions, and ambushes. This increasingly dangerous arena became even more treacherous in the aftermath of the US attacks on the Abdi House on 12 July (which is discussed below). It forced UNOSOM to launch ever shorter raids with increasingly less footprint on the ground. By October 1993, the entire city would start descending on UNOSOM forces on the ground in less than thirty minutes. At that point, the UN effectively lost control of the streets and its patrols virtually came to an end. Aideed successfully shaped a local environment where UN/US forces could no longer operate without sustaining and inflicting unacceptable levels of casualties.

Following the 5 June attacks, the abuse of civilian immunity became a systematic tactical means in the warlord's war plans.[173] Accordingly, the SNA sent non-combatants to the frontline to shield gunmen, get close to, and attack UN forces.[174] Using human shields was not only morally reprehensible but also a direct violation of the laws of armed conflict as

---

[170] Shultz and Dew 2006, 57–103.   [171] Peterson 2001, 99.

[172] Interview with Chuck Ikins (Somalia Task Force, Office of Secretary of Defence) in Washington, DC, 30 November 2004.

[173] Shultz and Dew 2006, 57–103; Peterson 2001, 112.

[174] Miller and Moskos 1995, 6; Bowden 2000, 142.

it deliberately abused Somali civilian immunity to launch attacks at enemy forces.[175] For example, on 17 June 1993, a combined UN force operation overran Aideed's headquarters in South Mogadishu. The resistance was fiercer than expected with civilians closing in on the peacekeepers and SNA gunmen hiding behind them. By strictly interpreting the existing RoE, the UN forces refused to shoot at civilians and as a result took heavy casualties themselves.[176] Admiral Howe recollects:

[w]e got a lot of UNOSOM forces killed in this particular incident ... because they wouldn't shoot at the women who threw hand grenades and who had gunners hidden in crowds. The Somalis used all types of tactics that we have seen in later wars.[177]

Unfamiliar with a local environment where the distinctions between soldiers and civilians were deliberately blurred, the restraint shown by the UN forces resulted in a disproportionate increase in their own risks. The presence of Somali civilians made it extremely difficult for peacekeepers to defend themselves without breaking existing RoE and killing non-combatants.

As a result, UNOSOM commanders relaxed the RoE by decreasing the levels of restraint to ensure higher levels of protection for UN forces.[178] UN forces were now permitted to shoot civilians who volunteered as human shields (and thereby became combatants), yet no such permission was given in cases where Somali non-combatants were forced by the SNA to act as human shields. UNOSOM forces thus had to distinguish between voluntary and forced civilian participation.[179] These adjustments to the RoE were justified by military necessity as a means to re-establish an equilibrium of risk in this new and complex security environment. At the same time, however, they provide a good illustration of the way in which Aideed's asymmetric and oftentimes reprehensible strategies started challenging the American values of safeguarding civilians while ensuring high standards of casualty-aversion. Given this local environment, did US forces comply with the laws of war and the moral idea of 'due care'?

UNOSOM II and the Law-Morality Nexus

As US frustrations mounted and the conflict escalated further, considerably less restraint was exercised by US QRF. Aideed's strategies forced the United States to face the trade-off between increasing protection for

---

[175] For a good, but more general discussion on human shields, ethics, and insurgency, see Gross 2015, 127–150. See also Bohrer and Osiel 2013, 782.
[176] KIA: 7; WIA: 56 (United Nations 1996, 391).
[177] Telephone interview with Jonathan Howe, 6 January 2005.   [178] Allard 1995, 36–37.
[179] United Nations 1996, 52.

US soldiers and decreasing it for Somali civilians.[180] Over the following months, concerns for US casualties were prioritised over civilian protection to such an extent that US QRF subsequently operated in manners that increasingly inflicted civilian casualties and thus sparked a debate whether US operations violated international humanitarian law.[181] For example, on 17 June, US helicopter gunships and UN artillery attacked the Digfer Hospital in southern Mogadishu, where SNA forces and Aideed were suspected to have taken refuge, and from where snipers were shooting at UN troops. Unlike earlier instances, however, when UN command had gone to great efforts to ensure that all occupants had vacated the target building, the hospital came under immediate artillery and missile fire from United States and other contingents.[182] This was a clear violation of the 1949 Geneva Convention, under which the hospital should have been protected. If one party violates the neutrality of the hospital as the SNA did, then the other party cannot simply attack it. Instead, warnings must be given and protection for civilians provided.[183] Civilians must be given the opportunity to leave and force must be used in restrained and proportionate ways. UNOSOM II did neither and instead attacked with excessive force, firing missiles and artillery rounds into the building, which at that point contained 380 patients, 230 hospital staff, and 19 doctors.[184]

The attack on the Digfer hospital did not attract much attention at the time. It is an important incident, however, because it was the precursor of the manner in which US QRF were to operate in the subsequent months.

'Operation Michigan' and the Laws of War

The trends towards ever-decreasing restraint in US operations culminated in the Abdi House raid, code named 'Operation Michigan'.[185] On 12 July 1993, US helicopter gunships attacked and demolished a house belonging to a senior aide of Aideed and suspected to be an

---

[180] Bacevich 2002, 145; Peterson 2001, 100.   [181] Human Rights Watch 1995.
[182] African Rights 1993, 7–10.   [183] ICRC 1977.   [184] Sly 1993.
[185] The raid was a unilateral US operation approved up the American chain of command to the White House. Montgomery said, 'this operation was a US operation, approved at the very highest levels in Washington before being executed' (telephone interview with Thomas Montgomery, 24 June 2005). Jonathan Howe emphasised that 'this and all other US operations were approved all the way up to DC. But I don't know to what extent it was going through Annan in New York' (telephone interview with Jonathan Howe, 21 June 2005). The decisions on the specific conduct were taken by a very small circle of American UNOSOM II leaders in Mogadishu (telephone interview with Jonathan Howe, 6 January 2005; telephone interview with Thomas Montgomery, 16 March 2005).

SNA command and control centre.[186] Departing from previous practices when great efforts were employed to ensure that the occupants had abandoned the building before it was destroyed, no such warnings were given.[187] As a result of the attack, 54 Somali occupants were killed and another 161 injured.[188]

Admiral Howe and General Montgomery cited local intelligence sources that described the Abdi House as a command and control centre.[189] The objectives of 'Operation Michigan' were to respond to recent SNA attacks on UNOSOM II, decapitate the SNA leadership, disrupt its command capabilities, and drive Aideed's militia from its base of operations.[190]

The justifications given for not issuing early warnings were twofold. On the one hand, the Abdi House allegedly served as a pure military facility. Eliminating the SNA leadership and military command centre depended on maintaining an element of surprise.[191] Prior warnings in previous UNOSOM raids had ensured high levels of civilian protection but the downside was that it had allowed Aideed and his men to repeatedly slip away and evade capture. Howe and Montgomery argued that the means employed to ensure restraint in an urban conflict zone undermined UNOSOM's mandate to capture the fugitive warlord. Moreover, arguing that the Abdi House constituted a military target, no such early warning would be required legally.[192] On the other hand, providing advance notices of impending US attacks had allowed the SNA to prepare their defences, which had killed a number of UN troops in a chain of fruitless raids on Habr Gidr compounds in June and early July 1993.[193] According to Howe,

[t]he US military took this particular operation on and said that they could not operate with warnings first, it would be too risky for US soldiers to provide a warning in advance. It was a judgment of the military commanders who felt that they could not do any operation at all . . . and so all I can say is this was one time where there were differences about how we would do it and it was certainly

---

[186] Richburg 1993a.

[187] Peterson 2001, 130; telephone interview with Thomas Montgomery, 24 June 2005; telephone interview with Jonathan Howe, 21 June 2005.

[188] African Rights 1993, 5–7; Hirsch and Oakley 1995, 121. Aideed claimed that the actual figure was 73 dead and 234 wounded whereas UNOSOM II estimated the number of Somalis killed at twenty.

[189] Richburg 1993a; Peterson 2001, 130; telephone interview with Admiral Howe, 6 January 2005; telephone interview with Thomas Montgomery, 16 March 2005.

[190] Wright 1993.   [191] Telephone interview with Thomas Montgomery, 16 March 2005.

[192] Telephone interview with Jonathan Howe, 6 January 2005; telephone interviews with Thomas Montgomery, 16 March and 24 June 2005.

[193] Between 5 June and 11 July 1993, 37 UN troops were killed and 130 wounded in action (United Nations 1996, 391–392).

questioned from the civilian stand point. But the operation went ahead because we felt at this point that something needed to be done because a lot of bad things were happening at the time.[194]

Thus, American commanders argued that the risks to QRF would be too high if they continued issuing early warnings.

This compelled the UNOSOM leadership to weigh the question of the early warnings and the concern for civilian casualties with the risks involved for US QRF and the effectiveness of the military operation. Howe recollects:

[p]rior to the operations on 12 July, we had bent over backwards in all US/UN operations to provide warnings first before anything was done ... We did hope that innocent people would be protected. On the 12 July it is true though there was a discussion of this between myself (as the civilian in this) and the UN military planners who wanted to attack this place. When the military plan was presented during that meeting, I questioned 'why isn't there going to be a warning? Why aren't we going to – as we always had done before – warn everybody in the house to get out?' We civilians felt that we needed to continue this practice but the US military commanders felt that they could not do any operation at all ... so you're weighing then the value of the military operation, weighing of a whole number of factors and yes it was the military's judgment that prevailed.[195]

Referring to the hostile local conditions, the UNOSOM II leadership concluded that military necessity and concerns for US casualties over-ruled concerns for Somali civilians. As Head of UNOSOM II, Howe could have overruled the military commanders in this particular question. By failing to do so, he effectively endorsed the departure from previous UNITAF and UNOSOM II practices.[196]

If early warnings had previously been an effective means to ensure that innocent life could be spared, then the situation on the ground had escalated to such an extent that, according to US commanders, it no longer permitted US QRF to operate in ways that ensured high standards of civilian protection and zero tolerance. Given Aideed's asymmetric stance, US commanders had to choose between increasing risks to their soldiers and increasing the risks to Somali civilians. Starting with the Abdi House raid, their concern for US casualties prevailed over civilian lives.

The attitude among the senior US military on 12 July 1993 was summed up in Montgomery telling Robert Oakley, UNITAF's Special Envoy (in October 1993), that 'we've got all the bad guys in one place,

[194] Telephone interviews with Jonathan Howe, 6 January and 21 June 2005.
[195] Telephone interview with Jonathan Howe, 6 January 2005.
[196] Montgomery denied that any such meeting took place but did not reject Howe's claim that he as the US military commander argued that the risks for US soldiers would be too high (telephone interviews with Thomas Montgomery, 16 March and 24 June 2005).

let's get rid of them.'[197] Montgomery and Howe tried to downplay the significance of their decision by insisting that the 'precision air strike hit a key military planning cell', that 'no innocent people were killed in the incident' because it was directed at a 'war council',[198] and that 'SNA reports about civilian casualties were pure propaganda'.[199] In other words, they justified the dropping of the advance warning system by referring to military necessity and the assumed absence of civilians from the property. According to their account of the Abdi House raid, the attacks on this military target were discriminate and proportionate.

The problem was that US QRF did not eliminate a war council, but instead attacked a peace meeting that was attended by elders and civilians from Aideed's Habr Gidr clan and a number of other sub-clans.[200] The building was consequently occupied by non-combatants rather than combatants. Tragically, the purpose of the clan elders' meeting that day was to force Aideed to enter peace negotiations with UNOSOM. According to Bowden,

[a]ll leaders and elders of Habr Gidr clan [were present], most of whom were opposed to the military posture that Aideed was taking against the UN. The meeting was about forcing Aideed to comply with UNOSOM II.[201]

In other words, US QRF killed civilians rather than militias belonging to Aideed's SNA.[202]

Although Howe and Montgomery strongly contest this view, insisting that the raid was 'legitimate' and 'not a violation of warfare', and that no 'innocent people were killed in the incident',[203] UNOSOM II has failed to produce any evidence to substantiate their claims that the Abdi House was indeed a legitimate military target where no civilians were present.[204]

---

[197] Interview with Robert Oakley in Washington, DC, 15 June 2005.

[198] Zinn 2003b, 440–441.

[199] Human Rights Watch 1995, 4; telephone interview with Thomas Montgomery, 16 March 2005; telephone interview with Jonathan Howe, 6 January 2005.

[200] Cann 2000, 174; David Keane 2002.   [201] Bowden interview on David Keane 2002.

[202] De Waal 1998, 138; Drysdale 1994, 203–204.

[203] Telephone interview with Thomas Montgomery, 16 March 2005; telephone interview with Jonathan Howe, 6 January 2005.

[204] Peterson 2001, 127; de Waal 1998, 138. In the first interviews conducted with Howe and Montgomery in January and March 2005 respectively, both argued that there was no peace meeting taking place and emphasised that this was a war meeting. When presented with claims to the contrary from sources within UNOSOM in June 2005, they changed their accounts slightly, claiming, in the case of Howe that 'there were two meetings going on and the one with the elders was several blocks away' (21 June 2005). Montgomery, interviewed three days later, suddenly changed his previous account too: 'As I said, Admiral Howe told me not a long time ago that the elders were meeting elsewhere ... He told me last time I saw him that the [elders] meeting this refers to was elsewhere and unrelated to the Abdi House meeting' (telephone interview with Thomas Montgomery, 24 June 2005).

By contrast, sources within and without UNOSOM II have provided evidence indicating that civilians were attending the meeting.[205]

Yet, besides these indications, no hard evidence could be uncovered that could substantially challenge the accounts given by UNOSOM II commanders that – at the time of the attack – they believed the Abdi House to be a military target. Did the raid on the Abdi House therefore constitute a violation of the laws of war? According to the doctrine of double effect, the harm inflicted on these non-combatants would be legally permissible as long as their deaths were unintended, indirect, and proportionate; and – furthermore – as long as the attacking forces had done 'everything feasible to verify' that the object attacked was neither civilians nor a civilian object.[206]

On the legal requirements of discrimination and intention, the assessment of the Abdi House raid is relatively clear: if the raid was conducted in good faith (that it was indeed aimed at a military target), then the accidental killing of civilians would not have violated IHL. Based on the statements by UNOSOM decision-makers, 'Operation Michigan' satisfied this principle of discrimination: as the Abdi House was thought to be a military target at the time, the deaths of and injuries to non-combatants were unintended.

One of the legal questions that then remains is whether the raid nevertheless breached the proportionality rule enshrined in Additional Protocol I to the Geneva Conventions. According to the latter, an attack aimed at the weakening of the enemy military must not cause harm to civilians or civilian objects that is excessive in relation to the concrete and direct military advantage.[207] This creates a legal obligation for military commanders to consider and weigh the potential effects on civilians with the anticipated military advantage – something that UNOSOM leaders did. It means that the legitimacy of a military target does not provide an unlimited licence for the use of force. Rather, principles of military necessity and civilian protection require the attacking party to seek to avoid or to minimise civilian casualties and prohibit disproportionate attacks.[208] The 12 July Abdi House raid arguably satisfied the principle of proportionality because the intention at the time of the attack was the destruction of a military facility which was assumed to be empty of non-combatants.

However, this interpretation was challenged on legal grounds from within UNOSOM II. According to Ann Wright, Head of UNOSOM Justice Division, US QRF operated in the way they did not because

---

[205] Wright 1993; Peterson 2001, 120–130.   [206] Walzer 1992, 153; ICRC 1977.
[207] ICRC 1977.   [208] Gutman and Rieff 1999, 195–198.

UNOSOM II leaders believed the Abdi House to be exclusively occupied by combatants (evidence suggests that a civilian presence was actually assumed),[209] but because concerns for US casualties were prioritised over the safeguarding of civilians. In a confidential (and hitherto unpublished) memo written to Howe and Montgomery on 13 July 1993,[210] Wright argued that the attack was disproportionate for it ruled out any possibility to discriminate between legitimate and illegitimate targets:

The [legal] issue boils down to whether the [UNSC] [Security Council] resolution's directive authorizing UNOSOM to 'take all necessary measures' against those responsible for attacks against UNOSOM forces meant for UNOSOM to use lethal force against all persons without the possibility of surrender in any building suspected or known to be SNA/Aideed facilities or did the SC allow that persons suspected to be responsible for attacks against UNOSOM forces would have an opportunity to be detained by UNOSOM forces and explain their presence in an SNA/Aideed facility and then be judged in a neutral court of law to determine if they were responsible for attacks against UNOSOM forces or were mere occupants of a building, suspected or known to be an SNA/Aideed facility? Are military tactics that largely prevent possible injury to UN military forces during military combat situations (helicopter rockets against a building) appropriate when those tactics rule out any possibility for persons, particularly non-combatants, inside the building being detained, questioned and if necessary put before a court for their activities rather than facing the arbitrary lethality of powerful and anonymous weaponry? . . .
    In previous attacks the short prior notice of impending attack, somehow gave persons in attacked buildings the option to choose between life and death as it was their decision to either stay in the building or to come out and be detained by UN forces. This is the first incident where no option was given . . .
    Of course, if UN forces are fired upon by occupants then they would be authorized to return fire. In these operations sufficient time and forces should be built into the operation so that persons inside a facility are as much as possible accurately identified and photographed. It is important to the UN's credibility that we confirm through accurate, believable means when military operations result in death and/or capture of persons suspected of attacking UN personnel or facilities. Conducting a military operation in lightning speed without taking time

---

[209] The presence of civilians in such gatherings (women, for instance cook meals and serve tea) is a common Somali tradition, something that UNOSOM II leaders were aware of in principle – even though they adamantly deny that they knew of the presence of civilians. Furthermore, the discussion which took place within UNOSOM II prior to the raid and which was described by Howe clearly indicated that civilians were actually suspected to be present in the building. Otherwise the discussion regarding the early warning that Howe said took place between himself and Montgomery prior to the raid, would seem illogical (see telephone interviews with Jonathan Howe, 6 January and 21 June 2005). Thus, any subsequent claim by American commanders that they were unaware of any civilian presence seems slightly implausible.

[210] Wright 1993. Both, Howe and Montgomery first denied the existence of this memo (telephone interview with Jonathan Howe, 6 January 2005; telephone interview with Thomas Montgomery, 16 March 2005), but later admitted that they actually received it.

to identify those who were found at a target site undercuts UN credibility when we can not with accuracy state how many persons were killed or injured, who they were and why they were in the facility.

The 'precision combined air and ground attack' was arguably meant to kill the occupants of the building in that there was no warning to depart the building. While the SC has given UNOSOM the authority to 'hold persons accountable for attacks against UNOSOM forces and to take all necessary measures against those responsible', UNOSOM should anticipate that some organizations and member states will characterize a deliberate attack meant to kill the occupants without giving all the building occupants a chance to surrender as nothing less than murder committed in the name of the UN.[211]

The memo raises a number of legal issues. Regarding proportionality, it argues that by employing tactics that significantly decreased possible risks to US service personnel (no advance warning issued), the nature of the attack was disproportionate for it ruled out the possibility for surrender.

Not granting any choice between 'life and death' to the occupants arguably violated Article 57(2) of the First Additional Protocol to the Geneva Conventions, which defines the rule of proportionality as it relates to civilian casualties in the course of military action. It requires that 'effective advance warning shall be given of attacks which may affect the civilian population, unless circumstances do not permit.'[212] In the case of the Abdi House raid, Wright contends, there were clear alternatives to its destruction without advance warning; for example, rather than killing all the occupants, US QRF could have tried to detain them, place them before a court, and thereby allow civilians to remain unharmed. These alternatives, however, the memo argues, were ignored because of concerns for US casualties.[213] It therefore might have been possible to detain the occupants rather than killing them, if other methods of engagement had been chosen and if higher risks to US forces had been accepted.

Yet, IHL is silent on this issue. From a legal point of view, no such obligation exists. Contrary to Wright, American decision-makers within UNOSOM II have insisted that they believed to have attacked a military target where no civilians were present. Thus, the particular issue of proportionality did not arise. From a legal point of view, the issue at stake regarding the Abdi House was not proportionality at all.

Rather, the legal issue – also raised in the secret memo – was over the adequacy of efforts by US forces to obtain accurate intelligence about who exactly occupied the Abdi House in the first place. This refers directly to Article 57(2)(i) of the Additional Protocol I, which required

---

[211] Wright 1993, 1–3 (Lack of clear sentence structure in original).   [212] ICRC 1977.
[213] Wright 1993; Peterson 2001, 120.

US forces to do 'everything feasible to verify' that the target to be attacked was neither civilians nor civilian objects.[214] In the case of the Abdi House raid, this proved to be a controversial issue. Significant evidence exists that the meeting attacked was attended exclusively by civilian clan leaders and elders,[215] an indication that the local (i.e. Somali) intelligence provided was at best incorrect or at worst even corroborated. Furthermore, any Somali meeting – whether it was a war council or a peace meeting – would have always been attended by civilians, something that UNOSOM II decision-makers were aware of.[216] In fact, such awareness was evident in the discussions among US leaders in the lead up to the attacks. This stands in direct contrast to the repeated statements made by Howe and Montgomery who insisted that no civilians were present and that the intelligence gathered had provided clear indications of a war council taking place.[217] The question therefore arises over the adequacy of efforts undertaken to verify who occupied the Abdi House in the first place. Was it sufficient to exclusively rely on local Somali intelligence to fulfil the legal requirement to do 'everything feasible to verify' the target or would this have required additional steps (taken, for instance, by US forces) to confirm that the local intelligence was in fact correct? As was shown in detail in Chapter 1, the problem with Article 57(2)(i) is twofold. On the one hand, there is the imprecision and vagueness of what exactly is meant by the requirement to do 'everything feasible'. This leaves the door sufficiently open for competing legal interpretations to arise. On the other hand, nowhere in the law does it state that 'everything feasible' needs to include any additional risks to be taken by the attacking forces. The laws of war are silent on this issue.

On both of these issues, the controversy over the Abdi House raid revealed the indeterminable and permissive nature of the laws of war. IHL leaves an 'important space of indeterminacy' within which conflicting legal claims can compete for validation.[218] UNOSOM commanders and their own Head of Justice Division were able to produce opposing claims by referring to the very same legal framework. Thus, the Abdi House not only provides a good example of the scope for conflicting judgments over the permissible limits set by the laws of war but also shows the limits of the existing legal framework to provide sufficient protection for non-combatants.

---

[214] ICRC 1977.   [215] Human Rights Watch 1995; Cann 2000, 174; David Keane 2000.
[216] Telephone interview with Jonathan Howe, 6 January 2005; telephone interviews with Thomas Montgomery, 16 March and 24 June 2005.
[217] Telephone interview with Jonathan Howe, 6 January 2005; telephone interviews with Thomas Montgomery, 16 March and 24 June 2005.
[218] Wheeler 2003, 210.

'Operation Michigan' and Walzer's Idea of 'Due Care'

From the point of view of Walzer's idea of 'due care', the legal framework which protects civilians is too permissive. Instead, civilians have the moral right that 'due care' is taken with their lives.[219] In practical terms, this morally obliges commanders to take active steps to reduce the risks to civilians even if it means increasing (within limits) the risks to their own soldiers.[220] This requirement to increase the combat risks of soldiers in order to spare civilian lives is what differentiates the moral idea of 'due care' from existing laws of war. The question therefore arises whether applying these moral standards to the Abdi House raid leads to a different judgement than the one based solely on legal criteria.

From a 'due care' perspective, the two key moral concerns are over the intelligence used and the type of attack deployed. The exclusive reliance on local Somali intelligence for such an important military raid, aimed at decapitating the SNA, is highly problematic, especially since US gunships killed civilians rather than enemy soldiers. The local intelligence therefore was incorrect, potentially it could have even been corroborated. Not double-checking the intelligence through US sources was morally irresponsible, and the use of US intelligence verification could have significantly reduced the chances of error that subsequently killed so many Somali civilians. Whether such a step would have required placing US soldiers under higher risks or whether other means of intelligence gathering could have been used can be debated. But from a moral point of view, taking additional steps would have allowed for better information on who was occupying the building in the first place.

The second moral issue concerns the type of attack chosen. Even if US decision-makers did not believe that the Abdi House was a peace meeting, they nevertheless would have been aware that any military meeting by Aideed always had a significant civilian presence. This was due to Somali culture and also a way for Aideed to try and deter any US attack.[221] Furthermore, the attack took place in a densely populated area, which made collateral damage very likely. These circumstances made the decision to drop the advance warning, to not deploy US ground forces, and to instead fire missiles into a building all the more problematic. It meant that US forces essentially minimised their own risks while maximising those faced by innocent Somali civilians. It was the exact opposite from what the idea of 'due care' would require.

From a 'due care' perspective, increasing the combat risks soldiers face needs to be accepted, provided that this saves innocent lives, and

---

[219] Walzer 1992, 152–159.   [220] Walzer 1992, 152–159.
[221] Gross 2015, 127–150; Bohrer and Osiel 2013, 782.

provided that such tactics neither generate disproportionate amounts of risks to soldiers, nor that they endanger the overall military objectives.[222] Would this have been possible?

Of course, issuing advance warnings and sending US ground forces (or soldiers abseiling from helicopters) into a densely urbanised environment would have been significantly more risky than using helicopter gunships to fire missiles into the building unannounced. To continue operating in the same way as US QRF had done prior to the Abdi House raid was seen as too risky by US commanders, especially because of the early warning.[223] This is not an unreasonable assumption. Yet, instead of dropping the advance warning *and* shifting from ground forces to helicopter missiles, there would have been a third option that was not chosen: US command could have stopped the advance warning and still have deployed ground forces.

On the downside, dropping the advance warning would not have permitted civilians to vacate the area before the attack. On the upside, it would not have alerted enemy forces to slip away or to put up defences, and it would have allowed US forces to retain the important element of surprise. This would have in a way increased the risks to civilians, but also reduced the risks to US ground forces. And while using ground forces instead of missiles would have generated higher risks to US soldiers, the risks would not only have been lower than if the raid had been announced, but it would have also significantly increased the ability of the US military to differentiate between enemy soldiers and civilians.

In other words, instead of just two military options (an announced operation with ground forces or an unannounced operation with missiles), this third option would have fulfilled the requirements of 'due care': US QRF could have accepted higher combat risks and thereby avoided harming Somali civilians, without exposing themselves to disproportionate risks. Would such an increase in combat risks have jeopardised the overall US interests in Somalia or the UNOSOM II mission? Maybe, but not very likely. Rather, it was the very casualty-averse modus operandi chosen by US forces that made the Abdi House raid mark the turning point in the conflict and that ultimately led to the US defeat in Somalia. As the next section will show, the effects of the Abdi House raid were so catastrophic that – from a military necessity point of view – operating in a less casualty-averse way would have saved the mission and ultimately US interests in the Somali conflict.

---

[222] Johnson 2006, 189; Walzer 1992, 156.
[223] Telephone interview with Jonathan Howe, 6 January 2005; telephone interviews with Thomas Montgomery, 16 March and 24 June 2005.

'Operation Michigan' deliberately disregarded these moral conditions of the 'due care' test because it ensured minimal US casualties and maximum risks to Somali civilians. By prioritising concerns for their own forces over the protection of civilians, US QRF operated in ways that – while not violating the laws of war – failed to meet the conditions set by the 'due care' test.

Thus, from this moral point of view, US QRF were required to make a positive effort to avoid harming Somali civilians. Yet, they failed in this obligation. At the moment when Aideed's asymmetric strategy forced US commanders to face the trade-off between increasing the risks to civilians and reducing it for their own forces, they decided to prioritise the safety of their military personnel over the lives of innocent Somalis. US tactical decisions were the exact opposite from the moral requirements set out by the idea of 'due care'.

The 12 July 'Operation Michigan' became the single most important event as the decisions taken, the operation conducted, and consequences proved disastrous for UNOSOM interests in Somalia. Admiral Howe admitted that the new modus operandi, including dropping the short notice policy on 12 July, did not remain an exception but became the new modus operandi: 'After 12 July, there were not any more warnings.'[224] As a result, this choice of tactics seen for the first time on 12 July continued to dominate US operations until 3 October 1993.

The Effects of the Abdi House Raid

The killing of Habr Gidr clan elders served to undercut the growing internal opposition to Aideed and solidified his leadership. With the advocates of reconciliation assassinated, the Abdi House raid rallied the entire clan as well as other Somalis behind Aideed.[225]

Any question of SNA accommodation with the United States was overtaken by the impact of the carefully planned attack which, according to Oakley and Hirsch, 'affected the Somali attitudes as much as the attack on Pakistanis had influenced attitudes with UNOSOM'.[226] The event galvanised the Somalis' hatred towards America.[227] From that day, the entire clan, including those who had been opposed to Aideed's posture against the UN, were basically at war against the United States.[228] US personnel, Oakley recalls,

[224] Telephone interview with Jonathan Howe, 6 January 2005.
[225] Bacevich 2002, 144; Human Rights Watch 1995, 3.
[226] Hirsch and Oakley 1995, 121.   [227] David Keane 2000.
[228] Peterson 2001, 127, 130.

[w]ere only attacked thereafter. Before 12 July, the US would have been attacked only because of association with the UN, but the US was never singled out until after 12 July.[229]

If UNSCR 837 had turned the UN into a player in the Somali power struggle, then 'Operation Michigan' turned most Somalis against the United States in particular.

Considerable evidence suggests that Aideed decided to deliberately target Americans, calculating that the US inability to sustain casualties was the Achilles heel of their involvement in Somalia.[230] SNA spokesman Abdi Abshir Kahiye said that following the air strike 'there was no more United Nations, only Americans. If you could kill Americans, it would start problems in America directly.'[231]

The SNA attacks doubled in the month of July and again in August, killing four US soldiers on 8 August and wounding six more on 22 August.[232] Howe's frustration with the lack of success led him to badger Washington for special operations forces to capture Aideed. After some hesitation, President Clinton finally authorised the deployment of four hundred US Rangers and Delta Force personnel (known as Task Force Ranger [TFR]) on 23 August 1993. TFR's mission was to support UNOSOM in apprehending Aideed and his lieutenants.

Between 30 August and 2 October 1993, these Special Operations Forces conducted six raids that proved increasingly successful (destroying weapons caches, detaining some of Aideed's lieutenants, but failing to apprehend Aideed himself). Based on intelligence which reported that a meeting of high-ranking SNA officials was to take place at a specific location in South Mogadishu, a seventh raid was ordered for 3 October.

The tactical plan called for elements of TFR to assault the target with the intention of capturing SNA officials and, hopefully, Aideed. In the initial stages, the operation was successful: task force soldiers descended onto the objective, isolated the target, and captured twenty-four SNA members. Then, as TFR was removing the detainees by road, rocket-propelled grenades brought down two special operations helicopters and TFR found itself trapped and surrounded by SNA forces and ordinary Somalis.[233]

This, according to Bowden, was the moment Aideed had been waiting for:

After six raids of TFR, Aideed had come up with a strategy to counter the superior forces: he believed that if he could shoot down one of these helicopters he could

---

[229] Interview with Robert Oakley in Washington, DC, 30 November 2004.
[230] Record 2002, 13–14.   [231] Cited in Richburg 1993b.
[232] United Nations 1996, 298.   [233] Bowden 2000.

force the Americans to stay put and trap them in one spot because he knew that they wouldn't abandon the crew of the downed helicopter.[234]

The fact that US QRF and TFR almost exclusively operated with helicopters that could insert and extract teams with speed was not lost on the SNA strategists. They interpreted this as an indication of the US reluctance to place forces on the ground and of the Americans' general unwillingness to die. For them, the helicopters were not only symbols of American arrogance, but also of US casualty-aversion.[235] In strategic terms, the SNA conceived – according to Awaleh, Aideed's chief strategist – the helicopters 'as the US centre of gravity' that permitted for operations in a relatively riskless manner.[236] Aideed later confirmed this strategic reasoning in his meeting with General Toni Zinni. Zinni recalls:

I talked to Aideed at length personally about the day of the battle in Mogadishu and the tactics involved ... He said that they had watched those dangerous men at the airfield and how they operated and he made the determination that the helicopters were the vulnerability, or the center of gravity. And so when they held a meeting he put people on the roofs of the houses around the meeting place with machine guns and rocket launchers and they were to concentrate all their fire on the helicopters. He really believed if he shot a helicopter down, that it would cause the Americans to gather around the helicopters, and that he could fix them and pin them in one area. The reaction force, he said, always came out of the airfield ... 'so we watched where the reaction forces came from [and] we put in an ambush, and it was only activated when we held meetings, so it would engage the reaction force or slow it down or stop it'.[237]

Once the helicopters had crashed, US forces (operating with the twin elements of surprise and momentum) lost the initiative. It marked the turning point in the conflict, the moment when Aideed succeeded in rebalancing the levels of vulnerability between the Americans and his SNA. He knew that with US forces pinned down on the ground the advantage of urban warfare would be on his side.[238]

The entire US mission changed from an assault planned for 19 minutes to a rescue operation that turned into a 27-hour firefight in which Aideed dictated the terms of the conflict. With seemingly the entire city descending on the crash sites and attacking the rescue convoys, US forces were vastly outnumbered and found themselves fighting for their very survival. Abdi Queybdid, Aideed's Defence Minister, reflects on how

---

[234] Interview with Mark Bowden on David Keane.   [235] Bowden 2000, 166.
[236] Awaleh interview on David Keane 2002.
[237] Zinni, Anthony D. interview on Cran, 1998.   [238] Bowden 2000, 166.

Aideed's biggest weapon was to tell his people: 'Just kill one American and they will go away.' It was a belief by every Somali that the Americans were afraid to die.[239]

And as Somalis proved on 3 October, they were willing to die in large numbers in order to kill one American. At least five hundred were killed.[240]

The public outcry and political backlash in the United States, however, was not in relation to the numbers of Somalis killed but the comparatively small number of US casualties. Eighteen soldiers lost their lives, 84 were wounded, pilot Michael Durant was captured, and video footage appeared on US television networks of a dead American being dragged through the streets of Mogadishu.[241]

Under immense pressure for an immediate exit from Somalia,[242] President Clinton announced a major change in his political course, arguing that the administration would undergo one more attempt at political reconciliation involving all Somali factions and that US forces would be withdrawn.[243] By reversing his policy and ending the hunt for Aideed, Clinton conceded that while the United States had won the battle on 3 October, it had effectively lost the war with Aideed.

In contrast to the casualty-averse political class in Washington, Task Force Ranger, Delta, and the QRF had fought courageously and self-lessly. They had heroically prevailed against the odds and in a hostile environment. Following the Ranger creed never to leave a fallen soldier/comrade behind on the battlefield, they had accepted the risks of combat to rescue their fellow warriors.[244] Epitomising their status as 'niche warriors', two Delta Force soldiers had roped themselves down to protect the survivors of one of the downed helicopters. They were aware of the risks they were taking with their own lives and – facing overwhelming opposition – both were killed. Yet, in recognition of their extraordinary valor, they posthumously earned the Congressional Medal of Honor, the highest military decoration given to soldiers.[245] Like most of the eighteen American casualties on that day, their death was incurred during the various rescue attempts rather than as a result of the helicopter crashes.

By following their humanistic warrior creed and accepting the risks of urban warfare, these 'niche warriors' significantly increased the American death toll and thereby indirectly helped create a situation that Clinton conceived as politically untenable.[246] The level of risk accepted by these

---

[239] Interview with Abdi Queybdid on Keane 2002.   [240] Wheeler 2000, 198.
[241] 'Horror Comes Home'.   [242] Gentry 2011, 242; Gartner 2008, 95–101.
[243] Brunk 2008, 301–320.   [244] Cran 1998.   [245] Bowden 2000.
[246] Murray 2007, 557.

'niche warriors' was considered too high by the American people and their commander-in-chief.[247] In other words, Aideed did not exploit the casualty-aversion of American 'niche warriors', but of the US public and political class. It was the politicians in particular who proved to be casualty-averse, not the US SOFs on the ground who were outraged at Clinton for not letting them finish their job.[248]

This became clear when Oakley and Zinni were sent back into Somalia on 9 October in order to prepare for 'Operation Somali Shield'.[249] Admiral Howe – who had not been informed of the change in US foreign policy yet – received Oakley by proclaiming:

'Look, we're winning.' But I [Oakley] said, 'John, do you remember Lebanon? Do you remember Vietnam? Politically, the war is over. It no longer matters what happens here on the battleground.'[250]

General Garrison, as Michael Smith shows, was equally eager to exploit the military advantage gained by his men over the last 27 hours.[251] But it was not just the two US commanders who needed some time to understand that the events on 3–4 October had decided the political outcome of the wrestling match. The other one was General Aideed. His SNA had suffered such tremendous losses that he only realised his political victory halfway through the meeting with Oakley and Zinni.[252]

Despite the effort to restart the political process, however, the US had effectively ended its operations and ambitions in Somalia and literally sat out the time in Mogadishu until the last US forces had withdrawn by the end of March 1994. The day the Americans evacuated, the Marine in charge of the withdrawal reflected on what the taking down of the flag meant. Raised by UNITAF back in December 1992 in memory of the 241 Marines killed in Beirut in 1982, the flag was now placed onto the last American helicopter that was about to take off from the UNOSOM compound. The same Marine had been a young soldier in the chopper evacuation off the roof of the American embassy in Saigon in 1975. Standing on the tarmac in Mogadishu 19 years later, he turned around to a Reuters journalist standing next to him and said: 'The last evacuation was anything but orderly, at least this one's orderly. But it's still Vietnam,

[247] Dauber 2001; Record 2002, 10–12.
[248] 'Clinton's Quick and Dirty Route to a Fiasco in Somalia', *The Guardian*, 17 March 1994; Record 2002, 12; David Keane 2002; Michael Smith 2006, 190.
[249] Though politically unable to remove Howe, the Clinton administration marginalised him with the appointment of Oakley (Cann 2000, 175).
[250] Interview with Robert Oakley in Washington, DC, 30 November 2004.
[251] Michael Smith 2006, 190.
[252] Interview with Robert Oakley in Washington, DC, 15 June 2005.

it's happening all over again.'[253] Only two years after President Bush's claim that the United States had buried the ghosts of Vietnam (and Lebanon), the latter cast their shadows again.

Conclusion

The chapter investigated how the interactive dynamics underpinning the asymmetric conflict in Somalia during UNITAF and UNOSOM II exacerbated the trade-off between US casualty-aversion and civilian protection.

UNITAF was characteristic for its lack of such a Ringkampf. Driven by the ghosts of Vietnam and Lebanon, the guiding assumptions of the United States were humanitarian and therefore geared towards establishing cooperative relations with potential adversaries rather than seeking confrontation. The benign security environment allowed UNITAF to operate in ways that ensured both low US casualties and high levels of respect for the principle of non-combatant immunity. This was not surprising as, from the perspective of military effectiveness, the tension between the US norms of casualty-aversion and civilian protection only manifests itself when militaries pursue ambitious military goals. Under UNITAF, this tension did not arise because UNITAF's mission was limited and US forces did not try to do much to resolve the underlying causes of the conflict.

If the guiding assumption behind UNSCR 794 was geared towards avoiding a potential Ringkampf between UNITAF and General Aideed, then the ambitious Resolution 814 set a different tone. Although it could be argued that the changed mandate was responsible for bringing UNOSOM II into an open Ringkampf with Aideed, the chapter has argued that a military confrontation was not a foregone conclusion. The confrontation was rather the outcome of US and UN policy decisions and American military operations on the ground.

Following the attacks on 5 June 1993, relations between UNOSOM II and Aideed spiralled out of control and resulted in an all-out war. Aware of US sensitivities, Aideed employed asymmetric tactics and strategies which presented UNOSOM II commanders with the dilemma that a choice had to be made between US casualty-aversion and civilian protection. Starting with the 12 July Abdi House raid, this led the US military to adopt operating procedures that prioritised US casualty-aversion over Somali civilian protection. Therefore, American forces

---

[253] Telephone interview with Aidan Hartley, 12 February 2005.

ended up employing tactics and strategies that reduced US risks while simultaneously increasing the risks to Somali civilians.

This finding has legal, moral, and strategic implications. From a legal standpoint, even though the Abdi House raid (the key turning in the conflict with regards to the US mode of combat and Somali attitudes) and subsequent US operations did not violate IHL, the fact that large number of Somali civilians could be killed in the process demonstrates the limits of the existing legal framework to provide sufficient levels of protection for non-combatants.

This legal permissiveness, however, has not eliminated moral judgments associated with the use of force. From the perspective of Walzer's idea of 'due care', the question arises whether a higher standard of civilian protection could have been achieved by accepting greater risks to US military personnel. The chapter showed that marginal increases in the levels of risk to US soldiers with some certainty would have increased civilian protection. Yet no such positive steps were taken. Instead, US QRF operated in a casualty-averse manner that maximised rather than minimised the risks faced by non-combatants. US operations during UNOSOM II therefore failed to meet the moral conditions set out by the idea of 'due care'. An acceptance of higher risks to US soldiers instead could have saved civilian lives.

This failure also had significant impact on the strategic outcome of the conflict – the increasingly more ferocious nature of US operations led to such horrendous levels of civilian casualties that it first alienated Aideed's sub-clan and eventually most Somalis. This culminated in the infamous 'Battle of Mogadishu' which brought American involvement in Somalia to an end. In other words, disregard for the moral restrictions set by the idea of 'due care' created repercussions for US strategic objectives.

The empirical findings on Somalia demonstrate the need to take the role of the adversary and the dynamic interaction of asymmetric warfare into account. It was Aideed's asymmetric strategy that exacerbated the trade-off within US warfare between casualty-aversion and civilian protection, thereby forcing the Americans to make a choice between these two norms. This confirms the shortcoming of existing approaches that investigate the trade-off between US casualty-aversion and civilian protection without recognition of the important fact that the 'enemy has a vote, too.'

More generally, the impact of Somalia on the US use of force has commonly been referred to as the 'Somalia syndrome', the 'Mogadishu effect', or the reluctance 'to cross the Mogadishu line'. These terms all conceive the impacts of Somalia as reinforcing the Vietnam and Lebanon syndromes and therefore the Weinberger-Powell doctrine. Following

Somalia, a general reluctance emerged in the White House and the US military to place US soldiers in harm's way in places where either no perceived vital US national security interests were at stake or the environment did not play to American technological strengths.

This was reflected in the very casualty-averse way the United States engaged in subsequent conflicts throughout the 1990s.[254] Here, the axiom of casualty-aversion reinforced by the Somalia experience, guided policy-makers in their employment of military power. In the first specific event that followed the crossing of the Mogadishu line, the USS Harlan County (with two hundred US troops on board) was turned away from the dock in Port-au-Prince (Haiti) by an angry mob.[255] This was followed by reluctance to send US ground troops to Bosnia and Kosovo, and by not giving any serious consideration to sending US troops into Rwanda.[256] And whenever the United States intervened in a conflict, it emphasised the use of cruise missiles and aircraft armed with precision guided missiles rather than inserting ground troops as a means to reduce the likelihood of US casualties to zero.

Yet, the Ringkampf in Somalia not only affected US warfare but also the strategic thinking of American adversaries. The general message picked up by the latter was that if the Americans take a hit, they run. Subsequent half-hearted and technology-driven American interventions seemed to confirm that the US public lacked heroism and the will to sacrifice.

Anyone that has watched the United States in its approach to war, particularly over the last ten years, has learned that if you can defeat the technology – if you can defeat the American will – then you have a chance.[257]

Following the powerful images of the mighty US military power rolling over Iraq two years earlier, the images of Mogadishu showed disadvantaged adversaries a way to defeat such military might.

Upon the arrival of UNITAF in December 1992, Aideed had claimed that he had learnt the lessons of Vietnam and Lebanon. After 3 October 1993, it was Osama Bin Laden, who updated Aideed's line by claiming that he had not only learnt the lessons of Vietnam and Lebanon, but also of Somalia. Expressing his 'surprise at the collapse of American morale', Bin Laden interpreted the firefight in Mogadishu as

---

[254] Cornish 2003, 121; Western and Goldstein 2011, 48–59.
[255] Shawcross 2001, 102–103.
[256] Moskos 1996, 136–137; Melvern 2000; Shawcross 2001, 125–168; Wheeler 2000, 208–241; Brunk 2008, 301–320.
[257] Allard on Cran, 1998.

proof that 'the Americans are a paper tiger.'[258] Interviewed by John Miller in 1998, he said that

We have seen in the last decade the decline of the American government and the weakness of the American soldier who is ready to wage cold wars and unprepared to fight long wars. This was proven in Beirut when the Marines fled after two explosions. It also proves that they can run in less than twenty-four hours, and this was repeated in Somalia ... [There] they forgot about being the world leader and the leader of the new world order. [They] left, dragging their corpses and their defeat.[259]

---

[258] Cited in Record 2002, 14.   [259] Cited in Bernard Lewis 2001, 62–63.

5   The US War in Afghanistan

The Americans must know that the storm of airplanes will not stop, God willing, and there are thousands of young people who are as keen about death as Americans are about life.

Suleiman Abu Gaith, spokesperson of Bin Laden

We have entered a new type of war. It's a war against people who hate freedom.

George W. Bush

Vietnam and Mogadishu still cast their shadows on the whole issue of ground deployments abroad.

Paul Kennedy

Introduction

The chapter investigates the relationship between US casualty-aversion and civilian protection in the case of the US warfare in Afghanistan (October 2001–March 2002).[1] It analyses the interaction between the American military and Taliban/al-Qaeda forces and the extent to which this conflict posed specific legal and moral challenges to the US ability to wage war in a casualty-averse and humane manner.

The examination is guided by the question of whether the US military conducted Operation Enduring Freedom (OEF) in ways that secured the values of both American casualty-aversion and Afghan civilian protection. Or did the asymmetric strategies of al-Qaeda and the Taleban force the American military to adopt operating procedures that stressed force protection over the protection of civilians in the target state? And if so, what were the legal, moral, and strategic consequences?

The chapter first examines the approach taken by American political and military decision-makers towards casualty-aversion in the post–9/11 world. In particular, it investigates the extent to which such attitudes

---

[1] After this date, US military operations in Afghanistan came to an end until after the Iraq war in 2003.

towards American casualties have differed from those present during United Task Force (UNITAF) and the United Nations Mission in Somalia (UNOSOM II). This is followed by an examination of US concerns for the safeguarding of non-combatants during OEF. The chapter then focuses on the asymmetric strategies implemented by the Taliban and al-Qaeda in response to the US-led intervention. Here, particular emphasis is placed on how enemy perceptions of American casualty-aversion and the need for civilian protection shaped the military response of Mullah Omar and Osama Bin Laden.

The chapter then discusses the possible inequalities of risk between US military personnel and Afghan civilians in OEF. It critically assesses US military operations in order to identify the reasons for and circumstances under which collateral damage occurred. It examines these reasons and circumstances in the context of the asymmetric strategies employed by the Taliban and al-Qaeda to see how far they exacerbated the tension between American concerns for casualties among its own forces and among Afghan non-combatants. Finally, the chapter analyses the extent to which US operations complied with International Humanitarian Law (IHL), i.e. the legal restraints on the use of force. Drawing on Walzer's idea of 'due care',[2] it then asks whether higher levels of civilian protection could have been achieved by marginally increasing the risks to US military personnel.

US Casualty-Aversion after 9/11

The reasons for US casualty-aversion during the interventions in Somalia, Bosnia, and Kosovo, it is often argued, were located in the humanitarian nature of US involvement.[3] Humanitarian interventions were conflicts where no perceived vital US national interests were at stake.[4] Thus, the assumptions among American military and political decision-makers were that because the US public would not tolerate large numbers of military casualties, the American military had to intervene in ways that would ensure low risks to US forces.[5]

By contrast, the US intervention in Afghanistan in response to 9/11 was not born out of humanitarianism (though humanitarian rationales were in play) but out of a perceived threat to US survival.[6] Al-Qaeda

---

[2] Walzer 1992, 156.   [3] Mueller 1996, 31; Bacevich 2002, 143.
[4] Walzer 2004, 100–101.
[5] Hirsch and Oakley 1995, 41–44; Dauber 2002, 66–90; McCrisken 2003, 189.
[6] Elshtain 2003, 1–45; *The 9/11 Commission Report: Final Report of the National Commission on Terrorist Attacks upon the United States* (New York: W. W. Norton & Company, 2004), p. xvi; Zambernardi 2010, 25.

was regarded (at least) by the US government at the time as a genuinely existential threat to the United States and the American way of life.[7] Vice President Richard Cheney emphasised this point five days after 9/11 when he pointed to the magnitude of the threat posed by the al-Qaeda network:

The world increasingly will understand what we have here are a group of barbarians, that they threaten all of us, that the U.S. is the target at the moment, but one of the things to remember is if you look at the roster of countries who lost people in the bombing in New York, over 40 countries have had someone killed or have significant numbers missing ... So it's an attack not just upon the United States but upon, you know, civilized society.[8]

In his address to a Joint Session of Congress on 20 September 2001, US President George W. Bush stated that

On September the 11th, enemies of freedom committed an act of war against our country on a single day – and night fell on a different world, a world where freedom itself is under attack ... This is not, however, just America's fight. And what is at stake is not just America's freedom. This is the world's fight. This is civilization's fight. This is the fight of all who believe in progress and pluralism, tolerance and freedom.[9]

In subsequent media appearances, key members of the US government such as Vice President Cheney, Secretary of Defense Donald H. Rumsfeld, Secretary of State Colin Powell, Attorney General John Ashcroft, as well as leading Democrats (the attacks killed partisan politics and resulted in a temporary surge in national unity)[10] conveyed a clear understanding that the United States and the world were at war with an existential threat.[11] According to their statements, America, the self-proclaimed 'city upon a hill', was forced (yet again) into a struggle between good and evil that endangered the very survival of civilisation, liberty, and democracy. By framing the 9/11 attacks in this context, the

---

[7] Bacevich 2005, 200–201; Walzer 2004, 33–50; Wheeler 2002, 215.

[8] www.whitehouse.gov/vicepresident/news-speeches/speeches/vp20010916.html, accessed on 29 July 2006.

[9] www.whitehouse.gov/news/releases/2001/09/20010920-8.html, accessed on 2 July 2005.

[10] 'Special Report September 11th 2001: America's Longest War', *The ECONOMIST*, 2 September 2006, p. 20.

[11] www.whitehouse.gov/news/releases/2001/09/20010911-10.html; www.state.gov/s/p/re m/5505.htm; www.whitehouse.gov/news/releases/2001/09/20010912-8.html; www .whitehouse.gov/news/releases/2001/10/20011007-8.html; www.defenselink.mil/spee ches/2001/s20010927-secdef.html; www.whitehouse.gov/vicepresident/news-speeches /speeches/vp20010916.html; http://usinfo.state.gov/is/international_security/terrorism/ sept_11/sept_11_archive/Powell_A_Terrible_Terrible_Tragedy_Has_Befallen_My_Nation .html, all accessed on 1 July 2005.

Bush Administration appealed to Americans' long-held sense of mission and duty that was bestowed upon them by history.[12]

Adding to the perception that the United States was confronting an existential threat was the nature of the adversary. Al-Qaeda's tactical success in transforming the enemy's civilian infrastructure into an operational platform for its attacks alerted American decision-makers.[13] Speaking at West Point, President Bush emphasised that

> In defending the peace, we face a threat with no precedent. Enemies in the past needed armies and great industrial capabilities to endanger the American people and our nation. The attack of 9/11 required a few hundred thousand dollars in the hands of a few dozen evil and deluded men.[14]

Cheney's analysis also reveals a high degree of alertness about the challenge posed by the asymmetric nature of the adversary. In an interview on 16 September 2001, the Vice President asserted:

> In terms of the sophistication of [the 9/11 attacks], it's interesting to look at, because clearly what happened is you got some people committed to die in the course of the operation, you got them visas, you got them entered into the United States. They came here. Some of them enrolled in our commercial aviation schools and learned to fly, courtesy of our own capabilities here in the United States. Then what they needed in order to execute was some degree of coordination, obviously, in terms of timing. But they needed knives, cardboard cutters, razor blades, whatever it was, and an airline ticket. And that's it. They then were able to take over the aircraft and use our own, you know, heavily loaded with fuel large aircraft to take over and use it.[15]

Al-Qaeda exposed the vulnerability of American civil society to an attack by an enemy which possessed strategic creativity and a willingness to sacrifice.[16] Instead of using twenty-first century military technology, the terrorist network employed primitive weapons to hijack civilian airliners and to transform the latter into rockets and their jet fuel into explosives. Thereby, as Herfried Münkler points out, Mohammad Atta and his accomplices

---

[12] Tony Smith 1995; Coker 1989.

[13] Münkler 2003, 10; John Gray 2003, 81, 84; www.whitehouse.gov/news/releases/2003/02/20030213-3.html, accessed on 12 October 2006.

[14] www.whitehouse.gov/news/releases/2002/06/20020601-3.html, accessed on 2 July 2005.

[15] www.whitehouse.gov/vicepresident/news-speeches/speeches/vp20010916.html, accessed on 29 July 2006.

[16] For example, Mohammed Atta, the planner of the 9/11 attacks, had studied at the Technical University of Hamburg-Harburg for several years. The topic of his thesis was 'The careful preservation of a multi-confessional quarter in the traditionally tolerant Syrian city of Aleppo'. See Reuter 2002, 15.

[a]ttacked the USA by using its own speed – from the concentration and intensity of air transport to a media system which broadcast the catastrophe of 11 September 2001 to the whole world in real time – as a weapon against it.[17]

This ability to turn the enemy's infrastructure into a platform within which attacks can be prepared *and* executed constituted a significant evolution of asymmetric warfare.[18] As Chapter 3 has shown, the strength of classical asymmetric strategies, such as guerrilla warfare, lay in the deceleration of violence, the creative use of space, and the support by the indigenous population against an outside invader.[19] Without the local support, the guerrilla would be unable to move freely as fish in the sea and instead would fall prey to the adversary. For a long time, this precondition limited the applicability of classical asymmetric warfare to the defensive. Yet, the 9/11 attacks showed how al-Qaeda's strategic creativity found a way of overcoming these constraints. It revealed how the American civilian infrastructure could serve as the functional equivalent of the sea in which its sleeper cells could swim.[20] The will to sacrifice, courage, and the exploitation of the enemy's civilian infrastructure therefore allowed al-Qaeda to transform conventional asymmetric warfare from a defensive into an offensive strategy. And while conventional asymmetric warfare tended to direct violence against the weak points of the enemy's military capabilities, the new form of asymmetric violence deliberately bypassed the enemy's military capabilities and aimed directly at civilian morale and life.

Moreover, al-Qaeda used suicide attacks as a means to intensify the psychological impact of their attacks dramatically. Operatives who turn their own bodies into weapons link the successful use of force to their own certain death. Attacks of the kind executed on 9/11 are only possible by renouncing any means of escape. In other words, suicide bombers compensate for their military inferiority by giving up any chance of survival.[21]

Given the nature of the enemy and the national security interests at stake, we would therefore expect US political and military decision-makers to have adopted a less casualty-averse strategy in Afghanistan than in Somalia, Bosnia, or Kosovo. In fact, a greater public willingness to spill American blood in the wake of the 9/11 atrocities was expected by several commentators.[22] Michael Barone, for example, predicted that

---

[17] Münkler 2003, 10.   [18] Freedman 2002a, 37–47; John Gray 2003, 81, 84.
[19] T. E. Lawrence 1962; Mao Zedong 1992; Giap 1977.   [20] Crawford 2003, 12.
[21] Reuter 2002.
[22] Krauthammer 2002; 'After September 11: A Conversation', *The National Interest*, 65/S, Special Issue (Thanksgiving 2001).

Americans are more willing to take casualties than almost anybody in our media thinks. Many of the constraints that people not only in the Clinton Administration but in the first and second Bush Administrations felt that they were operating under in foreign policy and in military policy probably never applied as much as they thought. But clearly they don't now. Americans will have some considerable staying power in this war against terrorism.[23]

Writing in *The Washington Post*, Charles Krauthammer went even further by claiming that

America is allergic to casualties – but only in wars that do not matter. Our history over the last century suggests a general theory of casualties: America's capacity to sustain casualties is near infinite, as long as the wars are wars of necessity.[24]

Put differently, 9/11 was conceived as ending the period of humanitarian interventions in which the absence of any major national interests had effectively made casualty-aversion the watchword of American military operations.[25] After 9/11, it would seem easier to justify to the American people that US soldiers could be placed in harm's way considering the threat al-Qaeda posed and the vital interests at stake.

Contrary to this logical assumption, however, the reality of American operations in Afghanistan in 2001 and 2002 suggested something very different. US combat operations bore a strong resemblance to the casualty-averse manner in which 'Operation Deliberate Force' and 'Operation Allied Force' had been waged.[26] US decision-makers deliberately chose a 'light footprint', i.e. an overall strategy that placed surprisingly few US military personnel in harm's way.[27] Instead, overwhelming American airpower provided fire support for local indigenous anti-Taliban forces whose operations were eventually coordinated by a handful of American Special Operations Forces (SOF) on the ground.[28] In fact, by the time of the fall of the Taliban regime in late November 2001 – nearly two months into the conflict – the US had placed no more than 316 SOF and 110 CIA operators on the ground.[29] By the end of June 2002, the numbers of ground forces had grown to 7,500; another 47,500 troops remained under Central

---

[23] Cited in 'After September 11: A Conversation', p. 116.   [24] Krauthammer 2002.
[25] Zambernardi 2010, 25–26.   [26] Conetta 2002a; Record 2002, 17.
[27] Ignatieff 2003a, 77–92; Shaw 2005, 27–28.
[28] Stephen Biddle 2002; McInnes 2003, 165–184.
[29] Woodward 2002, 25. In late November, two Marine Corps units of more than one thousand personnel had arrived in the country and had set up Camp Rhino. Yet, in contrast with SOF and CIA operatives, the Marines did not serve as active fighting units. Instead, they were primarily used to interdict some road traffic and to carry out supply missions for SOF. See O'Hanlon 2002, 64.

Command (CENTCOM) elsewhere.[30] But between October 2001 and March 2002 (the date after which major US operations in Afghanistan ceased until 2003),[31] the United States had placed significantly fewer US boots on the ground in the whole of Afghanistan to bring about regime change and to hunt down Osama Bin Laden and Mullah Omar than it had placed into the Somali capital of Mogadishu alone during the hunt for Mohamed Farah Aideed.[32] By the end of Operation Enduring Freedom following Operation Anaconda in March 2002, no more than forty US casualties had occurred, less than half of which were combat related.[33] In the same period, more humanitarian relief workers and journalists were killed than US military and intelligence personnel.[34]

This raises the question whether the US military adopted a different approach to casualties in Afghanistan than, for example, in Somalia, given that it was fighting a war in self-defence. Or, was the overall American strategy born out of a similar casualty-aversion that had shaped America's humanitarian interventions in the 1990s?

The material and sources collected through the close examination of the planning and decision-making period between 11 September and the beginning of OEF on 7 October 2001 reveals a concern with casualties that was similar to the one that had gripped American decision-makers in the 1990s.[35] Casualty-aversion was an ever-present consideration in the minds of those involved in the decision-making process. Other factors (such as geography, timing, logistics, and the deterrent effects of past invasions of Afghanistan) were also important,[36] but these had the general effect of confirming the already casualty-averse inclinations of key decision-makers.[37]

As a consequence the number of US ground troops was extremely limited and the key military emphasis was placed on the use of air

---

[30] Cordesman 2002, 9.
[31] Paul Rogers, 'The "War on Terror": Current Status and Possible Development', available at www.oxfordresearchgroup.org.uk, accessed on 13 September 2006.
[32] Telephone interview with Aidan Hartley, 12 February 2005; see also Hersh 2005, 146–147.
[33] Cordesman 2002; O'Hanlon 2002, 66.
[34] Peter Falk, 'Appraising the War against Afghanistan', available at www.sscr.org/sept11/essays/falk_text_only.htm, accessed on 15 November 2004.
[35] Record 2002, 11.
[36] Freedman 2002a, 43; Naylor 2005, 24–25; Woodward 2002, 115, 193; DeLong 2004, 23; Cordesman 2002, 19.
[37] Naylor 2005; Woodward 2002, 25; interview with Jeffrey Starr in Washington, DC, 15 June 2005; telephone interview with David Gray, 28 February 2005; interview with Peter Bergen in Washington, DC, 4 December 2004; interview with Bruce Pirnie in Washington, DC, 21 December 2004; interview with Carl Conetta in Washington, DC, 4 December 2004.

power.[38] Using new information and precision technologies in combination with local indigenous allies in the Northern Alliance/United Front allowed the US military to destroy its opponents at a distance without exposing more than a handful of US soldiers to risky close combat.[39] According to Michael Scheuer, the former head of the CIA's Bin Laden unit,

The Tenet Plan [which mapped out the nature of American operations] was used because it made sense to a US mindset – using the power of money and few Americans while having foreigners die for us; and not because it had drawn on the US government's vast repository of Afghan knowledge.[40]

General Michael DeLong, Deputy to General Tommy Franks at CENTCOM, candidly put it,

[t]he money offered to the Northern Alliance commanders] was indeed a fortune. But from our perspective, it was still less than it would have cost to put even one U.S. battalion on the ground. In that sense, it was a bargain – and more importantly, it would help keep thousands of U.S. soldiers out of harm's way.[41]

Although DeLong's statement has yet remained the bluntest admission of the role of casualty-aversion from a key US official, several commentators have confirmed the importance of this consideration for top level decision-makers.[42] For example, Carl Conetta, the Director of the 'Project on Defense Alternatives', concluded that

[t]he administration was deterred from making more use of US troops by the prospect of increased US casualties that this would entail. America's acute post-cold war sensitivity to combat casualties may still prevail, 11 September notwithstanding.[43]

In similar vein, Bob Woodward's *Bush at War* uncovers the doubts among members of the National Security Council about the readiness of the American people to tolerate casualties.[44] Bush's public speeches, filled with heroic rhetoric about sacrifice and glory, concealed the administration's uncertainty about the extent to which the public would tolerate these sacrifices despite 9/11.[45] Emphasising the factor of casualty-aversion, Andrew Bacevich argued that

---

[38] McInnes 2003, 165–184; Ignatieff 2003a, 112; Record 2002, 11; Shaw 2005, 80–81; Conetta 2002a.

[39] Hurka 2005, 50; Anonymous [Michael Scheuer] 2004, 35; Coker 2003, 22–29.

[40] Anonymous [Michael Scheuer] 2004, 29, 35.   [41] DeLong 2004, 25.

[42] Stephen Biddle 2002; O'Hanlon 2002; Shaw 2002; Elshtain 2003.

[43] Conetta 2002b.   [44] Woodward 2002.

[45] Woodward 2002; see also Smucker 2004; Naylor 2005, 16.

[e]ven at the time of Afghanistan the conventional wisdom [among decision-makers] was that the American people were casualty-averse. So the concern that Americans even after 9/11 would not tolerate casualties meshed nicely with the conviction on the part of senior Pentagon people that this new high tech airpower intense war was more effective anyway.[46]

In other words, the available sources reveal the extent to which the Bush administration approached OEF in a state of high uncertainty about how far the American people would accept casualties even in a post–9/11 world.[47]

Jeffrey Record writes that such an air-power–dominant way of waging war, in which ground forces were mainly functioning as liaison to and target spotters for indigenous allies,[48]

[was] an inherently attractive way of war, especially for a society that value[d] the individual as highly as America [did]. It also permit[ted] a casualty-phobic political and military leadership to wage war effectively – i.e., to achieve decisive strategic effects without paying the blood price traditionally associated with attainment of those effects.[49]

These casualty-averse attitudes among key American decision-makers were at odds with the attitudes towards such risks prevailing among US SOF. Contrary to the post-Vietnam political and military leadership, these 'niche warriors' were prepared to accept extraordinary risks because war for them has retained its humanistic dimension.[50] Considering the central role played by 'niche warriors' in OEF, their exceptional level of humanism relative to the rest of the US military generated tensions with the post-heroic leadership in Washington, DC.

During early years of the Afghanistan war, the political and military quest for minimum casualties overrode the warriorhood of these forces. SOF in cooperation with CIA operatives were liaising with proxies and coordinating the indigenous ground war element with US aerial bombardment. Yet, even though their role was celebrated as truly unconventional – merging a thirteenth-century army on horseback with twenty-first-century net-centric warfare[51] – the US military in reality waged a rather conventional campaign against al-Qaeda and the Taliban.[52] The conventional approach, which was dictated by the casualty-averse attitudes of the American leadership failed to deploy SOF most

[46] Telephone interview with Andrew Bacevich, 26 January 2005.
[47] Zambernardi 2010, 25–26; Boettcher and Cobb 2006, 835; Interview with Carl Conetta in Washington, DC, 4 December 2004; Michael Smith 2006, 214; Der Derian 2001; Stephen Biddle, 2002, 56.
[48] Michael Smith 2006, 219.   [49] Record 2002, 19–20.
[50] Adams 1998, 25; Coker 2002b, 80–83; McRaven 2004, 61–78.
[51] Freedman 2002a, 43; DeLong 2004, 47.   [52] Stephen Biddle 2002.

effectively.[53] With few exceptions (the most prominent ones were the raids on an airbase southwest of Kandahar on 20 October 2001, on Mullah Omar's housing compound outside Kandahar the next day, and during 'Operation Anaconda' in March 2002), the primary task of US 'Niche Warriors' was not necessarily to engage their adversary actively but rather serve as liaison and coordinator between the local allies and US aircrews.[54] Most critically, they were prevented from fully participating in the high-risk cave searches around Tora Bora, a decision exposing the full tension between 'Niche Warriors' lust for heroic battle and a casualty-phobic leadership.[55]

In December 2001, the Secretary of Defense commissioned a secret report on the way SOF have been used in the past and should be used in the War on Terror. Written by Professor Richard Schultz, the report concluded that risk-aversion among senior military commanders had prevented SOF from being deployed effectively.[56] The military leadership, Schultz emphasised, had effectively become 'Somalia-ized'[57]:

The firefight in Mogadishu had a profound impact on the willingness of the US to use SOF on offensive counter-terrorist missions for the rest of the decade. It reinforced an already jaded view. For the mainstream military, the lesson of Somalia was that here was yet another example of those reckless SOF units attempting operations that end up in disaster.[58]

Anxious about the high-risk manner in which 'Niche Warriors' tend to operate, the Joint Chiefs tended to insist on fail-safe requirements which – given the nature of unconventional warfare – were difficult to meet. These attitudes prevented 'Niche Warriors' from being deployed effectively. Put differently, political and military concerns for zero tolerance prevented US SOF from fighting in a less casualty-averse manner. 'Niche Warriors' in that sense were policed by post-heroic standards that were diametrically opposed to their humanism.

Reflecting on the casualty-averse attitudes taken by American decision-makers, Michael O'Hanlon opined that

[i]t is supremely ironic that a tough-on-defense Republican administration fighting for vital national security interests appeared almost as reluctant to risk American lives in combat as the Clinton administration has been in humanitarian missions.[59]

---

[53] Hersh 2001b; Michael Smith 2006, 205–237.
[54] Coker 2003, 58; Record 2002, 19–20; Robin Moore 2004.   [55] O'Hanlon 2002, 68.
[56] Michael Smith 2006, 232–234.   [57] Michael Smith 2006, 233.
[58] Cited in Michael Smith 2006, 233.   [59] O'Hanlon 2002, 68.

In humanitarian interventions, casualty-aversion had been the overriding factor in US considerations because of the humanitarian nature of the intervention. After 9/11, when the United States found itself fighting a perceived war of survival (i.e. a war fought in self-defence with vital interests at stake), American decision-makers nevertheless adopted a similar casualty-averse approach.[60] The obsession with avoiding military casualties that had characterised US warfare since Vietnam and Lebanon and that was strengthened during the 1990s therefore continued during the first leg of the War on Terror.[61]

What, then, were the implications of this for civilian protection in OEF? Did the American military, in making war more riskless for itself, make it less humane for Afghan non-combatants? This question is important as it asks how the United States balanced its military responsibility to defeat al-Qaeda and the Taliban at low costs to its own military personnel with its legal and moral responsibilities to minimise the harm suffered by non-combatants. To answer this question, the next section examines the attitudes of US decision-makers towards Afghan civilian protection during OEF, the extent to which US military practices complied with the laws of war, and – beyond this – the extent to which they met the moral requirement of 'due care'.

US Attitudes towards Civilian Protection

In the weeks following the terrorist attacks on September 11, 2001, three principal positions emerged among American political elites and decision-makers with regard to the levels of protection that should be afforded to Afghan civilians.

First, there were those who insisted that neither legal nor moral principles should restrain US military practice; especially that the United States should not be restrained out of concern for civilian casualties in Afghanistan. This attitude resulted from the deeply felt anger and sense of vulnerability caused by 9/11. In the immediate aftermath of the terrorist attacks, the most prominent supporter of this moral position was Senator John McCain who stated that

Issues such as Ramadan or civilian casualties, however regrettable and however tragic ... have to be secondary to the primary goals of eliminating the enemy.[62]

Senator McCain, who later retracted this moral position, echoed a realist perspective which holds that no restraint should be placed on the conduct

---

[60] Bellamy 2006, 180–198; Record 2002, 11.   [61] Kennedy 2001, 64.
[62] Buettner 2001, 14; Crawford 2003, 12.

of war when the survival of the state is at stake.[63] He essentially argued that the terrorist attacks had placed America into such a dire situation (reminiscent of Michael Walzer's idea of 'supreme emergency')[64] that any means could be employed without concern for civilian protection.[65] Under such conditions, violence did not have to be discriminate, nor proportionate to the harm inflicted, nor would it need to take into consideration the principle of double effect.[66] The adaptation of a McCainian moral position would have resulted in the overriding of the principle of non-combatant immunity and therefore would have constituted a fundamental break with the gradual humanising trend that has characterised US warfare since the end of World War II. As was shown in Chapter 1, this process towards strengthening American compliance with the laws of war was slow to develop and only accelerated significantly after the Vietnam War. By the time of the 1991 Persian Gulf War, however, adherence to the principle of non-combatant immunity had become one of the central features of contemporary American warfare.[67]

Other American leaders such as Donald H. Rumsfeld argued that since the al-Qaeda network (and the Taliban regime that harboured it) started the war, they were necessarily responsible for all the death and destruction that ensued as a consequence.[68] Such a view implied that the particular circumstances involved in the reason for war (*jus ad bellum*) might override certain considerations of restraint in war (*jus in bello*). Furthermore, it echoed General William T. Sherman's claim that 'war is hell'.[69] This moral position, first expressed at the height of the American Civil War, holds that because the Union forces did not start the war, the ultimate responsibility for all the harm inflicted on innocent civilians rested with the Confederacy.[70] According to Sherman, 'those who brought war into our country deserve all the curses and maledictions a people can pour.'[71] In contrast, Union forces – waging a defensive war – bore no responsibility for the non-combatant deaths it inflicted. By putting forward this rationale, Sherman famously tried to justify the Union's strategy of terror against the enemy's infrastructure and civilian population (in particular during his March to the Sea and the burning of Atlanta in September 1864).[72]

There was a strong echo of Sherman's 'war is hell' rationale in a statement Donald Rumsfeld made in early December 2001. Discussing Afghan civilian casualties that were caused by the American bombing

---

[63] Forde 1992, 62–84.   [64] Walzer 1992, 259.   [65] Crawford 2003, 12.
[66] Walzer 1992, 251–268.
[67] Coker 2001, 1–45; Ignatieff 2000c, 197–201; Shaw 2005, 4–28; Farrell 2005, 177–179.
[68] Bellamy 2006, 180.   [69] Walzer 1992, 32.
[70] Walzer 1992, 32; Chris H Gray 1997, 116–118; Weigley 1973, 149–152.
[71] Sherman cited in Walzer 1992, 32.   [72] Weigley 1973, 128–152.

campaign, the Secretary of Defense disavowed any US responsibility for non-combatant deaths:

We did not start this war. So understand, responsibility for every single casualty in this war, whether they are innocent Afghans or innocent Americans, rests at the feet of al-Qaeda and the Taliban.[73]

In this situation Secretary Rumsfeld accepted Sherman's argument in an attempt to transfer responsibility for any civilian casualties caused by the US military onto al-Qaeda and the Taliban on the ground that they initiated the war.[74] Adapting a 'war is hell' argument would have been extremely problematic as neither IHL nor Just War theory absolves the defending party from its responsibility for the harm it inflicts on civilians.[75] In other words, irrespective of the Taliban's and al-Qaeda's guilt in starting the war by launching terrorist attacks on America, the US military was still legally obliged to comply with the laws of war. This attempt to pin responsibility for civilian suffering in OEF on al-Qaeda and the Taliban, however, was the exception rather than the rule among US officials (including Donald Rumsfeld, who only appears to have employed it on this one occasion).[76]

By contrast, the vast majority of key American decision-makers from the outset articulated a clear distinction between combatants and non-combatants and emphasised high levels of respect for the principle of non-combatant immunity.[77] For instance, in an ABC interview on 25 October 2001, Rumsfeld stated that

I know for a fact that we are just being enormously careful. We are doing every-thing humanly possible to try to avoid collateral damage. We are focusing every-thing on military targets.[78]

He also added that

I can't imagine there's been a conflict in history where there has been less collateral damage, less unintended consequences.[79]

---

[73] Available at www.defenselink.mil/transcripts/2001/t12042001_t1204sd.html, accessed on 1 December 2004.
[74] Bellamy 2005, 277; Crawford 2003, 10; Wheeler 2002, 217.
[75] Johnson 1984, 22; Bellamy 2005, 277; Walzer 1992, 32–33; Skerker 2004, 32–35.
[76] Crawford 2003, 12.
[77] Renz and Scheipers 2012, 34; Crawford 2003, 13–14; Lane 2001; see also 'Secretary of Defense Donald Rumsfeld updates the world on the war against terrorism', NewsHour with Jim Lehrer Transcript, 7 November 2001, available at www.pbs.org/newshour/bb/military/july-dec01/rumsfeld2_11–7.html, accessed on 19 April 2006.
[78] Rumsfeld in ABC Interview, 25 October 2001. Available at www.defenselink.mil/tran scripts/2001/t10252001_t1024usa.html, accessed on 1 December 2004. See also Elshtain 2003, 67.
[79] Cited in William Arkin 2002.

Before the beginning of OEF, President Bush and General Tommy Franks, the Commander-in-Chief at CENTCOM, had already emphasised that the military operation was not directed against the Afghan people, but against the regime and the terrorists it harboured.[80] Their statements were framed fully in the language of the Geneva Conventions, claiming that discrimination and proportionality were of utmost importance and that 'great care' was being taken.[81] For example, General Richard Myers, the Chairman of the Joint Chiefs of Staff, asserted that

[t]he last thing we want are civilian casualties. So we plan every military target with great care. We try to match the weapon to the target and the goal is, one, to destroy the target, and two, to prevent any [of] what we call 'collateral damage' or damage to civilian structures or the civilian population.[82]

The official rhetoric of key military and political decision-makers therefore clearly indicated that ensuring high levels of respect for civilian protection was a central element in US operations.[83]

Similar to American reasoning during UNITAF, the US military during OEF operated under the assumption that high levels of respect for non-combatant immunity would ensure the benevolence of the local population and thereby reduce the danger to US forces.[84] According to Jeffrey Starr, the Assistant Deputy Secretary of Defense for South Asia,

[f]or the United States the principle of non-combatant immunity was important for several reasons. Military planners wanted to see a surgical war, as not to alienate Afghan civilians and to subsequently get the United States dragged into the nightmare the Soviets got into.[85]

Asserting the distinction between combatants and non-combatants, the US conduct of war was designed to closely follow conditions set by IHL.

Despite 9/11 being declared a turning point, a date that changed America and the world and that brought an abrupt end to the 'holiday from history',[86] attitudes towards casualty-aversion and civilian protection among key US decision-makers seem to have largely remained

---

[80] Elshtain 2003, 10; Roberts 2002.
[81] 'Fact Sheet: US Military Efforts to Avoid Civilian Casualties', US Department of State, 25 October 2001, available at http://usinfo.state.gov/is/Archive_Index/U.S._Military_Efforts_to_Avoid_Civilian_Casualties.html, accessed on 19 April 2006.
[82] Richard Myers in ABC interview on 22 October 2001, available at www.defenselink.mil/transcripts/2001/t10222001_t1021jcs.html, accessed on 2 December 2004.
[83] Conetta 2002a; Shaw 2002; Crawford 2003, 12.
[84] DeLong 2004, 23; Renz and Scheipers 2012, 34.
[85] Interview with Jeffrey Starr, in Washington, DC, 15 June 2005.
[86] Ignatieff 2003b; 'Special Report September 11th 2001: America's Longest War', p. 20; www.whitehouse.gov/news/releases/2003/02/20030213–3.html, accessed on 12 October 2006.

unaffected. But the question is whether the US military was capable of waging OEF in ways that secured both these values in an environment in which its enemy was using asymmetric strategies.

The Strategic Thinking of al-Qaeda and the Taliban

Since his first-ever television interview in 1997, Osama bin Laden has repeatedly argued that the overall strategic objective of al-Qaeda was to end the Muslim suffering at the hands of the so-called Jewish Crusaders and therefore expel the infidels from the holy lands.[87] The 1998 founding statement of bin Laden's terrorist network, for example, reads that

[t]he ruling to kill the Americans and their allies – civilians and military – is an individual duty for every Muslim who can do it in any country in which it is possible to do it, in order to liberate the al-Aqsa Mosque [Jerusalem] and the Holy Mosque [Mecca] from their grip, and in order for their armies to move out of all the lands of Islam, defeated and unable to threaten any Muslim.[88]

This and subsequent articulations of bin Laden's militant doctrine of global Jihadism emphasised the fight against the United States over the fight against local regimes or a particular occupation force.[89] It essentially argued that before a Caliphate (an Islamic state based on shariah law) could be established, Muslims needed to defend the entire Muslim world against the imminent military threat posed by the United States and its allies.[90]

As part of the mission to liberate the Islamic world, bin Laden and Ayman al-Zawahiri, often regarded as bin Laden's closest advisor and the Number Two of the network, conceived the war in Afghanistan to be located at the forefront of their holy war.[91] The previous Afghan war against the Soviet Union had served as a means of initiation for the Mujahideen – the Arab holy warriors like the al-Qaeda chief himself – and as the ideological birthplace of global Jihadism.[92] For Osama Bin Laden, according to Michael Scheuer, 'Afghanistan was the vanguard and the shield of Islam against the United States, just as it were against the Soviet Union.'[93] The remote Hindukush Mountains were the soil upon which the Soviet superpower had been defeated by the late 1980s, and the al-Qaeda leadership seemed convinced that a similar success could be repeated against the American invaders. The American withdrawal from

---

[87] See Hegghammer 2006, 11–32; Bergen 2002, 1–23.
[88] Cited in Halliday 2002, Appendix 1.   [89] Bergen 2002, 1–23.
[90] Hegghammer 2006, 11–32.   [91] Ibid.
[92] Coll 2004b; Rashid 2000; Kaplan 1989; Bergen 2002.
[93] Anonymous [Michael Scheuer] 2004, 144.

Somalia – placed in the historical context of Vietnam and Lebanon – was seen as proof that it was possible to expel a superpower from a Muslim country.[94] In fact, statements by bin Laden suggested that fighting the Americans was expected to be easier because of their casualty-averse nature. In 1997, for example, he told Robert Fisk that

Our battle against America is much simpler than the war against the Soviet Union, because some of our Mujahideen who fought here in Afghanistan also participated in operations against Americans in Somalia – and were surprised at the collapse of American morale. This convinced us that the Americans are a paper tiger.[95]

Al-Qaeda was hoping that in reaction to the 9/11 terrorist attacks, the United States would be dragged into another Afghan war. Such an invasion would put infidel forces on the ground, that is, within reach for al-Qaeda's holy warriors, and thereby set the scene for protracted guerrilla warfare on a territory more conducive to al-Qaeda and Taliban strengths.[96] With the Americans 'unprepared to fight long wars', such a conflict would allow al-Qaeda to inflict enough American casualties to force the superpower into another humiliating defeat. US casualty-aversion was seen as the centre of gravity of American warfare.

Anticipating an American intervention in response to 9/11, the al-Qaeda and Taliban leadership assassinated Ahmad Shah Massoud, the leader of the Northern Alliance in Afghanistan on 9 September 2001.[97] An attentive student of Mao's writings and an immensely skilled as well as popular leader, Massoud was killed by two al-Qaeda suicide bombers, dressed as television journalists.[98] Al-Qaeda's assassination of Massoud cannot be conceived merely in the context of the ongoing Afghan civil war, but needs to be understood in the wider context of the war with the United States that was to unfold two days later. The killing of Massoud had been planned for months in advance, with the two concealed al-Qaeda operatives conducting interviews with other Northern Alliance leaders (such as Dr Abdullah Abdullah) only to slowly gain the trust of Massoud.[99] Jeffrey Starr recalled:

When Massoud was assassinated on 9 September 2001 – something that was planned for months if not a full year – no one in Washington knew what it meant. Massoud was the most likely person to keep the Northern Alliance together as … a collection of militias and warlords. To decapitate him was aimed at turning the

[94] Bernard Lewis 2001, 62–63; Record 2002, 13.   [95] Cited in Bodansky 1999, 89.
[96] Rogers 2002, 30. Anonymous [Michael Scheuer] 2004, 63.
[97] Molly Moore 2001; Bergen 2002, 74.   [98] Rashid 2000; Robin Moore 2004, 64.
[99] Michael Smith 2006, 213.

Northern Alliance into its fractious elements, i.e. the killing of Massoud was designed to put the Northern Alliance into chaos.[100]

Michael Scheuer agrees that

[t]he killing of Massoud was a deliberate plot to deny the United States a local ally by killing the head of the Northern Alliance ... Massoud *was* the Northern Alliance.[101]

Expecting an American military response to the imminent terrorist attacks in New York and Washington, al-Qaeda and the Taliban practically decapitated their domestic opposition and robbed the United States of an important local ally.[102]

If bin Laden and Mullah Omar had hoped that the assassination of Massoud would make strategic cooperation between the Americans and the Northern Alliance difficult to such an extent that the Americans would be forced to place more of their own forces on the ground, they must have been disappointed. The Americans waged OEF from afar, that is, they effectively used the various factions of the Northern Alliance as a substitute for American boots on the ground.[103] A couple of SOF and CIA operators were strategically inserted with indigenous warlords to coordinate the latter's offensive with the US bombing campaign. Most of these SOF teams were not even supposed to directly engage the enemy.[104] Instead, they were equipped with SOFLAM (Special Operation Forces' Laser Markers), i.e. invisible laser designators to mark enemy positions at a range of two hundred meters to ten kilometres using an integrated global positioning system (GPS) and to designate targets for US aircraft circling above at heights between 15,000 and 22,000 feet.[105]

This American strategy effectively denied al-Qaeda and the Taliban the type of close range combat with the infidels that they had hoped for. Al-Qaeda forces in particular grew increasingly frustrated by their inability to kill Americans.[106] This became apparent in the two large battles in Tora Bora and in the Shah-i-Kot valley. Following the collapse of the

---

[100] Interview with Jeffrey Starr in Washington, DC, 15 June 2005.

[101] Anonymous [Michael Scheuer] 2004, 33–34 (Italics added).

[102] Bergen 2002, 72–75; Coll 2004a.   [103] Hersh 2005, 122; Cordesman 2002, 151.

[104] Coker 2003, 58; Record 2002, 19–20; Robin Moore 2004; Michael Smith 2006, 217–220.

[105] Bowden 2002; Robin Moore 2004, 5–8; Hakansson 2003, 93–99; Finlan 2003, 101.

[106] An important difference in combat motivation and fighting skills existed between al-Qaeda fighters and most Taliban forces. The former tended to be highly trained, motivated to sacrifice themselves as holy warriors, whereas the latter vacated the battlefields quickly and were more prone to change sides. See Stephen Biddle 2002, 4–25; Record 2002, 9; Naylor 2005, 15–16; Cordesman 2002, 17.

Taliban regime in late November 2001, the battle of Tora Bora was anticipated to finally provide an opportunity to engage American forces on the ground.[107] Yet even though two additional US Marines Corps units were already on the ground at Camp Rhino by the end of November 2001, they were withheld from any high risk cave fighting at the battle of Tora Bora.[108] Refusing to place its own forces in harm's way, the American military sent in its indigenous allies instead.[109] Frustrated by days of heavy bombing and a lack of opportunities to fight the Americans, al-Qaeda withdrew (negotiating their escape with Afghan warlords such as Ali Zaman, Younus Khalis, and Awol Gul, who were fighting on the side of the Americans).[110]

In contrast to Tora Bora, 'Operation Anaconda' in the Shah-i-Kot valley in March 2002 finally provided bin Laden's holy warriors the chance to engage the Americans directly.[111] Following the disastrous outcome at Tora Bora (which had exposed the unreliability, corruption, and different interests of the Northern Alliance),[112] the American military for the first time decided to place large numbers of its own forces on the ground and to place much less emphasis on its local allies.[113] According to Colonel John Mulholland, the Commander of US Special Operations in Afghanistan, these 'lessons of Tora Bora were directly applied to Anaconda'.[114] The US military concluded that its old strategies needed to be reconsidered as they had effectively allowed the enemy's leadership to escape.[115]

Assuming that al-Qaeda would again try to escape the valley as it had done in Tora Bora, the American military set up two defensive rings around the area. What they failed to anticipate, however, was that their

[107] Smucker 2004; Naylor 2005.   [108] Richard Cohen 2002; Michael Smith 2006, 226.
[109] O'Hanlon 2002, 64.
[110] Frantz 2001; Baker and Khan 2001; Hersh 2002, 36–40; Smucker 2004, 110; Cordesman 2002, 17, 27.
[111] Gordon 2002; Naylor 2005; Loeb and Graham 2002.
[112] During the offensive by the Northern Alliance and American military, al-Qaeda forces were able to escape in most cases because the Northern Alliance was neither interested in nor capable of defeating Bin Laden's forces (as opposed to the Taliban who were offering much less resistance and fighting skills). These were early signs of the growing divergence of interests between the Northern Alliance and the US military that came to the fore most strongly at Tora Bora. Whereas the latter not only wanted the Taliban regime toppled but also al-Qaeda defeated, the former was mostly interested in conquering, occupying, and holding the territorial gains they had just made. There were several instances when local generals negotiated the surrender of a city or when troops took payment that enabled al-Qaeda forces to escape unharmed. See Smucker 2004, 110; Record 2002, 18.
[113] Gordon 2002; Ricks 2002.
[114] John Mulholland, 'Campaign against Terror', PBS Frontline, www.pbs.org/wgbh/pages/frontline/shows/campaign/interviews/mulholland.html, accessed on 23 October 2004.
[115] Naylor 2005, 23–24.

adversary behaved in the opposite manner. Given that US military forces were within reach for the first time, al-Qaeda relished the type of fight it had longed for. Thus, instead of trying to escape, they descended upon the valley from outside.[116] Several US commanders expressed their surprise at al-Qaeda's persistence, its ability to stay put, and its willingness to actually reinforce during 'Operation Anaconda'.[117] In the course of this battle, eight Americans were killed.[118] This shows the centrality of engaging and killing Americans in al-Qaeda's strategic thinking. Put differently, for nearly a decade the al-Qaeda leadership has conceived the American inability to fight costly, high casualty wars as the centre of gravity of contemporary US warfare. Accordingly, bin Laden's asymmetric strategic thinking has been based on finding ways of exploiting American casualty-aversion.

Besides attempts to try and exploit US casualty-aversion, bin Laden and Mullah Omar deliberately tried to blur the distinctions between combatants and non-combatants. Understanding the American imperative to spare civilian lives, al-Qaeda and the Taliban located their forces and military assets in densely populated areas, next to hospitals, on the roofs of school buildings, and inside mosques, and used human shields in an attempt to achieve a military advantage by exploiting their enemy's good faith compliance with the laws of war.[119] In doing so, they deliberately violated international norms.[120]

Taliban and al-Qaeda forces concealed themselves among the civilian population, co-located troops and military equipment into civilian areas in the hope of either shielding themselves from aerial bombardments, or if attacks were to take place, to produce collateral damage that could be exploited politically.[121] Examples could be found in Khost, where Taliban troops took over a building used by relief organisations. In Kabul, they placed two large anti-aircraft guns under a tree in front of the office of CARE International.[122] In cities like Kabul, Masar-i-Sharif or Kandahar, and villages like Ainger, Jebrael, Ainger, and Ishaq Suleiman, al-Qaeda and Taliban fighters launched attacks at US aircraft from within residential areas.[123] Mosques were also used

---

[116] Naylor 2005.   [117] Stephen Biddle 2002, 44.   [118] O'Hanlon 2000, 66.
[119] Branigin 2001; Cordesman 2002, 23, 35; Robin Moore 2004; Bellamy 2006, 180–198. For extensive examples, see Human Rights Watch 2002, 40–44; Bohrer and Osiel 2013, 782.
[120] Ignatieff 2002, 7; Wheeler 2002, 213; Human Rights Watch 2002.
[121] Dunlop 2001, 5; Barber 2010, 472–473.   [122] Dunlop 2001, 5.
[123] Human Rights Watch 2002; 'Taliban hiding in residential areas', *The Irish Times*, 24 October 2001, available at www.irishtimes.com/news/taliban-hiding-in-residential -areas-says-us-1.401234, accessed on 13 April 2016.

partially out of convenience because of the nature of the regime and its ideology, but partially out of tactical considerations.[124]

Furthermore, the Taliban and al-Qaeda forces used human shields (a practice that became more systematic the longer the conflict lasted).[125] While this practice has been condemned on legal and moral grounds for violating the principle of non-combatant immunity,[126] it nevertheless was employed by both Taleban and al-Qaeda forces as a means to stage attacks and to provoke and exploit civilian casualties. It is precisely for these reasons that the ICRC strictly prohibits the use of human shields on the grounds that

[t]he use of human shields requires an intentional co-location of military objectives and civilians or persons *hors de combat* with specific intent of trying to prevent the targeting of those military objectives.[127]

By deliberately and systematically hiding in civilian areas in order to evade US firepower and by using these human shields as platforms from which to launch attacks at enemy forces, the al-Qaeda network and Taliban regime not only directly bore responsibility for endangering civilians but also they deliberately violated the IHL principle of distinction which requires parties to 'distinguish between the civilian population and combatants'.[128] Specifically, they violated Article 51(7) of the Additional Protocol I to the Geneva Conventions. According to the latter,

The presence or movements of the civilian population or individual civilians shall not be used to render certain points or areas immune from military operations, in particular in attempts to shield military objects from attacks or to shield, favor or impede military operations.[129]

US adversaries therefore deliberately violated IHL by using the civilian population as cover and compromising its immunity from attack.[130] These asymmetric methods that intentionally abuse IHL to seek a military advantage against their enemy's good faith compliance with the laws became known as 'lawfare'. Coined by Charles J. Dunlop in November 2001, lawfare denotes battlefield behaviour that

---

[124] Interview with David Radcliffe in Washington, DC, 30 November 2004.

[125] Dorn 2010, 39; 'Afghanistan Taliban "Using Human Shields"', *BBC News*, 17 February 2010, available at http://news.bbc.co.uk/2/hi/south_asia/8519507.stm, accessed on 16 April 2016.

[126] Newton 2013.

[127] Henckaerts and Doswald-Beck 2005, Rule 97; see also www.icrc.org/customary-ihl/en g/docs/v1_rul_rule97, accessed on 3 April 2016.

[128] Human Rights Watch 2002, 23.   [129] ICRC 1977.

[130] Although neither the Taliban nor al-Qaeda are signatories to and have therefore ratified the Additional Protocol, the latter's provision are generally regarded as constituting customary law.

deliberately jeopardises the protection of the innocent. Writing at the height of OEF, Dunlop argued that using lawfare was

one ever more frequently embraced dimensions by U.S. opponents ... [and] a cynical manipulation of the rule of law and the humanitarian values it represents. Rather seeking battlefield victories, per se, challengers try to destroy the will to fight by undermining the public support that is indispensable when democracies like the U.S. conduct military interventions. A principle way of bringing about that end is to make it appear that the U.S. is waging war in violation of the letter or spirit of LOAC.[131]

In other words, hiding among the civilian population and using the innocent as human shields was a deliberate asymmetric method of lawfare by al-Qaeda and the Taliban to exploit the US norm of civilian protection.

Given that al-Qaeda and the Taliban were employing asymmetric strategies that were designed to exploit America's casualty-aversion and its sensitivity to targeting innocent civilians, how did such enemy behaviour impact on the US ability to wage OEF in a casualty-averse and humane manner?

Operation Enduring Freedom and the Law-Morality Nexus

This section examines how the US military responded to the asymmetric behaviour of its adversaries. This is first investigated through the lens of IHL and then through the perspective of Walzer's idea of 'due care'.

US Operations and International Humanitarian Law

To accomplish high levels of civilian protection, US forces made unprecedented use of precision-guided weapons compared with previous military operations. About 60 per cent of all the US bombs dropped during OEF were so-called 'smart bombs' – guided by lasers or GPS systems – compared to 30 per cent during NATO's intervention in Kosovo ('Operation Allied Force') and just 6.5 per cent of such weapons during the 1991 Gulf War ('Operation Desert Storm').[132] While this reflects the steady shift towards the increased usage of precision weapons, it has also been an indication of the importance attached to the use of lethal force with maximum restraint towards the innocent.[133]

---

[131] Dunlop 2001, 4.
[132] O'Hanlon 2002, 63; Conetta 2002a; Bender, Burger, and Koch 2001, 20; Cordesman 2002, 8, 10–11, 76. Cordesman's figures are 56 per cent in Afghanistan, 35 per cent in Kosovo, and 7–8 per cent in Desert Storm.
[133] Cordesman 2002, 10.

Moreover, the United States developed a sophisticated target approval system to ensure highest levels of compliance with IHL.[134] Similar to US practices during the 1990s, legal advisors oversaw every stage of the bombing campaign and provided ongoing counsel about whether specific targets were prohibited as well as whether the weapons systems used were proportionate.[135] These systematic checks not only approved specific targets, but also assigned the ammunition to be used accordingly. In most cases, computer modelling was used to predict potential collateral damage that particular targets and weapons systems would cause. Based on such simulations, it could be determined which option should be chosen in order to maximise effectiveness while simultaneously minimising the harm inflicted on civilians.[136] RAND's Bruce Pirnie, who reviewed the Pentagon's operations in Afghanistan, recalled that

> [w]e had legal advice available within operation centers to help keep us within the laws of warfare. They were valid at all times and all our commanders were obligated to act within those rules . . . [Each commander] had legal advice to assist him in making these decisions.[137]

Integrated into every aspect of OEF, military lawyers provided the level of legal scrutiny seen in 'Operation Desert Storm' and 'Operation Allied Force'.[138] Rules of Engagement (RoE) dictated that for every potential target, the estimated probable collateral damage to the surrounding people and structures had to be assessed and that for critical ('high' in military jargon) probabilities the personal authorisation of the Secretary of Defense had to be obtained.[139] This information was then reviewed during daily video conferences between Rumsfeld, Myers, and Franks in order to certify that targets did not breach IHL.[140] These developments have been interpreted as indicative of the extent to which compliance with the legal norm of civilian immunity has become internalised in the operations of the US military.[141]

There is ample evidence that this approval system had profound effects on targeting practices in Afghanistan. According to one air force commander, 'there has been a decision by people running this war to rely on

---

[134] Bellamy 2006, 187–191; Roblyer 2003.
[135] Roblyer 2003, 17; Bellamy 2005, 288; Ignatieff 2000c, 197–201; Renz and Scheipers 2012, 34.
[136] Ricks 2001b, 111; Roblyer 2003, 16–17.
[137] Interview with Bruce Pirnie in Washington, DC on 21 December 2004.
[138] Farrell 2005, 159–160.
[139] Bradley 2003; United States Department of Defense, 'News Transcript: Background Briefing on Targeting', available at www.defenselink.mil/transcripts/2003/t03052003 _t305targ.html, accessed on 19 April 2006; Cordesman 2002, 113.
[140] Roblyer 2003.
[141] Wheeler 2002, 211; Eric Schmitt 2001; Farrell 2005, 154–164, 179.

the advice of lawyers to a greater extent than they have before.'[142] These controls often frustrated pilots and planners who were widely cited as complaining that the tight restrictions hampered their ability to fight the war.[143] The concern among American military staff was that the high level of respect for non-combatant immunity was undermining US bombing efforts.[144] Several military sources complained that the bombing campaign had deliberately been slowed down because military lawyers frequently ruled out potential targets due to legal restrictions and normative concerns.[145] Critics charged that targeting opportunities were lost to such an extent that it compromised US operations.[146] As one officer summed up, '[t]he whole issue of collateral damage pervaded every level of operation. It is shocking, the degree to which collateral damage hamstrung the campaign.'[147] For example, when commanders located high profile targets, CENTCOM occasionally refused to approve the target on the grounds that it might be a deliberate trick and that the target might contain non-combatants.[148] One such incident occurred early on in the air campaign when US military personnel operating a Predator Unmanned Aerial Vehicle (UAV) believed that they had Mullah Omar in their sight. According to Seymour M. Hersh, the Predator Drone identified a car convoy carrying the Taliban leader and permission was immediately requested from CENTCOM for a full-scale fighter bomber attack. It was at that point that a military lawyer to General Franks turned down the request.[149] CENTCOM later learned from an operative on the ground that Omar had indeed been in the convoy.

Concern was also voiced that legal concerns prevented the United States from securing the maximum advantage from its technological capabilities.[150] In Afghanistan, innovations in information technology and net-centric warfare potentially decreased the 'sensor to shooter cycle' (the time from the identification of targets by SOF, the communication of the coordinates via laptops and satellites, to the dropping of laser/GPS guided missile by aircraft circling overhead) to just twenty minutes on average – a time unprecedented in the history of warfare.[151] During Operation Desert Storm, by contrast, it had taken an average

---

[142] Cited in Wheeler 2002, 211; DeLong 2004, 67–73.
[143] Stephen Biddle 2002; Ricks 2001b, 111; William Arkin 2002.
[144] William Arkin 2002.
[145] Stephen Biddle 2002; Interview with Terry Pudas in Washington, DC, 17 June 2005.
[146] Roberts 2002.   [147] Cited by Ricks 2001b, 111.
[148] Ricks 2001b, 111; DeLong 2004, 38–39.
[149] Hersh 2001a. According to Franks, 'My JAG (Judge Advocate General) doesn't like this, so we're not going to fire.' See Hersh, 2001a.
[150] Ricks 2001, 111.   [151] Roblyer 2003; Cordesman 2002, 110–112.

eighty minutes to complete the same cycle.[152] However, the legal scrutinising that was required in each individual case by the target approval
system cost opportunities to engage legitimate targets.[153] This created
considerable frustration among SOF and Air Force commanders as they
felt that several opportunities to kill enemy fighters were lost.[154] In other
words, US military personnel felt that the full effects of the new net-
centric warfare were not realised due to concerns for civilian
protection.[155] Andrew J. Bacevich assessed this particular issue in the
following way:

> There was also a problem of rules of engagement in this post–9/11 environment
> that would facilitate the rapid decision-making and targeting on those occasions
> when they had intelligence: bumping up against old executive orders that prohib-
> ited assassinations, and military lawyers were consulted ... so the process of
> responding quickly to a tactical opportunity just wasn't what it needed to be.[156]

At the same time, however, these complaints give credence to the claim
that the US military put serious effort into following the principles set out
by the laws of war.

Sensitive to the explosive potential that images of civilian deaths could
have on US public opinion and relations with the Islamic world, the Bush
Administration went a long way to minimise civilian casualties.[157] It was only
after Operation Anaconda in March 2002 – and partially as a result of the
overall assessment of OEF – that these strict RoE were relaxed.[158]
The incident that began to indicate that initial hesitations had started to
fade was the Hellfire[159] strike by an unmanned Predator drone against al-
Qaeda suspects in Yemen on 4 November 2002.[160] From that point
onwards, US forces started to feel less inhibited by the strict constraints
imposed by their RoE.[161] But in the period under study here
(October 2001–March 2002), no major change in these strict RoE occurred.

The rules imposed by the target approval system ensured a relatively
low figure for Afghan civilian deaths. Admittedly, it is difficult to arrive at

[152] Bowden 2000.   [153] Hersh 2001a; Cordesman 2002, 110; Roblyer 2003.
[154] Erwin 2002, 55; Westhusing 2002, 128–135; interview with Terry Pudas in
Washington, DC, 17 June 2005; see also William Arkin 2002.
[155] Hersh 2005, 121–151; Bowden 2000; Stephen Biddle 2002; Interview with Terry Pudas
in Washington, DC, 17 June 2005.
[156] Telephone interview with Andrew Bacevich, 26 January 2005. See also Hersh 2001a;
Roblyer 2003.
[157] Falk, 'Appraising the War against Afghanistan'; Cordesman 2002, 110.
[158] Roblyer 2003; DeLong 2004, 67–73.
[159] AGM-114 Hellfire Missiles are used to arm Predator UAV vehicles for armed reconnaissance and interdiction.
[160] DeLong 2004, 67–73.
[161] Telephone interview with Andrew Bacevich, 26 January 2005.

a reliable estimate of the overall number of civilians killed during OEF, partially because of the Pentagon's continuing refusal since the end of the Vietnam War to issue such figures in public.[162] In addition, US adversaries tend to manipulate statistics of casualties and collateral damage for political purposes.[163] The Taliban, for example, produced grossly exaggerated claims of Afghan civilian deaths, arguing that as many as 6,000 fatalities occurred in the first 5 months.[164] The general estimates of collateral damage ranged from one to ten thousand civilian fatalities for the period between October 2001 and March 2002.[165] For those estimates of 3,500 civilian casualties or more, and especially the Taliban figures of six thousand, however, there are significant grounds for doubting their accuracy.[166]

The most accurate and publicly available figures[167] were produced by the Project on Defense Alternatives, which estimated that between one thousand and 1,300 civilians were killed in the first three months of OEF.[168] Compared with figures from US interventions in the 1990s, the aggregate number of non-combatant fatalities in Afghanistan therefore remained more or less within the range seen in the Gulf War, Bosnia, and Kosovo.[169] In comparison to the American intervention in Somalia under UNOSOM II (see Chapter 4), however, the aggregate number of civilian deaths in OEF was considerably lower.

This indicated that the importance of civilian protection seen in US interventions during the 1990s continued after 9/11 even though the United States no longer conducted a humanitarian intervention, but found itself fighting a perceived war of survival instead. Furthermore, it shows that the American military was able to wage war in a manner that ensured not only extremely low numbers of US casualties but also high levels of respect for the principle of non-combatant immunity.[170]

However, a number of important concerns arose in relation to the proportionality principle and the level of civilian protection achieved. First, OEF failed to set new standards for accuracy. According to the Project on Defense Alternatives, although a higher proportion of

---

[162] Interview with Bruce Pirnie in Washington, DC, 21 December 2004; see also Roblyer 2003; Stephen Biddle 2002.

[163] Cordesman 2002, 36.   [164] Kind 2002; O'Hanlon 2002, 66.

[165] Herold 2002; Todenhofer 2002, 1, 7; Mandel 2004, 29–30; Kind 2002; Bearak 2002, A-1; Rogers, 'The "War on Terror"'; Conetta 2002a.

[166] The figure of 3,767 was given by Herold 2001. The figure of 10,000 was produced by Mandel 2004. For a strong critique of these estimates, see Jeffrey C Isaac, 'Civilian Casualties in Afghanistan: The Limits of Herold's "Comprehensive Accounting"', available at www.indiana.edu/~iupolsci/docs/doc.htm, accessed on 2 November 2004.

[167] Falk, 'Appraising the War against Afghanistan'; Roberts 2002.

[168] Conetta 2002a; Filkins 2002; Farrell 2005, 183; Mandel 2004, 29.

[169] Shaw 2005, 10; O'Hanlon 2002, 66.   [170] Elshtain 2003, 65–67.

Precision Guided Missiles (PGM) were used in Afghanistan compared to Kosovo and the first Iraq War, the aggregate number of civilian casualties in Afghanistan was higher than in Bosnia as well as Kosovo. Second, the rate of civilian casualties per bomb dropped and missile expanded was higher in Afghanistan than in Kosovo (the underlying reasons will be discussed in detail).[171] This not only indicates a deterioration from the standards set during 'Operation Allied Force', but also reversed the trend of the 1990s towards progressively lower numbers of civilian casualties per bomb dropped.[172]

The question therefore arises whether all appropriate means were taken by the US military to minimise civilian harm. When confronted with this question from the press, the Pentagon routinely responded in two ways. First, the DoD systematically emphasised that it sought to minimise the level of harm and injury to civilians as much as possible.[173] To give an example: On 29 October, Rumsfeld declared that the military was acting in full compliance with IHL and emphasised that 'no nation in human history has done more to avoid civilian casualties than the US has in this conflict.'[174] Second, whenever civilians were injured or killed US officials asserted that such harm, though regrettable, was either unavoidable or unintended.[175] In the case of the former, the Pentagon repeatedly argued that despite great care being taken, collateral damage was inevitable in war.[176] See for instance Rumsfeld's press statement that 'war is ugly':[177]

There has never been a conflict where people have not been killed, and this is the case here. There is ordnance flying around from three different sources. It's flying around from us, from the air down; it's flying around from the al-Qaeda and the Taliban up, that lands somewhere and kills somebody when it hits; and there's opposition forces and al-Qaeda forces that are engaged in shooting at each other. Now in a war, that happens. There is nothing you can do about it.[178]

The alternative argument to the claim that war's ugly nature makes civilian casualties unavoidable was to emphasise that they were purely unintended, i.e. that they were not deliberately targeted. In such cases,

---

[171] Conetta 2002a.   [172] Conetta 2002a.   [173] Elshtain 2003, 9–25, 69.

[174] www.defenselink.mil/transcripts/2001/t10292001_t1029sd.html, accessed on 12 April 2005.

[175] www.defenselink.mil/transcripts/2001/t10152001_t1015sd.html, accessed on 12 April 2005; www.defenselink.mil/transcripts/2001/t12042001_t1204sd.html, accessed on 12 April 2005.

[176] www.defenselink.mil/speeches/2001/index.html, accessed on 12 April 2005; Duclaux and Aldinger 2002.

[177] www.defenselink.mil/transcripts/2001/t10292001_t1029sd.html, accessed on 12 April 2005.

[178] www.defenselink.mil/news/Oct2001/t10292001_t1029sd.html, accessed on 11 April 2005.

Rumsfeld tended to refer to civilian casualties as 'unintended effects of this conflict' or as being caused by 'ordnance end[ing] up where it should not.'[179]

By following these lines of argument Pentagon officials implicitly asserted the doctrine of double effect – as enshrined in the laws of war – by stating that harm to Afghan civilians was both unavoidable and unintended. But while the US military claimed to follow the principles of discrimination, proportionality, and double effect, the question remains whether an even higher standard of civilian protection could have been achieved by accepting greater risks to American soldiers.

US Operations and Walzer's Idea of 'Due Care'

The reason why this question is important lies in the legal and moral principles governing the balancing of risks between soldiers and civilians. The problem with the existing legal principles, as Chapter 1 has shown, is their permissiveness. The provisions of the laws of war leave what critics have termed an 'important space of indeterminacy' within which rival legal claims compete for validation.[180] This demonstrates more generally the limits of the existing legal framework to provide sufficient protection for non-combatants.[181] In other words, one of the problems of IHL is its inability to provide a clear answer to the question of whether everything has been done to spare civilian lives. This indeterminacy of the legal framework has been particularly apparent in relation to the targeting of dual-use facilities.[182] In effect, this indeterminacy has resulted in a permissiveness that allows states to perform acts that are likely to have evil consequences: any military act can be justified and any injury to non-combatants excused as unintentional collateral damage provided that it can be shown that it hit a legitimate military target.[183]

Yet, even if the conduct of war was considered clean and humane from a legal point of view, it would not necessarily follow that it fulfilled all moral requirements.[184] Inflicting collateral damage or targeting dual-use facilities in Afghanistan remains a sensitive moral issue. The book therefore draws on the more restrictive moral interpretation found in Michael Walzer's idea of 'due care'.[185] As shown in Chapter 1, the idea of 'due care' expects soldiers not only to refrain from intending to harm civilians,

---

[179] www.defenselink.mil/news/Oct2001/t10292001_t1029sd.html, accessed on 11 April 2005.
[180] Wheeler 2003, 214.   [181] Thomas W Smith 2002, 360–361; Rowe 2000.
[182] Rowe 2000.   [183] Bellamy 2005, 288.   [184] Ignatieff 2000c, 199.
[185] Bellamy 205, 287–289; Walzer 1992, 151–159; Wheeler 2002, 208–210; Lee 2004, 235–236.

but also to take positive steps to reduce the threat to non-combatants as far as possible, even if that means accepting a 'marginal' increase of risk to their own lives.[186] At the same time, however, protecting civilians should not require sacrificing the military objective or accepting excessive risks to soldiers' lives.[187]

To address whether 'due care' was taken with Afghan civilians, we need to understand how and why collateral damage occurred during the early phase of OEF. We can then assess whether increasing the risks to American aircrews as well as Special Operations Forces/CIA operatives could have reduced civilian harm. According to the available sources, non-combatant casualties in Afghanistan resulted from the following four causes.[188] First from the mix and technical characteristics of the weapons employed; second, from prioritising an aerial campaign over ground operations; third, from a combination of US focus on so-called targets of opportunity and the use of unreliable intelligence; and fourth, from the mistreatments and revenge killings committed by American allies in the Northern Alliance/United Front.

The mix and technical characteristics of the weapons employed   According to the Project on Defense Alternatives, even though the percentage of 'smart weapons' used in OEF clearly increased compared to the first Gulf War, Bosnia, and Kosovo, it did not lead to fewer civilian casualties.[189] Instead, OEF incurred a higher rate of civilian casualties than US operations in the Balkans during the 1990s not only per bomb dropped but also in absolute terms.[190] Estimates are that the aggregate civilian death toll during OEF was twice as high and the rate of civilians killed during OEF even up to four times higher than during 'Operation Allied Force'. Statistically, this amounts to about one civilian casualty for every twelve bombs dropped over Afghanistan compared to the 1999 war where about one non-combatant was killed for every forty-six bombs dropped.[191] This constituted a distinct deterioration of the high standards set during 'Operation Allied Force' and contradicted the notion professed by American leaders that OEF was 'cleaner' and 'more precise' than more recent US campaigns.[192]

One key reason for this development was a switch in emphasis within the category of 'smart weapons' from laser-guided bombs to bombs

---

[186] Walzer 1992, 152–159.   [187] Ibid.; Hart 1963, 130.   [188] Conetta 2002a.
[189] Conetta 2002a; Bellamy 2006, 180–198.   [190] Human Rights Watch 2003b.
[191] Conetta 2002a.
[192] www.defenselink.mil/transcripts/2001/t10292001_t1029sd.html, accessed on 12 April 2005; www.defenselink.mil/transcripts/2001/t10152001_t1015sd.html, accessed on 12 April 2005; Schmitt and Dao 2011; Ricks 2001a.

directed by Global Positioning System (GPS).[193] The latter are generally much cheaper than the former, can be used in all weather conditions, and can be launched from greater distances.[194] But while GPS-guided missiles are clearly more accurate than 'dumb bombs', they are – under ideal conditions – generally less accurate than laser guided munitions.[195] GPS-directed weapons such as 'Joint Direct Attack Munitions' (JDAM) tend to be less accurate than laser-guided bombs.[196] Therefore, a detailed investigation by the Project for Defense Alternatives into the smart weapons mix used by the American military in OEF, argues,

[w]hat we have seen in the Afghanistan campaign relative to Operation Allied Force is an increase in the percentage of 'smart weapons' but a sharp decrease in the percentage of those that are laser guided.[197]

According to the report, the aggregate effect of this switch within the category of 'smart bombs' from laser-guided to GPS-directed weapons was a reduction in the average accuracy of the smart weapons mix used in OEF compared to 'Operation Allied Force'.[198]

Further harm to Afghan civilians was caused by the use of depleted uranium weapons and cluster bombs (though used on a much lesser scale than in both 'Operation Allied Force' and 'Operation Iraqi Freedom').[199] Due to the level of contamination, these weapons cause lasting damage to

---

[193] During Operation Allied Force, of all the bombs dropped and missiles expanded, 30 per cent were laser guided 'smart bombs' and 70 per cent 'dumb bombs'. By contrast, during OEF, 20 per cent of all the bombs used were laser guided, 40 per cent GPS guided (i.e. 60 per cent were 'smart bombs'), and 40 per cent 'dumb bombs' (Conetta 2002a; Zehfuss 2006, 8).

[194] www.globalsecurity.org/military/systems/munitions/intro-smart.htm, accessed on 14 October 2006.

[195] Conetta 2002a; Michael Schmitt 2005, 449, 461; Richter and Pae 2001; 'Smart Bombs Made Dumb? Did Faulty Batteries Cause Failure of Precision Guided Weapons?', cbsnews.com, 6 December 2001; Air Force Pamphlet 14–210: USAF Intelligence Targeting Guide (Washington, DC: HQ USAF, February 1998); Crawford 2003, 18.

[196] Michael Schmitt 2005, 449, 461; www.fas.org/man/dod-101/sys/smart/jdam.htm, accessed on 14 October 2006; www.news24.com/News24/World/Iraq/0,,2-10-1460_1 335530,00.html, accessed on 14 October 2006; Conetta 2002a. This is the case under ideal conditions; under less favourable climatic conditions, however, laser-guided bombs can lose lock and because they are not 'fire and forget', they require pilots to maintain an aim on the target. This makes GPS-guided weapons less dependent on ideal weather conditions and less prone to human errors. At the same time, however, laser-guided weapons tend to have a smaller warhead, which results in less collateral damage inflicted per bomb dropped. See, for example, www.globalsecurity.org/military/systems/munitions/intro-smart.htm, accessed on 14 October 2006.

[197] Conetta 2002a.   [198] Richter & Pae 2001; Conetta 2002a; Human Rights Watch 2003b.

[199] A small number of 'Daisy cutters', the largest conventional bomb in the US arsenal, was also used. Yet, these bombs were mostly dropped in remote areas (especially on cave complexes) so that they did not result in collateral damage (Uranium Medical Research Centre 2005, 277–284; Bellamy 2006, 180–198).

the surrounding environment as well as long-term public health issues. According to Bellamy, the use of such weapons in or near populated areas was both indiscriminate (the nature of the weapon not only affects combatants) and disproportionate (the long-term costs exceeded short-term military benefits).[200]

OEF also saw an increased percentage of cluster bomb usage that surpassed the numbers used in Kosovo.[201] Even though these specific weapons were generally used against enemy troop concentrations, airfields, or defence units, they generally were old weapons with a high failure rate that in some incidents were dropped on areas close to non-combatants.[202] Examples of major incidences where cluster bombs were used in areas adjacent to those used by civilians occurred in Ishaq Suleiman on 31 October, in Qala Shater, a suburb of Herat, on 22 October, and in the village of Ainger on 17 November 2001.[203] According to Human Rights Watch, such practices were responsible for killing about twenty-five civilians.[204] The use of cluster bombs in any other than remote areas was both indiscriminate and disproportionate.

Even more problematic, however, were the indiscriminate effects of such weapons.[205] Each unexploded submunition effectively becomes a landmine, that is, an inherently indiscriminate weapon.[206] Estimates about the failure rate of submunitions to explode upon impact range between 5 and 22 per cent.[207] Complicating things further, the cluster bombs were of the same yellow colour as the aid packages dropped by US aircraft, thereby increasing the risk of killing civilians who might accidentally mistake the former for the latter. Evidence presented by community-based surveys suggests that at least 127 civilians were killed by such unexploded ordnance.[208] Having dropped cluster bombs, America had a special responsibility to remove the threat to non-combatants posed by unexploded submunitions. However, as Bellamy shows in a detailed discussion, the US government failed to do everything feasible to protect non-combatants from this particular threat. Bearing the responsibility for delivering cluster bombs, the US omission to clear such weapons constitutes breach of the idea of 'due care'.[209]

These examples show that higher levels of civilian protection could have been achieved by employing a mix of more discriminate and

---

[200] Bellamy 2006, 191–197.
[201] The proportion of cluster bombs used was about 10–15 per cent, compared with 7 per cent in the 1999 Balkans campaign (Conetta 2002a).
[202] Bellamy 2006, 180–198.   [203] Human Rights Watch 2002, 40–44.
[204] Human Rights Watch 2002, 21–23.   [205] Bellamy 2006, 191–197.
[206] Crawford 2003, 18–19.   [207] Cordesman 2002, 45; Fassihi 2001.
[208] Shaw 2005, 27; Human Rights Watch 2002, 25.   [209] Bellamy 2006, 196.

accurate weapons. On these accounts, therefore, the United States failed the 'due care' test. This failure, however, was not due to US casualty-aversion but due to the American preference for cheaper, yet less accurate weapons and a failure to protect civilians from unexploded ordnance. In these cases, a higher level of civilian protection would not have required an increase of the risks to American military personnel. Instead, a different choice of weapons system would have been sufficient to save civilian lives due to the mix and technical characteristics of the weapons employed.

US preference for aerial campaign over ground operations   Appreciating the American imperative to spare civilian lives and wage OEF humanely, the al-Qaeda network and the Taliban regime – wherever the opportunity existed – systematically tried to exploit US compliance with the principle of non-combatant immunity and to leverage this into a tactical advantage.[210] This strategy created dilemmas for any military wanting to satisfy the idea of 'due care'. Given the asymmetric nature of the adversary, how was the United States to discriminate between combatants and non-combatants? And what level of risk should the US military accept in order to increase the chances of distinguishing between enemy soldiers and civilians?[211]

US decision-makers recognised this exploitation of this asymmetry of moral concerns as a major challenge. Three weeks into the war Rumsfeld, for example, acknowledged that

[t]hey are actively using mosques and schools and hospitals for locations for command and control and for barracks and for their various activities. They're putting artillery pieces around schools and in residential areas, hoping they will not be hit because there will be collateral damage ... It is not an easy job when those images are all across the globe. It's a hard job.[212]

Despite this recognition, however, the collateral damage that occurred in urban areas was among the major factors that contributed to a higher rate of civilian casualties in Afghanistan.[213]

The reason for this lay in the US military utilising its improved precision technology to pursue goals and enemy targets that would not have been pursued in the past. For instance, besides targeting military facilities and front-line troops, US aircraft also targeted suspected al-Qaeda and

---

[210] Branigin 2001; Ignatieff 2002, 7; Human Rights Watch 2002, 44; Bellamy 2006, 180–198.

[211] Crawford 2003, 17.

[212] www.defenselink.mil/transcripts/2001/t10252001_t1024usa.html, accessed on 10 July 2005.

[213] Conetta 2002a.

Taliban leaders as well as enemy cadres in residential areas. American commanders pursued enemy fighters even when they used civilian infrastructure as cover (though, for political reasons, mosques were not targeted).[214] According to Conetta,

[the United States] attempted things that have never ever been attempted with these weapons. For instance: picking out individual structures and small groups of al-Qaeda fighters in the middle of populated neighborhoods. This cannot be done without having some – even if small degree of – collateral damage. It can be perfectly accurate but it would still kill those around the target area. It's a matter of how this new capacity is spent.[215]

This departure from less ambitious practices as seen in Bosnia and Kosovo directly increased the levels of civilian casualties. In other words, the asymmetric nature of the enemy on the one hand, the availability of a larger percentage of 'smart bombs', and the technological innovations of net-centric warfare on the other resulted in a more ambitious targeting practice by the US military.[216]

Pursuing enemy targets in urban areas was problematic with regard to questions of 'due care'. Although the United States did not intend to cause civilian harm and was careful not to attack Afghan civilians directly, it nevertheless attacked Taliban and al-Qaeda fighters who were using Afghan civilian infrastructure such as hospitals and densely populated urban areas as cover.[217] For example, US aircraft attacked enemy forces hiding in residential areas during attacks on Kabul, Khanabad, on a convoy in Khost, and on the villages of Qalai Niazi as well as Kakarak.[218] In the process, several hundred civilians were killed.[219]

According to the laws of war, the collateral damage caused in this process was permissible provided that targets were legitimate, that is, that they were military targets and that the civilian harm caused was neither intended nor excessive in relation to the military advantage secured from such strikes.[220] Most US bombing operations in urban areas fulfilled these legal conditions. The sophisticated target approval system set up at the beginning of the war ensured high levels of compliance with the laws of war. The biggest problem, however, was that the resulting civilian harm was nevertheless foreseeable.[221] On the one hand,

---

[214] Barber 2010, 472–473; Stephen Biddle 2002, 1–44.

[215] Interview with Carl Conetta in Washington, DC, 4 December 2004.

[216] Conetta 2002a; Stephen Biddle 2002, 1–44.

[217] Human Rights Watch 2002, 40–44; Ignatieff 2002, 7; Zehfuss 2006, 7–8; Bellamy 2006, 180–198.

[218] Conetta 2002a; Cordesman 2002.   [219] Gall 2002; Filkins 2002.

[220] Zehfuss 2006, 8; Wheeler 2003, 198.

[221] Hurka 2005, 50; Patricia Owens 2003, 595–616; Wippman and Shue 2002, 559–579.

precision guided missiles were never as precise as their name suggests. However smart they were, they did not always work as intended. Due to technological malfunctions some inevitably hit the wrong buildings and people.[222] On the other hand, precisely hit enemy military targets in residential areas automatically tended to inflict civilian casualties. According to Shaw, these

> Western massacres are indeed 'accidental' in the sense that they are not specifically intended and that efforts are made to avoid them. However, the risk of repeated small massacres of civilians is an understood feature of the way the West fights its wars.[223]

In other words, strict compliance with the laws of war permits that enemy non-combatants are exposed to the risks of war. Moreover, these risks are understood by US military planners as well as legal advisors and are programmed into the risk analysis of war.[224]

Applying the less permissive moral 'idea of due care', the question arises whether alternative ways existed of destroying enemy military objectives located in residential areas that would have reduced the risks to Afghan civilians even if it meant a marginal increase to the risks faced by US military personnel.[225]

Similar to 'Operation Allied Force', US military aircraft during OEF aimed at enemy targets in populated areas from the safe altitude of at least 15,000 feet.[226] The prime reason for this precautionary measure was that the Pentagon was fearful of Soviet SA7 and anti-aircraft artillery, which had been used with devastating effects against the Soviet Union in the 1980s.[227] Reliance on high-altitude and long range bombing kept the aircrews safe, but – so the narrative goes – inevitably led to errors of targeting and delivery that killed innocent non-combatants.[228] The logically inverse argument would be that higher levels of precision might have been achieved by reducing the altitude and thereby increasing the risks to US fighter jet crews. This is based on the assumption that lowering the altitude of US fighter pilots would automatically result in higher levels of accuracy.[229] Walzer, for example, implicitly asserted this notion when he argued that

> [i]f we are bombing military targets in a just war, and there are civilians living near these targets, we have to adjust our bombing policy – by flying at lower altitudes – so to minimise the risks we impose on civilians.[230]

---

[222] Shaw 2005, 84–85.   [223] Ibid., 86.   [224] Patricia Owens 2003, 595–616.
[225] Wheeler 2002, 213; Bellamy 2005, 288; Walzer 2004, 16–18.
[226] Bowden 2000, 62; Ignatieff 2000c, 197–201.
[227] Coll 2004b, 1–34; telephone interview with Milton Bearden, 21 June 2005.
[228] See for example Shaw 2005, 86.   [229] See for example Walzer 2004, 17.
[230] Walzer 2004, 17.

Similar claims have been voiced with reference to NATO's bombing campaign over Kosovo in 1999.[231] There are, however, indications that a change in altitude would not have had any significant effect on the level of precision. With regards to GPS-guided bombs, for instance, changing the height of the aircraft is not a factor that changes accuracy. In the case of GPS-directed bombs, which made up the largest share within the category of smart weapons used,[232] a change to the altitude of US aircrews would not have affected the weapon's accuracy.[233] In the case of OEF, most civilians killed in urban areas were killed because of ambitious US targeting practices. Moreover, collateral damage in residential areas was also caused by technological malfunctions (technological failure during OEF occurred in approximately 5–10 per cent of all bombs dropped).[234] Taken together, these two major causes of harm to civilians would not have been minimised by changing the levels of risk to US fighter pilots.

Instead, as prominent critics such as Richard A. Clarke, Michael Ignatieff, Nicholas J. Wheeler, Alex Bellamy, Carl Conetta, and Seymour M. Hersh charged, the United States could have spared significant numbers of unintended but foreseeable civilian casualties had it relied less on the bombing strategy and more on placing its own troops on the ground.[235] They point out that the negative effects of the campaign on civilian protection could have been reduced had Washington not decided to overthrow the Taliban by relying predominantly on aerial bombardment.[236] This assessment is in line with the findings of a government investigation into several incidents that claimed civilian lives. The results were reported by the *New York Times*, suggesting that one key factor in collateral damage was the government's preference for a predominant air campaign over a ground operation.[237] The report suggests that America's preference for 'out-of-harm's way air strikes instead of riskier ground operations' not only forced the military to rely on local Afghan intelligence, but also 'cut off a way of checking the accuracy of [the latter]'.[238] The suggested alternative of sending additional ground forces, however, was ruled out because of US casualty-aversion.[239]

---

[231] Farrell 2005, 156–162; Ignatieff 2000c, 197–201.   [232] Conetta 2002a.
[233] Michael Schmitt 2005.   [234] Eason 2001.
[235] Hersh 2005, 146; Richard Clarke 2004; Conetta 2002b; Wheeler 2002; Ignatieff 2003a, 19; Bellamy 2006, 180–198.
[236] Hersh 2005, 146; see also Richard Clarke 2004; Conetta 2002b; see also Mandel 2004, 40–46.
[237] Filkins 2002; Sewall 2002, 7.   [238] Filkins 2002.
[239] Elshtain 2003, 68–69; Naylor 2005, 8–183; Michael Smith 2006, 226.

These findings were buttressed by another internal military analysis of OEF. In 2003, the Pentagon's Office of Special Operations and Low-Intensity Conflicts (SOLICs) asked Hy S. Rothstein, a former Special Forces officer and an expert in unconventional warfare, to assess the war in Afghanistan. The subsequent report produced a devastating critique of the administration's strategy, in particular the overwhelming reliance on heavy aerial bombing.[240] Arguing that the initial bombing campaign against a conventional enemy (the Taliban before their regime was toppled) proved a success, Rothstein concluded that the campaign was a failure against the unconventional al-Qaeda network (and Taliban forces only *after* their regime had been toppled). Failing to adjust its conventional response towards an unconventional adversary, 'snatched defeat from the jaws of victory'.[241] It concluded that the bombing campaign was not the best way to try and hunt down the al-Qaeda leadership.[242] Rothstein's assessment is strongly supported by the findings of Steven Biddle's review of OEF. Biddle shows how despite the hype about net-centric warfare, the US bombing campaign was not unconventional at all, but rather waged like a classical twentieth-century air campaign: 'It was conducted like an orthodox air-ground theatre campaign in which large firepower decided a contest between two land forces.'[243]

Crucially, Rothstein's report argues that reliance on heavy aerial bombing resulted in large numbers of civilian casualties.[244] An entirely different American military strategy could have achieved a higher level of civilian protection. The failure to adjust to an unconventional adversary in a truly unconventional way on the ground not only cost the United States some of the fruits of victory but it also imposed additional and avoidable humanitarian costs on Afghan civilians.[245] Rothstein suggests that the number of civilian casualties from October 2001 until the end of March 2002 could have been significantly lower and that further incidents of collateral damage might have been avoided if SOFs had been allowed to wage a truly unconventional war.[246] Such an unorthodox strategy would have reduced the reliance on US aerial firepower and emphasised the need for an unconventional ground campaign.[247] Rothstein was subsequently asked by the Pentagon to soften his findings.[248]

---

[240] Hersh 2005, 147–151.
[241] 'The Other War: Pentagon's Own Report on Afghanistan Invasion Blasts US War Strategy', 17 April 2004, available at http://ia300224.us.archive.org/3/items/dn2004-0407/dn2004-0407-1_64kb.mp3, accessed on 1 September 2006.
[242] Hersh 2004.   [243] Stephen Biddle 2002, 6; Hersh 2004.
[244] 'Bush's Afghan Problem', *The New Yorker*, 5 April 2005.
[245] Hersh 2004; see also Stephen Biddle 2002.   [246] Hersh 2005, 147–151; Hersh 2004.
[247] Hersh 2004.   [248] 'Bush's Afghan Problem'; Hersh 2005, 151.

In similar vein, the 'Project on Defense Alternatives' suggested an alternative approach to America's key reliance on aerial bombardment. It argued that such an approach would have taken more time, but would have been less costly and would have avoided many of the negative impacts on non-combatants.[249] In agreement with the subsequent findings of both Rothstein and Biddle, the report argued that the bombing campaign was inherently flawed for it focused primarily on the Taliban rather than the al-Qaeda network (the Taliban fought a front-line trench warfare against the Northern Alliance which made them obvious targets for the American air force; whereas al-Qaeda fought an unconventional campaign).[250] Thus, the conventional aerial bombardment proved effective as a means to kill the Taliban but not to defeat al-Qaeda.[251] As a result, the US strategy was not only ill-adjusted to kill the main enemy,[252] but also imposed a lot of unnecessary humanitarian costs on Afghan civilians.[253] A more feasible strategy with less negative side effects on non-combatants, Conetta suggests, would have limited OEF to more SOF on the ground and very selective air strikes against al-Qaeda. Yet, such an alternative approach would have required the United States to place considerably more American SOF on the ground.[254]

Therefore, it can be argued that by placing US soldiers at higher risks and by choosing an altogether different (unconventional) strategy, a higher level of civilian protection could have been achieved. This is not to say that the United States did not try very hard to minimise Afghan civilian casualties. But while attempts were made to spare civilians, serious doubts exist whether all appropriate measures were taken and every effort was made to reduce civilian casualties. According to the reports by the Pentagon, Rothstein, and Conetta, a potentially higher degree of civilian protection could have been achieved by placing more US soldiers at greater risks.[255] Instead, an overall strategy was relied upon that questions the administration's assurances to have exhausted all measures to minimise collateral damage. Clear alternatives to the

---

[249] Conetta 2002b; for Rothstein's similar assessment, see Hersh 2004.

[250] Conetta 2002b.

[251] Three to four thousand Taliban were killed and another seven thousand taken prisoners. Regarding al-Qaeda, estimates are that six to eight hundred were killed. Yet, most of the al-Qaeda fighters, together with its leadership and the Taliban government, survived and escaped into Pakistan (Conetta 2002b).

[252] Biddle and Rothstein showed how the integrated warfare between US SOF, aircrews, and local proxies worked well against untrained and ill-motivated Taliban trenchlines, but not against hardened Taliban members and especially not against al-Qaeda fighters (Stephen Biddle 2002, 13–25; Hersh 2004).

[253] Conetta 2002b.   [254] Conetta 2002b.

[255] Hersh 2004; Conetta 2002b; see also Stephen Biddle 2002.

airpower-dominated warfare existed but were ruled out on the grounds of American concern for military casualties. At a time when the risks to US forces were already very reduced, placing more than just a handful of SOF on the ground would have increased US risks only marginally without jeopardising the overall mission objectives. Yet, the risks of combat were effectively transferred from US military personnel to the civilian population in Afghanistan. On these accounts, the US campaign failed the 'due care' test.

Targets of opportunity and unreliable intelligence   Due to a lack of infrastructure and fixed enemy objects of strategic significance, the US Air Force (USAF) had attacked most available fixed targets within one week of the start of the campaign.[256] As a result, the vast majority of US air strikes focused on targets of opportunity or emerging targets.[257] Anthony Cordesman assessed that in the course of OEF, the USAF and US Navy (USN) attacked 2,500 targets of opportunity with a 65 per cent hit rate.[258] Such targets were usually designated by ground-based special operations teams, air controllers or spotters who were inserted with local allies of the Northern Alliance/United Front.[259]

When targeting errors occurred, they tended to have their roots in intelligence and verification failures rather than in smart bombs missing their targets or technological malfunctions.[260] This meant that while most bombs hit their prescribed targets correctly, the selected targets themselves turned out to be wrong. The misidentification of targets was a particular problem in Afghanistan as the United States depended to an unusual degree on intelligence from local Afghans.[261] This turned out to be far from reliable and in many cases was malicious and politically motivated.[262] It made the American bombing campaign susceptible to the playing out of local rivalries that were either irrelevant or even detrimental to US military objectives.[263]

As a result of this flawed and often politically motivated intelligence provided by local indigenous allies, US aircraft launched a number of

---

[256] DeLong 2004, 39; Grant, 2002, 15.   [257] Roblyer 2003.

[258] Cordesman 2002, 106–107.

[259] Stephen Biddle 2002, 25; O'Hanlon 2002, 62; Hersh 2005, 122; Robin Moore, 5–8; Freedman 2002a, 43.

[260] Sewall 2002, 7; Filkins 2002. This is not to deny that smart bombs missing targets or technological malfunctions were insignificant (the contrary was shown earlier). Yet, the harm inflicted on civilians from intelligence failures was considerably higher.

[261] Naylor 2005, 8–183; Ignatieff 2003a, 77–108.

[262] Cordesman 2002, 17; Bellamy 2006, 180–198; telephone interview with Milton Bearden, 21 June 2005.

[263] Cryer 2002; Bellamy 2005, 289.

strikes on civilian targets as well as friendly forces.[264] The most prominent examples were the American bombing of a convoy (20 December) as well as a village in Paktia (16 November 2001) and the targeting of the village of Pul-e-Khumri (14 December 2001).[265] On 21 December 2001, US aircraft attacked Afghan tribal elders, causing interim President Hamid Karzai to publicly ask the United States to refrain from launching military operations based solely on the intelligence of local sources.[266] And the new Afghan Foreign Minister, Dr Abdullah, called for the United States to re-evaluate its procedure for determining targets and launching attacks –

'This situation has to come to an end. Mistakes can take place, human errors are possible, but our people should be assured that every measure was taken to avoid such incidents.'[267]

Applying the provisions set out by IHL, these bombing failures did not breach the principle of discrimination. For US aircraft, even though they attacked civilian targets directly instead of enemy combatants, did not do so deliberately.[268]

At the same time, however, the focus on targets of opportunity required that military action had to take place immediately owing to the risk of losing the target entirely. In such situations firm confirmation of the identity of the respective target proved impossible. But rather than refraining from hitting an unconfirmed target, the US military occasionally shortcut the targeting process and relied on unverified intelligence, thereby trading time for accuracy.[269]

Such collateral damage could have been significantly reduced if the United States had not only refrained from shortcutting the targeting process but had also accepted higher risks to its own forces or simply refrained from striking the target.[270] From the perspective of the idea of 'due care', the attacker is morally obliged to refrain from striking a target in cases where a target's identity is in doubt due to incomplete and unverified intelligence. Arguments of military necessity and military advantages alone (even in cases of emerging high profile targets) cannot serve as justification because such unverified strikes, according to Robert Cryer, are 'essentially blind' and therefore inherently indiscriminate.[271] In the end, the reason for America's inability to provide its own intelligence and its subsequent reliance on local indigenous allies stemmed

[264] Bellamy 2006, 188; Dana Priest 2002; Bearak 2002; Cordesman 2002, 33.
[265] Filipov 2001; Sadaqat 2001; Sengupta 2001.
[266] 'Karzai Calls for US military policy review', *The Guardian*, 2 July 2002.
[267] 'Karzai Calls for US military policy review', *The Guardian*, 2 July 2002.
[268] Roblyer 2003; Zehfuss 2006, 8.   [269] Roblyer 2003.   [270] Bellamy 2006, 180–198.
[271] Cryer 2002, 50.

from a lack of US forces on the ground which – in turn – was the result of the casualty-averse attitudes of the Bush Administration. Bellamy, for example, concludes that

> [i]n order to protect their own forces, the US military relied heavily on unverified intelligence provided by Afghans ... rather than placing American troops on the ground to search for and verify military targets.[272]

Put differently, by taking risks with target verification in order to strike at targets of opportunity, the United States put concerns for its own forces ahead of the concerns for non-combatants. As a consequence, it was simply not enough to devise an entire system of legal scrutinising if the number of SOF on the ground were too few to ensure that the process of information gathering remained unflawed in the first place. At the end of the day, precision-guided munitions are only as accurate as the intelligence on the ground. In other words, to provide unbiased intelligence and to verify the information gathered by local indigenous allies, much larger numbers of US forces were needed on the ground. By choosing an air campaign, however, the US military reduced its opportunity to do precisely that.

It seems highly unlikely that placing additional US military forces on the ground (and thereby marginally increasing the risks to US military personnel) would have jeopardised the overall military objectives. Making things worse, the Marines who had arrived by late November were withheld from actively fighting the enemy or collecting and verifying the intelligence provided by allied Afghan warlords.[273]

Furthermore, early on in the campaign Secretary Rumsfeld admitted that the United States lacked sufficient human intelligence of its own and announced that he would deploy more troops into the country to assist with the process of target selection and approval.[274] This suggests that decision-makers in Washington were aware of the problems resulting from unreliable intelligence provided by its allies. Yet, despite this recognition and Rumsfeld's announcement to send more American forces on the ground, none of these forces ever arrived due to concerns for US casualties.[275] Yet, at the same time, US targeting mistakes continued unabated.

Based on this evidence, US practice in this case did not satisfy the 'due care' test as the military – aware of the source of the problem – failed to adjust its operational practices accordingly. Small increases to the risks of American military personnel by placing or using more available forces on the ground would have neither endangered America's overall strategic

---

[272] Bellamy 2005, 289.   [273] O'Hanlon 2002, 64.   [274] Loeb 2001; Cryer 2002, 50.
[275] 'Rumsfeld Defends Bombing Campaign', *BBC News*, 5 November 2001; Bellamy 2006, 192.

objectives nor posed excessive levels of risk to US forces, but would have reduced the harm inflicted on innocent Afghans. Here, the US prioritised casualty-aversion over civilian protection.

The mistreatments and revenge killings committed by US local allies   Shortly after 9/11, US political and military decision-makers agreed not to deploy significant numbers of ground troops to combat al-Qaeda and the Taliban, but to forge an alliance with local forces in the Northern Alliance/United Front instead.[276] By systematically integrating with its indigenous allies, the US military campaign not only transferred the risks of ground combat onto Afghan forces, but also relied on an Afghan way of war that had a long record of deliberately killing non-combatants.[277] During two decades of civil war, warlords like General Abdul Rashid Dostum had engaged in revenge killings, rape, looting, and massive human rights violations.[278]

There is ample evidence to suggest that these local allies prosecuted their war against the Taliban and al-Qaeda in precisely this fashion. Several substantial allegations of mistreatment of civilians and prisoners in the hands of allied warlords occurred.[279] Northern Alliance forces engaged in a considerable number of revenge killings against non-combatants after the fall of Masar-i-Sharif, Kunduz, and Kabul during which an estimated one thousand civilians were killed.[280] It has been claimed that more than eight hundred Taliban deaths alone occurred due to postwar reprisals and the killing of Taliban prisoners in sealed containers.[281]

Pentagon officials were strongly aware of the inhumane record of their new allies.[282] According to David Radcliffe, who at the time worked for the Pentagon's counter-terrorism unit, decision-makers had no illusion of their way of fighting:

---

[276] Michael Smith 2006, 214–215.   [277] Nojumi 2002, 226.

[278] Scholl-Latour 2002; Coll 2004b; Rashid 2000.

[279] 'Physicians for Human Rights calls for End to Stalling Investigation into Afghan Mass Graves', available at www.phrusa.org/research/afghanistan/report_graves_newsweek .html, accessed on 4 December 2004; Peter Falk, 'Appraising the War against Afghanistan', available at www.sscr.org/sept11/essays/falk_text_only.htm, accessed on 15 November 2004; Roberts 2002; Scholl-Latour 2002, 118.

[280] Cryer 2002, 37–83.

[281] 'Physicians for Human Rights calls for End to Stalling Investigation into Afghan Mass Graves'; Human Rights Watch 2004; North 2004; 'Taliban Prisoners died in sealed containers', *The Scotsman*, 12 December 2001; 'Dozens of Taliban prisoners died in airtight containers: report', *Agence France Press*, 11 December 2001; '600 bodies discovered in Mazar-i-Sharif', *Agence France Press*, 22 November 2001.

[282] DeLong 2004; Michael Smith 2006, 218–219; Franks 2004; telephone interview with Milton Bearden, 21 June 2005.

They had often killed prisoners in containers and the US had a strong awareness of these legacies. It was very clear to the Pentagon that these guys had blood on their hands, that there was a clear record of switching sides and their abuses against civilians. We were not dealing with a bunch of choir boys but with a bunch of bloody and vicious fighters.[283]

But this historical record did not cause any concern for those involved in the planning stages and the conduct of OEF.[284]

Given the knowledge of the indiscriminate nature of their indigenous allies, the question arises whether a greater commitment of US ground forces would have contributed to a higher level of protection of prisoners of war (POWs) and non-combatants. Posing this question is not to argue that the US military should be held responsible for any of the war crimes committed by the Northern Alliance/United Front. Here, the laws of war clearly attribute responsibility to those who actively commit the crime. However, since the US military not only took the decision to transfer the risks of combat onto its Afghan allies, but also knew the latter's practices in the past, it should have taken positive steps to encourage greater respect for the principle of non-combatant immunity.

Robert Cryer for instance reveals how, during the later stages of OEF, US troops took a more direct control of the proceedings on the ground. They started encouraging allied forces to accept surrender, to take prisoners, and to build POW camps. As a result, the treatment of POWs and non-combatants improved considerably.[285] This suggests that an earlier and larger deployment of US ground forces would have contributed to the protection of ex-combatants and non-combatants.

But due to the reluctance of key decision-makers to place more US forces in harm's way and its reliance on indigenous allies, the risks of harm to Afghan civilians were increased. The moral argument can be made that had the US placed its own forces on the ground rather than outsourcing the ground war to the Northern Alliance, a higher level of respect for both Afghan non-combatants and enemy prisoners could have been achieved. The failure to accept modest increases to the risks faced by US military personnel indirectly allowed for the violations of the laws of war by the Northern Alliance to happen. Demonstrating clear appreciation for the inhumane record of their allies arguably created certain moral obligations for American decision-makers to prevent atrocities from happening. Higher levels of civilian protection could have been achieved by either using US forces instead of Afghan proxies, or by at least enforcing

---

[283] Interview with David Radcliffe in Washington, DC, 30 November 2004.
[284] Interview with Jeffrey Starr in Washington, DC, 15 June 2005; interview with Wade Ishimoto in Washington, DC, 18 December 2004.
[285] Cryer 2002, 64–65.

humane conduct upon its allies. On this account, therefore, the United States also failed the 'due care' test.

These four principle causes of collateral damage resulted in OEF's failure in setting new standards of accuracy and in achieving less harm to non-combatants. Thus, while US operations during OEF generally complied with the provisions set by IHL, the US operation nevertheless failed the 'due care' test.

Conclusion

The chapter has shown that although the United States in 2001 and 2002 fought OEF as a war of survival with vital national security interests perceived to be at stake, US decision-makers did not adopt a different approach to casualty-aversion from American humanitarian interventions. The pervasiveness of US casualty-aversion that had been so characteristic of US interventions during the 1990s continued despite 9/11. This overriding concern for American casualties resulted in a US strategy that refrained from placing more than a few hundred US forces on the ground in Afghanistan. Instead, the risks of ground combat were transferred to local indigenous allies in the Northern Alliance/United Front.

The chapter then investigated the implications of this high standard of casualty-aversion for Afghan civilian protection. It was found that strict RoE and a sophisticated target approval system ensured an extremely discriminate and largely proportionate use of force that was in compliance with the laws of war and that translated into low levels of civilian harm similar to the numbers incurred during US operations of the 1990s. Thus, OEF provides an example of a US war waged in ways that not only met the standards of minimal casualties but also respect for the principle of non-combatant immunity.

At the same time, however, the chapter has argued that an even higher level of civilian protection could have been achieved. This higher standard was not met because the US military failed to take all appropriate measures and to make every effort to reduce civilian casualties. This moral argument was developed by applying Walzer's idea of 'due care' to US operations in Afghanistan. In particular, the chapter investigated the four major causes of collateral damage that occurred between October 2001 and March 2002 in relation to the conditions set by the 'due care' test. This examination revealed that the US campaign failed the 'due care' test, i.e. it failed to take sufficient positive steps to reduce the level of harm to non-combatants.

All major causes of collateral damage identified in the chapter could have been mitigated in ways that would have required either the employment of a different weapons mix or the acceptance of a marginal increase of the risks to which US soldiers were exposed. Furthermore, it was shown that such increases would have neither exposed the lives of US soldiers to disproportionate risks, nor endangered the overall campaign against al-Qaeda and the Taliban. The US military, however, failed to accept such marginal increases because of casualty-aversion.

6   The US War in Iraq

No Iraqi is worth the life of any US military person.

Paul Wolfowitz

War is no pastime; it is no mere joy in daring and winning, no place for irresponsible enthusiasts.

Clausewitz

Looking at both the 1991 and 2003 wars, the only feature that marks the two wars as ostensibly 'revolutionary' is the low ratio of US combat fatalities.

Carl Conetta

The US counterinsurgency field manual is the counterrevolution in military affairs.

David Kilcullen

Introduction

On 1 May 2003, standing on the flight deck of the USS Abraham Lincoln, President George W. Bush announced in a nationally televised address that 'major combat operations in Iraq have ended.'[1] Operation Iraqi Freedom (OIF) was immediately hailed as a historical accomplishment, an unprecedented military success. A relatively small, highly mobile and technologically advanced US-led coalition force (consisting of troops from the United States, United Kingdom, Australia, and Poland) had taken minimal casualties and in just three weeks had swept across hundreds of kilometres of hostile territory, captured the capital Baghdad, and toppled the Ba'athist government of Saddam Hussein. Exhilarated by the apparent success of 'Shock and Awe', American political and military decision-makers believed that accomplishing the mission's stated political objectives, the true measure of victory, was imminent: Saddam's forces appeared defeated, the alleged weapons of mass destruction (WMD)

---

[1] Available at www.whitehouse.gov/news/releases/2003/05/2003050115.html, accessed on 1 December 2014.

would soon be discovered, Al-Qaeda cells believed to be operating in Iraq would be captured or killed, and reconstruction and democratisation would soon be underway with the assistance of the Iraqi people.[2]

As it turned out, however, American hopes for a lighting victory were quickly dashed. Rather than marking the end of the war, President Bush's 'Mission Accomplished' speech merely marked the beginning of a vicious insurgent guerrilla campaign that eventually threw Iraq into a full-scale civil war.[3] Besides the removal of Saddam Hussein, the US invasion did not accomplish any of its stated or tacit political objectives: at home, voter dissatisfaction with the Bush Administration's handling of the war, fuelled further by images of the Abu Ghraib scandal, cost the Republican Party its majorities in both the House of Representatives and the Senate, and led Secretary of Defense, Donald Rumsfeld, to resign his post in 2006. In post-Saddam Iraq, no WMDs were discovered while US forces found themselves bogged down in an ever-worsening asymmetric quagmire which – by the time of US withdrawal eight years later – had turned into the most costly war the US had fought since Vietnam: 3,482 US soldiers had been killed, another 32,222 wounded, and estimates of Iraqi civilian casualties resulting from direct and indirect violence ranging between 109,000 and five hundred thousand.[4]

The capacity to win the battle against Saddam's regime in a mere few weeks was thrown into stark relief by the failure to win the overall asymmetric conflict that followed. Failing to adequately respond to the insurgency in the first few years, the Pentagon eventually introduced the COIN manual in late 2006, the most far-reaching overhaul of US military strategy with regards to the norms of casualty-aversion and civilian protection since the end of the Vietnam War. Its purpose was to provide a strategy for victory in Iraq, and – as its authors made clear – it aimed at nothing less than a complete reversal of the long-held preference for risk-transfer from US soldiers to enemy civilians.[5] According to its key architect, it amounted to a 'counter-revolution in military affairs'.[6]

The purpose of this third and final case study of the book is to empirically evaluate this violent clash between American military forces and its adversaries in Iraq between 2003 and 2011. The chapter first provides

---

[2] Fontenot, Degen, and Tohn 2005; Keegan 2004; Boyne 2003; Franks 2004.

[3] 'Annan: Iraq Close to Civil War', USA Today, 27 November 2006.

[4] Figures available at www.defense.gov/news/casualty.pdf, accessed on 2 November 2014; Hagopian 2013; 'The War in Iraq: 10 years and counting', available at www .iraqbodycount.org, accessed on 17 November 2014; Leigh 2010.

[5] Herz 2007, 114.   [6] Cited Ricks 2009, 163.

a historical background to the war, with a particular focus on US strategic decisions taken in the run-up towards OIF. The main bulk of the chapter then examines the three distinguishable combat phases that characterised the course of OIF: the overthrow of Saddam Hussein's regime (19 March–1 May 2003), the insurgency (May 2003–December 2006), and the so-called 'surge' (January 2007–December 2011).

By investigating each of the three combat phases in turn, the case study advances understanding of how the US norms of casualty-aversion and civilian protection were impacted upon by its adversaries in Iraq. For each combat phase, the chapter evaluates US military operations through the prism of International Humanitarian Law (IHL) and examines whether American forces started prioritising casualty-aversion over the safeguarding of Iraqi civilians. Finally, by drawing on the moral idea of 'due care', the chapter examines whether – in each of the three combat phases – lower numbers of Iraqi civilian deaths could have been achieved if marginal increases to the risks faced by US soldiers had been accepted and if different military strategies had been chosen.

The chapter concludes by relating the empirical findings back to the theoretical framework of the book, by showing how the conflict in Iraq has impacted on US warfare, and by comparing its findings to the US interventions in Somalia and Afghanistan.

Background to the War in Iraq

While the US invasion of Afghanistan largely received global approval, the Bush Administration's decision and justification to go to war over Iraq as part of the 'Global War on Terror' proved to be highly controversial among global publics, academics, and the international community. According to President Bush and British Prime Minister Tony Blair, the objective of OIF was to 'disarm Iraq of weapons of mass destruction, to end Saddam Hussein's support for terrorism, and to free the Iraqi people'.[7] The 9/11 attacks – while not necessarily changing the world – certainly changed America's geostrategic view of the world. Framed by a rising neoconservative ideology, the fear of globally operating apocalyptic terrorists networks, equipped with WMDs and supported by rogue regimes like Saddam Hussein's, led to the new military calculus of pre-emptive war inside the inner circle of Washington's political powerbrokers.[8] According to this

---

[7] Available at http://georgewbush-whitehouse.archives.gov/news/releases/2003/03/200303 22.html, accessed on 2 December 2014.
[8] Schmidt and Williams 2008, 191–220.

view, later termed the 'Bush Doctrine',[9] Iraq's failure to take the 'final opportunity' to disarm itself of alleged nuclear, biological, and chemical weapons, and to stop harbouring and supporting terrorist organisations constituted an intolerable threat to world peace and thereby generated an ethical duty for the US military to act pre-emptively.[10]

This casus belli was questioned by some sections within the United States,[11] but was more strongly opposed across the globe, including some of America's long-standing allies France, Germany, and New Zealand who argued that there was no evidence of WMDs inside Iraq and that the findings of the newly resumed UN weapons inspections did not justify a military invasion.[12] On 15 February 2003, a month before the beginning of OIF, there were worldwide protests against the looming Iraq War, including a rally of three million people in Rome, which is listed in the Guinness Book of Records as the largest anti-war rally in history.[13] Overall, an estimated 36 million people across the globe took part in almost three thousand protests against the war between 3 January and 12 April 2003.[14]

While the global controversy over the Iraq War was visible in the media, in parliaments and on the streets, an altogether different controversy rained behind closed doors inside the Pentagon in the run-up towards the Iraq War. Here, a fierce discussion was raging over how to strategically conduct the upcoming military operation against Saddam Hussein's regime. It boiled down to two major issues: first, over whether the model of the concurrent Afghanistan War – airpower with low number of American boots on the ground – was to serve as the blueprint for Iraq or whether a much larger invasion force, similar to the 1991 ODS, was required.[15] The second issue was over how much attention military

[9] The 'Bush Doctrine' was outlined first outlined publicly in September 2002 and entailed the three main elements of pre-emption, acting alone if necessary, and the spread of freedom. For details, see www.informationclearinghouse.info/article2320.html, accessed on 1 December 2014.

[10] Schmidt and Williams 2008, 191–220; The focus of this book and indeed chapter is not on questions of 'jus ad bellum', but rather on 'jus in bello'. Thus, it is concerned with the justness of the conduct of the war, not the justness of the reason to go to war itself. For a good examination of these jus ad bellum controversies over Iraq, see O'Driscoll 2008.

[11] Prior to the war, polls showed 22 per cent of Americans to be against the war and 72% in favour: www.pewresearch.org/2008/03/19/public-attitudes-toward-the-war-in-iraq-200 32008/, accessed on 30 November 2014.

[12] Available at www.theguardian.com/world/2003/mar/06/france.germany, accessed on 20 November 2014.

[13] Available at https://web.archive.org/web/20040904214302/www.guinnessworldrecords .com/content_pages/record.asp?recordid=54365, accessed on 20 November 2014.

[14] Available at http://socialistworker.co.uk/art/5932/Anti-war+protests+do+make+a+differ ence, accessed on 20 November 2014.

[15] Rumsfeld 2002.

planners should bring to fighting the war as opposed to winning the peace.[16] These controversies merit revisiting briefly, for they reveal decision-makers' attitudes towards casualty-aversion and are important for shaping the subsequent course of the Iraq War.

As detailed records now show, the decision to go to War in Iraq was taken soon after 9/11 and planning for OIF became the Pentagon's central focus by November 2001.[17] As Chapter 5 has shown, notwithstanding the official rhetoric, the US leadership remained highly uncertain about Americans' willingness to accept sacrifice in spite of the events of 9/11. This had not changed by the time the Bush Administration turned its focus on Iraq in late 2001.[18] For US decision-makers, the original war plan for Iraq (OPLAN 1003–98) which had called for as many as five hundred thousand US troops in total, was unacceptable.[19] In the lead up to OIF, therefore, the plan was recast at least six times with each new draft calling for fewer boots on the ground. In the end, OIF was executed with 148,000 US troops (out of which 78,000 were ground forces).[20]

Why did the US leadership in the end decide to invade with 148,000 rather than five hundred thousand troops? The answer lies in the outcome of the fierce debate inside the Pentagon over the question of the appropriate force size.[21] As Dennison shows in a detailed study, the debate occurred between senior civilian leaders within the Office of the Secretary of Defence and the Office of Force Transformation on the one side and the senior military leadership at CENTCOM on the other.[22] While the latter group argued for an adherence to the traditional and time-tested approach of overwhelming mass and larger troop deployments, similar to those during the successful 1991 Persian Gulf War, the former group advocated net-centric warfare with an emphasis on high technology combat systems, air forces, and small numbers of ground forces.[23]

This debate had its origins prior to 9/11 when Secretary Rumsfeld, Arthur K. Cebrowski, and John J Garstka had started to transform the US military along the lines of net-centric, risk-averse warfare. Net-centric warfare, as shown in Chapter 2, was the outgrowth of the so-called RMA of the 1990s and inherently structured around risk-free US warfare.[24] Before this backdrop, the seemingly swift overthrow of the Taliban

---

[16] Dennison 2006, 1–34.

[17] Clark 2003, 130; Ricks 2006; www.cbsnews.com/news/plans-for-iraq-attack-began-on-9-11/, accessed on 19 November 2014.

[18] Boettcher and Cobb 2006, 835.   [19] Gordon and Trainor 2006, 4.

[20] Woodward 2004, 287.   [21] Clark 2003, 1819.

[22] Dennison 2006, 1–34; Clark 2003, 18–19.

[23] Cordesman 2003, 148159; see also Franks 2004, 373.

[24] Der Derian 2001, 120; Bacevich 1996, 47. The Office of Force Transformation, which drove the nucleus of netcentric warfare, was set up in October 2001.

regime in Afghanistan by the end of 2001 – seen by proponents and critics alike as the first litmus test for Rumsfeld's transformation agenda – played into Secretary of Defense's hands right at the time when the planning of Operation Iraqi Freedom turned into its hot phase. Exhilarated by the swift triumph in Afghanistan and driven by a casualty-averse agenda,[25] Rumsfeld steadfastly rejected the operational plans by senior Pentagon planners, insisting on further reductions of US forces for the Iraq war plan. And he eventually resolved the internal debate by removing all officers in the Joint Staff who did not share his transformation agenda.[26] As a consequence, the invasion of Iraq came to be modelled on the same net-centric, casualty-averse approach as OEF – albeit – in the absence of equivalent Iraqi indigenous ally to the Northern Alliance – with more ground forces than in Afghanistan.

Moreover, while few military planners doubted a decisive military victory in Iraq, the prognosis for the postwar phase was far less certain.[27] And yet, within an administration that repeatedly declared that it 'did not do nation-building',[28] military planners were directed to spend significantly more time and energy considering how to implement the military campaign than how to win the peace at war's end.[29] The extent to which the planning for the end of hostilities was considered comparatively unimportant by the leadership around Rumsfeld can be seen in the amount of time and staff dedicated to this task: while planning for the combat phase in Iraq began in late November 2001, planning for the postwar phase only commenced on 20 January 2003, less than two months prior to the beginning of the war.[30]

Even more disconcerting, based on a detailed CIA intelligence report, the postwar plan assumed a 'best-case' scenario: that US forces would be greeted as liberators by the Iraqi people, that Iraq's oil production would almost entirely cover the costs of reconstruction, that Iraqi security forces would patrol the streets and ensure public order, that US forces would withdraw within less than a year, and that political authority would be handed over to an interim government dominated by pro-US exiles. In other words, the CIA report and the Pentagon planning for the postwar stage assumed not only that the overthrow of Saddam Hussein meant the end of the Iraqi will to fight but also that the Iraqi state as a security provider would continue to function more or less as before.[31]

---

[25] Boettcher and Cobb 2006, 834–835.   [26] Hersh 2005, 251253.
[27] Rosen 2005; Sifry and Cerf 2003, 281–353.
[28] Available at www.usnews.com/news/national/articles/2008/10/10/new-army-manual
-shows-wars-softer-side-with-focus-on-nation-building, accessed on 2 December 2014.
[29] Keen 2006, 108; Hooker 2005, 6.   [30] Woodward 2004, 76.
[31] Hooker 2005, 3738; Gordon and Trainor 2006, 498–499; Keegan 2004, 209.

The reasons for why these optimistic expectations prevailed in the postwar plan are unclear.[32] What is interesting to note, though, is how the plan's optimistic assumptions were in sync with the principle logic driving the idea of net-centric warfare at the time: its two main architects, Cebrowski and Garstka, assumed that the information advantage of this new mode of warfare would generate a battlefield superiority so overwhelmingly in favour of the US military that enemy forces would have no choice but to drop their weapons. Net-centric warfare would break the enemy's will to resist and would enable the US to take Clausewitz out of war.[33]

These decisions were important. While the military strategy allowed US and coalition forces to swiftly overwhelm Iraqi forces in a casualty-averse manner, the low number of US forces deployed came to haunt US efforts in the aftermath when a mass army of soldiers, not speed and technology, was required for securing victory. Moreover, the lack of ground forces in combination with an unrealistic and inadequate postwar strategy, generated a power vacuum that sparked chaos and unrest, fuelling what subsequently turned into a large-scale, full-blown insurgency.

At the same time, the early successful combat phase in Afghanistan and the detailed accounts of the planning phase in the run-up towards the invasion of Iraq both show that 9/11 it did not alter the key concerns surrounding the US mode of warfare.[34] By early 2002, US officials felt that US operations in Afghanistan had revealed to the fullest the parameters of this 'new mode of warfare': the use of high-tech warfare to avoid quagmires like Vietnam, Lebanon, or Somalia and its ability to strictly limit casualties to both, US forces and enemy civilians.[35] President Bush outlined the prospect of this new mode of warfare in April 2003:

We've applied the new powers of technology ... to strike an enemy force with speed and incredible precision. By a combination of creative strategies and advanced technologies, we are redefining war on our terms. In this new era of warfare, we can target a regime, not a nation.[36]

The US President's claim that the US had 'redefined war' by developing a capacity for a new type of rapid, decisive, low cost warfare lead the Administration to raise expectations about the 'costless' nature of the War in Iraq. And by emphasising the capacity to 'target a regime, not

---

[32] Ample warnings were issued regarding the volatile nature of the post-Saddam situation prior to OIF. For an overview, see Diamond 2005, 281–283; Fallows 2004.

[33] Interview with John Garstka in Washington, D.C., 18 December 2004.

[34] Woodward 2004; Conetta 2004, 4; Kahl 2007b, 16–18.   [35] Rumsfeld 2002.

[36] 'Bush's Speech: Remarks by President Bush at Boeing, St. Louis, Missouri' *Voice of America News.*

a nation', the US President's rhetoric confirmed the importance attached to conducting a surgical military operation that was respectful of the principle of non-combatant immunity.

With hindsight it might be easy to dismiss these optimistic accounts, especially given the subsequent course of the situation in Iraq after May 2003. But at the time when the planning phase for OIF took place, the Bush Administration understood its operations in Afghanistan not only as a success story (the Taliban had been overthrown, US forces had been largely withdrawn, an interim government installed, and reconstruction was underway) but also as a blueprint for how to embark on the overthrow of Saddam Hussein. How, then, did OIF unfold and to what extent were US forces able to wage this first combat phase with low risks to both US military personnel and Iraqi civilians? And how did the strategy of Saddam's forces impact on the normative balance between US casualty-aversion and civilian protection?

The Toppling of Saddam's Ba'athist Regime (19 March–1 May 2003)

The airstrike on the Presidential Palace in Baghdad on 19 March 2003 marked the opening shot of what was largely a conventional interstate war between the US-led 'Coalition of the Willing' and the military forces of the Iraqi state. The following day, US ground forces moved into southern Iraq, occupied the Basra region and engaged in the Battle of Nasiriyah on 23 March 2003. US Special Forces launched an amphibious assault from the Persian Gulf to secure the oil fields while the 173rd Airborne Brigade was dropped near the city of Kirkuk where they joined Kurdish rebels to fight the Iraqi army in the north. Massive airstrikes across the country and against Iraqi command and control centres threw the defending army into chaos and prevented an effective resistance against invading coalition ground forces. On 9 March, three weeks after the beginning of the war, Baghdad was occupied without much resistance. This was followed on 10 April by the fall of Kirkuk, and of Tikrit on 15 April. Iraqi President Saddam Hussein and the central leadership went into hiding as coalition forces completed the occupation of the country.[37] On 1 May 2003, President Bush made his famous 'Mission Accomplished' speech.

During this initial and largely conventional phase of the war, US forces undertook considerable efforts to spare civilian lives and to adhere to IHL. From the outset, US leaders repeatedly emphasised that OIF was not directed against the Iraqi people but aimed 'merely' at regime change

---

[37] Rogers 2013, 1.

and that US forces went out of their way to avoid 'collateral damage'.[38] For instance, resonating Secretary Rumsfeld's assertion during the Afghan War that 'no nation in human history has done more to avoid civilian casualties than the United States has in this conflict',[39] Joint Chiefs of Staff Chairman General Myers reassured in February 2003 that

[i]n our targeting [in Iraq], we'll go to extraordinary lengths to protect noncombatants and civilians and facilities that should not be struck. And we always do that.[40]

Similarly, a senior CENTCOM official stated that

the ability to be that [much] more precise, intuitively tells me that there should be fewer casualties ... The precision capability that now exists allows us to keep civilian casualties to a lower number than we've ever seen in the past.[41]

On the eve of the war Admiral Timothy Keating, who led the US naval effort, promised that

the campaign will be unlike any we have seen in the history of warfare, with breathtaking precision, almost eye-watering speed, persistence, agility, and lethality.

President Bush reiterated the Admiral's claims when he spoke to the nation on the night the war began.[42] Ten days later, General Franks summarised the US effort as 'an incredibly precise military operation':

I think you have seen time and time and time again military targets fall while the civilian infrastructure remains in place. And it's the same with civilian lives.[43]

In essence, US decision-makers argued that the use of military force was directed against the Iraqi regime, not against the Iraqi people and that historically unprecedented efforts were undertaken to respect the legal principle of non-combatant immunity.[44]

This rhetoric was backed up in practice by considerable efforts to respect Iraqi civilian immunity.[45] For instance, prior to their deployment in Iraq, US soldiers had to undergo additional training in the laws of war, particularly regarding the respect for non-combatant immunity as found in the Rules of Engagement (RoE).[46] Moreover, the decision was made in the Pentagon prior to the invasion – and largely observed throughout – to

---

[38] For example, see http://edition.cnn.com/2003/US/03/19/sprj.irq.int.bush.transcript/ and www.defense.gov/transcripts/transcript.aspx?transcriptid=2141, both accessed on 28 July 2010.
[39] Nelson 2001.   [40] Lauer and Couric 2003.   [41] Porth 2003.
[42] 'Bush speaks to nation as explosions hit Baghdad', *Chicago Sun-Times*, 20 March 2003.
[43] Franks 2003.   [44] Thomas 2006, 10.   [45] Zehfuss 2010, 547–548; Thomas 2006, 10.
[46] Crawford 2007b, 206.

actively avoid the targeting of dual-use facilities (with few exceptions) even when such action would have been permitted by IHL.[47] For example, Iraqi television and radio stations as well as the electrical grid were left untouched.[48] This is significant because it indicates that the Pentagon in this first combat phase imposed restrictions on the use of force that went beyond what was legally required and what was done in previous US military operations, indicating the importance attached to civilian protection.[49] Here, the Pentagon's self-imposed restraint was reflective of the previous controversies over the targeting of dual-use facilities in Kosovo and Afghanistan.

Outside this 'no-strike' list, military targets on the Pentagon's list were vetted by military lawyers for compliance with IHL.[50] Here, military lawyers weighed the proportionality of strikes according a collateral damage estimate matrix that considered the target's military purpose, its protected status, the types of weaponeering, and anticipated civilian costs.[51] These legal procedures were designed not only to check and approve specific targets, but also to assign the ammunition to be used accordingly. In most cases, computer modelling was used to predict potential collateral damage that particular targets and weapons systems would cause.[52] Thus, US damage limitation efforts, as Carl Conetta examined,

> pertain[ed] not to technological capabilities, *per se,* but instead to the choice of targets and the care exercised in attacking them. US efforts along these lines include[d] vetting targets with DoD lawyers and relying on computer simulations – the so-called 'bug splat' program – to predict the likely 'spill over' or collateral effects of an attack.[53]

Based on such simulations, several of the potential targets were abandoned for humanitarian reasons while for others the risks for Iraqi civilians were deliberately reduced by changing the timing of the attacks and the types of weapons used.[54]

Further reflecting these efforts to minimise the harm to Iraqi civilians, over two-thirds (68 per cent) of the munitions dropped by the US military were precision-guided.[55] This percentage of smart precision-guided ammunitions was historically unprecedented: about 60 per cent of all the US bombs dropped in Afghanistan were so-called 'smart bombs', compared to 30 per cent during 'Operation Allied Force' in 1999 and just

---

[47] Johnson 2006, 191; Kahl 2007b, 16.   [48] Dennison 2006, 12.
[49] Johnson 2006, 191.   [50] Kahl 2007b, 16; Thomas W Smith 2008, 152.
[51] Crawford 2007b, 206; Conetta 2004.   [52] Roblyer 2003, 16–18; Kahl 2007b, 16.
[53] Conetta 2003b, emphasis in original.   [54] Kahl 2007b, 16–18.
[55] Conetta 2003b. For a good account of the 'imprecision' of 'smart bombs', see Zehfuss 2010, 548–550.

6.5 per cent of such weapons during the 1991 'Operation Desert Storm' (ODS).[56] And in direct comparison with the 1991 ODS, significantly less ordnance was dropped in Iraq in 2003.[57] While this reflects the steady shift towards the increased usage of precision weapons, it has also been an indication of the importance attached to the use of lethal force with maximum restraint towards the innocent.[58] In other words, from the outset of OIF, considerable efforts were undertaken by the Pentagon to comply with the legal protection afforded to Iraqi civilians.

These precautionary measures resulted in relatively low numbers of civilian deaths during the first combat phase in Iraq. While exact figures remain contested, the most accurate estimates suggest that between 3,200 and 4,300 Iraqi non-combatants were killed between the beginning of the war on 19 March 2003 and the toppling of the Saddam regime on 1 May 2003.[59] As detailed research by several scholars (including those highly critical of the US War in Iraq) shows, these civilian casualties were inflicted largely in accordance with the protection afforded by IHL, i.e. they were proportionate and were caused unintentionally and indirectly.[60]

Yet, in absolute numbers (and in proportion to the overall Iraqi combat deaths – estimated to be between 10,800 and 15,100), OIF incurred more civilian casualties than during the 1991 Operation Desert Storm – despite the lesser amount of ordnance dropped, the significant advancements of US military technology since, and the higher ratio of high-quality air munitions used in 2003.[61] This marked difference can largely be explained with the difference in military objectives for which the 2003 campaign was fought (the more ambitious objective of regime change in Iraq over the limited objective to liberate Kuwait while leaving Saddam's regime in place) and with where US ordnance was dropped (engaging the Iraqi leadership and military in populated areas in 2003 as opposed engaging Iraqi forces in the dessert in 1991).[62] But it nevertheless raises the question over the circumstances under which innocent Iraqis were killed and whether this number could have been reduced had US forces been exposed to higher combat risks.

---

[56] Conetta 2003b.

[57] In OIF, US aircraft delivered 29,900 munitions (19,948 guided, 9,251 unguided). During ODS, 227,000 munitions were dropped (14,825 guided, 212,175 unguided). See *Operation Iraqi Freedom: By Numbers* (Shaw AFB, South Carolina: CENTAF, Assessment and Analysis Division, 30 April 2003); Eliot Cohen 1993, 533–544.

[58] Thomas 2006, 1–33.

[59] Shaw 2005, 122. For a good overview of the discussion and reliability of civilian casualty figures for this period, see Roberts 2010, 115–136.

[60] Kahl 2007b, 36–37; Crawford 2007b; Zehfuss 2010.   [61] Conetta 2003b.

[62] Thomas 2006, 10; Conetta 2004.

The vast majority of Iraqi civilian deaths between 19 March and 1 May 2003 were caused in three distinct areas. First, hundreds of civilian casualties were inflicted when US aircraft engaged more fluid and emerging targets in urban areas, i.e. so-called targets of opportunity (Iraqi military and political leaders).[63] Second, the use of cluster bombs on enemy military targets in remote as well as densely populated urban areas killed hundreds of innocent Iraqi non-combatants.[64] And third, lowering the threshold of the use of force and the vague formulation of the RoE resulted in numerous civilian deaths during urban operations.[65] While civilian casualties caused by these three factors (which will be examined in detail) did not constitute a violation of IHL,[66] the moral question arises as to whether more could have been done to save civilian lives – in particular if the combat risks to US military personnel had been increased.

In Iraq, as in Afghanistan, US decision-makers chose strategies and tactics that ensured highest levels of force protection.[67] The assumption driving these decisions was the infamous 'body-bag syndrome', the internalised belief among US decision-makers that the American public would not tolerate high numbers of American military casualties.[68] The same casualty-averse attitudes that had determined the US mode of warfare throughout the 1990s and – as the previous chapter has shown – the early phase of the war in Afghanistan, was impacting US operations in Iraq in 2003.[69]

Critiques of the idea that the US military in Iraq acted in a casualty-averse manner have pointed to the large amount of ground forces which – in sharp contrast to ODS in 1991 or Afghanistan in 2001 – became involved from of the beginning (during ODS, the four-day ground invasion only followed the 30-day bombing campaign; during OEF only a few hundred forces were placed on the ground).[70] Yet, despite this comparatively heavy footprint moving into Iraq on the second days of the invasion, the actual risks to which the US army was exposed had been significantly reduced well before the first shot was fired: over a decade of US policed no-fly zones, repeated bombardments, UN weapons inspections, and strict sanctions on weapons imports had ensured that Iraq's armed forces never regained the strength they enjoyed prior to 1991, that their equipment lacked maintenance and modernisation, and that their soldiers lacked training in modern techniques of war. One might even argue that

[63] Human Rights Watch 2003b.   [64] Human Rights Watch 2003b.
[65] Human Rights Watch 2003b.
[66] Kahl 2007b; Human Rights Watch 2003b; Zehfuss 2010; Crawford 2007b.
[67] Ricks 2006, 66; Shaw 2005, 107–109; Boettcher and Cobb 2006, 834–835.
[68] Herz 2007, 58.   [69] Woodward 2004; Conetta 2004.   [70] Jon L Anderson 2004.

the first Gulf War never ended in 1991 because the US never actually stopped fighting the first Gulf War.[71] In very crude terms, this was reflected in the estimated reduction of Iraqi combat forces between 1991 and 2003: during ODS, Iraq possessed the 6th largest military force in the world (900,000).[72] In early 2003, experts estimated that Iraqi forces were down to around 360,000, at best 40 per cent of the 1991 Gulf War levels.[73] At the same time, it was believed that within this figure, some significant force was retained in the Republican Guard (comprising around 70,000 elite forces).[74] Overall, though, this meant that the 2003 ground offensive occurred at a time when decision-makers in Washington already knew that the risks to US army personnel were very low. Operating in a net-centric-information form of warfare, US decision-makers were confident, would make the toppling of Saddam's regime relatively costless.[75]

By operating along a largely conventional defensive strategy (rather than defaulting to systematic asymmetric strategies), the Iraqi military was no match for US military might, in particular US airpower, which was key to triggering the sudden collapse of the Iraqi military. The brunt of US fire power was directed specifically at the Republican Guard units and a handful of stalwart regular divisions that formed part of a defensive ring south of Baghdad. Iraqi military preparations and troop deployments only occurred by mid-February 2003 (in 1991 Iraqi units were well dug in and dispersed five months earlier), indicating a lower level of preparation. This, combined with a more rapid and forceful application of US airpower, meant that Iraqi forces had little time to adapt and thereby incurred extremely heavy losses within the first two weeks of OIF.[76] Conservative estimates are that in the second week alone (seen as the tipping point of the bombing campaign) Iraq lost over 1 per cent of its soldiers.[77]

Under heavy and lethal bombing from US aircraft and unable to retaliate the attacker by force, Iraqi desertion levels reached as high as 90 per cent in some units by early April, often precipitated by or even led by the desertion of officers.[78] Other factors contributing to the desertion

---

[71] Jon L Anderson 2004, 21, 62; US and in particular British bombing raids on Iraq increased significantly in late 2002 and early 2003, i.e. prior to the beginning of the war (Michael Smith 2005; Shah 2002.

[72] http://articles.latimes.com/1991-03-06/news/mn-359_1_north-korea, accessed on 30 November 2014.

[73] www.cfr.org/iraq/iraq-iraqs-prewar-military-capabilities/p7695, accessed on 30 November 2014.

[74] www.cfr.org/iraq/iraq-iraqs-prewar-military-capabilities/p7695, accessed on 30 November 2014.

[75] Shaw 2005, 124.   [76] Conetta 2003b, 5.   [77] Conetta 2003a, 5.

[78] Conetta 2003a, 5.

included the severe disenchantment with the military circumstances since 1991, poor and erratic leadership at the national level, growing doubts about the survivability of the Hussein regime, and the effects of US electronic and psychological warfare.[79] As a result, with a few exceptions, Iraqi resistance was low to minimal, enabling the US forces to achieve a quick and nearly costless victory.

Until the toppling of Saddam's statue in central Baghdad and President Bush declaring 'Mission Accomplished' on 1 May 2003, US forces had incurred 148 fatalities (43 of which were non-hostile).[80] This figure amounts to 39 per cent of the overall number of US casualties incurred during ODS (382 KIA [235 of which were non-hostile] and the latter only involved ground forces, traditionally the most costly form of war,[81] in the last few days).[82] The average ratio in combat deaths between Iraqi and US soldiers in 2003 therefore ranged between 70–90 to 1. For the US military this meant that less than one-tenth of 1 per cent of its deployed forces were killed in the overthrow of the Saddam regime.[83] These figures not only demonstrate the military imbalance during OIF but also show the extremely low levels of combat risk faced by US military personnel.

This means that in spite of the more ambitious objective of regime change in 2003, US forces incurred significantly less casualties than during the more limited campaign 1991. And yet, with regards to the number of Iraqi civilian deaths, more were killed by US forces in 2003 than in 1991. Thus, when looking at the absolute fatality numbers among US soldiers and Iraqi civilians in both the 1991 and 2003 war, the only feature that makes 'Shock and Awe' stand out is the low number of US combat fatalities.[84] Given the high level of casualty-aversion on the one hand and the public statements by US leaders on the other hand that 'every effort to spare innocent civilians from harm' had been taken, the question arises whether more civilian lives could have been saved by exposing US soldiers to higher combat risks. Would a less casualty-averse approach have reduced the levels of risk to civilians in the three key areas where collateral damage occurred? The three key circumstances under which the vast majority of civilians casualties occurred were the use of cluster bombs, the pursuit of 'targets of opportunity', and the specific formulation of the RoE.[85] Each of these will be examined in turn.

During OIF, significantly less cluster bombs were used than during ODS, both in absolute terms and in proportion to the overall weapons

---

[79] Conetta 2003a.
[80] http://icasualties.org/Iraq/Fatalities.aspx, accessed on 2 August 2010.
[81] Conetta 2003a.   [82] Couchon 2003.   [83] Conetta 2004.   [84] Conetta 2003b.
[85] Human Rights Watch 2003b.

mix. In 1991, US forces employed around 57,000 cluster bombs (about 25 per cent of all the bombs and missiles used), whereas in 2003, this number had dropped to approximately 1,500 cluster bombs (about 5 per cent of all the ordnance dropped).[86] Despite this reduction in OIF, cluster bombs killed several hundred Iraqi civilians. The problem with the use of cluster bombs was the indiscriminate effects of such weapons – they are area weapons that do not individually target an objective but spread bomblets over 10–18 acres. As Michael Walzer argued,

> The use of cluster bombs is wrong ... because these bombs ... cannot be utilized with any degree of precision; they are inherently indiscriminate and discrimination is a moral duty ... Cluster bombs leave behind large numbers of unexploded bomblets which continue to kill and maim long after the battle or war is over.[87]

Each unexploded submunition effectively becomes a landmine, that is, an inherently indiscriminate weapon. Estimates about the failure rate of submunitions to explode upon impact in Iraq in 2003 range between 4 and 20 per cent.[88]

Within the US military, significant differences existed regarding the use and quality of cluster bombs that on aggregate explain the large number of civilian casualties.[89] In contrast to previous practices, the US Air Force reduced the danger to Iraqi civilians by dropping fewer, yet more accurate cluster bombs in or near populated areas. The vast majority of air-dropped cluster bombs were in remote areas and directed against Iraqi troop concentrations, air defence systems, and airfields. According to Human Right Watch, these practices and the improved failure rate of cluster bombs used (4 per cent) constituted 'a dramatic improvement over that in the 1991 Iraq War, Yugoslavia, as well as Afghanistan'.[90] By contrast, US ground forces used much larger numbers of cluster munitions against military targets in populated areas. Most problematically, these cluster munitions tended to be outdated, less accurate, and with a significantly higher failure rate (of around 16 per cent).[91] In other words, the combination of less reliable and less accurate cluster munition and the tendency to deploy the latter consistently in populated areas virtually guaranteed the loss of civilian lives – something that is reflected

---

[86] Conetta 2004. At the same time, more cluster bombs were used in Iraq between 20 March and 9 April 2003 than during the first 6 months of US operations in Afghanistan (Human Rights Watch 2003b, 56).
[87] Walzer 2009, 49.   [88] Human Rights Watch 2003b, 55–60; Cordesman 2003, 45.
[89] Human Rights Watch 2003b, 55–84.   [90] Human Rights Watch 2003b, 59.
[91] Human Rights Watch 2003b, 80–84.

in the majority of civilian casualties killed by cluster ammunition as being caused by US ground forces rather than the US Air Force.[92]

Once cluster ammunition has been dropped, the high failure rate means that unexploded submunitions, so-called 'duds', effectively become anti-personnel landmines. Having used cluster bombs, the US military had a moral responsibility to remove the threat to non-combatants posed by unexploded submunitions. Bearing the responsibility for delivering cluster bombs, the US omission to clear such weapons means that the US failed the 'due care' test.[93] This failure, however, was not due to US casualty-aversion but due to the failure to protect civilians from unexploded ordnance. In these cases, a higher level of civilian protection would not have required an increase of the risks to American military personnel. Instead, a different choice of weapons system would have been sufficient to save civilian lives.

The situation, however, would have looked very differently in the cases in which collateral damage occurred through the targeting of the Iraqi leadership. Here, US attempts to target key Iraqi individuals hiding in residential areas through the use of PGMs contributed significantly to a higher rate of civilian casualties. As a detailed Human Rights Watch Report revealed, not a single of the fifty of such attacks on 'targets of opportunity' between 19 March and 1 May 2003 succeeded because the Pentagon relied on intercepts from satellite phones (which tended to be inaccurate) and local intelligence (which tended to be incorrect and falsely corroborating). Furthermore, in most of these fifty cases, the detailed scrutinising by military lawyers was bypassed due to perceived time constraints.[94] As the report concluded,

every single attack on leadership failed . . . [because] the intelligence and targeting methodologies used to identify potential leadership targets were inherently flawed and led to preventable deaths.[95]

It was in the pursuit of high profile, yet fluid targets from the air that many of the civilian casualties occurred.[96] Applying the provisions set out by IHL, these bombing failures did not breach the principle of discrimination, for US aircraft, even though they ended up hitting civilian targets instead of enemy combatants, did not attack them deliberately and directly.

At the same time, however, the focus on 'targets of opportunity' required that military action had to take place immediately owing to the risk of losing the target entirely. In such situations firm

---

[92] Human Rights Watch 2003b, 92.   [93] Bellamy 2006, 191–196.
[94] Human Rights Watch 2003b; see also Zehfuss 2010, 553.
[95] Human Rights Watch 2003b, 22.   [96] Crawford 2007b, 208.

confirmation of the identity of the respective target proved impossible. But rather than refraining from hitting an unconfirmed target, the US military relied on unverified intelligence, thereby trading time for accuracy.[97] Such collateral damage could have been significantly reduced if the United States had accepted higher risks to its own forces in order to verify and confirm each target or if it had simply refrained from striking the target. From a moral perspective, the attacker is obliged to refrain from striking a target in cases where a target's identity is in doubt due to incomplete and unverified intelligence. Arguments of military necessity and military advantage alone (even in cases of emerging high profile targets) cannot serve as justification because such unverified strikes are 'essentially blind' and therefore inherently indiscriminate.[98] In the end, the reason for America's inability to provide its own intelligence stemmed from a lack of US forces on the ground which – in turn – was the result of the casualty-averse attitudes of the Bush Administration. Put differently, by taking risks with target verification in order to strike at 'targets of opportunity', the United States placed concerns for its own forces ahead of the concerns for non-combatants. While such practices did not violate IHL, they nevertheless failed to meet the 'due care' test.

Where the US Air Force did *not* pursue fluid, emerging targets and therefore the legal scrutiny by Pentagon lawyers was *not* bypassed, however, collateral damage still occurred. The reason for this lies in the imprecision of precision-guided missiles. As Zehfuss and Conetta show, even under test conditions, PGMs on average fall within the designed radius of 10 meters of the designated target only 50 per cent of the time.[99] So,

the precision claimed for these weapons is, even under test conditions, normally achieved *only every other time* … In 50 percent of cases [the PGM] will land *somewhere else*, more than 10 meters away from the target.[100]

While the use of PGMs in Iraq did not violate IHL, their use in urban contexts invariably caused large numbers of non-combatant casualties – even when they fell within the prescribed 10-meter radius.[101] The reason why this is important is that – similar to OEF – the availability of the 'precision' weapons have lead the US military to pursue more ambitious targeting practices in Iraqi cities than would have been done in the past:

---

[97] Crawford 2007b, 208–209; Zehfuss 2010, 553.   [98] Cryer 2002, 50.
[99] Zehfuss 2010, 547–550; Conetta 2004, 20–25.
[100] Zehfuss 2010, 548 (emphasis in original).   [101] Conetta 2004, 24.

This new technology is also used to strike at different targets – or rather structures and indeed people that would not previously have been considered targets for aerial warfare.[102]

Advances in precision-guided technology thereby resulted in civilians being exposed to bigger risks.

Pursuing enemy targets in urban areas like Baghdad, Tikrit, Kirkuk, Karbala, and An Nasiriyah was problematic with regards to questions of 'due care'. Although the US Air Force did not intend to cause civilian harm and did not aim to target Iraqi civilians directly, the resulting civilian harm was nevertheless foreseeable – in half the cases, at best, the PGMs missed their target, in the other half, they hit the military target but still killed innocent civilians.[103] For example, even when they hit their target, guided bombs in the 500–2,000 lb pound range (which accounted for around 60 per cent of the bombs dropped by British and American planes in the first phase of the war), were sufficiently powerful to cause some degree of collateral damage. The average 500 lb bomb kills everything within a radius of 20 meters; a 2000 lb bomb everything within a radius of 35 meters. And according to Pentagon estimates, the safe distance for unprotected troops from a 2000 lb bomb blast is 1000 meters, for a 500 lb bomb it is 500 meters.[104] What these figures help demonstrate is that engaging targets in urban or suburban areas had a built-in calculus of civilian casualties, even among those 50 per cent of the bombs that hit their predesigned targets. This is further evidenced by Pentagon policy that any bombing target predicted to generate more than thirty civilian casualties needed to be personally authorised by Secretary Rumsfeld. By July 2003, more than fifty of such strikes had been proposed and all of them had been approved.[105]

The availability of the 'precision'-guided weaponry lead to more ambitious targeting practices which in turn generated foreseeable collateral damage. Here, a less ambitious targeting strategy in urban centres could have reduced the risks to Iraqi civilians significantly, without necessarily having to expose US forces to higher levels of risk.

The third area that incurred large number of civilian casualties was caused by the specific RoE which had imprinted the key American emphasis on the norm of casualty-aversion over concerns for civilian protection. In contrast to OEF, the latter were loosened in Iraq to permit US soldiers to use force not only when they found themselves under attack, but also when they felt 'threatened with hostile intent'.[106] For

---

[102] Zehfuss 2010, 552.   [103] Zehfuss 2010, 547–550; Conetta 2004, 20–25.
[104] Conetta 2004, 24–25.   [105] Gordon 2003.
[106] Rothbart 2012, 122–128; Gentry 2011, 245.

instance, the 2003 RoE card handed out to all US soldiers allowed them to engage individuals who were 'exhibiting hostile intent towards Coalition Forces'.[107] Complicating this lowering of the threshold was that the question of 'intent' was open to a variety of interpretations that have ensured that US soldiers felt they could legally use force pre-emptively and under circumstances that previously would have deemed as impermissible.[108] This led to numerous yet avoidable deaths of Iraqi civilians, in particular at road blocks and during house to house searches.[109]

The problems stemming from the 'threatened with hostile intent' standard were further exacerbated by enemy tactics that started identifying US checkpoints and neighbourhood patrols as primary targets. The growing number of ambushes from within civilian residencies and the rise of suicide car attacks at checkpoints (including donkeys loaded with explosives)[110] thereby pushed US soldiers to interpret this standard so liberally precisely because insurgent tactics rendered even apparently benign scenarios into extremely dangerous ones.

Underlying this licence was the priority by the Pentagon to conduct operations with absolutely minimal risk to US troops.[111] In other words, the lowering of the threshold of the use of force in the RoE was designed to guarantee maximum safety to US forces. While the protection of Iraqi civilians was seen as an important objective in and of itself, the reality of allowing US military personnel to use force pre-emptively and when faced with hostile intent resulted in a transfer of combat risks from US soldiers to enemy civilians. In his book *Fiasco*, Thomas Ricks shows, how 'the emphasis on the use of force and on protecting US troops at all costs tended to push them towards harsh treatment [of civilians].'[112]

The vast majority of civilian casualties were incurred in these three areas. Overall, therefore, the US military operated in ways that tended to prioritise the lives of American military personnel over the safeguarding of Iraqi civilians.[113] Yet, despite this clear normative prioritisation, the US military managed to wage the war in ways that not only ensured low risks to US military personnel but that also complied with IHL.[114] On the one hand, this demonstrates the actual permissiveness of IHL for it allows

[107] Thomas W Smith 2008, 149–150; Rothbart and Korostelina 2011, 109–113.
[108] Rothbart and Korostelina 2011, 152; Rothbart 2012, 122–128.
[109] Crawford 2007b, 187–212.
[110] The use of animals such as mules and donkeys as delivery systems of explosives grew considerably after May 2003. On a less serious note, such asymmetric enemy tactics in opposition to the US Operation 'Shock and Awe' should find entry into strategic studies as 'Shock and Ee Aw'.
[111] Schwartz 2006.   [112] Ricks 2006, 266.   [113] Thomas W Smith 2008.
[114] Human Rights Watch 2003a.

for prioritisation of casualty-aversion over civilian protection[115] – and OIF still incurred low numbers of civilian casualties by historical standards. On the other hand, it demonstrates that more could have done to spare innocent Iraqi lives: in the case of cluster bombs and large numbers of collateral damage, this could have been achieved without higher risks to US forces but through a choice of different weapons systems and the pursuit of less ambitious targeting practices; in the case of fluid targets and loosened RoE, this could have been achieved by exposing US soldiers to higher combat risks. Therefore, while the US military adhered to IHL, it nevertheless failed the 'due care' test.

The Insurgency (May 2003–December 2006)

Had the US previously been fighting Saddam's conventional forces, then the rise of the insurgency following the toppling of Saddam's regime meant that the US military was now facing an entirely different, asymmetric adversary.[116] The beginning of the insurgency and the emergence of a different enemy employing asymmetric strategies took the US forces off guard.[117] Having declared that 'major combat operations have ended' and that 'in the battle for Iraq, coalition forces have prevailed', the Bush Administration was taken by surprise by the level of violent resistance that surfaced after the 1 May 2003.[118] The internalised logic of net-centric warfare (according to which enemy forces would – in recognition of the overall US military predominance – simply give up fighting)[119] on the one hand and the optimistic assumptions underpinning the CIA's and Pentagon's postwar plan (according to which Iraqis would greet Americans as liberators and that reconstruction would take place under peaceful conditions)[120] on the other had meant that the Bush Administration at first was unable to fathom, let alone acknowledge, that the insurgency had taken roots and was in fact flourishing.

For a long time, US leaders were, according to Bruce Hoffmann, in 'insurgency denial'.[121] As a result, the large scale looting on the streets of Baghdad, the growing levels of attacks against US forces, and the overall chaotic and violent situation following 1 May were first attributed to 'pockets of resistance' by elements of the ancient regime, i.e. to the postcursors of the war that just had ended. On 2 July 2003, President Bush,

---

[115] Kaempf 2009, 668–670.   [116] Herz 2007, 128.   [117] Ricks 2006; Kahl 2007a, 1.
[118] Kahl 2007a, 1.   [119] Interview Garstka.
[120] Hooker 2005, 37–38; Gordon and Trainor 2006, 498499.
[121] Bruce Hoffmann interview on The History Channel, 'Hardcore History: Iraq War – Insurgency and Counterinsurgency' (2005), available at www.youtube.com/watch?v= Pn8M9nq8wtA, accessed on 19 December 2014; see also Kahl 2007a, 4.

for example, stated that 'conditions are such that there are some who feel that they can attack us there. My answer is: bring them on.'[122] By November 2003 Paul Bremer, the US Head of the Provisional Coalition Authority of Iraq, confessed that the US still had no reliable information on the size, structure, and leadership of the various groups carrying out attacks.[123] It took the Bush Administration until early 2004 to recognise and acknowledge that what had been occurring in Iraq was in fact an insurgency which – at that point – had grown to an estimated twenty thousand fighters with a seemingly endless capacity to continue recruiting fighters from within and without Iraq.[124]

Early signs of the beginning of the insurgency were already visible during major combat operations in April 2003, when in towns and cities throughout southern Iraq US forces were not met by cheerful crowds but with fierce resistance. For instance, the first US fatality was a Marine shot by men driving a civilian pickup truck while the first suicide car bombing of a US checkpoint occurred ten days into the war.[125] In Samawah and Nasiriyah, US forces were attacked and killed not through tank units by the Republican Guard but through primitive roadside bombs, suicide car bombs, and guerrilla style ambushes that shared strong resemblance with the violence after 1 May.[126] But being caught in 'insurgency denial',[127] the Administration was unable to fathom these and subsequent attacks as something distinct from the war against Saddam and therefore saw no reason to rethink its original postwar plan.

The first steps in this plan included, as part of de-Ba'athification process,[128] the removal of large sections of Iraq's bureaucracy and the disbanding of the Iraqi military and police force in May 2003.[129] At times of peace, such a move might have been less problematic, but at a time when violence started to grow and when US military forces were far too few to fill the gap, this move created a vacuum that allowed the insurgency to take root and to establish itself. Weeks of virtual anarchy and looting, and the inability and unwillingness by US-led forces to control the situation further fuelled Iraqi resentment.[130] Additionally, the unexpectedly quick implosion of Saddam Hussein's regime meant that the invading forces never fully engaged and decisively defeated his army in any major

---

[122] Mockaitis 2012, 208.   [123] Beckett 2005, 27.   [124] Dennison 2006, 6.
[125] Kahl 2007a, 1.   [126] Keegan 2004, 148–153, 157–161; Dennison 2006, 25.
[127] Kahl 2007a, 4.
[128] The de-Ba'athification Commission together with the selection of the Governing Council were perceived by Sunni Arabs as discriminating, which further fuelled sectarian tension, see Hashim 2003, 1–22.
[129] Dodge 2007, 85–106.
[130] Instead of patrolling the streets, US forces barricaded themselves into highly protected compounds. Hashim 2006, 96.

battle;[131] the majority of Iraq's armed forces simply melted away, often with their weapons intact or secretly stored. Whether the insurgency (i.e. urban guerrilla strategy) was part of Saddam's overall strategic plan or not remains debated. There are signs that it was planned and that it started already during the first part of OIF (allegedly, Saddam ordered his forces to read *Black Hawk Down*).[132] But certainly, it grew massively after the fall of Saddam's regime. Irrespective of whether it was preplanned or not, the insurgency was fuelled by the chaos and relative anarchy following the collapse of Saddam's regime and the lack of US forces to step into the emerging power vacuum.

Who were the insurgents, what were their motivations, and what strategies did they employ? The nature, quality, goal, and strategy of the insurgency was multifaceted, complex, decentralised, and evolved over time. There was no overall leadership or unitary command structure. Instead, as TX Hammes showed, from the beginning, the insurgency was a coalition of the willing; it was a mixed bag.[133] There were at least a dozen major militant organisations and some forty distinct groups, sometimes loosely associated, oftentimes diametrically opposed to one another, but who gravitated towards one another to carry out attacks against their enemies, trade weapons or intelligence, and disperse, oftentimes to never cooperate again.[134]

The first wave of armed opposition was mostly Sunni Arab and predominantly emerged in the so-called Sunni triangle, especially in and around Baghdad, Falludjah and Tikrit (Anbar Province) from April/ May 2003 onwards. These militant Sunni groups were united only in their nationalistic opposition to the US presence and in their desire to return to the former status quo in which they had exercised power in Iraq. Some were drawn from the former regime, the Ba'ath Party, the paramilitary and the Republican Guard. Others were anti-Saddam nationalist parties resentful of the US presence; others were Islamist groups, oftentimes trained overseas (especially from Syria, Saudi Arabia, Yemen, and Sudan); others were made up of the large numbers of criminals who Saddam had released prior to the war who were paid to attack US forces.[135]

Shiite militia groups were to emerge later on, in a second wave of insurgent factions, from May 2004 onwards, in particular through the militia of Muqtada al-Sadr, the so-called Mahdi's Army, and various military factions maintained by Shiite exiled groups like the Iraqi

---

[131] Conetta 2003b.   [132] Human Rights Watch 2005; Beckett 2005; Burke 2003.
[133] Hammes 2005, 1–7.   [134] Beckett 2005.
[135] Human Rights Watch 2005; Scahill 2002.

National Congress and the Iraqi National Accord.[136] The situation was made even more complex by the tribal nature of Iraq with its extended clan and kinship system, and the growing involvement of foreign jihadist groups like al-Qaeda, who started to enter Iraq by July/August 2003 and whose aim it was to stir a civil war in Iraq.[137]

Similar to the decentralised and complex nature of these diverse violent factions, the motivations that drove the latter ranged from aggrieved individuals (whose relatives were killed by US forces in April/May 2003),[138] those who opposed the US occupation per se, those who retained a strong allegiance to the old regime, those driven by tribal affiliations, to those fighters entering Iraq with a fundamentalist jihadist motivation. The Washington-based Center for Strategic and International Studies (CSIS) estimated that less than 10 per cent of insurgents were non-Iraqi fighters.[139]

Over time, the targets of the insurgents' violence became more diverse. At first, between 2003 and 2007, they predominantly aimed at US forces.[140] From 2006 onwards, they also started targeting the new Iraqi government and its security forces. And finally – once the insurgency became supplemented with a civil war after the bombing of the al-Askari Mosque in Samara in February 2006 – violence was also aimed at the various Iraqi factions themselves.[141] Thus, the insurgency was an asymmetric armed conflict against the US and its foreign allies, a war of attrition against the US-supported Iraqi government, as well as a sectarian conflict among the different ethnic groups within the Iraqi population. Whatever the motivation of any particular group, the overall aim was to sow divisions between the Iraqis and the Coalition, among Iraqis themselves, and to raise the costs of US and Western presence.[142]

Over time, the weapons used and the asymmetric tactics employed also became more sophisticated. While early attacks with assault-rifles and RPGs were oftentimes amateurish and demonstrated poor training and planning among the attackers (who often got killed in return by US forces), the insurgents began adopting more sophisticated tactics in

---

[136] There were also Kurdish armed groups, however, these remained largely peaceful during the period of US occupation and presence.

[137] Hammes 2005, 1–7.   [138] Conetta 2003b, 3–4.

[139] Whitaker and MacAskill 2005; Human Rights Watch 2005.

[140] 'Meeting Resistance: New Doc Follows Iraqis Fighting U.S. Occupation of Their Country', Democracy Now!, available at www.democracynow.org/2007/10/18/meeting_resistance_new_doc_follows_iraqis, accessed on 12 November 2014. The producers Molly Bingham and Steve Connors cite Pentagon reports claiming that between 2004 and 2007, 74 per cent of attacks by Iraqi insurgents targeted American-led occupation forces.

[141] Knickmayer 2010.   [142] Gentry 2011, 243; Hammes 2005, 1–7.

which they used IEDs, car bombs, suicide attacks, mortars, rockets, and rifle-propelled grenades.[143]

Materially disadvantaged against the world's mightiest military power, Iraqi insurgents took refuge in the cities where US firepower could not reach them without inflicting unacceptably high levels of civilian casualties. They blended into the civilian population in order to use the latter as cover from US attacks.[144] Reports describe in detail how insurgents deliberately occupied hospitals and travelled in ambulances, how they stored weapons in schools, cultural sites, and mosques.[145] Oftentimes, insurgents surrounded their mortar stations with school children to prevent US forces from firing at them. These practices regularly occurred in Baghdad, Fallujah, Husaybah, Ramadi, Qusayba.[146] Furthermore, many insurgent groups used women and children as human shields while firing their weapons from cover.[147]

Wearing civilian clothes, concealing themselves among the civilian population, co-locating troops and military equipment into civilian areas, and using human shields were insurgent tactics employed in the hope of either shielding themselves from attacks, or if attacks were to take place, to produce collateral damage that would alienate the Iraqi population and help win insurgent groups sympathisers and recruits.[148]

By deliberately and systematically hiding in civilian areas in order to evade US firepower and by using these human shields as platforms from which to launch attacks at enemy forces,[149] Iraqi insurgents not only directly bore responsibility for endangering civilians but also they deliberately violated IHL.[150] Armed insurgents have an obligation not to place civilians at risk. US adversaries therefore deliberately violated IHL by using the civilian population as cover and compromising its immunity from attack.[151]

These asymmetric methods that intentionally abuse IHL not only started to inflict high fatalities on US troops, but at the same time forced US soldiers to treat every encounter with Iraqi civilians as potentially hostile, thereby effectively undercutting the US military's ability to build rapport with the local populace. In other words, the insurgents' asymmetric strategy aimed at raising the costs of the American presence by

---

[143] Beckett 2005, 7–8.   [144] Human Rights Watch 2003b, 66–79.
[145] Human Rights Watch 2003b, 66–79.   [146] Shultz and Dew 2006, 197–258.
[147] Crawford 2013, 402; Shultz and Dew 2006, 197–258; Human Rights Watch 2005.
[148] Human Rights Watch 2005.   [149] Human Rights Watch 2003b, 66–79.
[150] Crawford 2013, 402; Henckaerts and Doswald-Beck 2005, Rule 97; www.icrc.org/cus tomary-ihl/eng/docs/v1_rul_rule97, accessed on 3 April 2016.
[151] Although neither the Taliban nor al-Qaeda are signatories to and have therefore ratified the Additional Protocol, the latter's provision are generally regarded as constituting customary law.

exploiting US sensitivities for civilian immunity and for US body bags.[152] Designed to overcome their own technological disadvantage, the insurgents' strategy sought to drag US forces into an environment where they were hard pressed to reassert their technological supremacy in ways that remained riskless to both US soldiers and Iraqi civilians. Lacking in numbers, US forces were obliged to engage their opponents on their opponents terms, forced to fight in close quarters and in unfamiliar urban landscapes where sheer numbers mattered and where sustaining higher casualties was unavoidable.

For the US military, this meant that they became increasingly vulnerable to a 'faceless' enemy whose urban guerrilla strategy succeeded in inflicting ever-larger numbers of casualties upon US forces. Over the summer months of 2003, IEDs, car bombs, and ambushes on US patrols and conveys numbered about a dozen every day and resulted, on average, in one US soldier killed and seven more wounded on a daily basis.[153] By October 2003, attacks increased to around fifty per day. In the first eight months of the insurgency alone, 347 US forces were killed.[154] By December 2006, insurgents had killed nearly three thousand US soldiers, making Iraq the most costly US war since Vietnam.[155]

While the lives of US soldiers were seen as the highest priced, but most difficult targets, insurgents also raised the political, economic, and military costs of the continued US presence by directing their attacks against 'softer' targets like the civilian members of the Coalition authorities, NGO workers, so-called Iraqi 'collaborators', Iraqi police and army recruits, and on economic targets such as power stations, oil installations, and pipelines.[156] The more coalition partners could be forced to withdraw and the more Iraqis could be convinced not to collaborate with the occupying powers, the higher the onus on US forces to step into the emerging gap and the higher the likelihood for insurgents to engage and kill US forces. This strategy was evident in the public beheadings of Japanese and Philippine NGO workers, which resulted in both governments to subsequently withdraw their forces from Iraq.[157]

At the same time that US forces started incurring historically large casualty figures, the intentional blurring of the distinctions between

---

[152] Gentry 2010, 11–30; Gentry 2011, 243; Kahl 2007b, 13.
[153] Human Rights Watch 2003a; see also www.globalsecurity.org/military/ops/iraq_casualties_notes.htm accessed on 11 November 2014.
[154] From May 2003 to March 2004, about 30.8 per cent of US fatalities were the results of bombs and IEDs; 14.3 per cent the result of mortars and RPGs; 10.5 per cent through small arms; 13.1 per cent through downed helicopters; the rest through non-hostile causes and accidents (Beckett 2005, 8).
[155] http://icasualties.org/Iraq/Index.aspx, accessed on 3 August 2010.
[156] Gentry 2011, 243; Gentry 2010, 11–30.   [157] Hegghammer 2006.

injure civilians.[173] The collateral damage caused therefore was generally
unintended (… h IHL), even though it was predictable
The US was not deliberately targeting
ly not doing enough to minimise the
.[175]

ns did not violate IHL and killed large
tary Rumsfeld believed, the US would
would] get tired of getting killed.'[176]
at after nearly four years of trying to
willingness of Iraqis to fight had not
weekly attacks by insurgents contin-
stance, by late 2003, the number of
twenty thousand. One year later, by
sand insurgents killed or captured by
owed no sign of coming to an end.
nth because US operations were too
large number of Iraqi civilians killed
struction of houses and livelihoods,
s and ensure basic levels of security
inary Iraqis against the US, thereby
heavy-handed approach and their
to an end with brute force, the
flames of the insurgency, denying
peace and achieving their political

through the battles in the insur-
ul. In 2004, US forces launched
cities – with Fallujah being the
in since Vietnam. In both urban
aused large numbers of collateral
rces managed to drive out the
ed away through tunnels or by
lation).[179] But because of the
S forces had to be withdrawn to
nsurgents to re-establish them-
ter. This forced the US military
on that same year, with large
lem, Stephen Biddle showed,

007a, 187–212; Shaw 2005, 111.
004.
05, 1–21.
Vautravers 2010, 445.

soldiers and civilians by Iraqi insurgents also made it more difficult for the
American troops to uphold civilian immunity.[158] The combined effects
stemming from a largely invisible enemy disguising himself in civilian
clothes and the rising risks to US forces meant that the American military
could no longer wage OIF in ways that ensured both norms of casualty-
aversion and civilian protection. Being forced to make a choice between
both norms, how did the US military respond?

After months of refusing to acknowledge the insurgency and faced with
growing US fatalities, Donald Rumsfeld and General Tommy Franks
finally recalibrated US tactics to deal with the insurgency. But by failing
to ascribe the causes of the insurgency to domestic discontent with foreign
occupation and instead blaming the eruption entirely on 'pockets of
resistance' and outside forces such as Al-Qaeda infiltrators, Iranian
operatives, and foreign jihadists, they labelled all insurgents as terrorists
and sought to bring an end to the insurrection with brute force. They
responded with a classical 'search and destroy' approach.[159] Thus, they
opted for a policy of massive coercion and enforcement rather than
directing their energies towards the humanitarian concerns of ordinary
Iraqis. Their approach, according to Ahmed Hashim,

can be characterised as one of coercion and enforcement rather than a hearts and
minds approach. The former focuses on collectively punishing those who deign to
rise up in revolt. The latter seeks to address the rebels' grievances, figuring out
which are legitimate and which are not, and slowly but surely looks to incorporate
the disgruntled community into the political process.[160]

Thus, at a time when the nature of the conflict in Iraq had fundamentally
changed by the rise of an asymmetric non-state adversary, the US military
leadership chose a conventional strategy against an unconventional
opponent.[161] This failure to adequately adjust on a strategic level was
perhaps unsurprising for a military that had been caught up in a post-
Vietnam cultural mindset, according to which the it 'does not do counterinsurgency'.[162]

Thus, at a time when ordinary Iraqis clamoured for basic police protection, law and order, clean water, electricity, or essential services,
US decision-makers chose what British allies called a 'baseball bat strategy' that emphasised the lives of US soldiers over the protection of Iraqi
civilians.[163] Transferring the risks of combat onto innocent civilians
meant that the overall US strategy was particularly inadequate and ill-

[158] Ricks 2009, 54–103; Gentry 2011, 243–244.   [159] Kahl 2007a, 4.
[160] Hashim 2006, 323.   [161] Kahl 2007a, 4.
[162] Biddle, Friedman, and Shapiro 2012, 21; Kahl 2007a, 1.
[163] Shaw 2005, 135; Gentry 2011, 244.

'was that insurgents had simply moved from the cleared areas to others, leading to deterioration elsewhere in a balloon-squeezing phenomenon that prevented security from improving overall'.[181] In other words, with too few military forces available on the ground, the US was caught in a vicious circle of having to clear an area which they were unable to hold and which forced them to return again and again.

The lack of US forces on the ground only allowed US forces to clear but never to hold any territory they gained. And the conventional strategy to crush the insurgency, with its emphasis on protecting US soldiers over Iraqi civilians caused excessive amounts of collateral damage that in turn only served to fan the insurgency.[182] This predicament demonstrated Rumsfeld's and Franks's inability to comprehend the role of the US military in creating and feeding the insurgency. It took US leaders until mid-2006 to realise that the growing number of non-combatant deaths was the central factor in alienating the Iraqi population and thereby increasing the strength of the insurgents.[183]

At this point, Iraq was on the brink of total disaster – it was a war the Americans were losing: over three thousand US soldiers had been killed with numbers of fatalities continuing to rise month by month; ninety civilians on average were being killed per day;[184] the Iraqi government itself was fuelling the violence with its own Shia death squads;[185] Al-Qaeda's Iraqi branch was recruiting hundreds of suicide attackers to launch attacks in Iraq; 5 million Iraqis – one-fifth of the overall population – had either fled the country or had become internally displaced; and the conventional sledgehammer approach by US forces was further fuelling Iraqi resentment.[186] According to the 'Failed States Index', Iraq was one of the world's top five most unstable states and polls of top US foreign policy experts showed that a mere 3 per cent still believed the US would be able to actually win the war in Iraq.[187] While sectarian and insurgent violence appeared to be spiralling out of control in Iraq, the Bush Administration was facing ever louder calls for withdrawal from Democrats in Washington who were newly in control of both Houses of Congress.[188]

It was only at this point that the perception of the US military forces started to shift: from a strategic point of view it now became essential to

---

[181] Biddle, Friedman, and Shapiro 2012, 22.   [182] Gentry 2011, 249.
[183] Ricks 2009, 29.
[184] www.iraqbodycount.org/database/ and http://icasualties.org/, both accessed on 1 January 2015.
[185] West 2009, 2.   [186] Bergen 2012.
[187] Available at http://foreignpolicy.com/images/TI3_Final_Results.doc, accessed on 20 December 2014; Tyson 2006.
[188] Simon 2008, 56–76.

actively save civilian lives.[189] This sea change led to a complete overhaul of the entire US strategy in Iraq and the subsequent introduction of a new counterinsurgency field manual in December 2006 ('the surge').[190]

The Surge (2007–2011)

The nucleus of what was published on 15 December 2006 as the new joint 'Army Field Manual 3-24/Marine Corps Warfighting Publication No. 3–33.5, *Counterinsurgency*' (the surge) can be traced back to the northern Iraqi city of Mosul in 2004. In contrast to the rest of the country, Mosul, one of the most dangerous cities in Iraq, was successfully pacified by twenty thousand US forces under the command of Lieutenant General David Petraeus. Applying classical counterinsurgency strategy, Petraeus managed to take over the city from insurgents, to hold it for several months, to organise local elections, and to begin implementing reconstruction projects. His efforts were only stymied when insurgents retook the city after his forces had been ordered out of Mosul to fight insurgents elsewhere in Iraq.[191]

After his tour in Iraq, Petraeus was assigned to run the US Army's Combined Arms Center at Fort Leavenworth, Kansas in 2006. Here, in light of the looming disaster in Iraq and with the positive lessons learned from his own experiences in Mosul, he assembled a team of top US military experts, scholars, and practitioners in the field and began revamping the Army's Counterinsurgency doctrine, something the military had not put any real thought into since the Vietnam War.[192] As Chapter 2 had already shown, ever since the Indochina War, the US military had shied away from even teaching counterinsurgency to its ordinary soldiers, leaving such 'operations other than war' and relevant expertise to US Marines and Special Forces.[193] This meant that by the time the US military invaded Iraq in 2003, it lacked a common understanding of the problems inherent in counterinsurgency campaigns. It had neither studied them, nor developed a doctrine and tactics to deal with them. As Sarah Sewall, one of the architects of the 2006 COIN manual put it: 'It is fair to say that in 2003, most Army officers knew   more   about   the   US   Civil   War   than   they   did   about

---

[189] Ricks 2009, 34.
[190] David Petraeus, US Army Counterinsurgency Field Manual, FM 3-24, 2006, available at http://usacac.army.mil/cac2/repository/FM_3-24.pdf, accessed on 1 February 2010.
[191] Bergen 2012.
[192] To help him, Petraeus recruited Iraq War veteran John Nagl, a Rhodes Scholar with a doctorate from Oxford who in 2002 published the book *Learning to Eat Soup with a Knife: Counterinsurgency Lessons from Malaya and Vietnam*. See Nagl 2005.
[193] Sewall 2007, xli; Kahl 2007a, 1.

counterinsurgency.'[194] *The U.S. Army/Marine Corps Counterinsurgency Field Manual* was written to fill that void and to turn the entire US military into an effective counterinsurgency force to reverse the looming defeat in Iraq.

By studying counterinsurgency theory (from Santa Cruz de Marcenado, to David Galula, Liddell Hart, Martin van Creveld, and Lorenzo Zambernardi) and history (in particular the wars in Algeria, Malaya, Vietnam, and El Salvador), Petraeus's team produced a manual that came to deeply inform how the US military would fight the wars in Iraq and – as of 2010 – in Afghanistan.[195]

The manual sets out by pointing to unsuccessful counterinsurgency practices such as failing to adopt unconventional warfighting strategies, overemphasising killing and capturing the enemy rather than making conditions secure for the populace, conducting large-scale operations as the norm, and concentrating military forces in large bases for protection.[196] This was, in fact, a good and sobering description of what the US military had been doing in Iraq for the past three years of the conflict and an explanation of why it was now losing the war.[197]

Successful practices, the new manual emphasised, focused on meeting the needs and ensuring the security of the population. The population rather than the insurgent movement thereby became the 'centre of gravity'. This meant that clearing, holding, and building areas became far more important than it was in a conventional war. Ensuring that people felt secure enough so they were not forced to have to side with the insurgents and, eventually, even felt secure enough to provide intelligence about them, became the prize. The manual also emphasises the paradoxical and often counterintuitive nature of counterinsurgency operations that were hardly typical of prevailing US military doctrine at the time: sometimes the more you protect your forces, the less secure you are; sometimes the more force you use, the less effective it is; sometimes doing nothing is the best reaction.[198]

Thus, at the heart of the surge doctrine lies the realisation that the US strategy in Iraq not only had remained too conventional (thereby failing to adequately adjust to the nature of the insurgency),[199] but also that it had been driven too heavily by concerns for the lives of US military personnel rather than the lives of innocent Iraqis.[200] And while US operations had largely complied with IHL, the emphasis on casualty-aversion had produced such an excessive number of civilian casualties

---

[194] Sewall 2007, xxi.   [195] Kahl 2007a, 1.   [196] Nagl, Petraeus, and Amos 2007.
[197] Biddle, Friedman, and Shapiro 2012, 21.   [198] Nagl, Petraeus, and Amos 2007.
[199] Sewall 2007, xxvii; Ricks 2009, 81, 134.
[200] Clegg 2012, 132; Biddle, Friedman, and Shapiro 2012, 21.

that the US was losing the 'hearts and minds' of ordinary Iraqis, was driving Iraqis into the arms of the insurgents, and, ultimately, was losing the war.[201]

If the US was to win the war in Iraq, then the hitherto imbalance between the norms of casualty-aversion and civilian protection needed to be reversed.[202] Because success in counterinsurgency operations ultimately hinges on protecting the civilian population, Sarah Sewall writes in the introduction to the COIN manual,

the field manual tells American troops something they may not want to hear: in order to win, they must assume more risks, at least in the short term. This is a radical message because it countermands decades of conventional US military practice.[203]

Military necessity now dictated that civilian protection had to be made the key priority, even at the cost of exposing US soldiers to higher combat risks.[204] The manual states explicitly that the standard of moral and ethical conduct

obligates soldiers and Marines to accept some risk to minimize harm to non-combatants ... proportionality and discrimination require combatants not only to minimize the harm to non-combatants but also to make *positive commitments* to ... assume *additional risks* to minimize potential harms.[205]

In this respect, the manual reads like an anti-Iraq textbook as it roundly rejects the long-held preference for risk-transfer from US soldiers to enemy civilians.[206] In arguing that US operations, despite their overall compliance with IHL, had not done enough to save civilian lives because of overriding concerns for the safety of US soldiers, the manual essentially comes very close to Walzer's 'due care' argument (even though the Pentagon's concern for civilian immunity here is not based on deontological humanitarian values).

In this sense, the manual reads like an open confession of how much higher civilian protection could previously have been had the US not operated in such casualty-averse ways. It directs American forces to make the security concerns of civilians their top priority, rather than their own safety or the destruction of the enemy. According to the manual, Sarah Sewall argues,

the real battle is for civilian support for, or acquiescence to, the counterinsurgents and host nation government ... killing the civilian is no longer just collateral damage. The harm cannot be easily dismissed as unintended. Civilian casualties

---

[201] Conetta 2007.   [202] Ricks 2009, 33, 156.   [203] Sewall 2007, xxvi–xxvii.
[204] Sewall 2007, xxvii; Clegg 2012, 132.
[205] Nagl, Petraeus, and Amos 2007, 244, 247; emphasis added.   [206] Herz 2007, 114.

undermine the counterinsurgency goals ... civilian deaths create an extended family of enemies – new insurgent recruits or informants – and erode the support for the host nation.[207]

The central goal now was to make the civilian population feel secure enough to engage in peaceful politics and thereby to marginalise the insurgent movements.

In other words, the 2006 COIN manual roundly rejects the long-held preference for risk-transfer from US soldiers to enemy civilians that had come to characterise US military operations since the post-Vietnam era. In that light, it not only reads like an anti-Iraq textbook, but also more generally like an anti-RMA and anti-net-centric warfare textbook. Reflecting its fundamental overhaul, David Kilcullen, one of the manual's authors, termed it 'the counterrevolution in military affairs.'[208] It constituted a revolutionary challenge to conventional US warfighting strategy and aimed at an overhaul of US military doctrine in light of the attacks on 9/11.

The surge was announced as an official change in US strategy in Iraq by President Bush in a television speech on 10 January 2007: 'America will change our strategy to help the Iraqis carry out their campaign to put down sectarian violence and bring security to the people of Baghdad.'[209] The major element of the strategy was a change in focus for the US military

to help Iraqis clear and secure neighborhoods, to help them protect the local population, and to help ensure that the Iraqi forces left behind are capable of providing the security ... This will require increasing American force levels. So I've committed more than 20,000 additional American troops to Iraq.[210]

Recognising that any successful counterinsurgency campaign requires a much larger presence of ground forces, the number of US soldiers in Iraq was increased significantly. Over the course of 2007, thirty thousand additional troops were deployed to Baghdad and Al Anbar Province, and by November 2007, US forces in Iraq peaked at 170,300.[211] To implement the new surge strategy on the ground, the president appointed General Petraeus as Commanding General of the Multinational Forces in Iraq on 10 February 2007.

---

[207] Sewall 2007, xxv.   [208] Cited in Ricks 2009, 163.
[209] Available at http://georgewbush-whitehouse.archives.gov/news/releases/2007/01/2007 0110-7.html, accessed on 3 January 2015.
[210] Available at http://georgewbush-whitehouse.archives.gov/news/releases/2007/01/2007 0110-7.html, accessed on 3 January 2015.
[211] Duffy 2008.

What effects did the implementation of the surge have? The new approach has certainly compromised the norm of casualty-aversion.[212] Petraeus's population-centric approach forced US soldiers out of their massively fortified bases into smaller, dispersed bases and into the Iraqi neighbourhoods through dismounted patrols to provide US security protection to threatened Iraqi civilians.[213] Exposing themselves to higher levels of combat risks than ever before, US forces started taking more casualties. In 2007, 904 US troops were killed, making it the deadliest year of the war for US military forces (this figure has gone down in subsequent years).[214] At the same time, however, and rather counterintuitively, the number of Iraqi civilian deaths caused by US operations in the first two years of the surge increased dramatically. According to conservative estimates, the years 2007 and 2008 each saw a 70 per cent increase in collateral damage caused by US forces (although these figures subsequently dropped).[215]

This spike in civilian casualties directly caused by US forces is surprising, given that the principle assumption underpinning the surge has been that accepting higher risks to US combat forces would lead to a reduction of risks to Iraqi civilians. Instead, the new population-centred approach led to a surge in casualties among US forces in 2007 *and* Iraqi civilians in 2007 and 2008. And even more bizarrely, in 2008, casualties among Iraqi civilians caused by US forces continued to grow by 70 per cent at a time when US combat casualties declined by over 60 per cent. How can this be explained?

Principally, four factors explain this rise in civilian casualties.[216] First, the adaption of the new COIN doctrine significantly increased the number of patrols by US troops out among the civilian population. Venturing out of their fortified bases and into Iraqi neighbourhoods brought US forces into more frequent hostile contact with insurgents who continued to employ tactics that exposed Iraqi civilians at risk.[217] In a way, this was to be expected; but this factor alone is insufficient in explaining the large rise in civilian casualties caused by US forces under the new COIN doctrine.

---

[212] Clegg 2012, 132.   [213] Duffy 2008.
[214] Figures available at http://icasualties.org/, accessed on 1 January 2015.
[215] www.iraqbodycount.org/analysis/reference/press-releases/12/, accessed on 12 July 2010. In 2006, US forces were directly responsible for 394–434 civilian deaths; in 2007, US forces directly caused between 669 and 756 deaths. These figures do not count those non-combatants killed in firefights, where the United States might claim civilians were caught in the crossfire. Those numbers have also increased: in 2006, between 544 and 623 were killed in Iraq during incidents involving insurgents and coalition military forces; in 2007, between 868 and 1,326 were killed in these circumstances.
[216] Crawford, Lutz, Lifton, Herman, and Zinn 2008.   [217] Duffy 2008.

The second and more important factor was the rather conventional manner in which US forces implemented the new doctrine on the ground. In spite of all the political and media attention surrounding the surge and despite US forces accepting higher combat risks to themselves, the US military has effectively continued to wage elements of its counterinsurgency war in a relatively conventional manner.[218] This is evidenced by the continued reliance of 'close air support' which has been responsible for causing the majority of civilian deaths by US forces during the surge. Already one of the major causes of non-combatant deaths until 2006, the tendency by US ground forces to call on helicopters and fixed wing aircraft to fire upon targets whenever they came in contact with insurgents increased significantly in 2007 and 2008. For instance, the number of airstrikes in Iraq, but in particular in Baghdad, increased fivefold from 2006 to 2007.[219] With US counterinsurgency operations increasing in areas of insurgent activities, US Air Force Colonel Gary Crowder explained, 'we integrated more airstrikes into those operations' in an attempt to overwhelm enemies through superior airpower.[220] This was problematic as close air support operations tended to be done on the fly, often with poor intelligence and without the legal vetting required during preplanned attacks.[221] Also, contrary to the rhetoric of exposing US forces to larger risks of combat, about half of the US forces were still primarily deployed to provide for force protection.[222] What this means is that the US military has only shifted half-heartedly into full counterinsurgency mode and that the relatively conventional elements within its counterinsurgency were responsible for causing the majority of Iraqi civilian deaths.

Third, the stress of urban combat, the prolonged rounds of duty, and the increasing risks when patrolling the streets have caused American soldiers to fire more quickly and aggressively in ambiguous situation. Exposing themselves more openly on the streets and entering and staying in the more violent neighbourhoods of Baghdad caused US forces to incur more casualties than before, which in return seemed to have made them more trigger happy.[223] This was not helped by their oftentimes growing contempt for Iraqi civilians.[224] The combination of contempt, fear, and fatigue resulted in a 'toxic brew' which has caused US soldiers to sometimes fire too quickly in ambiguous situations, thereby inflicting large numbers of civilian deaths.[225] Finally, despite the new restrictions imposed to the RoE since the beginning of the surge, the RoE still

---

[218] Londono and Paley 2008.   [219] Londono and Paley 2008; White 2008.
[220] White 2008.   [221] Crawford, Lutz, Lifton, Herman, and Zinn, 2008.
[222] Duffy 2008.   [223] Crawford, Lutz, Lifton, Herman, and Zinn, 2008.
[224] Roland C. Arkin 2010, 334–335.   [225] Crawford, Lutz, Lifton, Lifton and Zinn, 2008.

remained too permissive, allowing soldiers to continue using force when they feel threatened by hostile 'intent'.[226] What that means is that the implementation of the new counterinsurgency manual has resulted in a 'surge' in US military in 2007 as well as Iraqi civilian casualties in 2007 and 2008.[227]

But then, from the second half of 2007 onwards, something remarkable happened: the overall levels of sectarian violence between Iraqis and between Iraqis and US forces dropped dramatically across the country, and particularly in and around Baghdad (where over 80 per cent of the civilian and military casualties had occurred prior to the surge).[228] Monthly civilian fatalities fell from more than 1,700 in May 2007 to around 500 by December, to around 200 from June 2008 to June 2011. That constituted about one-tenth of the rate prior to the surge.[229] And besides making Iraq a less deadly place for Iraqis, the drop in overall violence also made Iraq a less threatening environment for US forces.[230] By the fall of 2006, the US military had suffered a monthly toll of almost one hundred dead and seven hundred wounded, peaking at a wartime high of 126 KIA by May 2007. By December 2007, monthly US military fatalities had declined to 23, and between June 2008 and June 2011, US casualties averaged at fewer than 11 per month, less than 15 per cent of the average rate seen between 2004 and mid-2007.[231] Viewed on an annual level, US casualties declined from 904 (2007), to 314 (2008), 149 (2009), 60 (2010), and 54 (2011).[232]

After the initial spike in casualties among Iraqi civilians and US forces had raised questions over the feasibility and success of the surge strategy, this was a remarkable turnaround from intense bloodshed to almost four years of relative calm. In retrospect, many have credited the surge for this outcome, arguing that the combination of thirty thousand additional US forces and different, less casualty-averse counterinsurgency methods, while initially exposing US forces to higher risks, ultimately reduced the levels of violence by suffocating the insurgency and destroying its ability to kill Americans or Iraqis.[233] According to this view, the normative shift from force protection to prioritising the safety of Iraqi civilians came at a short-term price of American lives but in the long run allowed US forces to increase the safeguarding of Iraqi civilians and thereby win Iraqi hearts and minds.[234]

---

[226] Gentry 2011, 245; Rothbart 2012, 122–128.
[227] Crawford, Lutz, Lifton and Zinn, 2008.   [228] Simon 2008, 57–76; West 2009, 2.
[229] Casualty-figures available at iCasualties.org, accessed on 13 December 2014.
[230] Bergen 2012.   [231] Biddle, Friedman and Shapiro 2012, 7.
[232] Figures available at http://icasualties.org/, accessed on 1 January 2015.
[233] Boot 2008; Kagan 2–9; Crider 2009, 81–89; McCain and Lieberman 2008.
[234] Clegg 2012, 132.

Given the proximity of the COIN manual's principles to Walzer's 'due care' argument, the reversal of the hitherto imbalance between the norms of casualty-aversion and civilian protection not only allowed the US military to snatch victory from the jaws of defeat in Iraq, but also more broadly validates the moral idea of 'due care' from a strategic point of view. Recognising that in spite of the overall compliance with IHL, US operations' pre-2007 normative prioritisation of casualty-aversion over civilian protection had caused such high levels of collateral damage that fuelled the insurgency, the change in emphasis on safeguarding civilians over the lives of US military forces allowed the Americans to turn the situation around. In other words, the proponents of the surge thesis would validate the findings of the previous two case studies on Somalia and Afghanistan.

This commonplace surge narrative, however, has been contested by a variety of alternative explanations which attribute the deduction of violence in post-2007 Iraq to events that were largely unrelated to the surge, including the Sunni tribal uprising against al-Qaeda in Iraq (the so-called 'Anbar Awakening'), the dynamics of sectarian cleansing, or the unilateral ceasefire by radical Shiite leader Moktada al-Sadr.[235] Each of these contending explanations attributes the decline in overall violence in Iraq to events that either predated the surge or that were unrelated to it. For instance, some researchers argue that violence in Iraq declined by mid-2007 because sectarian bloodshed had played itself out. According to this view, the sectarian violence, displaying elements of ethnic cleansing, came to an end once ethnically homogenous neighbourhoods had been set up by mid-2007. Thus, the fighting petered out as a product of its own dynamic rather than in response to the surge.[236]

On the contrary, proponents of the so-called Awakening thesis argue that violence did not decline because of the surge but because the Sunni insurgency abandoned its previous alliance with al-Qaeda in 2006 and subsequently allied itself alongside the US in exchange for payments as the so-called 'Sons of Iraq'.[237] According to this view, one big insurgent faction's decision to stop fighting had little to do with the surge itself but had resulted from resentment of al-Qaeda's excessive violence and its attempt to spearhead the Sunni insurgency.[238] Yet another explanation points to Shiite leader al-Sadr's surprise decision to order a unilateral

---

[235] Woodward 2008a; Thiel 2011, 1–9; West 2009, 22–27; Kingsbury 2014; Biddle, Friedman, and Shapiro 2012, 13–35; Stephen Biddle 2008.

[236] Weidmann and Salehyan 2013, 52–64; Agnew, Gillespie, Gonzalez, and Min 2008, 2285–2295.

[237] Phillips 2009, 64–84.   [238] Phillips 2009, 64–84; Simon 2008, 57–61.

ceasefire, arguably at the urging of his patrons in Iran who were interested in cooling down regional tensions to speed up US withdrawal.[239]

According to these views, the surge was only one factor and possibly not even a major one in the declining violence. Bob Woodward, for instance, expresses this view:

In Washington, conventional wisdom translated these events into a simple view: The Surge had worked. But the full story was more complicated. At least three other factors were as important as, or even more important than, the surge.[240]

Examining the different explanations and drawing on extensive declassified military datasets and interviews, Stephen Biddle and colleagues found that no unitary perspective alone can explain the decline in violence. Rather, they argue, the synergetic interaction between these factors, in particular between the surge and the Anbar Awakening, can best explain the reversal in violence in Iraq:

Without the surge, the Anbar Awakening would probably not have spread fast or far enough. And without the surge, sectarian violence would likely have continued for a long time to come ... Yet the surge, though necessary, was insufficient to explain 2007's sudden reversal in fortunes. Without the Awakening to thin the insurgents' ranks and unveil the holdouts to US troops, the violence would probably have remained very high until well after the surge had been withdrawn and well after US voters had lost patience with the war.[241]

In other words, rather than the surge or the Awakening alone, the synergetic interaction between these two factors generated the main source for the decline in violence that neither could have created alone. This means that the overall drop in sectarian violence that started to occur in Iraq was not solely caused by the new surge strategy. Shifting the priority from force protection to safeguarding civilians therefore contributed to the decline in violence, but only in synergy with other factors unrelated to the surge, such as the Anbar Awakening. In and of itself, the rebalancing of the norms within US warfare was a necessary but insufficient explanation for the reduction of violence.

This raises the question not only about the overall success of the new US strategy, but also about the feasibility of Walzer's idea of 'due care' as accepting higher levels of risk to US military personnel has not been sufficient to translate into higher levels of safety for Iraqi non-combatants. Does this mean that the idea of 'due care' simply does not work? Not necessarily. The problem with the way in which the surge has been implemented means that the US military – albeit

---

[239] Woodward 2008a.   [240] Woodward 2008b.
[241] Biddle, Friedman, Shapiro 2012, 10–11.

significant changes – still tended to operate in a too conventional manner that directly resulted in large numbers of civilian deaths as long as the overall situation in Iraq remained violent. Furthermore, it remains highly questionable if, after several years of inflicting high numbers of civilian deaths on the Iraqi population, the surge could still have brought about a change in Iraqi 'hearts and minds'.[242] In fact, there is no evidence that the 2007 turnaround occurred because Iraqi civilians changed their minds and decided to support the US or the Iraqi government. After years of sectarian violence, Iraq was a highly polarised society with highly mobilised sectarian identity groups that were unlikely to support sectarian rivals in response to an offer of better protection or services. When the Sunni insurgency changed sides, it did not do so by allying with the Shiite Government of Iraq but because the 'Sons of Iraq' programme was negotiated and paid for by US forces. And their goal was not to receive economic support or large-scale development projects, but American combat power to protect them from the Shiite government. The 2007 dynamics, therefore, appeared to have more to do with combat realignment than with winning hearts and minds.[243]

And yet, irrespective of what motivated Sunni insurgents to break ranks with al-Qaeda and to realign with US forces, the overall reduction of violence meant that for the Bush Administration, the first goal of the surge had been achieved: reduction of violence. Achieving the short-term benefits of violence reduction, however, came at the detriment of the second goal, namely political reconciliation among the various Iraqi factions. The decline in violence, so the initial American plan, would give the Iraqi government the breathing space needed to push for national reconciliation. And yet, the bottom-up strategies pursued through the surge and the Anbar Awakening had fostered the retribalisation of Iraq between Sunnis, Shiites, and Kurds which further undermined the authority of the central government and the cohesion of the country. Iraq became more divided politically. In other words, the attainment of the first goal of the surge created, as Steve Simon argued, 'an illusory short-term stability' through a strategy that 'systematically nourished domestic rivalries.[244] As long as US forces remained in the country, they managed to keep the lid on these sectarian rivalries. Once US forces had completed their withdrawal in 2011, sectarian violence re-emerged the following years.[245]

---

[242] Kahl 2007a, 5.   [243] Biddle, Friedman, and Shapiro 2012, 38.
[244] Simon 2008, 70.
[245] Figures available at www.iraqbodycount.org/database/, accessed on 12 January 2015.

Conclusion

The US war in Iraq lasted for nearly eight years and underwent three distinctive combat phases from the early overthrow of the Saddam regime (March–May 2003), the insurgency (May 2003–December 2006), to the surge (2007–2011). Over the course of this period, the dynamics of the conflict displayed what Clausewitz had described as the chameleonesque nature of war, changing from an initial conventional interstate conflict to the rise of an asymmetric non-state adversary whom US forces tried to defeat in a conventional manner, to the introduction the new counter-insurgency strategy which aimed at fighting an asymmetric adversary in an unconventional manner. War, as the conflict in Iraq showed, is never waged upon a lifeless object, but always on an enemy who responds.

By examining this interactive dynamic of the Iraq war, the case study focused on how the strategies of US adversaries exacerbated the US ability to operate in ways that ensured low risks to American military personnel and high levels of civilian protection. It critically evaluated US military operations through the prism of International Humanitarian Law (IHL) and examined whether American forces started prioritising casualty-aversion over the safeguarding of Iraqi civilians. Finally, by drawing on moral guidelines (such as those underpinning Michael Walzer's idea of 'due care'), the chapter examined whether lower numbers of Iraqi civilian deaths could have been achieved if marginal increases to the risks faced by US soldiers had been accepted and if different military strategies had been chosen. This has generated the following findings: while fighting a largely conventional interstate war against the forces of the Iraqi state, the US military complied with the provisions set by IHL for the protection of Iraqi civilians and succeeded in toppling Saddam's regime at minimal costs to the lives Iraqi civilians and American service personnel. At the same time, however, it was shown how US warfare displayed a normative prioritisation of casualty-aversion over civilian protection, which effectively resulted in a risk-transfer from US soldiers to Iraqi civilians. While such a risk-transfer neither violated IHL nor lead to excessive collateral damage, from a moral point of view this was problematic as US forces could have achieved an even higher level of civilian protection had they had accepted higher risks to themselves. Therefore, the chapter argued, the US military complied with IHL but failed the 'due care' test. On a strategic level, this failure was unproblematic during the conventional combat phase as collateral damage remained low and US forces succeeded in swiftly overthrowing the Iraqi regime. Yet, it became the central strategic problem during the second combat phase.

Once the US military faced a truly asymmetric adversary and for the first time started incurring large numbers of casualties, it proved not only incapable of adjusting to a counterinsurgency strategy but also unable to continue waging OIF in a manner that respected both norms of force protection and civilian immunity. Consequently, the US defaulted onto a 'search and destroy' mode of fighting that emphasised concerns for its own soldiers over the lives of innocent Iraqi. The resulting rise of civilian casualties, largely permitted under IHL, was in violation of the 'due care' test. While this moral violation (caused by the emphasis on force protection over the safeguarding of Iraqi civilians) had remained relatively unproblematic from a strategic point of view during the first combat phase, it now generated severe strategic repercussions as this US mode of warfare escalated the conflict, strengthened the insurgency and brought the US close to losing the war.

In response to the looming loss of the war, the new counterinsurgency manual recognised that the high levels of collateral damage – even when permitted under IHL – were detrimental to American military objectives in the conflict. In order to win the war over 'hearts and minds', the COIN manual argued, the existing imbalance between casualty-aversion and civilian protection inherent in US warfare needed to be reversed completely. Not only did this new priority for civilian protection demonstrate the extent to which the COIN manual essentially embraced Walzer's 'due care' argument, but it also reads like an open confession over the extent to which previous US operations were driven by primary concerns for the protection of its own forces at the expense of the lives of ordinary Iraqis. From the Pentagon's point of view, placing the protection of Iraqi civilians above concerns for US casualties now became a strategic imperative to win the war.

After an initial surge in casualties among US forces and Iraqi civilians, the chapter showed, the sectarian violence between Iraqis and violence against US forces declined dramatically. And yet, while some have attributed this reduction in violence exclusively to the surge strategy, the chapter revealed the overstatement of such claims. On the one hand, large elements of the new counterinsurgency strategy retained a heavy conventional footprint (which was responsible for inflicting large numbers of civilian deaths), indicating that US forces shifted only half-heartedly to a truly unconventional, less casualty-averse mode of warfare. On the other hand, even where such a strategic shift occurred, detailed research has shown that the new risk re-transfer from Iraqi civilians to US soldiers in and of itself has been a necessary but insufficient explanation for the reduction of violence. The latter, the chapter has shown, occurred only in synergy with other factors unrelated to the surge, such as the Anbar Awakening and the unilateral cease fire declared by militant Shiite leader al-Sadr. As a result, the normative change in US counterinsurgency can only partially explain the lull in violence on the streets of Iraq.

Judging from the Iraq war, one can neither overstate nor dismiss the importance of the 'due care' element of the surge. It neither constituted the sole reason for the deduction of violence, nor did it fail to impact on the safeguarding of ordinary Iraqis. It contributed to changing the security environment in Iraq while at the same time cementing (if not worsening) the sectarian division of the country which resurfaced as soon as US forces had withdrawn in 2011. Given that the sectarian violence started emerging two years prior to the surge and that the surge cemented rather than unravelled sectarianism, the interesting counterfactual question to ask is would an earlier US strategic adjustment to the insurgency in 2003 rather than in 2007 have shown a more clear-cut success? Would the impact of the normative rebalancing between US casualty-aversion and civilian protection have been more pronounced had it occurred four years earlier?

Conclusion

The book has investigated the interactive dynamics in asymmetric conflicts between the US military and semi-/non-state actors in the post–Cold War world. Its main objective has been to examine the implications of these asymmetric encounters for the US ability to wage wars with little risk to its own soldiers while at the same time providing high levels of protection for civilians in target states.

This research focus is important for it responds to the critical issues that have been raised by US military interventions over the last two-and-a-half decades. On the one hand, the American willingness to sacrifice large numbers of its citizens in the modern age has been replaced by the rise of casualty-aversion among military and political decision-makers following the wars in Vietnam and Lebanon. This process has been illustrated in Chapter 2 by examining the transformation of humanism as a force that traditionally allowed warriors to experience war as an act of self-realisation and to accept sacrifice. The demise in humanism and the subsequent reluctance to sustain significant military casualties is reflected in the existing literature where a conventional wisdom has developed that the American military has exhibited a high level of casualty-aversion in its interventions throughout the 1990s.[1] At the same time, however, the book has shown that pockets of humanism have survived in American Special Operations Forces (SOF). In contrast to the general intolerance among military and political leaders towards exposing American military personnel to the risks of combat, these 'Niche Warriors' continue to view war (and the acceptance of the risk of dying) in humanistic terms, that is, as a source of individual transformation.[2] Considering the central roles played by 'Niche Warriors' in the US interventions in Somalia, Afghanistan, and Iraq, the book has raised questions regarding the tensions between their humanism and the general casualty-aversion among

[1] Luttwak 1995 and 1996; van Creveld 1996; Coker 2002b; Ignatieff 1999 and 2000c; Record 2000.
[2] Toffler and Toffler 1994, 105–107; Coker 2002b, 80–83; Adams 1998, 9; Kibbe 2004, 109–110; Horn 2004, 3–34.

US leaders that has guided investigations in the empirical part of the book.

The systematic targeting of enemy civilians in modern industrial wars has been superseded by the strengthening of the principle of non-combatant immunity in the late 1980s and 1990s. This process, examined in Chapter 1, has elevated the avoidance of civilian casualties to one of the central norms of contemporary American warfare. The 1991 Persian Gulf War showed the extent to which the American military has come to adhere to the principle of non-combatant immunity.[3] Existing studies have referred to this growing American compliance with International Humanitarian Law (IHL) as the humanising trend in US warfare.[4] Reflecting these fundamental normative changes, the literature has identified casualty-aversion and civilian protection as the defining characteristics of contemporary US warfare.[5]

Based on the socio-historical analysis provided in Chapters 1 and 2, the book has illustrated the inherent normative tension between achieving zero tolerance and sparing the innocent from harm. This collision of norms lies at the heart of US warfare at the end of the Cold War and has raised the important question of whether it has been possible for the US military to wage today's wars in both a casualty-averse and humane manner.

Despite the growing recognition among key American decision-makers as to the importance of adhering to IHL, the book has illustrated how IHL remains too permissive regarding the risks to civilians. IHL allows states to perform acts that are likely to have highly negative consequences, such as the killing of civilians or the targeting of dual-use facilities, which in turn have sparked major controversies.[6] This criticism demonstrates more generally the limits of the existing legal framework to provide a sufficient framework for protecting non-combatants from harm.[7] Furthermore, it shows that even if the American conduct of war satisfied the conditions set by IHL (the legal indeterminacy of this particular issue was illustrated in Chapter 1),[8] it does not necessarily follow that all moral

---

[3] Thomas 2001; Shaw 2005, 83; Bacevich 1996, 37–48; Farrell 2005, 197.

[4] Coker 2001; Thomas 2001; Farrell 2005; Ignatieff 2000c.

[5] Walzer 2004; Ignatieff 2000c; Shaw 2005; Coker 2001; Wheeler 2002; Bacevich 1996, 37–48; Der Derian 2001.

[6] Crawford 2003, 555–558; Wheeler 2002, 209; Norman 1995, 83; Johnson 1999, 119–120, 130–133.

[7] Reus-Smit 2004, 360–361; Rowe 2000.

[8] Wheeler 2003, 210; Human Rights Watch 2000; Amnesty International, 'NATO/Federal Republic of Yugoslavia: "Collateral Damage" or "Unlawful Killings"? Violations of the Laws of War by NATO During Operation Allied Force', available at www.web.amnesty .org/ai/nsf/index/Eur700182000, accessed on 1 June 2006; 'Final Report to the Prosecutor by the Committee Established to Review the NATO Bombing Campaign

requirements have been fulfilled. The controversies over collateral damage and the targeting of dual-use facilities in recent American campaigns have shown that the legal permissiveness has not eliminated moral judgements of the use of US military power.[9] In fact, the legal permissiveness regarding collateral damage and dual-use targets raises the important moral question of whether an even higher level of civilian protection could have been achieved. By examining the issues of this law-morality nexus pertaining to the protection afforded to non-combatants, the book has drawn on Michael Walzer's idea of 'due care' as a moral framework to test if the US military has done everything possible to spare enemy non-combatants or whether American casualty-aversion has compromised the level of protection afforded to civilians.

A limited amount of material exists that discusses the relationship between US casualty-aversion and civilian protection.[10] However, this particular body of literature has generally failed to provide a systematic investigation of what happens when these norms come into conflict, and there is no detailed empirical investigation of how this collision of values has played itself out in relation to cases before and after the events of 11 September 2001.

Existing studies have shown that while the United States has striven to fight recent conflicts with little risks to both its own military personnel and enemy non-combatants, it has found it increasingly difficult to do so. Yet, existing sources have tended to view this difficulty as merely resulting from the moral and/or legal tensions inherent within the relationship between casualty-aversion and civilian protection.[11] This body of literature thereby neglected the important role played by enemy behaviour, a factor external to yet shaping US behaviour in turn. By not taking the role of the adversary – and thereby the notion of the interactive nature of war[12] – into account, the existing literature has failed to explore how the tension between these two conflicting American norms has been exacerbated by the behaviour of US adversaries.[13]

Therefore, the central argument put forward in Chapter 3 has been that any systematic investigation into the trade-off between American

Against the Federal Republic of Yugoslavia', available at www.un.org/icty/pressreal/nat 0061300.htm, accessed on 1 June 2006.

[9] Thomas 2001, 88; Ignatieff 2000c, 199; Johnson 2006, 189; Farrell 2005, 159–162.

[10] Walzer 2004 and 1992; Shaw 2005; Wheeler 2002; Ignatieff 2000c; Bellamy 2005.

[11] Walzer 2004 and 1992; Ignatieff 2000c; Shaw 2005; Wheeler 2002; Kahn 1999.

[12] Clausewitz 1984, 85–89; 1966b, 205–588; 1966a, 684–690; T. E. Lawrence 1962; Griffith 1992; Giap 1977, 23–55; MacDonald 1993.

[13] Clausewitz 1984, 86; Beyerchen 1992, 59–90; van Creveld 2000, 116; Skerker 2004, 27–39; Arreguin-Toft 2005.

casualty-aversion and civilian protection cannot ignore the particular dynamics generated by the interactive nature of war. Not to take these particular dynamics into account distorts not only the analysis of whether it has been possible for the United States to wage riskless and humane wars but also the investigation of whether more could have been done to spare civilians from harm.

The theoretical part of the book has been opened up for the empirical investigation of the American interventions in Somalia, Afghanistan, and Iraq. The monograph has compared these three interventions, in part, to understand if key American decision-makers adopted a different approach to casualty-aversion and civilian protection in 'disinterested'[14] wars (humanitarian interventions such as Somalia where no national security interests were at stake) and 'interested' wars (wars fought with vital national security interests at stake such as Afghanistan and Iraq).[15] While existing studies have tended to distinguish between the former and the latter by asserting that this difference had impacted on whether or not the Americans were willing to accept body bags and collateral damage,[16] this book has demonstrated that such assertions proved to be unfounded in the cases of Somalia, Afghanistan, and Iraq.

The reason for American casualty-aversion during the UNITAF and UNOSOM II missions in Somalia was located in the humanitarian nature of the American involvement.[17] This humanitarian intervention was a conflict where no perceived vital US national security interests were at stake.[18] Thus, the assumption among American military and political decision-makers was that because the US public would not tolerate large numbers military casualties, the American military had to intervene in ways that would ensure lowest possible risks to US forces.[19]

By contrast, the US interventions in Afghanistan and Iraq in response to the events of 11 September 2001 were not born out of humanitarianism (even though humanitarian rationales were at play) but out of a perceived threat to US survival.[20] The Bush and Obama Administrations essentially argued that the Taliban, al-Qaeda, and the regime of Saddam Hussein constituted an existential threat not just to the United States, but also to

---

[14] Krauthammer 2002.
[15] Mueller 1996, 31; Bacevich 2002, 143; Walzer 2004, 100–101; Dauber 2002, 68.
[16] Record 2002, 11; Kennedy 2001, 64; 'After September 11: A Conversation', p. 116; Krauthammer 2002.
[17] Mueller 1996, 31; Bacevich 2002, 143.   [18] Walzer 2004, 100–101.
[19] Hirsch and Oakley 1995, 41–44; Dauber 2002, 28; McCrisken 2003, 189.
[20] Elshtain 2003, 1–45; *The 9/11 Commission Report: Final Report of the National Commission on Terrorist Attacks upon the United States*, p. xvi.

freedom and democracy.[21] Detailed examination has revealed, however, that although the United States fought both Operation Enduring Freedom (OEF) and Operation Iraqi Freedom (OIF) as so-called 'interested' wars with clear national security interests at stake, American decision-makers did not adopt a significantly different approach to casualty-aversion (i.e. a less casualty-averse approach) from previous humanitarian interventions.[22] In Afghanistan, the concern for US casualties resulted in a strategy that refrained from placing more than a few hundred American forces on the ground.[23] Instead, the risks of ground combat were transferred to local indigenous allies in the Northern Alliance/United Front.[24] In Iraq, similar casualty-averse attitudes among key decision-makers dictated the adoption of a net-centric mode of warfare that – to US decision-makers at the time of planning for OIF – had proven to be successful in Afghanistan.

Thus, the pervasiveness of US casualty-aversion that had been so characteristic of American humanitarian interventions during the 1990s continued unabated despite the events of 9/11. This finding shows, in contrast to the existing literature, that the factor of casualty-aversion has remained largely unaffected irrespective of whether the United States has intervened on humanitarian grounds or for reasons of self-defence. This suggests that the post-heroic attitudes among American decision-makers before and after 9/11 have stemmed from the long-term impact that Vietnam, Lebanon, and Somalia have had on American humanism in general. With the Mogadishu effect reinforcing the Vietnam and Lebanon syndromes, the reluctance in the White House and the Pentagon to place US soldiers in harm's way has become a fundamental value among political and military decision-makers independent of the nature of the enemy or the type of conflict the United States has waged.

The book has found a similar phenomenon at work in relation to the level of protection afforded to enemy non-combatants. Even though key American decision-makers (in a way that was reminiscent of Walzer's 'Supreme Emergency')[25] identified al-Qaeda, the Taliban, and the regime of Saddam Hussein as an existential threat to US survival, their attitudes regarding the legal protection of Afghan and Iraqi civilians have not differed significantly from humanitarian interventions prior to

---

[21] www.whitehouse.gov/news/releases/2001/09/20010912-4.html, accessed on 1 July 2005; www.whitehouse.gov/vicepresident/news-speeches/speeches/vp20010916.html, accessed on 29 July 2006; www.whitehouse.gov/news/releases/2001/09/20010920-8 .html, accessed on 2 July 2005.

[22] Conetta 2002b; O'Hanlon 2002, 68.   [23] Woodward 2002, 25.

[24] Stephen Biddle 2002; McInnes 2003, 165–184; O'Hanlon 2002, 64.

[25] Walzer 1992, 259.

9/11.[26] The fact that American political and military leaders have continued to emphasise the centrality of sparing innocent Afghan and Iraqi lives suggests that the trend towards strengthening the norm of noncombatant immunity has remained largely unaffected by the types of enemies the United States has faced. This seems to suggest that, irrespective of whether the United States has waged 'disinterested' or 'interested' wars, compliance with the laws of armed conflict has become an intrinsic value in American warfare.

With US attitudes towards casualty-aversion and civilian protection largely unchanged, the nature of the relationship between the former and the latter have shown similar characteristics in US operations before and after 9/11. As a result, the events of 11 September 2001 – often referred to in the existing literature as the date when the world changed[27] – did not turn out to be a watershed in relation to the two central norms underpinning contemporary US warfare: the attitudes among American decision-makers towards civilian protection and casualty-aversion have remained largely unaffected during the 'Long War on Terror'.

With these values unchanged, the conflicts in Somalia, Afghanistan, and Iraq have provided ideal cases for a critical investigation of how conventionally weaker adversaries have identified these American values as the centre of gravity of US warfare and have sought to exploit them accordingly. In that sense, all three cases have been good examples of conflicts waged under conditions of asymmetry for they show how conventionally overmatched adversaries have tried to shape the conditions of combat in ways that deliberately manipulated the US compliance with IHL and its perceived inability to stomach the sight of its own blood. By identifying and targeting this American centre of gravity, Muhamed Farah Aideed, Mullah Omar, Osama bin Laden, al Zarqawi, and Iraqi insurgents have attempted to neutralise the unbridgeable technological advantage enjoyed by the American military.

In Somalia, General Aideed correctly interpreted the American preference for operations launched by helicopters as an indication of casualty-aversion.[28] Understanding the pervasiveness of the body bag syndrome in American society since the Vietnam War and Lebanon, the

---

[26] 'Fact Sheet: US Military Efforts to Avoid Civilian Casualties', US Department of State, 25 October 2001, available at
http://usinfo.state.gov/is/Archive_Index/U.S._Military_Efforts_to_Avoid_Civilian_C asualties.html, accessed on 19 April 2006; Richard Myers in ABC interview on 22 October 2001, available at www.defenselink.mil/transcripts/2001/t10222001_t1021j cs.html, accessed on 2 December 2004; Conetta 2002a; Shaw 2002; Crawford 2003, 12.

[27] Ignatieff 2003b.

[28] Awaleh interview on David Keane 2002; Bacevich 2002, 145; interview with General Zinni on Cran 1998.

Somali warlord created a hostile local environment in which mounting numbers of casualties were inflicted on US military forces. This strategy reflected his conviction that fears for casualties were the centre of gravity and thus constituted such a vulnerability in US operations that – if exploited successfully – could bring about an American withdrawal.[29] In addition, Aideed successfully exploited America's concerns for high levels of respect for the principle of non-combatant immunity. He accomplished this by launching attacks from densely populated areas, encouraging or forcing civilians to act as human shields, using crowd swarming attacks, and provoking reprisal massacres.[30] Thereby, he copied and refined some of the tactics used by Saddam Hussein during the 1991 Gulf War (Saddam had used foreigners and Iraqis as human shields at various strategic sites throughout the country)[31] to systematically manipulate and exploit the restraint expected from the US military to further his cause.

The effectiveness of Aideed's creative and innovative asymmetric strategy did not go unnoticed. Following the triumph of the 1991 Gulf War, the US military claimed to have overcome the 'body bag syndrome' and most military analysts at that time were convinced that the transformation brought about by the 'Revolution in Military Affairs' (RMA) had provided the US military with a recipe for invincibility for years to come.[32] In Somalia, however, the inconceivable happened: a warlord commanding young, drugged, yet highly experienced militias, equipped with no more than Kalashnikovs and rocket-propelled grenades (RPGs), brought the world's mightiest military power to its knees.[33]

Following the powerful images of the mighty US military power over Iraq two years earlier, the images from the Somali capital showed disadvantaged adversaries a way to defeat the world's remaining military superpower. The disastrous American intervention in Somalia became their learning ground. As a result, US adversaries throughout the 1990s tried to employ strategies that had either been successfully implemented or pioneered in Somalia. The general message was that if the Americans took a hit, they would start running. Subsequent half-hearted and technology-driven US interventions throughout the 1990s such as Haiti, Bosnia, or Kosovo (and the failure to intervene in the Rwandan genocide)

[29] Interview with Robert Oakley in Washington, DC, 30 November 2005; Peterson 2001, 96; Bowden 2000; Hirsch and Oakley 1995, 123.
[30] Lewis and Mayall 1996, 117; Peterson 2001, 112; Miller and Moskos 1995, 6; Bowden 2000, 142; Birnbaum 2002, 65–66.
[31] Bullock and Morris 1991, 111.
[32] For a good summary of these accounts, see Bacevich 2005, 33–35; Ignatieff 2000b; Chris H Gray 1997, 46.
[33] Bowden 2000.

seemed to confirm that the American people lacked the will to sacrifice. At the same time, US adversaries discovered that the effective use of the civilian population as human shields or cover could be turned into a tactical advantage and that provoking the United States into causing collateral damage or even reprisal massacres provided a powerful propaganda tool. Such a learning process could for example be found in the strategic thinking of Slobodan Milosevic (during the wars in Bosnia and Kosovo) or Saddam Hussein (throughout the 1990s).[34]

The book focused on two different semi-/non-state actors, the Taliban and al-Qaeda in Afghanistan as well as insurgents and al-Qaeda in Iraq. Since 1994, Osama bin Laden repeatedly acknowledged the fundamental effect that the US withdrawal from Somalia has had on his strategic thinking.[35] And during OEF following the attacks on 9/11, Taliban and al-Qaeda forces adjusted their strategies and tactics in Afghanistan to exploit the US centre of gravity. The book has found evidence which suggests that, where possible, they used the local population as cover (yet, unlike Aideed, they did not use human shields), located themselves and their military equipment in urban civilian areas, used Mosques and hospitals as operational headquarters, and systematically concealed themselves among the civilian population as cover from US attacks.[36] Furthermore, they based their overall strategy on the assumption that if the United States could be dragged onto the ground in Afghanistan, they would prevail as the Americans were viewed as lacking the stomach for high numbers of military casualties.[37]

In Iraq, similar reasoning was shown to have informed the asymmetric strategies employed by al-Qaeda and insurgent groups (though, surprisingly, to a much lesser degree by the strategy of Saddam's forces). Killing US military personnel and provoking US forces to inflict high levels of collateral damage would not only increase the political costs of the war for the US government but ultimately also lead to US withdrawal.

Approaching the case studies through the Clausewitzean metaphor of war as an interactive wrestling match has enabled the book to reveal not only how prevailing conditions of asymmetry compelled adversaries in Somalia, Afghanistan, and Iraq to adjust, but also how the latter adjusted in a manner that exploited the centre of gravity in US warfare. In other words, the two fundamental normative changes occurring in US humanism and humanity over the past thirty years – reflected in the emergence of US casualty-aversion and civilian

[34] Skerker 2004, 29–30; Ignatieff 2000c, 28, 195, 200; Dunlop 1999, 29.
[35] Lewis 2001, 62–63; Record 2002, 13.
[36] Human Rights Watch 2002, 40–44; Ignatieff 2002, 7.
[37] Lewis 2001, 62–63; Record 2002, 13.

protection respectively – simultaneously opened windows of opportunities that creative, yet unscrupulous, ruthless, and indiscriminate adversaries began to exploit systematically. This allowed the book to reveal the extent to which today's wars are essentially contestations – by both sides – over the norms of casualty-aversion and civilian protection.

Moreover, the book has shown how in Somalia, Afghanistan, and Iraq, the asymmetric strategies that aimed at exploiting the American centre of gravity created a local security environment that exacerbated the tension between these two American norms and turned them into a trade-off. As a result, in pursuit of its military objectives, the US military – to various degrees – faced the dilemma that it could no longer wage riskless wars *while also* ensuring highest levels of protection for enemy civilians. Enemy behaviour had shaped the conditions of combat in ways that compelled US decision-makers to either accept likely compromises to non-combatant immunity (if the emphasis was placed on the safety of US military personnel) or accept higher risks to its own military personnel (if the emphasis was placed on the safeguarding of civilians).[38] Thus, the asymmetric strategies employed by its adversaries presented the US military with two options: to forgo discrimination to achieve its military objective with low levels of risk to its own forces or to forgo its reluctance to place its own military personnel in harm's way to achieve the goal of a higher level of protection for civilians.

In other words, the inherent tension that exists within the US mode of war between the two norms of casualty-aversion and civilian protection turns into a devilish dilemma once the particular interactive dynamics of asymmetric conflicts are taken into account. The two norms have opened new areas of vulnerability that have been systematically exploited by non-state adversaries, who have identified the two norms of casualty-aversion and civilian protection as the centre of gravity of US warfare. It is this strategic behaviour by non-state adversaries that exacerbates the tension inherent in these two norms, forcing US decision-makers to have to choose between exposing innocent civilians to larger risks and increasing the combat risks to its own soldiers in the pursuit of their military goals.

Against this backdrop, the book examined the origin and nature of this dilemma, it investigated the ways in which the US has responded to this dilemma, and assessed the legal, moral, and strategic consequences. Has the US military been able to wage these post–Cold War asymmetric conflicts in ways that achieved highest levels of casualty-aversion while also safeguarding innocent civilians? Or did the asymmetric strategies

---

[38] Bacevich 2002, 145; Peterson 2001, 100.

employed by its non-state adversaries force US decision-makers to decide on one norm at the expense of the other? And if so, what were the legal, moral and strategic consequences of such decisions?

The book has made the following findings. The United Task Force (UNITAF) mission avoided large scale military clashes with local actors because, driven by the ghosts of Vietnam and Lebanon, the United States sought to work with the warring parties rather than directly against them.[39] The benign security environment that resulted from very limited US military objectives never presented US commanders with the dilemma of having to choose between the values of casualty-aversion and civilian protection. UNITAF therefore was conducted in ways that ensured both low US casualties and high levels of respect for the principle of non-combatant immunity.

Yet, despite the absence of a full-blown conflict, the US military nevertheless took a wrestling stance and occasionally confronted both warlords with overwhelming firepower. During these operations, tactics and strategies were employed that reduced the risks to Somali civilians significantly. The UNITAF leadership accepted potentially higher risks to US military personnel (for instance by issuing advance warnings of all military operations) in order to ensure the safeguarding of the Somali population.[40] This reduction of risk to the indigenous population was regarded as the key component in avoiding alienation and confrontation, which in return ensured low risks to American military personnel. Due to these careful operating procedures, 'Operation Restore Hope' not only adhered to the laws of armed combat, but also met the conditions set by the 'due care' test.

Once the confrontation started to escalate during the United Nations Mission in Somalia (UNOSOM II) and US military objectives changed, Aideed created a local security environment that forced the American military and political leadership to decide between increasing the risk to its own soldiers and increasing the risks to Somali civilians. This led the US military to adopt operating procedures that prioritised US casualty-aversion over Somali civilian protection. Therefore, American forces ended up employing tactics and strategies that reduced US risks while simultaneously increasing the risks to Somali civilians.

This development raised important legal issues as to whether the United States was complying with IHL; but it was even more controversial when judged in moral terms. From a legal standpoint, it can be argued

---

[39] Lippman and Gellman 1993; Mersiades 2005, 206–208; Hirsch and Oakley 1995, 104.
[40] Dworken 1993, 1–27; Interview with Robert Oakley in Washington, DC, 30 November 2004.

that the 12 July Abdi House raid did not find US Quick Reaction Forces (QRF) operating in violation of the Geneva Conventions. However, from a moral point of view, the question is whether a higher standard of civilian protection could have been achieved by accepting greater risks to US military personnel. Drawing on Walzer's idea of 'due care', the Somalia case showed that marginal increases in the levels of risk to US soldiers would have increased civilian protection during the Abdi House raid. Yet, no such positive steps were taken to reduce the threat to civilians. Instead of following alternative paths, such as capturing rather than killing occupants (some of whom the evidence suggests were suspected by US military leaders of being civilians), US QRF operated in a casualty-averse manner that maximised rather than minimised the risks faced by non-combatants.[41]

US operations after the 12 July attack, for the same reasons, did not meet the moral conditions set out by the idea of 'due care'. US troops refrained from taking positive steps to increase their chances to distinguish between combatants and non-combatants and to thereby reduce the threat to civilians. An acceptance of higher risks to US soldiers instead could have saved civilian lives. Based on these findings, the UNOSOM II mission, while adhering to IHL, failed to comply with the moral criteria set by the 'due care' test. This failure also had significant impact on the strategic outcome of the conflict – the increasingly more ferocious nature of US operations led to such horrendous levels of civilian casualties that it first alienated Aideed's sub-clan and eventually most Somalis. This culminated in the infamous 'Battle of Mogadishu' which brought American involvement in Somalia to an end. In other words, disregard for the moral restrictions set by the idea of 'due care' created repercussions for US strategic objectives.

The investigation of OEF has found that the official rhetoric by US political and military leaders – emphasising the centrality of high levels of respect for the principle of non-combatant immunity – was actually accomplished through strict RoE and a sophisticated target approval system. These measures ensured an extremely discriminate and largely proportionate use of force that was in compliance with IHL. Thus, OEF provides an example of a US war waged in ways that not only met the standards of minimal casualties but also respect for the principle of non-combatant immunity.

Yet, while US operations during OEF generally complied with the provisions set by IHL, the moral question nevertheless arises whether the US military took all appropriate means to minimise civilian harm.

---

[41] De Waal 1998, 139; Peterson 2001, 112; Wright 1993.

Having investigated the four principal causes of non-combatant casualties, it was shown that considerable scope existed to decrease the risks of war faced by Afghan civilians further. The chapter has demonstrated that in three out of the four principal causes of collateral damage, the American military actually failed the 'due care' test. Here, casualty-aversion prevented the US military from reducing the threats faced by enemy non-combatants further. This means that an even higher level of civilian protection could have been achieved during OEF by increasing the risks to US military personnel. Thus, while the American conduct of war in Afghanistan generally adhered to IHL, it failed to meet the less permissive conditions set by the 'due care' test. While favouring casualty-aversion over civilian protection was morally indefensible, prioritising the former over the latter was also strategically imprudent. It allowed al-Qaeda to escape from the Battle of Tora Bora, to strategically withdraw (alongside remainders of the Taliban regime) from Afghanistan in early 2002, and to subsequently return to Afghanistan in form of a full-blown insurgency the American military was forced to engage from 2003/04 onwards.

During OIF, while fighting a largely conventional inter-state war against the forces of the Iraqi state, the US military complied with the provisions set by IHL for the protection of Iraqi civilians and succeeded in toppling Saddam's regime at minimal costs to the lives Iraqi civilians and American service personnel. At the same time, however, US warfare displayed a normative prioritisation of casualty-aversion over civilian protection that effectively resulted in a risk-transfer from US soldiers to Iraqi civilians. While such a risk-transfer neither violated IHL nor led to excessive collateral damage, from a moral point of view this was problematic as US forces could have achieved an even higher level of civilian protection had they had accepted higher risks to themselves. Therefore, the US military complied with IHL but failed the 'due care' test. On a strategic level, this failure was unproblematic during the conventional combat phase as collateral damage remained low and US forces succeeded in swiftly overthrowing the Iraqi regime. Yet, it became the central strategic problem during the second combat phase.

Once the US military faced a truly asymmetric adversary and for the first time started incurring large numbers of casualties, it proved not only incapable of adjusting to a counterinsurgency strategy but also unable to continue waging OIF in a manner that respected both norms of force protection and civilian immunity. Consequently, the US defaulted onto a mode of fighting that emphasised concerns for its own soldiers over the lives of innocent Iraqi. The resulting rise of civilian casualties, largely permitted under IHL, was in violation of the 'due care' test. While this moral violation (caused by the emphasis on force protection over the safeguarding of Iraqi civilians) had remained relatively unproblematic from a strategic point of view during the first combat phase, it now generated severe strategic repercussions as this US mode of warfare escalated the conflict, strengthened the insurgency, and brought the US close to losing the war.

In response to the looming loss of the war, the 2006 counterinsurgency manual recognised that the high levels of collateral damage – even when permitted under IHL – were detrimental to American military objectives in the conflict. In order to win the war over 'hearts and minds', the COIN manual argued, the existing imbalance between casualty-aversion and civilian protection inherent in US warfare needed to be reversed completely. Not only did this new priority for civilian protection demonstrate the extent to which the COIN manual essentially embraced Walzer's 'due care' argument, but it also read like an open confession over the extent to which previous US operations had been driven by primary concerns for the protection of its own forces at the expense of the lives of ordinary Iraqis. From the Pentagon's point of view, placing the protection of Iraqi civilians above concerns for US casualties now became a strategic imperative to win the war.

After an initial surge in casualties among US forces and Iraqi civilians, the chapter showed, the sectarian violence between Iraqis and violence against US forces declined dramatically. And yet, while some have attributed this reduction in violence exclusively to the surge strategy, closer examination revealed the overstatement of such claims. On the one hand, large elements of the new counterinsurgency strategy retained a heavy conventional footprint (which was responsible for inflicting large numbers of civilian deaths), indicating that US forces shifted only half-heartedly to a truly unconventional mode of warfare. On the other hand, even where such a strategic shift occurred, detailed research has shown that the new risk re-transfer from Iraqi civilians to US soldiers in and of itself has been a necessary but insufficient explanation for the deduction of violence. The latter, the chapter has shown, occurred only in synergy with other factors unrelated to the surge. As a result, the normative change in US counterinsurgency can only partially explain the lull in violence on the streets of Iraq.

These findings on Somalia, Afghanistan, and Iraq have – to some extent – been counterintuitive. Asked whether violations of the existing legal framework were more prone to occur in a humanitarian intervention or in a war of survival, the most likely answer would have favoured the latter over the former. As the book has found, however, US operations generally have complied with IHL irrespective of their 'interested' (OEF and OIF) or 'disinterested' (UNITAF and UNOSOM II) nature.

Yet, even though US operations across all the combat phases examined in case studies were shown to have adhered to IHL, UNITAF and (to a qualified extent) the surge in Iraq (2007 onwards) were exceptions in that they did not fail to meet the 'due care' test. Here, concerns for casualty-aversion were deliberately subordinated to concerns over the safeguarding of the civilian population – with the result that US forces were able to achieve their overall military objectives. These two operations were exceptions. By contrast, US operations during UNOSOM II, OEF, and OIF (2003–2006), while complying with IHL, prioritised casualty-aversion over civilian protection. This not only led to a failure to meet more stringent moral requirements set out by the 'due care' test, but also caused the US military to fail in the pursuit of its overall strategic objectives. In other words, in those cases where US forces not only adhered to IHL but also met the 'due care' test, they were able to achieve their strategic objectives. Where they 'merely' complied with IHL while prioritising concerns for US military personnel over the safeguarding of civilians, US operations displayed a lack of strategic success in prosecuting post–Cold War asymmetric conflicts.

This empirical finding demonstrates the legal, moral, and strategic implications stemming from the prioritisation of the lives American soldier over the lives of innocent civilians. From a legal point of view, such preferences are not necessarily problematic as long as they do not lead to violations of IHL (and only very few, still legally controversial instances have been found). This, in turn, demonstrates the permissiveness of IHL for it allows for the fundamental transfer of combat risks from soldiers to civilians. From a moral standpoint, however, transferring the risks from military personnel to enemy non-combatants is highly problematic because the latter, who are entitled that 'due care' be taken with their lives, end up bearing the brunt of the brutality of war. By demonstrating in each of the case studies how less casualty-averse approaches by the US military would have resulted in positive effects in terms of the safeguarding of civilians (without jeopardising the overall military objectives and without exposing US soldiers to excessive risks), the book argued that operating procedures that prioritised the safety of American soldiers over innocent civilians were morally unacceptable. In all cases, the book illustrated that a marginal increase in the level of risks faced by US soldiers would have indeed resulted in higher levels of civilian protection. Strategically, this finding is important, as the levels of civilian protection in Somalia (with the exception of UNITAF), Afghanistan, and Iraq (with the qualified exception of the counterinsurgency) – even though they did not constitute a violation of IHL – were insufficient as they lead to a loss of hearts and minds among the enemy population, thereby ultimately causing the US military to fail in the pursuit of its military objectives. What this means is that formal compliance with IHL has proven to be insufficient for the US military to strategically prevail in today's asymmetric conflicts.

In other words, the uncomfortable finding of this book is that even highest levels of compliance with the laws of armed conflict on part of democratic states like the United States might simply not be enough to win the asymmetric wars of the twentieth-first century. But rather than endorsing the age-old Realist idiom that 'inter arma silent leges', the monograph showed that there now is a strategic need for democracies to adhere to stricter moral guidelines to protect innocent civilians to win today's asymmetric conflicts – even if this means a marginal increase in the combat risks to American soldiers. The big stumbling block, however, is that such a move is bumping up against the prevailing reluctance in the White House and the Pentagon to expose their soldiers to higher combat risks. Whether such a rebalancing of combat risks between US soldiers and innocent civilians will occur, time will tell. The message, however, is clear: unless such a move were to occur, the strategic losses and inconclusive conflicts like those experienced in Somalia, Afghanistan, and Iraq, are more likely to reappear in the future.

Given America's technological superiority, its adversaries in the future are likely to emulate the tactics and strategies pioneered by Aideed, al-Qaeda, the Taliban, and Iraqi insurgents. Under these conditions, US decision-makers will have to show fewer casualty-averse inclinations to achieve higher levels of civilian protection. Such a result, as the findings of this book suggest, will not be achieved by simple compliance with the laws of armed conflict, but will require US forces to operate more in line with the moral standards set by Walzer's idea of 'due care'.

Bibliography

Book, Journals, and Other Sources

'A Nation at War', The New York, *NY Times*, 2 April 2003, available at www .nytimes.com/2003/04/02/world/nation-war-casualties-us-military-has-no-c ount-iraqi-dead-fighting.html, accessed on 16 December 2016.

Adam, Hussein M. 1995. Somalia: A Terrible Beauty Being Born? In *Collapsed States: The Disintegration and Restoration of Legitimate Authority*, edited by William I. Zartman, 69–90. Boulder, CO: Lynne Rienner.

Adams, Thomas K. 1998. *US Special Operations Forces in Action: The Challenge of Unconventional Warfare*. London: Frank Cass.

African Rights. 1993. *Somalia: Human Rights Abuses by the United Nations Forces*. London: African Rights.

Africa Watch. 1993. Somalia beyond the Warlords: The Need for a Verdict on Human Rights Abuses. *Africa Watch*. V(2).

'After September 11: A Conversation', The National Interest, 65/S, Special Issue (Thanksgiving 2001).

Agnew, John, Gillespie, Thomas W., Gonzalez, Jorge, and Min, Brian. 2008. Baghdad Nights. *Environment and Planning A*. 40(10): 2285–2295.

Air Force Pamphlet 14–210: USAF Intelligence Targeting Guide. Washington, DC: HQ USAF, February 1998.

Albright, Madeleine. 2004. *Madam Secretary: A Memoir*. London: Pan Books.

Allard, Kenneth. 1995. *Somalia Operations: Lessons Learned*. Washington, DC: National Defense University Press.

Anderson, Jon Lee. 2004. *The Fall of Baghdad*. London: Penguin Books.

Anderson, Mary B. 1999. *Do No Harm: How Aid Can Support Peace – or War*. London: Lynne Rienner.

'Annan: Iraq Close to Civil War', USA Today, 27 November 2006.

Anonymous [Michael Scheuer]. 2004. *Imperial Hubris: Why the West Is Losing the War on Terror*. Washington, DC: Brassey's.

Arendt, Hannah. 1998a. *The Human Condition*. London: Chicago University Press.

    1998b. Introduction. In *The Warriors: Reflections on Men in Battle*, edited by Gray, J. Glenn, vii–xxiii. Lincoln, NE: Bison Books.

Aristotle. 1958. *The Politics*. Oxford: Oxford University Press.

Arkin, Roland C. 2010. The Case for Ethical Autonomy in Unmanned Systems. *Journal of Military Ethics*. 9(4): 332–341.

Arkin, William. 2002. Fear of Civilian Deaths May Have Undermined Efforts. *Los Angeles Times*, 16 January.

Aron, Raymond. 1953. *Der permanente Krieg*. Frankfurt: Fischer.

1980. On Dubious Battles. *Parameters*. X(4): 2–9.

Arquilla, John and Ronfeldt, David, eds. 1997. *In Athena's Camp: Preparing for Conflict in the Information Age*. Santa Monica, CA: RAND.

Arreguin-Toft, Ivan. 2005. *How the Weak Win Wars: A Theory of Asymmetric Conflict*. Cambridge: Cambridge University Press.

Atkinson, Rick. 1993. *Crusade: The Untold Story of the Persian Gulf War*. New York, NY: Houghton Mifflin.

Bacevich, Andrew J. 1996. Morality and High Technology. *National Interest*. 45: 37–48.

2002. *American Empire: The Realities and Consequences of US Diplomacy*. Cambridge: Harvard University Press.

2005. *The New American Militarism: How Americans Are Seduced by War*. Oxford: Oxford University Press.

Baker, Peter and Khan, Kamran. 2001. Deal-Making Let Many Leaders of Taliban Escape. *The Washington Post*, 17 December.

Barber, Rebecca J. 2010. The Proportionality Equation: Balancing Military Objectives with Civilian Lives in the Armed Conflict in Afghanistan. *Journal of Conflict and Security Law*. 15(3): 467–500.

Bartov, Omer. 1985. *The Eastern Front, 1941–1945: German Troops and the Barbarisation of Warfare*. New York, NY: Oxford University Press.

Baskir, Lawrence M. and Strauss, William A. 1978. *Chance and Circumstance: The Draft, the War, and the Vietnam Generation*. New York, NY: Knopf.

Baumann, Zygmunt. 2000a. *Liquid Modernity*. Cambridge, UK: Polity Press.

2000b. *Modernity and the Holocaust*. Cambridge, UK: Polity Press.

Bearak, Barry. 2002. Uncertain Toll in the Fog of War. *New York Times*, 10 February.

Beck, Ulrich. 1992. *Risk Society*. London: Sage.

World Risk Society. 1999. Cambridge, UK: Polity Press.

Beck, Ulrich, Giddens, Anthony, and Lash, Scott, eds. *Reflexive Modernization: Politics, Tradition and Aesthetics in the Modern Social Order*. Cambridge, UK: Polity Press.

Beckett, Ian F. W. 2005. *Insurgency in Iraq: A Historical Perspective*. Carlisle, PA: Strategic Studies Institute U.S. Army War College.

Bellamy, Alex J. 2005. Is the War on Terror Just? *International Relations*, 19(3): 275–296.

2006. *Just Wars: From Cicero to Iraq*. Cambridge, MA: Polity Press.

Bender, Bryan, Burger, Kim, and Koch, Andrew. 2001. Afghanistan: First Lessons. *Jane's Defense Weekly*. 19 December.

Bennett, Stephen E. and Flickinger, Richard S. 2009. Americans' Knowledge of US Military Deaths in Iraq, April 2004 to April 2008. *Armed Forces and Society*. 35(3): 587–604.

Berdal, Mats. 1993. *Wither UN Peacekeeping?* Adelphi Paper 281: 1–88. London: Brasseys for the IISS.

Bergen, Peter L. 2002. *Holy War, Inc.* New York, NY: Touchstone.

2012. How Petraeus changed the US military. CNN, 10 November, available at http://edition.cnn.com/2012/11/10/opinion/bergen-petraeus-legacy/, accessed on 20 December 2014.

Best, Geoffrey. 1983. *Humanity in Warfare: The Modern History of the International Law of Armed Conflict.* London: Methuen.

Beyerchen, Alan. 1992. Clausewitz, Nonlinearity, and the Unpredictability of War. *International Security.* 17(3): 59–90.

1997. Clausewitz, Non-linearity and the Importance of Imagery. In *Complexity, Global Politics, and National Security,* edited by David S. Alberts and Thomas J. Czerwinski. Washington, DC: National Defense University, available at www.dodccrp.org/html4/bibliography/c omch07.html, accessed on 21 September 2017.

Biddle, Stephen. 2002. Afghanistan and the Future of Warfare: Implications for Army Defense Policy. 1–58, available at www.strategypage.com/articles/AF GHANISTANANDTHEFUTURE/default.asp, accessed on 4 November 2004.

2008. Stabilizing Iraq from the Bottom Up – Statement before the Committee on Foreign Relations, United States Senate (2 April 2008), available at http://foreign.senate.gov/testimony/2008/BiddleTestimon y080402p.pdf, accessed on 12 December 2014.

Biddle, Steve, Friedman, Jeffrey A., and Shapiro, Jacob N. 2012. Testing the Surge: Why Did Violence Decline in Iraq in 2007? *International Security* 37 (1): 7–40.

Biddle, Tami D. 2004. *Rhetoric and Reality in Air Warfare: The Evolution of British and American Ideas about Strategic Bombing, 1914–1945.* Princeton, NJ: Princeton University Press.

Birnbaum, Michael. 2002. *Krisenherd Somalia: Das Land des Terrors und der Anarchie.* Munich: Heyne.

Blumenberg, Hans. 1985. *The Legitimacy of the Modern Age.* Cambridge, MA: MIT Press.

Bodansky, Yossef. 1999. *Bin Laden: The Man Who Declared War on America.* New York, NY: Random House.

Boettcher, Willam A. III and Cobb, Michael D. 2006. Echoes of Vietnam?: Casualty Framing and Public Perceptions of Success and Failure in Iraq. *Journal of Conflict Resolution.* 50(6): 831–854.

Bohrer, Ziv and Osiel, Mark J. 2013. Proportionality in Military Force at War's Multiple Levels: Averting Civilian Casualties vs. Safeguarding Soldiers. *Vanderbilt Journal of Transnational Law.* 46 (3): 747–822.

Boot, Max. 2002. *The Savage Wars of Peace: Small Wars and the Rise of American Power.* New York, NY: Basic Books.

2003. Sparing Civilians, Buildings, and Even the Enemy. *The New York Times,* 30 May.

2008. The Truth about Iraq's Casualty Count. Wall Street Journal, 3 May.

Bourke, Joanna. 2000. *An Intimate History of Killing: Face-to-Face Killing in Twentieth Century Warfare.* London: Granta Books.

Boutros-Ghali, Boutros. 1992a. *An Agenda for Peace: Preventive Diplomacy, Peacemaking and Peacekeeping.* New York, NY: United Nations.

1992b. Letter dated 8 December 1992 from the Secretary-General to President Bush of the United States Discussing the Establishment of a Secure Environment in Somalia and the Need for Continuous Consultation. In *The UN and Somalia, 1992–96: The UN Blue Book Series, Vol. VIII.* United Nations, 217. New York, NY: United Nations Department of Public Information.

Bowden, Mark. 2000. *Black Hawk Down.* London: Corgi Books.

2002. The Kabul-ki Dance. *The Atlantic Monthly.* November.

Boyne, Walter. 2003. *Operation Iraqi Freedom: What Went Wrong, What Went Right, and Why.* New York, NY: Tom Doherty Associates.

Bradley, Graham. Military Turns to Software to Cut Civilian Casualties. *The Washington Post,* 21 February 2003.

Branigin, William. Taliban's Human Shields. *The Washington Post,* 24 October 2001.

Braudy, Leo. 2003. *From Chivalry to Terrorism: War and the Changing Nature of Masculinity.* New York, NY: Alfred A Knopf.

Broder, John M. 2003. A Nation at War. *The New York Times,* 2 April, available at www.nytimes.com/2003/04/02/world/nation-war-casualties-us-military-has-no-count-iraqi-dead-fighting.html, accessed on 16 December 2016.

Brodie, Bernard. 1984. A Guide to the Reading of *On War.* In Von Clausewitz, Carl. *On War.* 641–712. Princeton, NJ: Princeton University Press.

Brunk, Darren C. 2008. Curing the Somalia Syndrome: Analogy, Foreign Policy Decision Making, and the Rwandan Genocide. *Foreign Policy Analysis.* 4(3): 301–320.

Bryant, Michael. 2016. *A World History of War Crimes: From Antiquity to the Present.* London: Bloomsbury.

Buettner, Russ. 2001. Stray US Bomb Kills 13: Friends and Foes Angered. *New York Daily News.* 29 October.

Buley, Ben. 2008. *The New American Way of War: American Culture and the Political Utility of Force.* London: Routledge.

Bullock, John and Morris, Harvey. 1991. *Saddam's War.* London: Faber & Faber.

Burke, Jason. 2003. The Iraqi Resistance Was Planned. The Observer. 29 June 2003.

'Bush Speaks to Nation as Explosions Hit Baghdad', Chicago Sun-Times, 20 March 2003.

'Bush's Speech: Remarks by President Bush at Boeing, St. Louis, Missouri' *Voice of America News.*

Cann, John. 2000. Somalia: The Limits of Military Power. *L'Afrique Politique.* 158–176.

Caputo, Philip. 1996. *A Rumour of War.* New York, NY: Owl Books.

Chaliand, Gerard. 1994. *The Art of War in World History from Antiquity to the Nuclear Age.* Berkeley, CA: University of California Press.

Church, George J. 1993. The Anatomy of a Disaster. *Time Magazine.* 18 October.

Clancy, Tom and Franks, Frederick M. 1997. *Into the Storm: A Study in Command.* New York, NY: Berkley Books.

Clark, Wesley. 2003. *Winning Modern Wars.* New York, NY: Public Affairs.

Clarke, Richard A. 2004. *Against All Enemies: Inside American's War on Terror.*
New York, NY: Free Press.

Clarke, Walter and Herbst, Jeffrey. 1996. Somalia and the Future of
Humanitarian Intervention. *Foreign Affairs.* 75(2): (March–April).

1997. *Learning from Somalia: Lessons from Armed Humanitarian Intervention.*
Boulder, CO: Westview.

Clegg, Mark. 2012. Force Protection and Society. *Defense and Security Analysis.*
28(2): 131–139.

Clinton, Bill 2005. *My Life.* London: Arrow Books.

'Clinton's Quick and Dirty Route to a Fiasco in Somalia', *The Guardian,* 17
March 1994.

Cohen, Elliot A. 1996. A Revolution in Warfare. *Foreign Affairs.* 75(2): 37–54.

2001. Kosovo and the New American Way of War. In *War over Kosovo,* edited
by Andrew J. Bacevich and Elliot A. Cohen, 38–62. New York, NY:
Columbia University Press.

1993. *GWAPS, Volume V: A statistical Compendium and Chronology.*
Washington, DC: Department of the Air Force.

Cohen, Richard. 2002. The Cost of Victory.... *The Washington Post,* 8 January.

Coker, Christopher. 1989. *Reflections on American Foreign Policy since 1945.*
London: Pinter Publishers.

1994. *War and the Twentieth Century.* London: Brassey's Lts.

2000a. Globalisation and Insecurity in the Twenty-First Century: NATO and
the Management of Risk. *Adelphi Paper,* 345.

2000b. *Waging War without Warriors? The Changing Culture of Military Conflict.*
London: Lynne Rienne.

2001. *Humane Warfare.* London: Routledge.

2003. *Empires in Conflict: The Growing Rift between Europe and the United States.*
London: The Royal United Services Institute.

2004. *The Future of War: The Re-Enchantment of War in the Twenty-First
Century.* Oxford: Blackwell, 2004.

2005. The Unhappy Warrior. *Royal United Services Institute Journal.* 150(6).

Coll, Steve. 2004a. Flawed Ally Was Hunt's Best Hope. *The Washington Post,* 23
February.

2004b. *Ghost Wars: The Secret History of the CIA, Afghanistan, and Bin Laden.*
New York, NY: Penguin Books.

'Commission of Inquiry Established by Security Council Resolution 885', 24
February 1994.

Conetta, Carl. 2001. Disengaged Warfare: Should We Make a Virtue of the
Kosovo Way of Warfare? *Project On Defence Alternatives.* 21 May, available
at www.comw.org/pda/0105bm21.html, accessed on 13 September 2006.

2002a. Operation Enduring Freedom: Why a Higher Rate of Civilian Bombing
Casualties? 18 January, available at www.comw.org./pda/0201oef.html,
accessed on 13 November 2004.

2002b. Strange Victory: A Critical Appraisal of Operation Enduring
Freedom and the Afghanistan War. Project on Defense Alternatives. 30
January, available at www.comw.org/pda/0201strangevic.html, accessed
on 12 November 2004.

2003a. Catastrophic Interdiction: Air Power and the Collapse of the Iraqi Field Army in the 2003 War. 26 September, available at www.comw.org/pda/full text/0309bm30.pdf, accessed on 2 September 2014.

2003b. Wages of War. 20 October, available at www.comw.org/pda/fulltext/0 310rm8exsum.pdf, accessed on 28 October 2014.

2004. Disappearing the Dead: Iraq, Afghanistan, and the Idea of a 'New Warfare'. *Project on Defense Alternatives*. 9, February 2004.

2007. More troops to Iraq? Time to just say No. 9 January, available at www .comw.org/pda/0701bm39.html, accessed on 1 June 2010.

Cordesman, Anthony H. 1998. *US and CENTCOM Strategy and Plans for Regional Warfare*. Washington, DC: Center for Strategic and International Studies.

2002. *The Lessons of Afghanistan: War, Fighting, Intelligence, and Force Transformation*. Washington, DC: The CSIS Press.

2003. *The Iraq War: Strategy, Tactics, and Military Lessons*. Washington, DC: Center for Strategic and International Studies Press.

Cornish, Paul. 2003. Myth and Reality: US and UK Approaches to Casualty Aversion and Force Protection. *Defence Studies* 3(2): 121–128.

Couchon, Dennis. 2003. Why US casualties were low, available at www.usato day.com/news/world/iraq/2003-04-20-cover-usat_x.htm, accessed on 2 August 2010.

Cran, William. 1998. PBS Frontline: Ambush in Mogadishu (29 September), available at www.pbs.org/wgbh/pages/frontline/shows/ambush/, accessed on 22 February 2005.

Crawford, Neta C. 2013. *Accountability for Killing: Moral Accountability for Collateral Damage in America's Post-9/11 Wars*. Oxford: Oxford University Press.

2004. Just War Theory and the US Counter Terror War. Available at www.A PSANET.ORG, 1(1), accessed on 12 December 2004.

2007a. Blame for Systemic Atrocity and When Soldiers 'Snap': Locating Collective and Individual Moral Responsibility. *The Journal of Political Philosophy*, 15(2): 187–212.

2007b. Individual and Collective Moral Responsibility for Systematic Military Atrocity. *The Journal of Political Philosophy*. 15(2): 187–212.

Crawford, Neta C., Lutz, Catherine, Lifton, Robert J., Herman, Judith L., and Zinn, Howard. 2008. The Real 'Surge' of 2007: Non-Combatant Death in Iraq and Afghanistan, available at www.carnegiecouncil.org/publications/arti cles_papers_reports/0003.html, accessed on 10 November 2014.

Crider, James R. 2009. A View from Inside the Surge. *Military Review*. 89(2): 81–89.

Crocker, Chester A. 1995. The Lessons of Somalia: Not Everything Went Wrong. *Foreign Affairs*. 74(3): 2–8.

Cryer, Robert. 2002. The Fine Art of Friendship: Jus in Bello in Afghanistan. *Journal of Conflict and Security Law*. 7(1): 37–83.

Daase, Christopher. 2001. Kleine Kriege und die Aktualitaet von Clausewitz. In *Vom 'traurigen' Notmittel Krieg*, edited by Joerg Calliess, 23–38. Loccum: Evangelische Akademie Verlag.

2003. 'Der Krieg ist ein Chamaeleon' – Zum Formenwandel politischer Gewalt im 21. Jahrhundert. In *Zivile Konfliktbearbeitung im Schatten der Terrors*, edited by Joerg Calliess, 17–36. Loccum: Evangelische Akademie Verlag.

Dauber, Cory. 2001. Images as Argument: The Impact of Mogadishu on US Military Intervention. *Armed Forces & Society* 27(2): 205–229.

2002. Implications of the Weinberger Doctrine for American Military Intervention in a Post-Desert Storm Age. In *Dimensions of Western Military Intervention*, edited by Colin McInnes and Nicholas J. Wheeler, 66–90. London: Frank Cass.

De Waal, Alex. 1998. US War Crimes in Somalia. *New Left Review*. I(230): 131–144.

Delaney, Douglas E. 2004. Cutting, Running, or Otherwise? The US Decision to Withdraw from Somalia. *Small Wars and Insurgencies*. 15(3): 28–46.

DeLong, Michael. 2004. *Inside CENTCOM: The Unvarnished Truths about the Wars in Afghanistan and Iraq*. New York, NY: Regney.

Dennison, Clayton. 2006. Operation Iraqi Freedom: What Went Wrong? A Clausewitzean Analysis. *Journal of Military and Strategic Studies*. 9(3): 1–34.

Der Derian, James. 2001. *Virtuous War: Mapping the Military-Industrial-Media-Entertainment Network*. Oxford: Westview Press.

2005. 'Virtuous War' and the Banality of Terror, available at www.globalagen damagazine.com/2005/jamesderderian.asp, accessed on 22 November 2005.

Der Derian, James and Wibben, Annik. 2003. *After 9/11*. Udis Production.

Diamond, Larry. 2005. *Squandered Victory: The American Occupation and the Bungled Effort to Bring Democracy to Iraq*. New York, NY: Times Books.

Dodge, Toby. 2007. The Causes of US Failure in Iraq. *Survival*. 49(1): 85–106.

Dorn, A. Walter. 2010. Warfighting, Counterinsurgency and Peacekeeping in Afghanistan: Three Strategies Examined in the Light of Just War Theory. In *War, Human Dignity and Nation Building: Theological Perspectives on Canada's Role in Afghanistan*, edited by Gary D. Badcock and Darren C. Marks, 16–70. Newcastle: Cambridge Scholars Publishing.

Dowden, Richard. 1993. Today's Reluctant Imperialists. *The Independent*. 9 March.

Dower, J. M. 1993. *War without Mercy: Race and Power in the Pacific War*. New York, NY: Pantheon Books.

Downes, Alexander B. 2006. Desperate Times, Desperate Measures: The Causes of Civilian Victimization in War. *International Security* 30(4): 152–195.

'Dozens of Taliban Prisoners Died in Airtight Containers: Report', Agence France Press, 11 December 2001.

Drysdale, John. 1994. *Whatever Happened to Somalia?* London: HAAN Associates.

Duclaux, Denise and Aldinger, Charles. 2002. Afghan Government Protests Attack: Inquiry Launched. Miami Herald. 2 July.

Duffield, Mark. 2001. *Global Governance and the New Wars: The Merging of Development and Security*. London: Zed Books.

Duffy, Michael. 2008. The Surge at Year One. Time Magazine. 31 January.

Duncan, Steven M. 1997. *Citizen Warriors: America's National Guard and Reserve Forces and the Politics of National Security.* Navato, CA: Presidio Press.

Dunlop, Charles J. 1999. Technology: Recomplicating Moral Life for the Nations Defenders. *Parameters.* 39(3): 24–53.

2001. *Law and Military Interventions: Preserving Humanitarian Values in 21st Conflicts.* Paper presented at the 'Humanitarian Challenges in Military Intervention Conference', Carr Center for Human Rights Policy Kennedy School of Government, Harvard University Washington, DC, November 29.

Durch, William J. 1996. Introduction to Anarchy: Humanitarian Intervention and 'State-Building' in Somalia. In *UN Peacekeeping, American Politics, and the Uncivil Wars of the 1990s,* edited by William J. Durch, 311–366. New York, NY: St. Martin's Press.

Dworken, Jonathan T. 1993. *Rules of Engagement (RoE) for Humanitarian Intervention and Low-Intensity Conflict: Lessons from Restore Hope.* Alexandria, VA: Center for Naval Analyses.

Eason, Gary. 2001. Why Bombing Can Go Wrong. *BBC.* 16 December.

Ehrenreich, Barbara. 1998. *Blood Rites: Origins and History of the Passions of War.* London: Virago Press.

Eikenberry, Karl W. 1996. Take No Casualties. *Parameters.* 26(2): 109–118.

Elbe, Stefan. 2003. *Europe: A Nietzschean Perspective.* London: Routledge.

Elias, Norbert. 1996. *The Germans.* Cambridge, MA: Polity Press.

1998. *The Civilizing Process: Sociogenetic and Psychogenetic Investigations.* Oxford, Basil Blackwell.

Ellis, Richard. 1993. Gun Gangs Rule Again on Streets of Somalia. *The Sunday Times,* 3 January.

Elshtain, Jean B. 2003. *Just War against Terror: The Burden of American Power in a Violent World.* New York, NY: Basic Books.

Enemark, Christian. 2014. *Armed Drones and the Ethics of War: Military Virtue in a Post-Heroic Age.* New York, NY: Routledge.

Enzensberger, Hans M. 1993. *Aussichten auf den Buergerkrieg.* Frankfurt: Suhrkamp.

Erwin, Sandra I. 2002. Naval Aviation. *Aviation Week & Space Technology.* 29 April.

Fairbairn, Geoffrey. 1974. *Revolutionary Guerrilla Warfare: The Countryside Version.* Harmondsworth, Middlesex: Penguin.

Falk, Peter. 'Appraising the War against Afghanistan', available at www.sscr.org/sept11/essays/falk_text_only.htm, accessed on 15 November 2004.

Fallows, James. 2004. Blind into Baghdad. The Atlantic Monthly (January/February).

Farrell, Theo. 1995. Sliding into War: The Somalia Imbroglio and US Army Peace Operations Doctrine. *International Peacekeeping,* 2(2): 194–214.

2005. *The Norms of War: Cultural Beliefs and Modern Conflict.* London: Lynne Rienner.

Fassihi, Farnaz. 2001. Death Lurks Underfoot. Star-Ledger. 23 December.

Filipov, David. 2001. Another Deadly, Errant US Attack Is Alleged. Boston Globe. 24 December.

Filkins, Dexter. 2002. Flaws in US Air War Left Hundreds of Civilians Dead. *New York Times*. 21 July.

Finlan, Alastair. 2008. *Special Forces, Strategy and the War on Terror: Warfare by Other Means*. London: Routledge.

2003. Warfare by other means: Special Forces, Terrorism and Grand Strategy. In *Grand Strategy in the War on Terrorism*, edited by Rich, P. B. and Mockaitis, T. R., 89–104. London: Frank Cass.

Fontenot, Gregory, Degen, E. J., and Tohn, David. 2005. *On Point: The United States Army in Operation Iraqi Freedom*. Annapolis: Naval Institute Press.

Forde, Steve. 1992. Classical Realism. In *Traditions of International Ethics*, edited by Terry Nardin and David R. Mapel, 62–84. Cambridge: Cambridge University Press.

Foucault, Michel. 1977. Nietzsche, Genealogy, History. In *Language, Counter-Memory, Practice: Selected Essays and Interviews*, edited by D. F. Bouchard, 139–164. Ithaca: Cornell University Press.

Franks, Tommy. 2003. United States Central Command Operational Update. *Federal News Service*, 30 March.

2004. *American Soldier*. New York, NY: Regan Books.

Frantz, Douglas. 2001. Hundreds of Qaeda Fighters Slip into Pakistan. *The New York Times*, 19 December.

Freedman, Lawrence. 2002b. *Kennedy's Wars: Berlin, Cuba, Laos, and Vietnam*. Oxford: Oxford University Press.

2002a. A new type of war. In *Worlds in Collision: Terror and the Future of Global Order*, edited by Booth, Ken and Dunne, Tim, 37–47. New York, NY: Macmillan.

Fussell, Paul. 1975. *The Great War and Modern Memory*. Oxford: Oxford University Press.

Gade, Emily K. 2010. Defining the Non-Combatant: How Do We Determine Who Is Worthy of Protection in Violent Conflict? *Journal of Military Ethics*. 9 (3): 219–242.

Gall, Carlotta. 2002. In Kabul, Rumsfeld Aide Regrets Toll in Raid. *New York Times*, 16 July.

Gartner, Scott S. 2008. The Multiple Effects of Casualties on Public Support for War: An Experimental Approach. *American Political Science Review*. 102(1): 95–106.

Gaudreau, Julie. 2003. The Reservations to the Protocols Additional to the Geneva Conventions for the Protection of War Victims. *International Review of the Red Cross*. 849 (March): 143–184.

Gelven, Michael. 1994. *War and Existence: A Philosophical Inquiry*. University Park: Pennsylvania State University Press.

Gentry, John A. 1998. Military Force in an Age of National Cowardice. *The Washington, DC Quarterly*. 21(4): 179–191.

2011. Casualty-Management: Shaping Civil-Military Operational Environments. *Comparative Strategy*. 30(3): 242–253.

2010. Norms as Weapons of War. *Defense & Security Analysis*. 26(1): 11–30.

Giap, Vo Nguyen. 1977. *How We Won the War*. Ypsilanti, MI: RECON Publications.

Gibbs, David N. 2000. Realpolitik and Humanitarian Intervention: The Case of Somalia. *International Politics*. 37: 41–55.

Gibson, James W. 2000. *The Perfect War: Technowar in Vietnam*. New York, NY: Atlantic Monthly Press.

Giddens, Anthony. 1984. *The Constitution of Society: Outline of the Theory of Structuration*. Cambridge, UK: Polity Press.

1985. *A Contemporary Critique of Historical Materialism, Vol. 2: The Nation-State and Violence*. Cambridge, UK: Polity Press.

1990. *The Consequences of Modernity*. Cambridge, UK: Polity Press,1990.

Gordon, Michael R. 2002. This Time, American Soldiers Join the Fray. *The New York Times*, 4 March.

2003. US Air Raids in 2002 Prepared for War in Iraq. *New York Times*, 20 July.

Gordon, Michael R. and Trainor, B. E. 2007. *Cobra II: The Inside Story of the Invasion and Occupation of Iraq*. New York, NY: Random House.

Goulding, Marrack. 1993. The Evolution of United Nations Peacekeeping. *International Affairs*. 69(3): 451–464.

Grant, Rebecca. 2002. *Afghan Air War*. Arlington: Aerospace Education Foundation, available at https://secure.afa.org/Mitchell/reports/0902afghan.pdf, accessed on 15 August 2005.

Gray, Chris H. 1997. *Postmodern War: The New Politics of Conflict*. London: Routledge.

Gray, Colin S. 1999. *Modern Strategy*. Oxford: Oxford University Press.

2007. Irregular Warfare: One Nature, Many Characters. *Strategic Studies Quarterly*. 1(2): 35–57.

Gray, J. Glenn. 1998. *The Warriors: Reflections on Men in Battle* Lincoln, NE: Bison Books, 1998.

Gray, John. 2003. *Al-Qaeda and What It Means to Be Modern*. London: Faber and Faber.

Green, Leslie C. 2000. *The Contemporary Law of Armed Conflict*. Manchester: Manchester University Press.

Greenwood, Christopher. 1993. Is There a Right of Humanitarian Intervention? *The World Today*. 49(2): 34–40.

Grenier, John. 2005. *The First Way of War: American War Making on the Frontier*. Cambridge: Cambridge University Press.

Griffin, Jasper. 1980. *Homer: On Life and Death*. Oxford: Clarendon Press.

Griffith, Samuel B. 1992. *Mao Tse-Tung on Guerrilla Warfare*. Baltimore: The Nautical and Aviation Publishing Company of America.

Gross, Michael L. 2006. Killing Civilians Intentionally: Double Effect, Reprisal and Necessity in the Middle East. *Political Science Quarterly*. 120(4): 555–579.

2009. Asymmetrical War, Symmetrical Intentions: Killing Civilians in Modern Armed Conflict. *Global Crime*. 10(4): 320–336.

2014. Just War and Guerrilla War. In *The Just War Tradition: The Practice of Authority and Authority in Practice*, edited by Anthony F. Lang, Jr, Cian O'Driscoll and John Williams, 213–230. Washington, DC: Georgetown University Press.

2015. *The Ethics of Insurgency: A Critical Guide to Just Guerrilla Warfare.* Cambridge: Cambridge University Press.

Gutman, Roy and Rieff, David. 1999. *Crimes of War: What the Public Should Know.* London: Castle House.

Habermas, Juergen. 1999. Bestialitaet und Humanitaet: Ein Krieg an der Grenze zwischen Recht und Moral. *Die Zeit* 29 April.

Hagerman, Edward. 1988. *The American Civil War and the Origins of Modern Warfare.* Bloomington, IN: Indiana University Press.

Hagopian, Amy. 2013. Mortality in Iraq Associated with the 2003–2011 War and Occupation. *PLoS Medicine* (15 October), available at http://journals.pl os.org/plosmedicine/article?id=10.1371/journal.pmed.1001533, accessed on 17 November 2014.

Hahlweg, Werner, Clausewitz and Guerrilla Warfare. 1986. In *Clausewitz and Modern Strategy,* edited by Michael I. Handel, 127–133. London: Frank Cass.

Hakansson, Kersti. 2003. New Wars, Old Warfare? Comparing US Tactics in Afghanistan and Vietnam. In *The Nature of Modern War: Clausewitz and His Critics Revisited,* edited by Angstrom, Jan and Duyvesteyn, Isabelle. Vaellingby: Swedish National Defense College.

Halim, Omar. 1996. A Peacekeeper's Perspective of Peacebuilding in Somalia. *International Peacekeeping.* 3(2): 70–86.

Halliday, Fred. 2002. *Two Hours That Shook the World.* London: Saqi Press.

Hammes, Thomas X. 2005. Insurgency: Modern Warfare Evolves into a Fourth Generation. *Strategic Forum.* 214: 1–7.

Handel, Michael I., ed. 1986. *Clausewitz and Modern Strategy.* London: Frank Cass.

2001. *Masters of War: Classical Strategic Thought.* London: Frank Cass.

Haney, Eric L. 2003. *Inside Delta Force: The Real Story of America's Elite Military Unit.* London: Corgi Books.

Hanson, Victor D. 2000. *The Western Way of Warfare: Infantry Battles in Classical Greece.* Berkeley, CA: University of California Press.

2001. *Why The West Has Won: Nine Landmark Battles in The Brutal History of Western Victory.* London: Faber & Faber.

Harley, David. 1999. *The Condition of Postmondernity.* Oxford: Blackwell Publishers.

Hart, Herbert Lidell A. 1963. *The Concept of Law.* Oxford: Clarendon Press.

Hartley, Aidan. 2004. *The Zanzibar Chest: A Memory of Love and War.* London: Harper Perennial.

Hashim, Ahmed S. 2003. The Insurgency in Iraq. *Small Wars and Insurgencies.* 14 (3): 1–22.

2006. *Insurgency and Counterinsurgency in Iraq.* London: Cornell University Press.

Hedges, Chris. 2002. *War Is a Force That Gives Us Meaning.* Oxford: Public Affairs.

Hegghammer, Thomas. 2006. Global Jihadism after the Iraq War. *Middle East Journal.* 60(1): 11–32.

Henckaerts, Jean-Marie and Doswald-Beck, Louise. 2005. *Customary International Humanitarian Law Vol 1: Rules.* Cambridge: Cambridge University Press 2005.

Herodotus. 2003. *The Histories*. London: Penguin Classics.

Herold, Marc W. 2001. A dossier on Civilian Victims of US Aerial Bombing of Afghanistan: A Comprehensive Accounting. 19 December 2001, available at www.pubpagesw.unh.edu/~mwherold/, accessed on 23 February 2003.

2002. Afghan Killing Fields. *The Guardian*, 12 February.

Herr, Michael. 1991. *Dispatches*. New York, NY: Vintage Books.

Herring, Georg C. 1986. *America's Longest War: The United States and Vietnam, 1950–1975*. New York, NY: Alfred A Knopf.

2000. Preparing Not to Fight the Last War: The Impact of the Vietnam War on the U.S. Military. In *After Vietnam: Legacies of a Lost War*, edited by Charles Neu, 56–85. Baltimore, MD: Johns Hopkins University Press.

Hersh, Seymour M. 2001a. The King's Ransom: How Vulnerable Are the Saudi Royals? *The New Yorker*. 22 October.

2001b. Escape and Evasion: What Happened when the Special Forces Landed in Afghanistan? *The New Yorker*.12 November.

2002. The Getaway. *The New Yorker*. 28 January.

2004. The Other War: Why Bush's Afghanistan Problem Won't Go Away. *The New Yorker*. 12 April.

2005. *Chain of Command*. New York, NY: Penguin Books.

Heuser, Beatrice. 2002. *Reading Clausewitz*. London: Pimlico.

Herz, Dietmar. 2007. *Die Amerikaner im Krieg*. Hamburg: Beck.

Hirsch, John and Oakley, Robert B. 1995. *Somalia and Operation Restore Hope: Reflections on Peacemaking and Peacekeeping*. Washington, DC: United States Institute of Peace.

Hobsbawm, Eric. 1998. *On History*. London: Abacus.

1999. *Age of Extremes: The Short Twentieth Century*. London: Abacus.

Hoffmann, Bruce, interview on The History Channel, 'Hardcore History: Iraq War – Insurgency and Counterinsurgency (2005), available at www.youtube.com/watch?v=Pn8M9nq8wtA, accessed on 19 December 2014.

Hooker, Gregory. 2005. *Shaping the Plan for Operation Iraqi Freedom: The Role of Military Intelligence Assessments*. Washington, DC: The Washington Institute for Near East Policy.

Horkheimer, Max and Adorno, Theodor W. 1973. *Dialectics of Enlightenment*. London: Allen Lane.

Horn, Bernd. 2004. Special Men, Special Missions: The Utility of Special Operations Forces – A Summation. In *Force of Choice: Perspectives on Special Operations*, edited by Horn, Bern, de B Taillon, J. Paul and Last, David, 3–34. London: McGill-Queen's University Press.

Horowitz, Michael C., Simpson, Erin M., and Stam, Allan C. 2011. 'Domestic Institutions and Wartime Casualties', *International Studies Quarterly*, 55 (2011), pp. 909–936.

'Horror Comes Home', Independent, 13 October 1993.

Howard, Michael. 1976. *War in European History*. Oxford: Oxford University Press.

1981. *War and the Liberal Conscience*. Oxford: Oxford University Press.

2000. *The Invention of Peace: Reflections on War and International Order*. London: Profile Books Ltd.

Howard, Michael, Andreopoulos, G. J., and Shulman, M.R., eds. 1994. *The Laws of War: Constraints on Warfare in the Western World*. London: Yale University Press.

Human Rights Watch. 1991. 'Needless Deaths in the Gulf War: Civilian Casualties during the Air Campaign and Violations of the Laws of War', available at www.hrw.org/reports/1991/gulfwar/INTRO.htm, accessed on 6 January 2017.

1995. *Somalia Faces the Future: Human Rights in a Fragmented Society*, 7(2) (April), available at www.hrw.org/reports/1995/somalia/, accessed on 19 December 2004.

2002. 'Fatally Flawed: Cluster Bombs and Their Use by the United States in Afghanistan', 14/7 (December), available at http://hrw.org/reports/2002/us -afghanistan/, accessed on 20 April 2006.

2003a. 'Hearts and Minds: Post-war Civilian Deaths in Baghdad Caused by US Forces', available at www.hrw.org/reports/2003/iraq1003/, accessed on 12 April 2010.

2003b. 'Off Target: The Conduct of War and Civilian Casualties in Iraq', 11 December, available at www.hrw.org/en/node/12207/section/1, accessed on 17 January 2010.

2004. '"Enduring Freedom:" Abuses by US Forces in Afghanistan', available at www.hrw.org/reports/2004/afghanistan0304/, accessed on 4 December 2004.

2005. 'A Face and a Name: Civilian Victims of Insurgent Groups in Iraq', available at www.hrw.org/reports/2005/iraq1005/index.htm, accessed on 15 April 2016.

2006. 'Civilian Deaths in the NATO Air Campaign', available at www.hrw.org/ reports/2000/nato/, accessed on 1 June 2006.

Hurka, Thomas. 2005. Proportionality in the Morality of War. *Philosophy and Public Affairs*. 33(1): 34–66.

Hyde, Charles K. 2000. Casualty Aversion: Implications for Policy Makers and Senior Military Officers. *Aerospace Power Journal*. 14 (2): 17–27.

Hynes, Samuel. 1998. *The Soldiers' Tale: Bearing Witness to Modern War*. London: Pimlico.

ICRC. 1977. Additional Protocol to the Geneva Conventions of 12 August 1949, and relating to the Protection of Victims of International Armed Conflicts (Protocol 1), available at www.icrc.org/eng/assets/files/other/icrc_002_0321. pdf, accessed on 4 April 2017.

1987. Commentary of 1987 on the Protocol Additional to the Geneva Conventions, available at https://ihl-databases.icrc.org/applic/ihl/ihl.nsf/Co mment.xsp?action=openDocument&documentId=D80D14D84BF36B92 C12563CD00434FBD, accessed on 3 January 2017.

1997. *Spared from the Spear: Traditional Somali Behaviour in Warfare*. Nairobi: International Committee of the Red Cross.

Ignatieff, Michael. 1999. *The Warrior's Honour: Ethnic War and the Modern Conscience*. London: Vintage.

2000a. Battle without Blood, available at www.salon.com/books/int/2000/05/ 04/ignatieff, accessed on 2 April 2004.

2000b. The New American Way of War. *The New York, NY Review of Books.* 47 (12), available at www.nybooks.com/articles/12, accessed on 18 September 2003.

2000c. *Virtual War: Kosovo and Beyond.* London: Chatto and Windus.

2002. Ethics and the New War. *Canadian Military Journal.* 2(4): 5–10.

2003a. *Empire Light: Nation-Building in Bosnia, Kosovo and Afghanistan.* London: Vintage.

2003b. Why Are We in Iraq? (And Liberia? And Afghanistan?). *New York Times,* 7 September.

International Independent Commission on Kosovo. *The Kosovo Report* (Oxford: Oxford University Press, 2000).

Isaac, Jeffrey C. 2002. Civilian Casualties in Afghanistan: The Limits of Herold's 'Comprehensive Accounting', available at www.indiana.edu/~iupolsci/docs/doc.htm, accessed on 2 November 2004.

Isaacs, Arnold R. 1997. *Vietnam Shadows: The War, Its Ghosts, and Its Legacy.* Baltimore, MD: Johns Hopkins University Press.

Isaacson, Walter. 1996. *Kissinger: A Biography.* New York, NY: Touchstone.

Joas, Hans. 2003. *War and Modernity: Studies in the History of Violence in the 20th Century.* Cambridge, UK: Polity Press.

Johnson, James T. 1981. *Just War Tradition and the Restraint in War: A Moral and Historical Inquiry.* Princeton, NJ: Princeton University Press.

1984. *Can Modern War Be Just?* New Haven: Yale University Press.

1991. *Just War and the Gulf War.* Washington, DC: Ethics and Public Policy Centre.

1999. *Morality and Contemporary Warfare.* Binghamton, NY: Vail-Ballou Press.

2006. The Idea of Just War: The State of the Question. *Social Philosophy and Policy.* 23(1): 167–195.

Joint Staff. 2002. Doctrine for Joint Urban Operations. *Joint Staff Publications,* III-06 (16 September).

Jünger, Ernst. 2007. *In Stahlgewittern.* Stuttgart: Klett-Cotta.

Kaempf, Sebastian. 2009. Double Standards in US Warfare: Exploring the Historical Legacy of Civilian Protection and the Complex Nature of the Moral-Legal Nexus. *Review of International Studies.* 35: 651–674.

2011. Lost through non-translation: Bringing Clausewitz's writings on 'new wars' back in. *Small Wars and Insurgencies.* 22(4): 548–573.

Kagan, Kimberley. 2009. *The Surge: A Military History.* New York, NY: Encounter Books.

Kahl, Colin H. 2007a. COIN of the Realm: Is there a Future for Counterinsurgency? *Foreign Affairs.* 86(6): 169–176.

2007b. In the crossfire or the crosshairs? Norms, civilian casualties, and the US conduct in Iraq. *International Security.* 32(7): 7–46.

Kahn, Paul W. 1999. War and Sacrifice in Kosovo. *Philosophy and Public Policy Quarterly.* 19(2): 1–6.

2002. The Paradox of Riskless Warfare. *Philosophy and Public Policy Quarterly.* 22(3): 2–9.

Kaldor, Mary. 1999. *New and Old Wars: Organized Violence in a Global Era.* Cambridge, UK: Polity Press.

Kaplan, Robert D. 1989. Afghanistan Post Mortem. *The Atlantic Monthly.* April.

2000. *The Coming Anarchy: Shattering the Dreams of the Post Cold War.* New York, NY: Random House.

2002. *Warrior Politics: Why Leadership Demands a Pagan Ethos.* New York, NY: Random House.

Kapteijns, Lidwien. 2008. The Disintegration of Somalia: Historiographical Essay. *An International Journal of Somali Studies.* 1: 11–51.

Karnow, Stanley. 1990. An Interview with General Giap. *New York Times Magazine*, 24 June 1990.

'Karzai Calls for US Military Policy Review', *The Guardian*, 2 July 2002.

Kaufmann, Whitley. 2003. What Is the Scope of Civilian Immunity in Wartime? *Journal of Military Ethics.* 2(3): 186–194.

Keane, John. 1996. *Reflections on Violence.* London: Verso.

Keane, David. 2002. *The True Story of Black Hawk Down.* The History Channel.

Keegan, John. 1978. *The Face of Battle.* New York, NY: Penguin Books.

1993. *A History of Warfare.* London: Pimlico.

2004. *The Iraq War.* Toronto: Key Porter Books.

Keen, David. 2006. *Endless War.* London: Pluto Press.

Kennedy, Paul. 2001. Maintaining American Power: From Injury to Recovery. In *The Age of Terror: America and the World after September 11*, edited by Strobe Talbott and Nayan Chanda, 53–80. New York, NY: Basic Books.

2002. The Eagle Has Landed: The New US Global Military Position. *Financial Times*, 1 February 2002.

Kennett, Lee. 1982. *A History of Strategic Bombing.* New York, NY: Charles Scribner's Sons.

Kibbe, Jennifer D. 2004. The Rise of the Shadow Warriors. *Foreign Affairs* 83(2): 101–115.

Kind, Laura. 2002. A Civilian Toll in Afghan War Likely Lower. *Philadelphia Inquirer.* February 12, 2002.

Kingsbury, Alex. 2014. Why the 2007 Surge in Iraq Actually Failed. *The Boston Globe.* 17 November.

Kinross, Stuart. 2004. Clausewitz and Low-Intensity Conflict. *The Journal of Strategic Studies.* 27(1): 35–58.

Knickerbocker, Brad. 2003. Pentagon's Quietest Calculation: The Casualty Count. *The Christian Science Monitor.* 28 January, available at www.csmonitor.com/2003/0128/p01s02-woiq.html, accessed on 3 March 2003.

Knickmayer, Ellen. 2010. Blood on Our Hands. *Foreign Policy* (25 October), available at http://foreignpolicy.com/2010/10/25/blood-on-our-hands/, accessed on 3 January 2015.

Kovic, Ron. 1977. *Born on the Fourth of July.* New York, NY: Pocket Books.

Krauthammer, Charles. 2002. America, Battle-Tested. *The Washington Post*, 18 January.

Krepinevich, Andrew F. 1988. *The Army in Vietnam.* London: Johns Hopkins University Press.

2001. Military Experimentation: Time to Get Serious. *Naval War College Review.* 54(1): 76–89.

Kull, Steven and Destler, I. M. 1999. *Misreading the Public: The Myth of a New Isolationism.* Washington, DC: Brookings.

Lane, Earl. Few Civilian Casualties Expected: Military Targets Focus on Attack. *Newsday*, 9 October 2001.

Laqueur, Walter. 1977. *Guerrilla: A Historical and Critical Study*. London: Weidenfeld & Nicolson.

Lauer, Matt and Couric, Katie. 2003. General Richard Myers, Chairman, Joint Chiefs of Staff, discusses preparing for a possible war with Iraq. *Today Show, NBC-TV*. 27 February.

Lawrence, Philip K. 1999. *Modernity and War: The Creed of Absolute Violence*. London: Macmillan.

Lawrence, Thomas E. 1962. *Seven Pillars of Wisdom: A Triumph*. Harmondsworth: Penguin.

1994. Guerrilla Warfare. In *The Art of War in World History from Antiquity to the Nuclear Age*, edited by Gerard Chaliand, 880–891. London: Berkley University Press.

Lazar, Seth. 2010. The Responsibility for Killing in War. *Philosophy and Public Affairs*. 38(2): 180–213.

Lee, Steven. 2004. Double Effect, Double Intention, and Asymmetric Warfare. *Journal of Military Ethics*. 3(3): 233–251.

Leigh, David. 2010. Iraq War Logs Reveal 15,000 Previously Unlisted Civilian Deaths. *The Guardian*, 22 October.

Lewis, Bernard. 2001. The Revolt of Islam. *The New Yorker*. 19 November.

Lewis, Ioan M. 1993. Misunderstanding the Somali Crisis. *Anthropology Today*. 9 (4): 1–3.

2002. *A Modern History of the Somali: Nation and State in the Horn of Africa*. Oxford: James Currey.

Lewis, Ioan and Mayall, James. 1996. Somalia. In *The New Interventionism 1991–1994: United Nations Experience in Cambodia, Former Yugoslavia and Somalia*, edited by Mayall, James, 94–126. Cambridge: Cambridge University Press.

Lewis, Jonathan and Steele, Ben. 2001. *Hell in the Pacific: From Pearl Harbour to Hiroshima and Beyond*. London: Channel 4 Books.

Lewy, Guenter. 1980. *America in Vietnam*. Oxford: Oxford University Press.

Lieven, Anatol. 2001. Soldiers Before Missiles: Meeting the Challenge from the World's Streets. *Carnegie Endowment for International Peace Policy Brief*, 1(4): 1–8.

Lindqvist, Sven. 2002. *A History of Bombing*. London: Granta Books.

Linklater, Andrew. 1998. *The Transformation of Political Community*. Cambridge, UK: Polity Press.

2002. The Problem of Harm in World Politics: Implications for the sociology of States-Systems. *International Affairs*. 78(2): 319–338.

2004a. Norbert Elias, The 'Civilising Process' and the Sociology of International Relations. *International Politics*. 41(1): 3–35.

2004b. The 'Civilizing Process' and the Sociology of International Relations. *International Politics*. 41(1): 3–35.

2010. Global Civilizing Processes and the ambiguities of human connectedness. *European Journal of International Relations*. 16(2): 155–178.

Linklater, Andrew and Stephen Mennell. 2010. Norbert Elias, The Civilizing Process: Sociogenetic and Psychgenetic Investigations – An Overview and Assessment. *History and Theory* 49 (October): 384–411.

Lippman, Thomas and Gellman, Barton. 1993. A Humanitarian Gesture Turns Deadly. *The Washington Post*, 10 October.

Loeb, Vernon. 2001. Technology Changes Air War Tactics. *The Washington Post*, 28 November.

Loeb, Vernon and Graham, Bradley. 2002. American Troops Play Greater Role in Latest Offensive. *The Washington Post*, 5 March 2002.

Logevall, Fredrik. 1999. *Choosing War: The Last Chance for Peace and the Escalation of War in Vietnam*. London: University of California Press.

Londono, Ernesto and Paley, Amit R. 2008. In Iraq, a surge in US airstrikes. *The Washington Post*. 23 May 2008.

Luttwak, Edward. 1995. Towards a Post Heroic Warfare. *Foreign Affairs* 74(3): 109–122.

1996. A Post-Heroic Military Policy: The New Season of Bellicosity. *Foreign Affairs* 75(4): 33–45.

Lyall, Jason. 2010. Do Democracies Make Inferior Counterinsurgents? Reassessing Democracy's Impact on War Outcomes and Duration. *International Organization*. 64(1): 167–192.

Lyons, Terrence and Samatar, Ahmet I. 1995. *Somalia: State Collapse, Multilateral Intervention, and Strategies for Political Reconstruction*. Washington: Brookings Institute.

MacDonald, Peter. 1993. *Giap: The Victor in Vietnam*. London: W. W. Norton & Company.

Mack, Andrew. 1975. Why Big Nations Loose Small Wars: The Politics of Asymmetric Conflicts. *World Politics*, 27(2): 175–200.

Maier, Karl 1993. US Forces Ready to Step Up Action against Somalis. *The Independent*. 9 January.

Mandel, Michael. 2004. *How America Gets Away with Murder*. London: Pluto Press.

Mann, Michael. *States, War and Capitalism: Studies in Political Sociology*. Oxford: Blackwell, 1988.

2003. *Incoherent Empire*. New York, NY: Verso.

Mao Zedong. 1992. On Guerrilla Warfare. In *Mao Tse-Tung on Guerrilla Warfare*, edited by Samuel B. Griffith, Baltimore: The Nautical & Aviation Publishing Company of America.

Maren, Michael. 1993. Cleaning up from the Cold in Somalia. *Somalia News Update*. 20 September, available at www.etext.org/Politics/Somalia.News .Update/Volume.2/snu-2.25, accessed on 13 November 2004.

Mathews, Jessica T. 1997. Power Shift. *Foreign Affairs*, 76(1): 50–66.

Mayall, James, ed. *The New Interventionism 1991–1994: United Nations Experience in Cambodia, Former Yugoslavia and Somalia*. Cambridge: Cambridge University Press, 1996.

Mayer, Chris. 2007. Nonlethal Weapons and Noncombatant Immunity: Is It Permissible to Target Noncombatants? *Journal of Military Ethics*. 6(3): 221–231.

Mazower, Mark. 1999. *Dark Continent*. London: Penguin Books.

McCain, John and Lieberman, Joe. 2008. The Surge Worked. *Wall Street Journal*. 10 January.

McCrisken, Trevor B. 2003. *American Exceptionalism and the Legacy of Vietnam: US Foreign Policy since 1974*. London: Palgrave Macmillan.

McInnes, Colin. 2002. *Spectator Sport Warfare: The West and Contemporary Conflict*. London: Lynne Rienner.

    2003. A Different Kind of War? September 11 and the United States. In *The Nature of Modern War: Clausewitz and His Critics Revisited*, edited by Jan Angstrom and Isabelle Duyvesteyn, 165–184. Vaellingby: Swedish National Defence College.

McInnes, Colin and Wheeler, Nicholas J., eds. 2002. *Dimensions of Western Military Interventions*. London: Frank Cass.

McNamara, Robert S., Blight, James G., and Brigham, Robert K. 1999. *Argument without End: In Search of Answers to the Vietnam Tragedy*. New York, NY: Public Affairs.

McRaven, William H. 2004 Special Operations: The Perfect Grand Strategy? In *Force of Choice: Perspectives on Special Operations*, edited by Bern Horn, J. Paul de B Taillon, and David Last, 61–78. London: McGill-Queen's University Press.

'Meeting Resistance: New Doc Follows Iraqis Fighting U.S. Occupation of Their Country', Democracy Now!, available at www.democracynow.org/2007/10/18/meeting_resistance_new_doc_follows_iraqis, accessed on 12 November 2014.

Melvern, Linda. 2000. *A People Betrayed: The Role of the West in Rwanda's Genocide*. London: Zed Books.

Mersiades, Michael. 2005. Peacekeeping and Legitimacy: Lessons from Cambodia and Somalia. *International Peacekeeping*. 12(2): 205–221.

Miller, Laura L. and Moskos, Charles. 1995. Humanitarians or Warriors? Race, Gender, and Combat Status in Operation Restore Hope. *Armed Forces and Society*. 21(4): 615–637.

Minear, Larry; Scott, Colin, and Weiss, Thomas G. 1996. *The News Media, Civil War and Humanitarian Action*. Boulder, CO: Lynne Rienner.

Mitchell, Reid. 1997. The GI in Europe and the American Military Tradition. In *Time to Kill: The Soldier's Experience of War in the West 1939–1945*, edited by Paul Addison and Angus Calder, 304–318. London: Random House, 1997.

Mockaitis, Thomas R. 2012. *The Iraq War: A Documentary and Reference Guide*. Oxford: Greenwood.

Moore, Molly. 2001. Bombing Injures Afghan Guerrilla Leader. *The Washington Post*, 11 September.

Moore, Robin. 2004. *Task Force Dagger: The Hunt for Bin Laden*. London: Macmillan.

Moran, Daniel. 2002. *Wars of National Liberation*. London: Cassell.

Morris, Errol. 2003. *The Fog of War*. Culver City, CA: Sony Picture Classics.

Moskos, Charles. 1996. Casualties and the Will to Win. *Parameters* 26(4): 136–139.

    2002. Our Will to Fight Depends on Who Is Willing to Die. *Wall Street Journal*, 20 March.

Mueller, John. 1990. *Retreat from Doomsday: The Obsolescence of Major War*. New York, NY: Basic Books.

Changing Attitudes towards War: The Impact of the First World War, *British Journal of Political Science*, 21(1) (1991), pp. 1–28.

The Perfect Enemy: Assessing the Gulf War, *Security Studies*, 5 (Autumn 1995).

Policy Principles for Unthreatened Wealth Seekers, *Foreign Policy*, No. 102 (Spring 1996).

Münkler, Herfried. 2003. The Wars of the 21st Century. *International Review of the Red Cross* 85(849): 7–22.

2004. *Die Neuen Kriege*. Hamburg: Rowohlt.

2006. *Vom Krieg Zum Terror: Das Ende des Klassischen Krieges*. Zurich: Vontobel-Stiftung.

2014. *Der Wandel des Krieges: Von der Symmetrie zur Asymmetrie*. Weilerswirst: Velbrueck.

Murray, Leonie. 2007. Somalia and the 'Body Bag Myth' in American Politics. *International Politics*. 44(5): 552–571.

Nagl, John A. 2005. *Learning to Eat Soup with a Knife: Counterinsurgency Lessons from Malaya and Vietnam*. Chicago, IL: Chicago University Press.

Nagl, John A., Petraeus, David H, and Amos, James F. 2007. *The U.S. Army/Marine Corps Counterinsurgency Field Manual*. Chicago, IL: Chicago University Press.

Nash, Gary B. and Jeffrey, Julie R., eds. 1994. *The American People: Creating a Nation and a Society*. New York, NY: HarperCollins.

Naylor, Sean. 2005. *Not a Good Day to Die: The Untold Story of Operation Anaconda*. New York, NY: Berkley Books.

Nelson, Craig. 2001. Concern Grows over US Strategy, Tactics in Afghanistan. *Cox News Service*, 29 October.

Neu, Charles E. 1995. The Unfinished War. *Reviews in American History*. 23(1): 144–152.

2000. *After Vietnam: Legacies of a Lost War*. Baltimore: Johns Hopkins University Press.

Newton, Michael. 2013. Human Shields as Unlawful Lawfare, available at www .css.ethz.ch/en/services/digital-library/articles/article.html/163434/pdf, accessed on 16 April 2016.

Nietzsche, Friedrich. 1981. *Thus Spoke Zarathustra: A Book for Everyone and No One*. Middlesex: Penguin Books.

1995. *On the Genealogy of Morals*. Cambridge: Cambridge University Press.

Noble, Keith B. 1993. Troops in Somalia Raid Big Arsenal. *The New York Times*, 12 January 1993.

Nojumi, Neamatollah. 2002. *The Rise of the Taliban in Afghanistan, Mass Mobilization, Civil War, and the Future of the Region*. New York, NY: Palgrave.

Norman, Richard. 1995. *Ethics, Killing and War*. Cambridge: Cambridge University Press.

North, Andrew. 2004. US Condemned for Afghan 'Abuses'. *BBC News*. 8 March 2004, available at www.news.bbc.co.uk/1/hi/world/south_asia/3541839.stm, accessed on 4 December 2004.

O'Brien, Tim. 1999. *If I Die in a Combat Zone: Box Me Up and Ship Me Home*. New York, NY: Broadway Books.

O'Driscoll, Cian. 2008. *Renegotiation of the Just War Tradition and the Right to War in the Twenty-First Century*. New York, NY: Palgrave.

O'Hanlon, Michael. 2000. *Technological Change and the Future of Warfare*. Washington, DC: Brookings Institution.

    2002. A Flawed Masterpiece. In *The War on Terror*. New York, NY: Council of Foreign Relations Book.

Oakley, Robert B. and Tucker, David. 1997. *Two Perspectives on Interventions and Humanitarian Operations*. Carlisle: Strategic Studies Institute.

Olson, James S. and Roberts, Randy. 1991. *Where the Domino Fell: America and Vietnam, 1945–1990*. New York, NY: St. Martin's Press.

Operation Iraqi Freedom: By Numbers. Shaw AFB, South Carolina: CENTAF, Assessment and Analysis Division, 30 April 2003).

Otunnu, Olara A., and Doyle, Michael W., eds. 1998. *Peacekeeping and Peacemaking for the New Century*. Oxford: Rowman and Littlefield.

Owens, Bill. 2000. *Lifting the Fog of War*. New York, NY: Farrar, Straus, and Giroux.

Owens, Patricia. 2003. Accidents Don't Just Happen: The Liberal Politics of High Technology Humanitarian War. *Millennium: Journal of International Studies*. 32(3): 595–616.

Paret, Peter. 1976. *Clausewitz and the State*. Oxford: Oxford University Press.

    1986. Clausewitz. In *Makers of Modern Strategy from Machiavelli to the Nuclear Age*, edited by Peter Paret, 186–216. Oxford: Clarendon.

Parker, Geoffrey, ed. 2005. *The Cambridge History of Warfare*. Cambridge: Cambridge University Press.

Perlez, Jane. 1992. Mission to Somalia; Expectations in Somalia? *The New York Times*, 4 December.

Peterson, Scott. 2001. *Me against My Brother: At War in Somalia, Sudan, and Rwanda*. London: Routledge.

Phillips, Andrew. 2009. How Al Qaeda Lost Iraq. *Australian Journal of International Affairs*. 63(1): 64–84.

Phillipson, Coleman. 1911. *The International Law and Custom of Ancient Greece and Rome*. London: Macmillan.

'Physicians for Human Rights calls for End to Stalling Investigation into Afghan Mass Graves', available at www.phrusa.org/research/afghanistan/report_gra ves_newsweek.html, accessed on 4 December 2004.

Pick, Daniel. 1993. *The War Machine: The Rationalisation of Slaughter in the Modern Age*. New Haven: Yale University Press.

'Plans for Iraq Attack began on 9/11', CBS News, 4 September 2002, available at www.cbsnews.com/news/plans-for-iraq-attack-began-on-9-11/, accessed on 19 November 2014.

Plaw, Avery. 2010. Upholding the Principle of Distinction in Counter-Terrorist Operations: A Dialogue. *Journal of Military Ethics*. 9(1): 3–22.

Porch, Douglas. 2001 *The Wars of Empire*. London: Cassell & Co.

Porth, Jacquelyn S. 2003. Coalition to Make Painstaking Effort to Avoid Iraqi Civilian Damage. *Washington, DC File*. US Department of State. 6 March 2003.

Powell, Colin L. 1992. Why Generals Get Nervous. *New York Times*, 8 October
1992.
Price, Richard and Reus-Smit, Christian. 1998. Dangerous Liaisons? Critical
International Theory and Constructivism. *European Journal of International
Relations*. 4(3): 259–294.
Priest, Andrew. 2009. From Saigon to Baghdad: The Vietnam Syndrome, the
Iraq War and American Foreign Policy. *Intelligence and National Security*. 24
(1): 139–171.
Priest, Dana. 2002. In War, Mud Huts and Hard Calls. *Washington Post*, 20
February 2002.
Prins, Gwyn and Tromp, Hylke. 2000. *The Future of War*. Leiden: Martinus
Nijhoff Publishers.
Rabkin, Jeremy. 2011. Can We Win a War If We Have to Fight by Cosmopolitan
Rules? *ORBIS*. 55(4): 700–716.
Ransdell, Eric. 1992. Strangers in a Strange Land. *US News and World Report*. 21
December 1992.
Rapoport, Anatol. 1968. *Clausewitz: On War*. Harmondsworth, Middlesex:
Penguin.
Rashid, Ahmed. 2000. *Taliban: Militant Islam, Oil, and Fundamentalism in Central
Asia*. Yale: Nota Bene Book.
Record, Jeffrey. 1996. Vietnam in Retrospect: Could We Have Won? *Parameters*.
26(4): 51–65.
    2000. Force Protection Fetishism: Sources, Consequences, and Solutions.
    Aerospace Power Journal. 14(2): 4–11.
    2002. Collapsed Countries, Casualty Dread, and the New American Way of
    War. *Parameters*. 32(2): 4–23.
Reid, Tim. 2003. US Defence Spending to Top $500bn by 2010. *The Times*, 1
February.
Reisman, Michael W. 1997. The Lessons of Qana. *Yale Journal of International
Law*. 22: 381–399.
Remarque, Erich M. 2000. *Im Westen Nichts Neues*. Cologne: Verlag Kiepenheuer
& Witsch.
Renner, Major R. A. 2004. America's Asymmetric Advantage: The Utility of
Airpower in the New Strategic Environment. *Defence Studies*. 4(1): 87–113.
Renz, Bettina and Scheipers, Sibylle. 2012. Discrimination in Aerial Bombing:
An Enduring Norm in the 20th Century? *Defence Studies* 12(1): 17–43.
Reus-Smit, Christian, ed. 2004. *The Politics of International Law*. Cambridge:
Cambridge University Press.
Reuter, Christoph. 2002. *Mein Leben ist eine Waffe – Selbstmordattentaeter:
Psychogramm eines Phaenomens*. Munich: Random House.
Richburg, Keith B. 1993a. UN helicopters assault in Somalia targeted Aideed's
top commanders. *Washington Post*. 16 July.
    1993b. In War on Aideed, UN battled itself. *Washington Post*, 6 December.
Richter, Paul and Pae, Peter. 2001. High-Tech U.S. Bombs Are Precise but Not
Perfect. *Los Angeles Times*, 24 October 2001.
Ricks, Thomas E. 2001a. Bull's-Eye War: Pinpoint Bombing Shifts Role of GI
Joe. *The Washington Post*, 2 December 2001.

2001b. Target Approval Delays Cost Air Force Key Hits. *Journal of Military Ethics*. 1(2): 109–112.

2002. Battle Sends Broader Message of U.S. Resolve. *The Post*. 5 March.

2006. *Fiasco: The American Military Adventure in Iraq*. London: Penguin.

2009. *The Gamble*. New York, NY: Penguin.

Roberts, Adam. 1993. Humanitarian War: Military Intervention and Human Rights. *International Affairs*. 69(3): 429–449.

2002. Counter-Terrorism, Armed Forces and the Laws of War. *Survival*. 44 (1): 7–32.

2010. Lives and Statistics: Are 90% of War Victims Civilians? *Survival*. 52(3): 115–136.

Roberts, Adam and Guelff, Richard, eds. 1999. *Documents on the Laws of War*. Oxford: Oxford University Press.

Roblyer, Dwight A. 2003. Beyond Precision: Issues of Morality and Decision Making in Minimizing Collateral Casualties, available at www.dtic.mil/docs/citations/ADA424627, accessed on 19 April 2006.

Rogers, Paul. 2002. The War on Terror – One Year on. *RUSI Journal*. 147(5): 28–33.

'The "War on Terror": Current Status and Possible Development', available at www.oxfordresearchgroup.org.uk, accessed on 13 September 2006.

2013. Iraq, a War Foretold. *Open Democracy*, 22 March.

Rorty, Richard. 1989. *Contingency, Irony, and Solidarity*. Cambridge: Cambridge University Press.

Rosen, Gary, ed. 2005. *The Right War? The Conservative Debate on Iraq*. New York, NY: Cambridge University Press.

Rothbart, Daniel. 2012. The Politics of Civilian Identity. In *Civilians and Modern War: Armed Conflict and the Ideology of Violence*, edited by Daniel Rothbart, Karina Valentinovna Korostelina, and Mohammed D. Cherkaoui, 115–129. New York, NY: Routledge.

Rothbart, Daniel and Korostelina, Karina. 2011. *Why They Die: Civilian Devastation in Violent Conflict*. Ann Arbor, MI: University of Michigan Press.

Rowe, Peter. 2000. Kosovo 1999: The Air Campaign – Have the Provisions of Additional Protocol I Withstood the Test?. *International Review of the Red Cross*. 837: 147–164.

Rubinstein, William D. 2004. *Genocide*. Harlow: Pearson Education Ltd.

'Rumsfeld Defends Bombing Campaign', *BBC News*, 5 November 2001, available at http://news.bbc.co.uk/2/hi/south_asia/1638455.stm, accessed on 10 October 2005.

Rumsfeld, Donald H. 2002. Transforming the Military. *Foreign Affairs*. 81(3), available at www.foreignaffairs.com/articles/58020/donald-h-rumsfeld/transforming-the-military, accessed on 19 November 2014.

2014. DOD News Transcript, 14 September, available at www.defense.gov/Transcripts/Transcript.aspx?TranscriptID=2391, accessed on 2 December 2014.

Rutherford, Andrew. 1979. *Literature of War: Five Studies of Heroic Virtue*. London: Macmillan.

Sadaqat, Jan. 2001. Afghan elder warns Karzai over convoy bombing. *Reuters*. 23 December.

Sahnoun, Mohamad. 1994. *Somalia: The Missed Opportunities*. Washington, DC: United States Institute of Peace Press.

Scahill, Jeremy. 2002. A Day that shook Iraq: Saddam grants 'complete and final amnesty' to all prisoners. 20 October, available at www.iraqjournal.org/jour nals/021020.html, accessed on 2 December 2014.

Schering, Walter M. 1939. *Wehrphilosophie*. Leipzig: Johann Ambriosius Barth.

Schmidt, Brian C. and Williams, Michael C. 2008. The Bush Doctrine and the Iraq War: Neoconservatives versus Realists. *Security Studies*. 17(2): 191–220.

Schmitt, Eric. 2001. A Nation Challenged: The Chiefs; Bush's Troika Seeking Blend of Military and Civilian Decision-Making. *New York Times*, 24 October.

and Dao, J. 2001. Use of Pinpoint Air Power Comes of Age in New War. *The New York Times*, 24 December.

Schmitt, Michael N. 2005. Precision Attack and International Humanitarian Law. *International Review of the Red Cross*. 87(859): 445–466.

Scholl-Latour, Peter. 2002. *Kampf dem Terror – Kampf dem Islam?* Munich: Propylaeen.

Schram, Stuart R. 1969. *The Political Thought of Mao Tse-Tung*. Harmondsworth: Pelican Books.

Schwartz, Michael. 2006. The American Rules of Engagement from the Air. 11 January, available at www.tomdispatch.com/post/48180/, accessed on 3 March 2010.

Schwenkenbrecher, Anne. 2014. Collateral Damage and the Principle of Due Care. *Journal of Military Ethics*. 13(1): 94–105.

Scott, Richard. 1966. Draft-dodging in the US now socially acceptable. *The Guardian*, 12 April, available at www.theguardian.com/century/1960–1969/Story/0,,106464,00.html?redirection=century, accessed on 8 August 2012.

Sechser, Todd S. and Saunders, Elizabeth N. 2010. The Army You Have: The Determinants of Military Mechanization, 1979–2001. *International Studies Quarterly*. 54(2): 481–511.

'Secretary of Defense Donald Rumsfeld Updates the World on the War against Terrorism', NewsHour with Jim Lehrer Transcript, 7 November 2001, available at www.pbs.org/newshour/bb/military/july-dec01/rumsfeld2_11–7 .html, accessed on 19 April 2006.

Sengupta, Kim. 2001. Americans 'duped' into attack on convoy. *The Independent*. 24 December.

Sewall, Sarah. 2007. A Radical Field Manual. In *The U.S. Army/Marine Corps Counterinsurgency Field Manual*, edited by John A Nagl, David H. Petraeus, and James F. Amos, xxi–xliv. Chicago, IL: Chicago University Press.

2002. *Understanding Collateral Damage*. Conference paper presented in Washington, DC, 4 June.

Shah, Anup. 2002. Iraq was being bombed during 12 years of sanctions. *Global Issues*. 5 April, available at www.globalissues.org/article/107/iraq-was-being -bombed-during-12-years-of-sanctions, accessed on 1 November 2014.

Shaw, Martin. 1991. *Post-Military Society: Militarism, Demilitarisation and War at the End of the Twentieth Century*. Cambridge, UK: Polity Press.

2002. Risk-transfer Militarism, Small Massacres, and the historic Legitimacy of War. *International Relations*. 16(3): 343–360.

2003. *War and Genocide: Organized Killing in Modern Society*. Cambridge, UK: Polity Press.

2005. *The New Western Way of War*. Cambridge, UK: Polity Press.

Shawcross, William. 2001. *Deliver Us from Evil: Warlords and Peacekeepers in a World of Endless Conflict*. London: Bloomsbury Publishing.

Shue, Henry. 2011. Civilian Protection and Force Protection. In *Ethics, Law, and Military Operations*, edited by David Whetham, 135–147. London: Palgrave.

Shultz, Richard H. and Dew, Andrea J. 2006. *Insurgents, Terrorists, and Militias: The Warriors of Contemporary Combat*. New York, NY: Columbia University Press.

Shy, John and Collier, Thomas W. 1986. Revolutionary War. In *Makers of Modern Strategy from Machiavelli to the Nuclear Age*, edited by Peter Paret, 815–862. Oxford: Clarendon.

Sifry, Micah L. and Cerf, Christopher, eds. 2003. *The Iraq War Reader: History, Documents, Opinions*. New York, NY: Touchstone.

Simon, Steve. 2008. The Price of the Surge. *Foreign Affairs*. 87(3): 57–76.

Simons, Geoff. 1998. *Vietnam Syndrome: Impact on US Foreign Policy*. London: Macmillan.

Singer, Peter. 2009. *Wired for War: The Robotics Revolution and War in the 21st Century*. Penguin Books.

'600 Bodies Discovered in Mazar-i-Sharif', Agence France Press, 22 November 2001.

Skerker, Michael. 2004. Just War Criteria and the New Face of War: Human Shields, Manufactured Martyrs, and Little Boys with Stones. *Journal of Military Ethics*. 3(1): 27–39.

Sloyan, Patrick J. 1995. Mission in Somalia: Clinton called shots in failed policy targeting Aidid. *Newsday*, 5 December 1995.

Sly, Liz. 1993. UN Raises the Ante in Somalia Attacks. *Chicago Tribune*. 20 June 1993.

'Smart Bombs Made Dumb? Did Faulty Batteries Cause Failure of Precision Guided Weapons?', cbsnews.com, 6 December 2001.

Smith, Michael. 2005. RAF bombing raids tried to goad Saddam into war. *The London Times*, 29 May.

Smith, Michael. 2006. *Killer Elite: The Inside Story of America's Most Secret Special Operations Team*. London: Weidenfeld & Nicolson.

Smith, Stephen. 1993. *Somalie: La Guerre Perdue de l'Humanitaire*. Paris: Calmann-Levy.

Smith, Thomas W. 2002. The New Law of War: Legitimizing Hi-Tech and Infrastructural Violence. *International Studies Quarterly*. 46(3): 355–374.

2008. Protecting Civilians … or Soldiers? Humanitarian Law and the Economy of Risk in Iraq. *International Studies Perspectives*. 9(2): 144–164.

Smith, Tony. 1995. *America's Mission: The United States and the Worldwide Struggle for Democracy in the Twentieth Century*. Princeton: Princeton University Press.

Smolowe, Bill. Great Expectations. *Time*. 21 December 1992.

Smucker, Philip. 2004. *Al Qaeda's Great Escape: The Military and the Media on Terror's Trail*. Washington, DC: Brassey's, Inc.

Stacey, Robert C. 1994. The Age of Chivalry. In *The Laws of War: Constraints on Warfare in the Western World*, edited by Michael Howard, G. J. Andreopoulos, and M. R., Shulman, 27–39. London: Yale University Press.

Stetler, Russell, ed. 1970. *The Military Art of People's War: Selected Writings of General Vo Nguyen Giap*. London: Monthly Review Press.

Strachan, Huw. 2007. *Clausewitz in the Twenty-First Century*. Oxford: Oxford University Press.

Summers, Harry G. 1982. *On Strategy: A Critical Analysis of the Vietnam War*. Novato, CA: Presidio Press.

Svendsen, Adam D. M. 2010. Strategy and Disproportionality in Contemporary Conflicts. *Journal of Strategic Studies*. 33(3): 367–399.

'Taliban Hiding in Residential Areas', *The Irish Times*, 24 October 2001, available at www.irishtimes.com/news/taliban-hiding-in-residential-areas-says-us-1.4 01234, accessed on 13 April 2016.

'Taliban Prisoners died in sealed containers', *The Scotsman*, 12 December 2001.

Tannenwald, Nina. 1999. The Nuclear Taboo: The United States and the Normative Basis of Nuclear Non-use. *International Organisation*. 53(3): 433–468.

2007. *The Nuclear Taboo: The United States and the Non-Use of Nuclear Weapons since 1945*. Cambridge: Cambridge University Press.

The 9/11 Commission Report: Final Report of the National Commission on Terrorist Attacks upon the United States New York, NY: W. W. Norton & Company, 2004.

'The Other War: Pentagon's Own Report on Afghanistan Invasion Blasts US War Strategy', 17 April 2004, available at http://ia300224.us.archive.org/3/items/dn2004-0407/dn2004-0407–1_64kb.mp3, accessed on 1 September 2006.

'The Raid that Went Wrong: How an Elite US Force Failed in Somalia, The Washington, DC Post, 30 January 1994.

'The War in Iraq: 10 Years and Counting', available at www.iraqbodycount.org, accessed on 17 November 2014.

Thiel, Joshua. 2011. The Statistical Irrelevance of American SIGACT Data: Iraq Surge Analysis Reveals Reality. *Small Wars Journal*. April 2011: 1–9.

Thomas, Ward. 2001. *The Ethics of Destruction: Norms and Force in International Relations*. London: Cornell University Press.

2006. Victory by Duress: Civilian Infrastructure as a Target in Air Campaigns. *Security Studies* 15(1): 1–33.

Thucydides. 1974. *History of the Peloponnesian War*. London: Penguin.

Tilly, Charles, ed. 1975. *The Formation of National States in Western Europe*. Princeton, NJ: Princeton University Press.

Todenhofer, Juergen. 2002. It's a Lot Easier to Declare Victory Than to Earn It. *The Chicago Tribune*. 30 June.

Toffler, Alvin and Toffler, Heidi. 1994. *War and Anti-War: Survival at the Dawn of the Twenty-First Century*. London: Warner Books.

Townshend, Charles. 1997. People's War. In *The Oxford Illustrated History of Modern War*, edited by Townshend, Charles. Oxford: Oxford University Press.

Toynbee, Arnold J. 1957. *A Study of History*. Oxford: Oxford University Press.

Tyler, Patrick E. 1992. UN Chief's Dispute with Council Boils Over. *The New York Times*, 3 August.

Tyson, Ann S. 2006. Pentagon Cites Success of Anti-US Forces in Iraq. *The Washington Post*, 19 December.

United Nations. 1996. *The UN and Somalia, 1992–96: The UN Blue Book Series. Vol. VIII*. New York, NY: United Nations Department of Public Information.

Uranium Medical Research Centre. 2005. The Quantitative Analysis of Uranium Isotopes in the Urine of the Civilian Population of Eastern Afghanistan after Operation Enduring Freedom. *Military Medicine*. 170 (4): 277–284.

'US and UN at Odds over Somalia', Independent, 12 December 1992.

US Marine Corps. 1997. *Warfighting*. United States Government, Department of the Navy: Washington, DC.

'USA treiben Ruestungsspirale nach oben', Der Spiegel, 12 June 2006.

Van Creveld, Martin. 1991a. The Clausewitzean Universe and the Law of War. *Journal of Contemporary History*. 26(3): 403–429.

1991b. *The Transformation of War*. New York, NY: The Free Press.

1996. War. In *The Osprey Companion to Military History*, edited by Robert Cowley and Geoffrey Parker, 497–499. London: Osprey.

2000. *The Art of War: War and Military Thought*. London: Cassell.

2011. The Rise and Fall of Air Power. *The RUSI Journal*. 156(3): 48–54.

Vautravers, Alexandre. 2010. Military Operations in Urban Areas. *International Review of the Red Cross*. 92(878): 437–452.

Virilio, Paul. 2002. *Desert Screen: War at the Speed of Light*. London: Continuum.

Von Clausewitz. Carl. 1966a. Bekenntnisdenkschrift. In *Carl von Clausewitz: Schriften – Aufsaetze – Studien – Briefe*, edited by Werner Hahlweg, pp. 644–690. Goettingen: Vandenbeck & Ruprecht.

1966b. Meine Vorlesungen ueber den Kleinen Krieg, gehalten auf der Kriegs-Schule 1810 und 1811. In *Carl von Clausewitz: Schriften – Aufsaetze – Studien – Briefe*, edited by Werner Hahlweg, pp. 205–588. Goettingen: Vandenbeck & Ruprecht.

1984. *On War*. Translated by Michael Howard and Peter Paret. Princeton: Princeton University Press.

Walker, Frank. 2009. *The Tiger Man of Vietnam*. Sydney: Hachette Australia.

Walzer, Michael. 1992. *Just and Unjust Wars: A Moral Argument with Historical Illustrations*. New York, NY: Basic Books.

2004. *Arguing about War*. London: Yale University Press.

2009. Responsibility and Proportionality in State and Nonstate Wars. *Parameters* 39(1): 40–52.

Watts, Barry D. 1996. Clausewitzean Friction and Future War. *McNair Paper*. 52 (October 1996): 1–132. Washington, DC: Institute for National Strategic Studies, National Defence University.

Weidmann, Nisl B., and Salehyan, Idean. 2013. Violence and Ethnic Segregation: A Computational Model Applied to Baghdad. *International Studies Quarterly*. 57(1): 52–64.

Weigley, Russell F. 1973. *The American Way of War: A History of United States Military Strategy and Policy*. London: Collier Macmillan Publishers.

Weintraub, Stanley and Weintraub, Robelle. 1967. *Evolution of A Revolt: Early Postwar Writings of T E Lawrence*. Philadelphia: Pennsylvania State University Press.

Weiss, Thomas G. 2004. *Military-Civilian Interactions: Humanitarian Crises and the Responsibility to Protect*. Oxford: Rowman & Littlefield Publishers.

Wendt, Alexander. 1992. Anarchy Is What States Make of It: The Social Construction of Power Politics. *International Organization*. 46(2): 391–425.

Werrell, Kenneth P. 1992. Air Force Victorious: The Gulf War vs. Vietnam. *Parameters*. 22(2): 41–54.

West, Bing. 2009. Counterinsurgency Lessons from Iraq. *Military Review*. 89(2): 2–12.

Western, Jon and Goldstein, Josua S. 2011. Humanitarian Intervention Comes of Age: Lessons from Somalia to Libya. *Foreign Affairs*. 90(6): 48–59.

Westhusing, Ted. 2002. Target Approval Delays Cost Airforce Key Hits: Targeting Error, Killing Al Qaeda the Right Way. *Journal of Military Ethics*. 1(2): 128–135.

Wheeler, Nicholas J. 2000. *Saving Strangers: Humanitarian Intervention in International Society*. Oxford: Oxford University Press.

2002. 'Dying for Enduring Freedom': Accepting Responsibility for Civilian Casualties in the War against Terror. *International Relations* 16(2): 205–225.

2003. The Kosovo Bombing Campaign. In *The Politics of International Law*, edited by Christian Reus-Smit, 189–216. Cambridge: Cambridge University Press.

Whitaker, Brian and MacAskill, Ewen. 2005. Report attacks 'myth' of foreign fighters. *The Guardian*, 23 September.

White, Josh. 2008. US Boosts Its Use of Airstrikes in Iraq. *The Washington Post*, 17 January.

White House, Crafting Tragedy, available at https://georgewbush-whitehouse.ar chives.gov/ogc/apparatus/crafting.html#3, accessed on 6 January 2017.

Williams, Glenn F. 2005. *Year of the Hangman*. Pennsylvania: Westholme Publishing.

Wippman, David and Shue, Henry. 2002. Limiting Attacks on Dual-Use Facilities Performing Indispensable Civilian Functions. *Cornell International Law Journal*. 35 (3): 559–579.

Woodward, Bob. 2002. *Bush at War*. New York, NY: Simon and Schuster.

2004. *Plan of Attack*. Toronto: Simon & Schuster.

2008a. *The War Within: A Secret White House History 2006–2008*. Toronto: Simon & Schuster.

2008b. Why Did Violence Plummet? It Wasn't Just the Surge. *The Washington Post*, 8 September 2008, available at www.washingtonpost.com/wp-dyn/con tent/article/2008/09/07/AR2008090701847.html, accessed on 5 January 2014.

Wright, Anne. 1993. Legal and Human Rights aspects of UNOSOM military operations. 13 July.

Youssef, Nancy. 2006. Commander: Fewer Civilians Dying. *Philadelphia Inquirer*. 22 June.

Zambernardi, Lorenzo. 2010. Counterinsurgency's Impossible Trilemma. *The Washington Quarterly*. 33(3): 21–34.

Zehfuss, Maja. 2001. Constructivism in International Relations: Wendt, Onuf and Kratochwil. In *Constructing International Relations: The Next Generation*, edited by Jørgensen, K. E. and Fierke, K. M., 54–75. London: M. E. Sharpe.

2006. *Targeting Ethics*. Paper presented at the Annual ISA Convention, San Diego, 22–25 March.

2010. Targeting: Precision and the production of ethics. *European Journal of International Relations*. 17(3): 543–566.

2012. Killing Civilians: Thinking the Practice of War. *British Journal of Politics and International Relations*. 14(3): 423–440

Zinn, Howard, 2003a. *A People's History of the United States: 1492 – Present*. New York, NY: HarperCollins.

2003b. *The Twentieth Century: A People's History*. New York, NY: Harper.

Websites

http://articles.latimes.com/1991-03-06/news/mn-359_1_north-korea, accessed on 30 November 2014.

www.cbsnews.com/news/plans-for-iraq-attack-began-on-9-11/, accessed on 19 November 2014.

www.cfr.org/iraq/iraq-iraqs-prewar-military-capabilities/p7695, accessed on 30 November 2014.

www.defense.gov/news/casualty.pdf, accessed on 2 November 2014.

www.defense.gov/transcripts/transcript.aspx?transcriptid=2141, accessed on 28 July 2010.

http://edition.cnn.com/2003/US/03/19/sprj.irq.int.bush.transcript/, accessed on 28 July 2010.

http://icasualties.org/Iraq/Fatalities.aspx, accessed on 2 August 2013.

www.gallup.com/poll/18097/Iraq-Versus-Vietnam-Comparison-Public-Opinio n.aspx, accessed on 5 December 2016.

http://georgewbush-whitehouse.archives.gov/news/releases/2003/03/20030322 .html, accessed on 2 December 2014.

http://georgewbush-whitehouse.archives.gov/news/releases/2007/01/20070110 -7.html, accessed on 3 January 2015.

www.informationclearinghouse.info/article2320.html, accessed on 1 December 2014.

www.pewresearch.org/2008/03/19/public-attitudes-toward-the-war-in-iraq-200 32008/, accessed on 30 November 2014.

http://socialistworker.co.uk/art/5932/Anti-war+protests+do+make+a+differ
ence, accessed on 20 November 2014.

www.theguardian.com/world/2003/mar/06/france.germany, accessed on 20
November 2014.

www.usnews.com/news/national/articles/2008/10/10/new-army-manual-shows
-wars-softer-side-with-focus-on-nation-building, accessed on 2 December
2014.

https://web.archive.org/web/20040904214302/www.guinnessworldrecords.com/
content_pages/record.asp?recordid=54365, accessed on 20 November
2014.

www.whitehouse.gov/news/releases/2003/05/2003050115.html, accessed on 1
December 2014.

Index